Orphan Warriors

Orphan Warriors

THREE MANCHU GENERATIONS
AND THE END OF THE QING WORLD

Pamela Kyle Crossley

PRINCETON UNIVERSITY PRESS

PRINCETON, NEW JERSEY

Copyright © 1990 by Princeton University Press
Published by Princeton University Press, 41 William Street,
Princeton, New Jersey 08540
In the United Kingdom: Princeton University Press, Oxford

All Rights Reserved

Library of Congress Cataloging-in-Publication Data

Crossley, Pamela Kyle.
  Orphan warriors : three Manchu generations and the end of the Qing
world / Pamela Kyle Crossley.
     p.   cm.
  Bibliography: p.
  Includes index.
  ISBN 0-691-05583-1
  1. Manchus—Social life and customs. 2. China—History—Ch'ing
dynasty, 1644–1912. I. Title.
DS731.M35C76   1990
951'.03—dc20   89-34963
                                                       CIP

This book has been composed in Linotron Caledonia

Princeton University Press books are printed on acid-free paper,
and meet the guidelines for permanence and durability of the
Committee on Production Guidelines for Book Longevity of the
Council on Library Resources

Printed in the United States of America by Princeton University Press,
Princeton, New Jersey
10 9 8 7 6 5 4 3 2 1

For Ronnie

Contents

Acknowledgments

THOUGH it is fashionable today in Qing studies to point out how significant the Northeastern heritage is for understanding the political style,
social milieu and cultural vigor of China's last dynasty, it was very different when I started graduate studies at Yale. At that time the general thing
was to brush aside any questions of Manchu culture or language as having
little importance after the conquest of China, and perhaps precious little
even before. Discourse, if I may call it that, was awash with ideas like
"sinicization," hopelessly vague and unapologetically stamped with the
prejudices and assumptions of Chinese nationalist scholarship. My first
acknowledgment goes to the scholars who awakened me to the factual
lacunae, logical fallacies and historical improbabilities underlying the
conventional model of Qing sinicization: Jonathan D. Spence, Joseph
Francis Fletcher, Jr., and Beatrice S. Bartlett. As readers of this book
will note, I feel strongly that rejection of sinicization as a tool for the
analysis of Chinese history does not in and of itself resolve the complexities of the Manchu experience in China under the Qing dynasty, since
it may be doubted that there really ever was a "traditional" Manchu culture or that Manchus in China lived it. Indeed, it may only invite the
erection of a new straw man for toppling. The reality was far more subtle
and far more revealing of China's transition to "modernity." For a sensitivity to the intricacies involved in unravelling something of this aspect
of the dynasty's history, I owe a second debt to the scholars named
above.

It would be improper to consider this work a revision of my dissertation, but it certainly owes a great deal to concepts and materials I grap-
pled with at that time. Ying-shih Yü, Parker Po-fei Huang, Fred M. Don-
ner, Edward J. M. Rhoads and Lillian M. Li were all of very great help
to me, in different ways. I also benefitted from the aid of Kang Le, John
L. Withers II, Richard von Glahn, Kandice Hauf, Roger Thompson, Paul
Clark, Huang Chin-hsing, Joey Bonner, Leon Seraphim and Judith Whit-
beck. For critical aid, guidance to further reading, and continuing incentive I subsequently owe thanks to Jonathan Spence, Betsy Bartlett, Ed
Rhoads, Susan Naquin, Lillian Li, Benjamin A. Elman, Mark Elliott, Susan Blader and Ellen Widmer. While doing research in Taiwan, I became
indebted to Dr. Chiang Fu-ts'ung, Chuang Chi-fa and Ch'en Fang-mei
of the National Palace Museum archives; Professor Li Hsüeh-chih of the
Academia Sinica; and a special thanks is owed to Kuang Shu-ch'eng (Sibo

[Khantinggur] Kunggur), past president of the Manchu Association (*Manzu xiehui*) in Taipei. In the People's Republic of China, my work would not have been possible without the intercession and companionship of the faculty and staff of the Institute for Qing Studies (*Qingshi yanjiu suo*), especially Professors Dai Yi, Luo Ming and Mr. Zhang Kuan; and I am not alone in my gratitude to Liu Zhongying of the Number One (Ming-Qing) Historical Archives for all that she has done. I owe very special thanks to Professor Li Hongbin of the Institute for Qing Studies, and to Professor Yan Chongnian of the Peking Academy of Social Sciences. Finally, I am extremely grateful to those who have generously shared with me their work in progress over the years, from which I have benefitted greatly: Ed Rhoads, David Strand, Mark Elliott and Susan Blader.

In its own languorous fashion this study became a book, and this would not have been possible without the critical judgment of William Rowe, Evelyn Rawski, and John E. Wills, Jr. To a startling degree this work is a product of their stimulation. Margaret Case, my editor at Princeton, took a chance on this manuscript when it did not look like much. Finally I am indebted to Wendy Chiu for editing the manuscript, and to Jonathan Tyler for research assistance.

For aid during the extraordinary struggle to secure the photograph by John Thomson of the Canton bannermen, I am indebted to the Royal Asiatic Society, Clark Worswick, Steven White, the Asia Society, Sotheby's, Bill McCune, Greg Finnegan and Gene Garthwaite.

Of institutional support I have enjoyed more than my portion. I owe first mention to the superb research facilities and friendly environment of Yale University, but subsequently enjoyed the institutional support of Cornell University, for which I would like to thank T. J. Pempel, Sherman Cochran, Charles Petersen, Bernard Faure and James Cole, among many. The manuscript was finished at the Mary Ingraham Bunting Institute, Radcliffe College, where I am indebted to Elizabeth McKinsey, Anne Bookman, Faye Myenne Ng, Rikki Ducornet, Wendy Kaminer, Ellen Perrin and many, many others for their encouragement, friendship and support. Dartmouth College, and the History Department in particular, has been much more than understanding in the provision of leaves, incidental research funds, and a generally good environment for thinking and writing, for which I thank, as representatives, Dean Marysa Navarro and Chairman Kenneth E. Shewmaker. I am particularly beholden (and they are something to behold) to the Living Thesauri of Reed Hall: Jere Rogers Daniell II, Gene Ralph Garthwaite, Nancy Grant, Paul David Lagomarsino and Charles Tuttle Wood; and last but not least to the Amazing Talking Webster, Gail Vernazza.

During the time I thought of, researched, rethought, researched, wrote, researched, rewrote, researched, and again rewrote this, I was intermittently subsidized by the following generous entities: Yale University, the Yale Council for East Asian Studies of the Councilium for International and Area Studies, the National Defense Foreign Languages Fellowship Program, the Arthur F. Wright Memorial Fellowship, the Mrs. Giles Whiting Foundation, the American Council of Learned Societies and Andrew D. Mellon Foundation, the Wang Fellowships in Chinese Studies, and the National Academy of Sciences, Committee for Scholarly Communication with the People's Republic of China. I thank them.

Conventions

PEKING (for Beijing) and Canton (for Guangzhou) are considered by the author to be English words of good standing, like Munich, Jerusalem and the names of many other world cities; most other Chinese names and terms (except where they occur in the titles of treaties or published works) are romanized in accordance with the so-called *pinyin* system, with the exception of the names of authors living in and places in Taiwan, which are given in Wade-Giles. Japanese is romanized with the Hepburn system, Manchu with the Möllendorf system adapted by Jerry Norman in his lexicon and the editors of *Mambun rōtō*. For primary works in Chinese, citations are provided by *juan* and *ye*—for example, 1.2a for *juan* 1, *ye* 2 (*shang*) or simply *ye* 2a; for modern reprints by *juan*, colon, and page—for example, 1:15. It is hoped that by providing the *juan*, readers may follow up citations regardless of the edition they happen to be using. Periodicals are cited by volume (which is sometimes a year), colon, issue, colon, page—for example, *Minzu yanjiu* [Historical Studies] 1983:2:45–54. Archival sources are cited by collection name and box number. Names for all Chinese or Japanese persons featured in the book are provided with the family name first; authors who publish in English are cited by the name pattern they customarily use. Manchus are presented with their clan name first, in brackets [ ], unless it is unknown. In conventional usage, clan names were not a part of the personal name, but they are worth knowing. In all instances where two transliterations are provided in parentheses, the first is Manchu, the second Chinese.

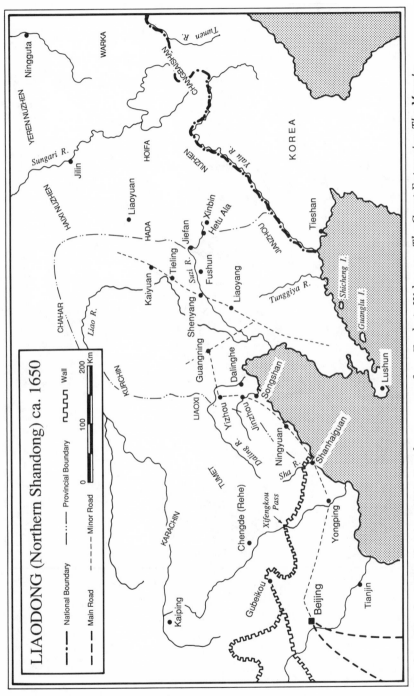

Liaodong (Northern Shandong) ca. 1650. Based upon a map from Frederic Wakeman, *The Great Enterprise: The Manchu Reconstruction of Imperial Order in 17th Century China,* Vol. 1, p. 40.

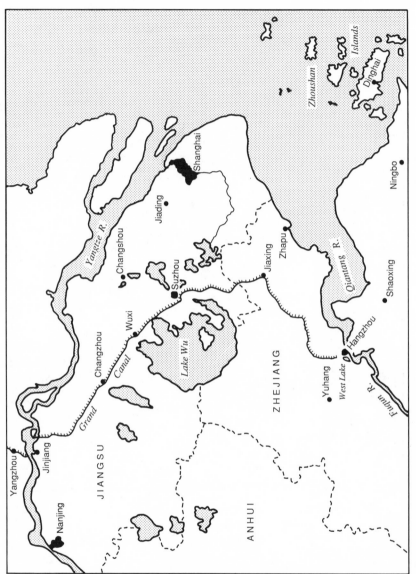

Zhejiang province ca.1850.

Orphan Warriors

Introduction

WHEN ONE CONSIDERS that the Manchu children Jinliang and Wenliang, growing up in the ruined banner quarter of Hangzhou in the 1880s, had as their childhood hero the Song dynasty martyr Yue Fei, new doors open one after another on the life of the "bannermen" of Qing China. Yue Fei, who was executed at the orders of the Southern Song court in 1142 because of his intractable opposition to the ceding of North China to the Jin Jurchens, was and is today the embodiment of Chinese patriotism. Jinliang and Wenliang, youngest sons of the Manchu printer and Taiping War veteran Fengrui, were of the people who claimed with all good sense to be the descendants of the Jurchens against whom Yue Fei had sworn his fatal enmity. They lived in a city where workingmen paid their respects to the memory of General Yue by spitting on and urinating on the kneeling iron figures of those who had plotted his demise. But the two Manchu boys centered their childhood fantasy world on Yue Fei, the god-hero of their home, Hangzhou on West Lake, and a great warrior, like their own ancestors. Jinliang in particular was believed marked by the spirit of the dead general. On the night of his birth in 1878, according to family legend, terrible sounds had rushed from Yue's temple north along the lake, into the banner quarter, into the family compound.

Jinliang's childhood conviction that he was a reincarnation of Yue Fei was not a happy one. The general's glory had been acquired at the cost of a hopeless and lonely struggle; his solitude could not be separated from his purity, and his literary image was best captured by the word *gu* that was inevitably associated with him. In his time the word, meaning "orphaned," or "solitary," or "unsupported," was a literary designation for the military ranks he held under the Song dynasty. But it was his *gujun*, "orphan army," that struggled on unsupported and unsupplied after the retreat south of the Yangzi River of the rest of the Song forces. "Orphaned warriors cannot last" (*gujun bu ke jiu liu*) became the motto of Yue's enemies at the Song court; his alienation from the court made his demise and the downfall of his people inevitable. Through the Qing period and the twentieth century, *gujun* has remained a common term for stalwart units persisting in battle without cover or adequate supplies.[1] It has a strangely exact cognate in the English phrase "forlorn hope." But the solitariness of the image had a special romantic resonance for the West Lake literati. Orphan Hill (Gushan) dominated the West Lake landscape and reinforced the imagery of Yue's persistence, which pervaded much of the poetic language of the entire West Lake and Hangzhou region. Poets from Song to Ming times demonstrated their fondness for it,[2] and Liu Zongshou, a Hangzhou literatus preoccupied with futile plans to protect the city from Manchu invasion in the summer of 1644, styled himself *caomang guchen,* "orphaned minister of the wilderness," in his petitions to the remnant Ming court in Nanjing.[3] Of course, more than local sentiment, romanticization of war heroes or even supernatural affinity drew Jinliang to the story of Yue Fei. In fact the Qing court had been promoting the cult of Yue Fei for a century and a half before Jinliang's birth; temples to the warrior god, like the four found in the vicinity of West Lake alone, were built with government funds, and prizes were awarded to his descendants from time to time. The Qing court had, in the middle eighteenth century, decided to emphasize the absolute value of loyalty over the relative value of cultural enmity, and all good bannermen were expected to revere this imperial demand together with many other demands with which it conflicted.

Jinliang's family enjoyed some status and some wealth in a community that since the conclusion of the Taiping War in 1864 had been coming to terms with a loss of legal definition, an ever-steeper decline in living standards, and a sense of abandonment by the Qing court in Peking. It was not, however, a world in which lines of identity had yet been fundamentally compromised. The violence and deprivations of the war years and the ensuing petitioning campaigns to the court for relief of the widowed and homeless reinforced old ties among the bannermen, and in some ways necessitated the forging of new communal relationships. At the same time it was clear enough, even to the child Jinliang, that the orphaned warriors of the former garrison communities could not last. Those who were by descent or by achievement members of the elite busied themselves with relief and reform projects of varying levels of practicality; the more humble, some of whom were desperately poor, turned to any despised urban trade and demi-trade for sustenance or lingered in perpetual unemployment. Whether high or low, whether busy or idle, Manchus of the later nineteenth century shared a peculiar set of traits and problems. Many harbored suspicions of Chinese neighbors who had threatened their lives or property in the Taiping War. Most were painfully aware that their present poverty and its incongruence with their formerly elevated status made them the butt of brutal witticisms in the popular entertainments of the time. There was a high rate of opium addiction. Some looked to foreign missionaries for solace or to foreign capitalists for employment. Most indulged in a nostalgia for the days of Manchu glory. For an articulate, self-identified elite, there was an emerging sense that even when the last legal barriers between the Manchus and

the Chinese had been removed, when the walls of the garrisons had finally crumbled to rubble and all external vestige of Manchu identity had
been erased, yet an irreducible source of differentiation would remain.
Like other traditional minorities undergoing the political modernizations
of their societies, the Manchus of China had come to a sense of ethnicity,
which in Jinliang's adulthood was expressed by the neologism *manzu*, the
"Manchu race."

This sense of racial identity was a relatively new thing to the Manchus.
The truth is that Manchu history is a classic illustration of the fundamental unviability of the notion that "race" is or ever can be a thing real in
itself; the reality, for Manchus, lay in the political, cultural and psychological power that "race" as a construct came to assume.[4] In the Northeastern cultural realm in which Nurgaci's (1559–1626 [ruled 1616–1626])[5]
army, the Eight Banners, was formed in the very early seventeenth century, culture was a matter of geography and manifestation. Chinese had
moved to the Liaodong frontier, particularly during the Ming period, and
had adapted themselves to local customs as necessary. Many natives of
the Northeast—particularly some of the Manchu ancestors, the Jurchens—had moved the other way, into the towns along the Ming frontier;
others moved between them as traders of horses, ginseng, pine seeds,
pelts and other desired Northeastern products. Nurgaci's Later Jin (*Hou
Jin*) state, ignoring the genealogical ties of the urbanized Jurchens with
peoples settled in tribal villages under their rule, classed the latter together with the "Chinese-martial" (*nikan, hanjun*), people of often indeterminable Chinese, Jurchen or Korean descent who inhabited the Ming
pale of Liaodong. They were brought into the Jurchen camp in the early
seventeenth century either by their own will or by being kidnapped by
Jurchen raiders. After 1601, when the "Eight Banners" (*jakūn gūsai,
baqi*) began to be formed, those incorporated were classed as Manchu,
Mongol or Chinese-martial on the basis of their cultural affinities, with
little reference to ancestors.

In its maturity, the Qing court deeply changed in its assumptions on
matters of identity. The eighteenth-century emperors, and particularly
the Qianlong emperor Hongli (r. 1736–1795), put a new emphasis upon
genealogy, encouraging Manchus to maintain or renew their acquaintance with the knowledges necessary, in his eyes, for their cultural and
spiritual health. Ironically, the court of the eighteenth century, in its insistence that race should determine culture, had begun to approach the
philosophy championed by dissident scholars of the early period of the
Qing conquest. There is no evidence that Hongli was successful in any
general sense in his campaign to hone the racial and cultural consistency
of the Manchus, though the imperial endorsement of the concept of racial

identity would have far-reaching consequences. Much more crucial in the actual shaping of a sense of Manchu identity was the Taiping War (1850–1864), in the course of which many marginal bannermen were permanently alienated from the communities while a conscious choice of loyalty or apostasy was forced on those who remained. All those readily identified as bannermen were subjected to the clearest pronouncements of racial differentiation, issuing from Chinese nativists, as well as to both threatened and actual extermination at the latter's hands. The war experience and its aftermath of official abandonment and economic destitution was the matrix in which Manchu racial and cultural sensibilities were forged; the Manchu ethnic consciousness that resulted was reinforced during the Republican Revolution of 1911/12 and its aftermath.

The Qing "world" invoked in the title of this work had particular components for the Manchus, around whom it was disintegrating in the nineteenth century. There was, at its center, the court (*chao*), which in most usage included the dynastic lineage, its rituals, the living emperor, his family, and all those about him involved in guiding the realm. The court was in the Forbidden City (*zijincheng*), which was in the Imperial City (*huangcheng*), which was in the Inner City (*neicheng*), which together with the Outer City (*waicheng*) comprised Peking, the center of the empire. Very few Manchus stationed outside the capital ever saw Peking, though most may have wanted to. Many had relatives or acquaintances who had travelled to the capital on some business or for an educational stint, or perhaps to be conducted to one of the smaller palaces within the Forbidden City and awarded a token of merit for accomplishment in education or military service, or for a belated recognition of a loyal or chaste ancestor. Back in the garrisons, word of the glory of Peking travelled quickly among the few thousands in any community, who generally lived as a tiny minority among the Chinese they were supposed to be occupying. More than their ancestral territories in the Northeast, Peking (which was the point of legal registration for all mobilized bannermen in the early Qing period) was the spiritual home of the Manchus of China. There was, equal with the court and the capital, an invisible unifying power for the Manchus in their clans, which constituted the history of the dynasty and of the Manchu people themselves. As court-endorsed symbols of identity and as the matrix of family lore, clans worked on many levels to supply a definition and a direction for Manchus in the nineteenth century. But the world of the Manchus was also founded upon each garrison, as an independent and enduring entity. After the early eighteenth century it was uncommon for Manchus to move away from the garrison in which they were born. Though particular conditions varied from garrison to garrison, in general bannermen learned to speak the local dialects as their own tongue, to adopt many of the social values, and to relish the local history. The result was a division of the Manchu landscape between those who had stayed in the Northeast (or returned there during the early Qing) and those who had immigrated to China, with further divisions between those settled in Peking and those in the provincial garrisons. In tension with these powers of diversification were the unifying bonds of the court and the capital, history and the clans. Imbalances in the dynamic interplay of these forces determined the cultural destiny of the Manchus, who in the nineteenth and into the twentieth century became aware of the gradual attenuation of the structures erected and fitfully reinforced by the Qing founders.

The Manchus and their changing political, social, cultural and economic status are fundamental problems in the history of the Qing dynasty. The most frequently encountered questions on the Manchus relate to their presumed "sinicization," specifically the ways in which the process of bannermen becoming urban and sinophone may have affected the military preparedness or the cultural personality of the Qing dynasty. The historical and theoretical difficulties of "sinicization" will be left for later parts of this work. What lies immediately before us is the problem of knowledge about the Manchus of China proper, or present-day China without the Northeast ("Manchuria"), Xinjiang ("Chinese Turkestan") or Tibet. This is a study of Manchu experience and sensibility in the late imperial period. It is fundamentally guided by the experiences and extant writings of three generations of members of the Suwan Gūwalgiya clan who lived at the Hangzhou and Zhapu garrisons in Zhejiang province from the very early Qing period to its last decades. They were not noblemen, nor did they experience the lower extremes of economic privation that many bannermen suffered during the dynastic period. Their perspectives on their experiences seem to cast light on the great issues of Manchu life in the Chinese provinces: the complex relationship they saw developing between themselves and individual Chinese as well as China as a society; the essential urbanism of Manchu life in China; their persisting unpreparedness for the violence that increasingly threatened their communities in the nineteenth and twentieth centuries; and the growing sense of a Manchu "people" with an identity and a destiny that was distinct from, and might even transcend those of, the Qing dynasty who created them. These are part of the texture of Manchu history that, I suspect, has been obscured for a long time by some received wisdom on the meaning of "sinicization," for Manchus and for other peoples in China.

The present work does not pretend to new accomplishments in the history of banner or garrison institutions. Materials for research on such topics are plentiful and have already been exploited in excellent institutional studies; more is possible in this vein, and will be accomplished.

The significance of Manchu culture and experience, like much else in China's late Qing social and cultural history, has not been particularly well reflected in the amount of material that is available for their research. The paucity of good information about Manchu life may have been felt as early as the eighteenth century, when the Mongol Sungyun (1751–1835) wrote, supposedly on the basis of his interviews with aged bannermen in the Northeast, "Record of One Hundred and Twenty Stories from Old Men" (*Emū tanggū orin sakda-i gisun sarkiyan*), published in 1791.[6] Three collections of documents from the garrisons provide a sampling of official history, together with bannerman poetry and memoirs. The earliest, "History of the Garrison of the Eight Banners at Jingzhou" (*Jingzhou zhufang baqi zhi*), was compiled under the editorship of Xiyuan in 1879. "History of the Eight Banners at Canton" (*Zhu Yue Baqi zhi*), compiled by Changshan and others between 1879 and 1884, dealt with banner life at the Canton garrison. The last, "Administrative History of the Eight Banners Garrison at Hangzhou" (*Hangzhou Baqi zhufang ying zhilue*), compiled by Zhang Dachang and others, was first published by the Zhejiang provincial printing office in 1893. The second and third of the above were partially utilized by the writing group that produced "Short History of the Manchus" (*Manzu jianshi*) in Peking in 1977, and all were extensively employed by Kaye Soon Im in her 1981 comparative administrative history, "The Rise and Decline of the Eight Banner Garrisons in the Ch'ing Period (1644–1911): A Study of the Kuang-chou, Hang-chou and Ching-chou Garrisons." The gazetteer of the Suiyuan garrison was produced in 1958, and recently the history of the Manchu community at Huhhot has been published.[7] The present study, which builds upon a foundation laid in my dissertation, in my published articles and unpublished papers, makes use of Zhang's collection on the Hangzhou garrison, as well as the local histories for Hangzhou, West Lake, Pinghu county in Zhejiang province, Peking, selected counties in Sichuan province, and various locations in the Northeast for the appropriate periods of the nineteenth and twentieth centuries. Archival material has come primarily from the Number One (Ming-Qing) Historical Archives in Peking, particularly the *Shenji ying* and Zhao Erxun collections. Where it has seemed responsible to do so, information from such sources has been augmented by literature, some fictional, written by or about bannermen, including the work of Lao She (Shu [Sumuru] Qingchun), Dun Lichen ([Fuca] Dunchang), [Feimo] Wenkang, and Wu Woyao. There are, however, certain peculiarities associated with the present research that must be pointed out, for it is an example of the historian's paradox of self-reference. "Draft History of the Qing" (*Qingshi gao*), or what in other circumstances might have represented the preliminary form of the standard reference history of the Qing dynasty, is here a primary document, since one of the subjects of this study was notorious for his participation in the 1927 and 1928 attempts to publish and distribute "Draft History." Indeed, the involvement of [Suwan Gūwalgiya] Guancheng (c. 1790–1842), Fengrui (1824–1906) and Jinliang (1878–1962) in writing and publishing documents related to garrison life dated back to the early nineteenth century, making them an unwieldy historical vehicle. They are producers of most of the documents through which we know them.

Like all biographies, case studies or local studies (elements of all three are combined here), this work must eventually confront the problem of its own representativeness. The reader will undoubtedly wonder at many points how much the main figures here resemble most other Manchus. The writer has wondered, too. Where it has been possible an attempt has been made to create a comparative context. But it should be understood that representativeness is a rather meaningless question, given the state of our present knowledge of Manchu cultural life in the middle and late Qing period. As indicated above, this is a field that still harbors a few excellent documents for study, but they are small in number. Beyond those resources, it is from a study such as the present one, based upon a wide range of circumstantial and often indirect information, that a sense of Manchu life in the nineteenth and twentieth centuries can be drawn. In its way, this study represents a limit (at present) of what is known of literate Manchu experience in the modern period. By default, the subjects are representative. That will change, probably quite soon.

Another consideration is still at hand, however. This study suggests (and I am confident that future works will confirm) that Manchus throughout their history (and very certainly in the nineteenth century) were never a simple, single category that could be distilled to a particular type. The origins of the Manchus were diverse, their class system was rigid and powerful, their geographical dispersion was vast, and as the dynasty passed its prime their economic and political differences became profound. This study argues that within that diversity there was coherence, both in the sense of unity and in the sense of orderly difference. Rather than forming a single group, there were within the late Qing Manchus constituencies of the poor, the middle class, the wealthy, diagonally divided by radically conservative, progressively moderate, and actively revolutionary convictions. For the Manchus as a group, however, there was also a coherent unity. A core of tradition and a controlling symbolic vocabulary combined with a shared history to provide the basis for Manchu self-identification in the nineteenth and twentieth centuries. In the case of the Suwan Gūwalgiya lineage of Hangzhou, there is evidence of an emerging Manchu articulate stratum, a "middle class," or what the authors of "Short History of the Manchus" describe as "new capitalists" among the bannermen, with an orderly difference from many other Manchus. Economically and culturally advantaged in comparison to the majority of Manchus, firmly established as local elites in their home community, cherishing an ancient connection with the nobility in Peking and an increasingly problematic identification with the court, these men are representative of a politically dynamic stratum of later Qing Manchu society that had a rather clear view of its relationship to other portions of Manchu and banner society. They are also writers with a point of view that lends itself to decipherment, but they are writers nonetheless—subjective, individualistic, and sometimes painfully eccentric. Representativeness among the Manchus, at this point, is an issue for which the best questions have not yet been devised, far less answered in a way that can be satisfactory.

Jinliang died in 1962. Until fairly recently he was well-known by his literary name, "Old Man of the Melon Patch" (*Guapu laoren*), for his supernatural and historical vignettes. In this regard he was a minor star in the constellation of Manchu writers on life and manners at the end of the Qing. But in the 1920s and very early 1930s Jinliang was notorious as one of the most energetic and more resourceful of the Qing loyalists who attempted, in the early Republican decades, to build a coalition that would restore the Qing empire to existence and its last emperor, Puyi, to the throne. The hopes of the group gradually diminished after their expulsion from Peking in 1924, and by 1931 their cause had been appropriated by the Japanese Guandong Army, the Kantōgun. In his own view, Jinliang had by the timing and circumstance of his birth (with or without the infusion of Yue Fei's spirit) lived a life that admitted of no other real outlet than literature. He often brooded, we know, upon the irony of being born to a prominent family, scion of one of the world's most honored clans, with all the talent and privileges that could be desired, in one of the most beautiful and cultured cities on earth, yet to live out one's last thirty years as a deprived and distrusted relic of the past, with no place in or understanding of the new order. Jinliang did not always live his life with exemplary wisdom, courage or style. His was, nevertheless, inarguably a life exquisitely posed to teach the hazards of surviving one's historical context.

PART ONE

Though there was great diversity in the life of the garrisons in the early nineteenth century, these differences represented variations upon basic themes established in the seventeenth and eighteenth centuries. Most immediate was the idealism of the Qianlong court (1736–1795), which had prompted a set of policies designed to promote standard Manchu speech, Manchu literacy, and accomplishment in the traditional military skills among the bannermen. Still fundamental, however, was the legacy of the conquest and the occupation, which demanded that bannermen in China be concentrated in garrison compounds, that they be permanently sustained by supplies of commodities and cash, and that they be bound to military service regardless of whether the state had occasion to actually employ them. By 1800 the purposes of many of these policies had faded, and their practicability was in permanent doubt. But the interdependency of the state and the garrisons had not yet dissolved.

CHAPTER I

Peace and Crisis

THE PACIFICATION and occupation of Xinjiang, the "New Dominion," in 1755 marked the end of the last great stage in Qing territorial expansion. That was a little more than a century after the first Manchu invaders had entered China through the Shanhai Pass in the spring of 1644 and pro- ceeded to seize control of the Ming capital at Peking. In systematic but often slow succession, the Qing court pursued its campaign of conquest to the limits of the former Ming empire (1368–1644), and beyond. Taiwan was annexed as the Manchus attempted to root out loyalist resisters who used it as a base from which to harry the shores of southeast China in the 1680s. The border stretches of Mongolia and the Yunnan-Guizhou fast- nesses were stabilized only in the late seventeenth and middle eigh- teenth centuries, respectively. Tibet was invaded in 1720, occupied in 1750 and under firm Qing control by the end of the century. And Xin- jiang, the acquisition of which nearly doubled the expanse of the empire, was conquered in stages during the middle eighteenth century. Banner horsemen had spearheaded and Manchu nobles had overseen the inva- sion of Ming China. When the conquest was secure it was the bannermen who were installed as the agents of occupation, in closed garrison com- munities where their activities were, at least in the regulations, strictly limited. Until the opening of Xinjiang, that portion of the banner popu- lation directly involved in the conquest—probably on the order of 120,000–150,000[1]—had been as mobile as the front itself, shifting in units from the Manchu ancestral lands in Northeast Asia to Peking, from Pe- king to the provinces of central and south China, from central China to the northwest China, southwest China and Xinjiang. With the ultimate expansion of the empire, massive population transfers ceased, and an un- precedented stability overcame the Manchus.[2] Cultural and social crises, of various appearances and severities, ensued.

At bottom the post-conquest difficulties of the bannermen were ques- tions of identity. Although in the eighteenth century lofty issues of cul- tural and spiritual well-being would come into play, in the earlier Qing period the concerns were rather more mundane. Livelihood and legal privilege were both mediated by the definition of "bannerman" (gūsai niyalma, qiren). In the nineteenth century, "bannerman" would be used ambiguously to indicate individuals of Manchu or sometimes Mongol heritage, as well as the complex group called Chinese-martial (nikan *cooha, hanjun*),[3] and it was generally assumed by the civilian, or non-banner, population that all bannermen received monthly stipends from the court. But in the seventeenth and eighteenth centuries, "bannerman" had been a rather precise term, excluding many of the individuals called by that name in later times. In this earlier context it denoted a man enrolled in one of the Eight Banners (*jakūn gūsa, baqi*), the socio-military organizations created under Nurgaci beginning as early as 1601 in order to "unite the various peoples under one rule"[4]—that is, to marshall the energies of and to control distribution of booty to the warriors of friendly or conquered tribes brought under Nurgaci's power. An early seventeenth-century bannerman might have been a Manchu, a Mongol, a Northeastern tribesman, a Korean or Chinese transfrontiersman,[5] who had joined Nurgaci's band either to avoid annihilation or to profit by the expansion of the Later Jin (*Hou Jin*) khanate (1616–1626); in 1685, a separate company was created for the "Russians" incorporated after the fall of Albazin, within the Romanov territories.[6] A bannerman was not, in these times, a member of the Manchu nobility, which by virtue of politically meaningful marriage had come to embrace a good number of men and women of Mongolian descent.[7] The imperial clan, who after the middle of the seventeenth century called themselves Aisin Gioro, were effectively the owners (*ejen*) of the banners before the reforms of Hung Taiji (1592–1643).[8] Through a process of entitlement the court extended the noble class, beginning with the so-called "Eight Great Houses" (*ba dajia*) and "Eight Colleagues" (*ba fen*) and continuing, with various degrees of reward and heritability, to the minor ranks with which loyal deeds were recognized to the end of the Qing era. The majority of non-noble bannermen were understood to be "common" (*irgen*).[9]

It would be misleading to consider commoners, here, to be "free," since in the traditional Manchu and early Qing context freedom was relative. Domestic servitude in various forms encumbered a good number of Manchus and Chinese-martial. The elite of the domestic slave world were the so-called bondservants (*boo-i aha, baoyi*), many of whom were incorporated into the Three Superior Banners as the personal or household servants of the imperial clan.[10] In less exhalted station, slaves also served the nobility as agricultural workers, household menials, bodyguards or secretaries. The origin of the slave class is obscure, dating to the pre-conquest period in which Jurchens, Koreans, tribal peoples of Northeast Asia, and settled Chinese were captured during warfare or traded among warchiefs.[11] On the eve of the conquest, it is probable that the number of bondservants rose dramatically as Qing control over western Liaodong was consolidated.[12] After the conquest, reduction to slave status within the banners was a judicial matter, reserved as punishment for serious offenses such as desertion, manslaughter and rape.

Military servitude was qualitatively a different experience from its agricultural and domestic parallels. The continued development of the banners and the refinement of an identity for the Manchus under Hung Taiji drew deeply, as did the evolution of a distinctive style for the Qing court, upon the Mongolian traditions that had been familiar in the Northeast since the Yuan dynasty (1260–1368). A Manchu would be distinguished by his skills. The cavalry was the heart of the conquest army, and Manchus, like Mongols and Turks before them, were expected to give precedence to their skills in horsemanship and archery, including the art of shooting from horseback (niyamniyambi, qishe) that had been the hallmark of all Inner Asian conquerors. A Manchu was, moreover, a man who used his skills exclusively to serve the sovereign. Formal discussions of servitude during the Qing period normally omit bannermen, but the fact is that the banners as institutions were derived from Turkic and Mongolian forms of military servitude, all enrolled under the banners considered themselves slaves of the emperor and called themselves so (aha, nucai) when addressing him, and all were legally bound to pursue military careers unless excused by the court. More fundamentally, the personal relationship of the Manchu soldier to his ruler was a continuation of the Mongolian tradition, a model of slave to owner: "The Mongol is the slave of his sovereign," a twelfth-century prisoner informed his Mameluk captor. "He is never free. His sovereign is his benefactor; [the Mongol] does not serve him for money."[13] The Turco-Mongolian institution of hereditary military slavery was clearly the guiding image in the state's elaboration of banner institutions and Manchu identity in the middle seventeenth century. For the bannermen, the state encouraged mediation of concepts like loyalty not through the Confucian conceit of parent and child that it applied to civil relations, but through the tradition of the owner and slave.[14]

The premise, however, was founded on a basic contradiction, and the Qing court understood as their Mongolian predecessors had understood the special status of a skilled, armed man in servitude. Aware of the limits of toleration for the ennui of slavery, the emperors required that the bannermen observe primarily the external forms of servitude. In turn, the bannermen cherished their ritual slavery as an emblem of their importance to and intimacy with the court. But rarely, it must be acknowledged, did the court push for more than ritual. Manchus were well compensated for their service, first with booty, then after the conquest with rice and cash. When bannermen came occasionally to view their salaries as insufficient to cover their expenses, they demonstrated their dissatisfactions—sometimes vocally, sometimes violently. Demands from the ranks for increased compensation and monetary gifts for the sustenance of their debts were usually addressed with promptness by the government. Educational policies of the later seventeenth and earlier eighteenth centuries, though couched in stern rhetoric, in fact were pressed upon the bannermen very gently. Government drafting of bannermen into the newly created language schools and military units of the middle nineteenth century was in reality a search for volunteers, who were paid well for their cooperation. As an individual, certainly, any bannerman was liable to be exposed to the extremes of the Qing regime's ability to punish or reward. As a group, however, the bannermen enjoyed, until the middle nineteenth century, the privilege of being the perceived foundation upon which the state was built, and thus were often sheltered from an emperor's wrath, demands for performance or inclinations to economize.

During the Qing period the meaning of "bannerman" and the meaning of "Manchu" were intertwined in constant ambiguity. But bannermen were bannermen before the Manchus were Manchus and, indeed, before the Qing was the Qing. The people from whom Nurgaci arose were called Jurchens (*jusen, nusen, nuzhen*) of the Jianzhou federation, once led by Nurgaci's ancestors.[15] During the last years of the sixteenth century, when Nurgaci began his campaigns, the Jurchens had been a culturally diverse and politically contentious collection of peoples. Some claimed among their ancestors the Jurchens who had created and sustained an empire in the Northeast and Northern China between 1115 and 1234. Some had lived close to the Chinese, both geographically and culturally, in Liaodong, the portion of the Northeast closest to the Great Wall. Others, particularly the group called the Hulun federation, were heavily influenced by the Mongols. Northeastern peoples of upper Jilin and Heilongjiang—some, like the Evenks (Solon) and Golds (Hezhe), close to the Manchus linguistically—had had their tribal affairs influenced very little by the Chinese, Mongol or Korean regimes, and seem never to have been caught up in the confederalizing that might had made them "Jurchen."[16] By 1635 Hung Taiji, the second khan of the Later Jin, announced that the majority of the banner populations were now melded into a new people, to be called not Jurchens but Manchus (*manju, manzhou*), a name whose meaning and source are still unclear. The new identity subsumed not only the majority of Jurchens, but also the acculturated descendants of Chinese and Korean transfrontiersmen. At the same time, some Jurchens became not Manchus in this process but Mongols or Chinese-martial.[17] The next year Hung Taiji created the Qing empire and declared himself emperor. With the surrender of the Chahar Mongols in 1635 he had become, by virtue of his earlier victory over Legdan Khan (1592–1634), the successor of the Mongolian khans back to Genghis. The Korean king, whose ancestors had been vassals of the Mongolian khans, was subjugated in 1637. The conquest of Ming China, with whom the Jurchens and then the Manchus had been at war off and on for nearly twenty years, was becoming a possibility (though Hung Taiji would not live to see it) and may well have figured in the redefinition of the Manchus. For the disparate Jurchen groups, the new name "Manchu" signified the khanate's intentions to create a new unity of purpose and identity for the peoples incorporated in the banners.

The early legal criteria, such as they were, for determining bannerman status were simple: a bannerman was a soldier of the khan, and later, of the emperors. But the banners had been the only centralized means the state had of regulating and administering its military population before the creation of the empire in 1635/36. Since bannermen's families were subsumed under the banner apparatus, the vast majority of this "banner" population was not combatant. Bannerman status entailed a share in the rewards of conquest; the state therefore limited the number of banner appointments available. Females, males who were handicapped or infirm, below the age of fifteen and over the age of sixty, or less than 1.56 meters in height were not eligible for service. Moreover, at any given point only a minority of eligible Manchu, Mongol or Chinese-martial commoners served actively in the banners, and could thus with precision be called "bannermen." For the pre-conquest period, actively serving Manchus probably comprised about a third of the Manchu male population.[18] For the post-conquest period, the ratio increased steadily, and after the early nineteenth century becomes incalculable because of changes in statutory definition of bannerman and a general decline in the rigor with which garrison records were kept. In the years prior to the conquest the non-serving majority was called, simply enough, "leftovers" (*yuding*). Typically, they were either sons over the age of fifteen eligible to serve but not yet appointed, or the younger brothers in a family who had yielded precedence for an appointment to an older sibling. In the middle seventeenth century, this population was recognized as *zidi*, or "sons and younger brothers." The *zidi* were often assigned agricultural duty in the early khanate and imperial periods. But they were also potential bannermen, and the state showed the same concern for their education and welfare that it showed for the actively serving population. They were the last component in the lineage-based system that had allowed the banners, through their constituent companies, to organize the populace. Rice, silver, and communications from above flowed through the serving bannermen to their wives, parents, *zidi* and the families of *zidi*; in turn, service to the emperor and obedience to the law was supposed to flow upward from those dependents through the bannermen.

The function of households and lineages in the early banner companies inevitably extended questions of banner affiliation to a population encompassing not only both sexes, all ages, and all classes, but also several cultures, all differences that the early banners accommodated rather deftly. The geographical origins of the New Manchus (*ice manju*), who were drawn from a variety of peoples including the Dagurs, Orochons, Evenks, Sibo and Gold peoples—all formerly tribal peoples of the region with varying degrees of historical and cultural affinity with the Manchus proper[19]—underscore the ancient division of the Northeast into two cultural worlds and the continuing reflection of the old boundaries in Qing Manchu life. The inner zone, primarily modern Liaoning province, had since Tang times (618–906) been subjected to a steady, if at first thin, Chinese influence; in Ming times (1368–1644) the region had been permitted to establish firm and important commercial ties with China proper, which had further opened the channels of Chinese immigration and cultural penetration in the area. A large portion, though not a majority, of the Jurchens who had begun to call themselves Manchu in the early seventeenth century came from this inner zone. Its heart was Mukden (Shenyang), which in 1625 became the seat of the Later Jin government and site of the early tombs of the Aisin Gioro clan. The outer region—primarily modern Jilin and Heilongjiang provinces—where tribal traditions remained strong, retained pockets that were only casually acquainted with the Chinese language and political order until the early twentieth century. Changbaishan, the great extinct volcano that became sacred to the Manchus and to the imperial clan, was located in such a corner of the old Jurchen world. The eighteenth-century court recognized it as the continuing link of the Qing Manchus with their past, and the outer region of the Northeast as a protected homeland where the old ways continued, at least in the thought of the Qianlong emperor, without the intrusion of Chinese language, religion, or urbanization.[20]

The cultural diversity that had marked the early banner population took on a different pattern after a settlement of a portion of the population in China. In Canton (where Manchus did not reside until the massive displacement of the Chinese-martial garrison population in order to make way for them in the middle eighteenth century), in the great cities of Zhejiang and Jiangsu provinces, in Fujian and many other regions, bannermen were susceptible to influence by and even sympathy with the local culture. There were, however, many parts of the country where the garrison communities proved relatively impermeable to Chinese influence. The bannermen of Xinjiang were by legend the stiffest.[21] During the Qianlong period they, more than most other bannermen, were aware of their role as conquerors; they had come most recently to their territory and even well into the nineteenth century found it the most difficult to keep pacified. They also learned to live as one people in a variegated cultural landscape: Muslims, Mongols, Manchus, Tibetans, Turks, Uigurs, Kazaks and Chinese of many provinces settled the "New Dominion," keeping their distance and their customs. Many of the Manchu bannermen who settled Xinjiang had previously been stationed at Xi'an, in a Shaanxi province that by Qing times had become isolated from China's centers of economic development; there they had been familiar with the dynamics of a provincial city with unresolved cultural differences.[22]

Curiously, in the regions where the Manchu population of Qing times was concentrated there was often the greatest change in the cultural life of the bannermen. Slightly more than half of all registered Manchus during the Qianlong period lived either in Peking or in the Northeast. During the initial period of conquest in the middle seventeenth century, there had apparently been no justification for the evacuation of the Manchu homeland; as many troops as seemed necessary were taken into China and the remainder were left behind to protect the home territories. The number of China-based bannermen had been augmented as the garrisons were created in the successively conquered regions, and Manchu families, as well as additional soldiers, were summoned from the Northeast into China. Those Manchus remaining in the Northeast had their numbers enlarged somewhat by the ongoing incorporation into the Eight Banners of the New Manchus, some groups of which were ultimately recognized as unincorporable and organized into irregular "hunting and fishing" (butha) banners.[23] In the late Kangxi period, as the court began its long rumination on the historical meaning of "Manchu," it gathered into the Manchu banners those it construed to have Manchu affinities but who had not yet been recognized as such.[24]

By the middle eighteenth century, the banners were no longer adequate for the accommodation of new cultural and social diversity among the bannermen. The garrison cultures, if they could have been systematically compared, would have presented a patchwork of adaptations and innovations, many disturbing to the court. Economic conditions varied sharply. Some communities had retained their land grants from the century before and lived off them securely. Others had lost their land or managed it ineffectively, and their inhabitants were declining to total dependence upon the rice and silver stipends. By the early eighteenth century, competition for banner company appointments and the hereditary captaincies had become intense. Bannermen were beginning to turn to thievery and begging in addition to a range of more conventional but, for bannermen, equally illegal trades. Desertion, always a problem, increased, and local populations often protected garrison fugitives. Provincial bannermen in poverty-stricken garrisons began flocking to Peking, closer to the accumulated wealth of the dynasty and the chances of sharing in its effects.

The Qianlong court, caught in a confusing nexus of economic, social and cultural changes throughout the garrison communities, took an aggressive posture toward the management of Manchu life and identity. Certainly the Qianlong emperor was under no illusion that the populations of the garrisons actually devoted themselves to lives of frugality and single-minded cultivation of the martial spirit. His father and grandfather had frequently inveighed in their own times against the military unpreparedness of the bannermen. But by the late eighteenth century the Eight Banners had lost their role as the mainstay of imperial power. The suppression of the Rebellion of the Three Feudatories in 1681 had forced a recognition of the importance of the Chinese auxiliary forces of the Green Standard, created in each province at the time of conquest as a police and maintenance force.[25] With the final victory in Xinjiang in 1755, the Eight Banners' mission of conquest seemed to have been achieved, though poorly planned and erratically financed attempts to awe Southeast Asia would mar the later part of the century. Hongli himself continued to scold garrison officials for gross dereliction of military duty, but it was clear even early in his reign that the real military role of the banners had diminished markedly. New forms of decay aroused Hongli's concern. Officials continually brought to the emperor's notice the convictions of banner officers who broke curfew, often for the express purpose of indulging in the forbidden pleasures of the Chinese cities in which they dwelt; who had illegally sold banner agricultural or grazing land, sometimes to settle their private debts to Chinese lenders; who had, in exchange for recommendations for appointment or promotion, extorted goods and money from their own bannermen, whom they were sworn to steward on behalf of the court. The officer class of the garrisons may have seemed to him a garden that, weeded, was only incited to the more furious production of offending flora. His displeasure was piqued not only by the turpitude of his soldiers but also by those hints he could glean of new attitudes and behavior, much of which represented a clear departure from *fe doro*, the "Old Way."

Hongli's reaction, as he became increasingly aware of the economic decline and cultural diversity among the bannermen, was conservative, restorationist, and in context probably impracticable. Once his great-great-grandfather Hung Taiji, anticipating an era in which the Manchus would experience, in post-conquest lassitude, the same cultural deshabillement that had afflicted their imperial Jurchen ancestors, had approvingly cited the policies of the restorationist Jin ruler Shizong (r. 1161–1191), who had forced his Jurchens to return to the Northeast for a period of reacclimation to rural, martial life. Hongli was canny enough to know that forced relocation might well spark rebellion among the bannermen. His hope, instead, was that Manchus might travel home in their minds and be reeducated in their communities. The emperor himself had been trained in the written Manchu and Chinese languages since childhood and in all probability was a true bilingual. In his ancestral language he wrote poems and edicts, and indulged his romantic interest in the history of the imperial clan by sponsoring the composition, in 1743, of "Ode to Mukden" (*Mukden i fujurun bithe, Shengjing fu*) in Manchu. In successive translations into European languages the work helped nurture the Enlightenment enthusiasm for the Oriental philosopher-king, for which Hongli was taken as a suitable model.[26] His reign period saw publication of "General History of the Eight Banners" (*Jakūn gūsai uheri ejetun bithe, Baqi tongzhi*) in 1739, "Comprehensive Genealogies of the Clans and Lineages of the Eight Banner Manchus" (*Manjusai mukūn hala be uheri ejehe bithe, Baqi manzhou shizu tongpu*) in 1745, "Ceremonies for the Manchu Worship of the Spirits and of Heaven" (*Manzhou jishen jitien dianli*) in 1781, and "Researches on Manchu Origins" (*Manzhou yuanliu kao*) in 1783. The emperor became strident in his insistence that Manchus reclaim mastery of their language, and that they be regularly examined in martial skills. It was all aimed at the protection of the Old Way, which he regarded as the definitive thread in Manchu life and history. If Hongli's reaction to the problem seems of greater magnitude than that of his father, the Yongzheng emperor (r. 1723–1735) or his grandfather, the Kangxi emperor (r. 1662–1722), it is partly because the problems were better reported and probably in actuality more widespread than had previously been the case.[27] This does not, however, explain the character of Hongli's response. Natural conservatism (not at all a negligible consideration) aside, the court might have profited by allowing the expensive garrison communities to privatize and assimilate. But the Qianlong age was one in which racial and cultural identity came under increasing scrutiny and control by the court. The emperor was bent on authentic *manjurarengge*, "Manchuness," that which would distinguish those whom the state identified as Manchus.[28]

Part of the Qianlong emperor's sweeping and unprecedented concern with the cultural condition of the Manchu populations was due to an ideological preoccupation with imperial universalism and the image of the Qing sovereign as a patron of certain of the nationalities under his rule. Like the Jurchen Jin dynasty from whom they claimed descent, the Qing derived part of their legitimacy from the traditions of their native world, Northeast Asia.[29] But the glory of the mature empire was based upon its power to integrate disparate languages, cultures, religions and national economies into an externally undelimited political order. A corollary of this was the increasing tendency of the court to enforce registrations among bannermen along rigid Manchu, Mongol and Chinese-martial lines. In fact the early banners had institutionalized the ambiguous history and blurred criteria of these or any cultural characterizations; in the final analysis, seventeenth-century registration as one of these three groups was based upon the language, religion, occupation and place of residence of the registered individual. By the eighteenth century, particularly during the Qianlong reign, this had changed. Economic and political pressures for the clarification of individual cultural identity increased in what was possibly direct proportion to the social factors obscuring many of the original criteria of *manjurarengge*, primarily language and religion. The response of the court was to develop a construction of race. Individuals argued their right to be considered Manchu on the basis of genealogy, not their own cultural skills and proclivities.[30] Hongli elaborated upon these developments by attempting to encourage and, whenever possible, to enforce a congruence of racial descent to real cultural life. This allowed him to raise to rather grand heights an ancient element of the Qing emperorship, one reaching to Nurgaci, and having earlier roots in the the khanship of the Mongols. Nurgaci had styled himself a parent, impartially nurturing the various peoples under his rule. In its original context this vocabulary denominated the paternalistic relationship between master and slave. The theme was followed up in later times, particularly in the Yongzheng emperor's confrontation with questions of origin, race and universal emperorship in "Record of Great Righteousness Resolving Confusion" (*Dayi juemi lu*), and developed into a more nearly Confucian ideology of benevolent, impartial rule.[31] In monumental epigraphs, in encyclopedic and symbolic literature, and in his personal behavior, Hongli manifested the universal king, and if his tomb—which is adorned with the wheels of the Buddhist universal king, the *čakravartin*—is any indication, he was as interested in the religious as in the secular dimensions of that role. The Manchu bannermen were, by their ascribed cultural particularism, designated living emblems of the emperor's universalism.

Cultural distinctness and integrity for the Manchus was only one, but certainly an indispensable, element in the Qianlong order. Hongli's program as attested by imperial edicts, commentary and the introductions to various volumes produced during his reign rested upon clear, minimal criteria of *manjurarengge*: skills in archery and horsemanship, and above all a mastery of the Manchu language, preferably in its spoken form. The emperor's proper eighteenth-century Manchu was not an ideal, but existed in exemplars such as [Dolar] Hailancha (d. 1793), a bannerman of common origins who had to wait long for his due recognition as a commander, [Gūwalgiya] Fude (d. 1776), or his nephew Eldemboo (1748–1805) who was evidently totally incapable in either spoken or written Chinese but drew much of the inspiration for his military strategy from a Manchu translation of the Chinese novel, "Romance of the Three Kingdoms" (*Sanguo yanyi*).[32] It may also have had some reflection in his fascination with [Niohuru] Heshen (1750–1799), a bodyguard whose crudity

in the estimation of many Chinese may have seemed to Hongli a vindi-
cation of his pristine Manchuness.[33] The fading generation these men
represented were by and large Northeastern natives who figured prominently in the major banner military operations in the Southwest during
the 1770s and 1780s. But this small group was no influence upon the
garrison populations, whose total numbers for the later eighteenth century probably hovered near three million.[34] The hundreds of garrisons
now scattered throughout the country's provinces ranged in size from
about five hundred individuals to perhaps as many as thirty thousand,
each a small world forbidden by law from intercourse with its surroundings. Within the garrisons, the actively enrolled bannermen lived together with their families, surviving from the proceeds of their land
grants and the monthly stipends provided by the court. Ambitious bannermen of modest means or origins were expected to pursue the court-
sponsored education that would allow them to receive degrees through
competition in the examinations where special quotas had been established for them, and thereby gain access to lucrative civil posts; or they
could achieve literacy and competence adequate to rise through the garrison command ranks, perhaps attaining the coveted assignment to Peking; or they could resign themselves to garrison life, with its evolving
mix of the traditional and the urban.

Hongli was determined that bannermen should revive "Manchu
speech, riding and archery (*guoyu qishe*)." In reemphasizing the Manchu
military arts in his reform campaigns, the emperor was to a certain extent
building on precedents. There was the still considerable but diminishing
strategic concern with military preparedness. The Kangxi emperor, concerned about the effects of urbanization upon the bannermen, had made
riding and archery part of the formal curriculum of instruction for all bannermen. In 1689 he had replied to a Manchu licentiate's (*shengyuan*) pe-
tition to be examined on riding and archery, "The Manchus take riding
and archery as the root (*ben*), and this was originally no impediment to
book learning. Those bannermen examined as provincial and capital candidates should also be required to [show proficiency in] riding and archery." Hongli retained these regulations and further stipulated that they
should apply to *zidi* as well as to actively serving bannermen. Since the
vast majority of these individuals would never exercise their skills on behalf of the state, it is tempting to surmise that Hongli had in mind an
exploitation of the banner schools for his ultimate goal of re-acculturation
of the Manchus. "We fear," the editors of "Researches on Manchu Origins" (*Manzhou yuanliu kao*) said on his behalf, "that in later days the
banner descendants will forget the old order, and do away with riding
and archery, taking up Chinese (*han*) customs." Hongli made a passing
mark in riding and archery a prerequisite to being admitted to the ex-

amination halls, and Gioro Manchus (cadet branches of the Aisin Gioro imperial clan) were rewarded for their achievement in riding and archery or punished for inadequacy.[35] In 1753 he instructed the bannermen at Canton, "Horsemanship and archery, as well as Manchu speech, are the foundation of the Manchus, and every bannerman's foremost duty." This was to remain a frequent, formulaic exhortation from the Qing emperors to the garrison communities until the Opium War.[36]

The consistency with which the succeeding emperors after Hongli put primary emphasis upon Manchu speech was characteristic of the shift in standards of identity from military servitude to cultural (and by implication spiritual) life. Emperors before Hongli had seen little reason to force bannermen in mass into an intense program of Manchu language study. Political interests had indicated the reverse policy. When China had been freshly conquered, the state had been in need of Manchus who could handle the bureaucratic apparati. In practice, this meant encouraging banner officers to learn Chinese, the better to oversee the work of the Chinese bureaucrats upon whom the regime was unavoidably dependent. But as, in the middle seventeenth century, the rewards of a bureaucratic career came to look very alluring in comparison to a bannerman's shrinking allowance, more and more Manchus sought to compete in either the regular examinations or the "translation" examinations that had been particularly established for them. Manchu degree aspirants all but ceased their study of Manchu thereafter. The late seventeenth century court had begun its bolstering of Manchu usage by requiring that students in the banner academies at Mukden and Peking be divided evenly between those who would study in Manchu and those who would study in Chinese. Hongli later extended such provisions, as he had the requirements of archery and horsemanship, to all categories of bannermen, including *zidi* and intendant servicemen.[37] The reeducation programs, in other words, targeted a far greater number of Manchus than had a real probability of exercising their language skills in an official capacity.

But economic and social conditions within the garrisons placed serious constraints upon the ability of most Manchus to master two cultures, whether the motivations were strategic, political or cultural. The inevitable result was court dissatisfaction with the failure of Manchus to claim true accomplishment in either their traditional culture or in that of the Chinese. From an early period the Qing court was wary about allowing inadequately educated bannermen to pervade the court and central bureaucracy. The Kangxi emperor, whose interests were more strictly utilitarian than those of Hongli, had noted in 1667 that the rights to inherit and to purchase degrees had resulted in a large number of *zidi* who knew only Chinese, or Manchus and Mongols who did not know Manchu or

Mongol, or individuals who were illiterate in all languages. As a result they were "useless to the state." The emperor suggested that the deficients should be divided into those who were willing to study, those who were willing to assume *zidi* status, and those willing "to follow the banners to court," or serve in a variety of guard and attendant's posts there. His son, the Yongzheng emperor, acknowledged the importance of voluntariness in such reforms. He recommended that the sons and grandsons of the Three Superior Banners should attend a school, at which the teaching should be "not too strenuous." Students would be over twenty years of age. Those who had some training in Manchu and Chinese would receive a stipend of two taels, or ounces (*liang*) of silver, and one picul (*shi*) of rice, as well as being posted with the rank of clerk (*bithesi*). For non-readers and members of the Imperial Guard (*hujun*), the stipend would be four taels, plus rice and rank. Court distrust of Manchu preparation probably led to favorable employment opportunies for middle-level Chinese-martial bannermen for a time.[38] Manjusri, a Manchu of the Aisin Gioro clan who in 1728 was assistant commander (*fudutong*) of the Bordered Yellow Mongolian Banner, wrote to protest that Manchus were not receiving equal appointments with the Chinese-martial candidates in the Capital Garrisons. Manchus and Chinese, Manjusri reminded the emperor, were after all equal in "talent." In response, the emperor noncommitally ordered that upon the announcement of a vacancy the Manchu, Chinese-martial and civilian Chinese should each recommend one candidate to the Board of Appointments (*li bu*).[39]

Hongli shared his ancestors' contempt for Manchus who tried to negotiate their way to partial familiarity with two cultures. Those who had the energy or ambition to compete in the bureaucratic examinations fared as poorly as incompetent soldiers in the emperor's estimation, for he considered that the cultural milieu that the bannermen had created for themselves was both bastard and sterile. According to the complaint of [Janggiya] Yinjishan (1696–1771), "They both pollute Chinese customs and forget our heritage. Asked about archery and horsemanship, they demur, saying 'I am a scholar,' but asked about literature they say 'I am a bannerman.' "[40] The emperor replied, "They have become useless people and incurred my great disgust."[41] At first, like his father and grandfather, Hongli had been inclined to encourage more effective study of Chinese. He deduced that Manchu was so much a part of the garrison environment that it was impeding the bannermen's expertise in Chinese; execution of the standing mandate to rule over the Chinese bureaucratic class required greater concentration in the classics. In 1741, Hongli had decreed that Manchu national degree holders (*jinshi*) who ranked highly should be employed as magistrates, and for this reason the study of civil, or "non-banner (*wairen*)," affairs should be emphasized. "From childhood the Manchus learn to speak Manchu," Hongli explained. "And since Chinese is generally understood (*tongshun*), everyone can translate it. After examination, [Manchus] can receive appointments as translators. Since written Manchu (*Qingwen*) is used so much less extensively anyway, what need is there of its special study?"[42] By the later seventeenth century bannermen had established the practice of memorializing the throne (and receiving rewards) whenever members of their families forewent the special examinations established for Manchus and achieved degrees through the normal examinations.

Later, on the basis of better information about the garrison conditions and Manchu performance, Hongli reconsidered the policies he had inherited and in his own right encouraged. He grew jaded on reports of Manchu success in the examinations, and increasingly called for a return to definitive Manchu skills. After 1765 he advised bannermen that they need no longer disturb him with notifications of their households' success in the examinations unless the candidates had also distinguished themselves at horsemanship and archery.[43] And again he stressed the primary importance of the Manchu language. "Speaking Manchu is the Old Way of the Manchus," Hongli admonished four Manchu officials of the Court of Colonial Affairs who had been unable to keep up their end of an audience in the winter of 1762. He demanded that henceforth banner officers recommended for duty in Peking would have as an unwaivable requirement the ability to speak Manchu; no other qualifications would override a failure in the language. In addition the officers within the garrisons, from whom the candidates for duty in the capital would be drawn, would be responsible for testing their subordinates in Manchu conversation. Those who were proficient should be encouraged to become perfect, those who were deficient should be given remedial instruction. "And as for those from among the provincial officers appointed to duty in the capital who arrive for their audience still unable to speak Manchu, I will hold their commanders responsible," the emperor warned.[44] It must be emphasized that Hongli did not construe his own cultural role and status as emperor as a model for the Manchus. His childhood education had conspicuously encompassed a certain training in the Confucian classics, and he liked to pose as a literary patron.[45] But for the bannermen Hongli frankly prescribed a program of re-immersion in their own language and customs. "Whether you have studied classical literature is a matter of no concern to me."[46]

It should not be thought that Hongli's exclusive motivation in promoting reeducation in Manchu was personal or ideological. In fact the Manchu language was still a significant component in the workings of some sectors of the Qing bureaucracy. State organs such as the Court of Colonial Affairs (*Tulergi golo be dasara jurgan, Lifan yuan*) and the Grand

Council (*Coohai nashūn i ba, Junjichu*), both of which represented Qing innovations in the imperial bureaucratic structure, continued in the use of documentary Manchu and Mongol, for reasons of strategy and of protocol.[47] Despite an insistence that bannermen preparing for service in the civil or military bureaucracies learn Manchu orthography, unfamiliarity with the spoken language still wreaked havoc with communications in those languages. In 1779 Hongli in exasperation ordered that translations of edicts issued in Mongolian should be submitted to him for grammatical review, as was already the practice for Manchu; thus the emperor proposed to augment his normal duties of edict review by becoming a Manchu and Mongolian language tutor as well. "The Mongolian princes are receiving Mongolian communications from the Court of Colonial Affairs that they cannot understand. Those who have translated the materials from Chinese into Mongolian do not know what spoken Mongolian sounds like, so that there is a great disparity between the spoken and written word. There has recently been the case of Tongda's translations into Manchu, which Adai, when he received them, could not completely understand. It is not the case that Adai does not know Manchu, but that Tongda rigidly followed the pattern of Chinese in his writing, departing utterly from the grammatical order (*shenli*) of Manchu. From this we can see that spoken Manchu (*Qingyu*) and written Manchu (*Qingwen*) are two distinct entities, not surprisingly in disagreement. Thus the Mongol princes do not understand the Mongolian of the Court of Colonial Affairs in accord with its [Chinese] meaning. For more than a century since the dynasty was founded, the *zidi* of the Manchu and Mongolian banners have lived, like their grandfathers and fathers, in Peking. As a consequence they not only do not understand spoken Mongolian, but Manchu also is being lost day by day, and the bannermen persistently refuse to study."[48]

These educational and professional problems revolved to a great extent around the unusual relationship of the written to the spoken language in Manchu. The spoken language, a readily recognizable descendant of its ancestral Jurchen, had been commonly used among the Jurchens of Nurgaci's time and the Manchu bannermen who invaded China in the middle seventeenth century.[49] But the vast majority of speakers were illiterate. Those who did learn to read and write dealt with a comparatively new device. Until the late sixteenth century Jurchen had been written in a script derived from Chinese (though not intelligible to a Chinese reader). Under Nurgaci, Manchu came to be written in a phonetic script, adapted (by a slow and possibly, for contemporaries, confusing process) from Mongolian.[50] Before Hung Taiji commanded the translation into Manchu of selected Chinese historical and philosophical works, there was virtually no literature in Manchu. Development of the Manchu corpus was encouraged by the Kangxi and Qianlong emperors, but by then the speaking of Manchu among the bannermen in China was already in decline. The court readily perceived at this point that spoken Manchu and written Manchu were two separate problems. Some bannermen spoke but did not read, some read but did not speak, too many could handle neither. Not everywhere, but in many garrisons, the speaking of Manchu had become a mannerism of the elderly.[51] Under such conditions, the reading of Manchu became laborious; many did not even attempt to learn the language in any form but simply memorized long translation passages for the examinations, a trick that did not deceive or amuse the emperors.[52] Chinese-speaking bannermen who had to learn to read Manchu for the sake of their promotions devised the rather bizarre device of reading the script as if it were ideogrammatic, like Chinese. The phonetic orthography of Manchu was in reading aloud substituted with the Chinese, word for word, so that the syllabary was stripped of all phonetic content. Thus the word *niyalma*, "man, person," would by many bannermen of the eighteenth century and after be called *ren*, the Chinese for "man." Since Manchu was written with a limited syllabary of sixty-seven characters, this method was at least as cumbersome as it would be for a Chinese speaker to habitually substitute spoken Chinese for written English words of the same or similar meaning.[53] But it was the exact reverse of the means by which Chinese script had been introduced, a thousand and more years before to the peoples of Northeast Asia, Korea and Japan, and it is unlikely that it seemed to its practitioners to be, on its face, ludicrous. It allowed those Manchus who adopted the method in the eighteenth century to part ways with the spoken language long before the requirements of the court would allow them to dispense with the written.

The spoken language was of equal and independent concern. Traditionally Jurchen/Manchu culture had been heavily dependent upon folk literature, and the ability to speak directly and forcefully remained a valued Manchu character trait until the end of the dynasty. In fact Manchu dialects lived in the garrisons, though rarely written and greatly changed by their contacts with Chinese. Hongli, however, was explicitly concerned with standardization and purification of Manchu speech. This was at least in part due to his emphasis upon the general standardization and codification of cultures throughout the realm. But he also had a particular interest in the role of language in the ancestral Manchu religion, shamanism. In Jurchen times shamanism had been integral to the clans and lineages and all their functions; through shamans the clans communicated with their individual spirits and sanctified their collective economic activities. The Qing emperors had maintained their intimacy with their own clan shamanism and amalgamated it to a certain extent with the Buddhist sects they patronized. Hongli clearly believed that the garrison Manchus of his time were neglecting the shamanistic rites. He reminded the court that shamanism was no less important to the Manchus than Buddhism or Confucianism. Once the secret, heritable traditions of the individual clans, the various shamanist rites used by the Manchus had now become incoherent. It was Hongli's conviction that the enforced distance of the lineages from one another that was part of the garrison system had led to distortion of worship. He was determined that order would be restored. In 1741 the emperor commanded that a compilation of shamanist rituals based on those of the imperial clan should be prepared for publication. The language, he noted, was crucial. Incantations used in the original ceremonies had all been in Manchu. But as decreasing numbers of young bannermen were familiar with the language, the liturgies had declined to a level of mumbo-jumbo that made those who understood the language wince. Princes were ordered to commit the utterances used in their own lineage rites to paper, and to bring them for Hongli's personal inspection. Those that were "nonsensical, incorrect, or unorthodox" would be edited, corrected or expunged, as necessary. They would be incorporated into the text, along with pictorial representations and explanations of the shaman's implements. Many of these items had been developed since the migration into China or had long ago lost their original terms, and the emperor was forced to a painfully revealing admission. "These we will have no choice but to call by their Chinese names."[54]

The dichotomy between written and spoken Manchu—or, as time went on, the more vexing problem of unspoken Manchu—was symbolic of the divided stream that the Qianlong court expected bannermen to swim as it became increasingly prescriptive in its concept of *manjura-rengge*. By slow but inexorable steps, the eighteenth-century Qing state was attempting to transform the Manchus from a pool of military servants to a population of cultural artifacts. There is no evidence that bannermen felt in sympathy with Hongli's aims, and in view of the many infelicities for garrison life that they implied, it is unlikely that bannermen were keenly aware of or inspired by the court's rhetoric. But they unquestionably grasped that economic contingencies were forcing the Qianlong court to pare a certain number of appointments from the banner rolls in the later decades of the eighteenth century. Those who could not produce genealogical evidence of Manchu ancestry were in some jeopardy of being consigned to the Chinese-martial banners, and from there to being struck off the lists of the court-supported population. Those who could produce such documentation were pressured to learn a language that may have been alien to them, to master skills that were irrelevant to their daily lives, and to practice a formalized version of what to them was possibly a little-understood and little-respected folk religion, all to the greater glory of the universal emperor, Hongli. Few Manchus of the eighteenth century could have imagined that they were identical with Chinese civilians. At the same time, it is clear that few Manchus of the period could claim to have fulfilled the Qianlong emperor's program for being Manchu. Somewhere between being Chinese and being Hongli's ideal lay the conditions of banner identity in the eighteenth century. Ironically, the strongest Manchu ties to their ancient folk traditions were in the clans, which the court had attempted to emasculate in all but their religious functions over the past century; and the Manchus' greatest alienation from their traditional way of life was the garrison, which the court had imposed upon them in an attempt to keep them free of Chinese influence. The true tests of Manchu self-definition lay ahead, in the coming conflicts with Europeans, with the Taiping rebels and with Chinese nationalists. At least one family, a Suwan Gūwalgiya lineage at Hangzhou, has left a testament of the process.

CHAPTER II

The Suwan Gūwalgiya

UNLIKE THE EMPEROR, the Manchus as a people made no statement of their policy regarding preservation of their identity. The evidence is that continuation of Manchu speech was of little consequence to the Manchus of China. Manchu-Chinese hybrid dialects abounded, but if it were the case that use of the language became awkward or dangerous, it was abandoned. The Manchu clans (*hala, mukūn, shi, zu*),[1] on the other hand, were not shed so easily. In many instances clan affiliation had social or political advantages. For the entitled nobility—that is, those who were not members of a branch of the imperial clan but enjoyed inherited meritory rank—clan affiliation was their main means of identification with the Eight Great Houses. They frequently memorialized the court on the eminence of their clans and, particularly in the nineteenth century, funded the printing of elaborate genealogies reifying their links to the founding group of the dynasty.[2] For others, the clans—as symbolic if not as social entities—were the means for the Manchus of maintaining access to the spirits and to the past. Hongli had seen *manjurarengge* as mediated by the Manchu language and religious rites. Manchus themselves saw it in the survival of the clans. In the early Qing period all Manchus and the court were in agreement on the utter dependence of Manchu history upon the clans and their names. For Manchu individuals, this tendency to see the clans as both the limits and the substance of Manchu identity was more powerful than the court's prescriptions for a total Manchu life, and the dynasty itself was seen as only an outcropping of the destiny of the clans.

On the basis of [Suwan Gūwalgiya] Jinliang's testimony it may be supposed that for a certain class of Manchu individuals this remained true well into the twentieth century. In Jinliang's youth, the glowing past of his clan and its association with the magnificence of the Qing had seemed to him a symbol of the continuing promise of the dynastic culture; in old age, he saw the decline and dispersal of his clan as corresponding to the ultimate dissipation of the imperial life-force. Jinliang did not know the imperial tutor Ikedan (1865–1923), whom he later eulogized as "the last loyal person in the court," until 1923 when the two discovered that they were fellow clansmen, both members of the great Suwan Gūwalgiya lineage whose branches in China proper traced their descent to Fiongdon, perhaps the closest and most famous comrade of the Qing founder Nurgaci. Ikedan and Jinliang considered writing together a group biography of the "loyal figures from our clan, in order to express our own loyalty." They had a model for such an enterprise, since the erstwhile regent Ronglu (1836–1903), also of their clan, had collated a partial hagiography of the Suwan Gūwalgiya, "Exemplary Biographies of Three Patriots of the Gūwalgiya Clan of Changbai" (*Changbai Guarjia shi san zhong liezhuan*) at the height of his suppression of the reform plans of the Guangxu emperor in 1898.[3] But Ikedan died before his work with Jinliang could begin. Like many others of Jinliang's plans during this period, the proposed genealogy came to nothing. "I tell you," Jinliang commented upon this episode, "the present decline and dispersal of our Manchu clansmen leaves me without any way to express myself. The very thought of it provokes me to uncontrollable weeping."[4] Clans, for most of the post-conquest period, were primarily symbols; but, as Jinliang's account attested, they were very powerful symbols indeed.

Manchu history prior to the conquest of China was a totality of the separate histories of the clans. The empire's history consequently found its genesis in that of the imperial clan, the Aisin Gioro. Clans and the equation of clan continuity with historical legitimation were so important to the Later Jin state created by Nurgaci that he and his descendants found it necessary to protect their supreme status within the state by actually inventing a clan and a clan history for themselves. Nurgaci assembled his Later Jin khanate out of the remnants of the old Jianzhou tribal federation (*aiman*), where elements of collegial rule were strong.[5] He had been dependent upon a close group of loyal retainers, who aided him not only in conquest but in governance thereafter; [Niohuru] Eidu (1561–1621), [Suwan Gūwalgiya] Fiongdon, [Donggo] Hohori (1561–1624), and others were remembered in Qing lore as the ancestors of the powerful Eight Great Houses. "Whenever the emperors wish to arrange marriages for their daughters, in the process awarding servants and slaves, they are most likely to pick a bridegroom from one of the Eight Great Houses," was how their role was later described by [Aisin Gioro] Zhaolian (1780–1833).[6] As khan, Nurgaci was anxious to protect the primacy of his own lineage. But like many other clans reconstituted in the wars of reunification, the clan with which Nurgaci was affiliated had a murky history, poorly documented before Nurgaci's own time.[7] The preponderance of the evidence indicates that his clan name was Gioro, and that it was a sixteenth-century reflex of the name that appears in the history of the Jurchen Jin dynasty three centuries before as Jiagu. In the historical records, their lineage could be traced to Möngke Temür, a powerful leader of the Jianzhou Jurchen federation who had died fighting another Jurchen band in northern Korea in 1433.[8] As an ancient clan the Gioro had many sub-branches and isolate lineages scattered across the

Northeast by Nurgaci's time, and in the course of his campaigns of unification a great many of them surfaced. It was important that none should be able to claim parity with his lineage. So Nurgaci created his own clan the Aisin Gioro—the Golden Gioro. Other branches were assigned prefixes of contrast, all equally improbable as real clan names: "Superior Gioro" (Silin Gioro), "Inferior Gioro" (Irgen Gioro), "Miscellaneous Gioro" (Tongyan Gioro), and so on.

There were two advantages of this innovation. First, the imperial clan was now distinct, historically as well as politically, from all other Gioro. To prevent a surplus of claims upon Aisin Gioro privilege over time, the Aisin Gioro name was strictly limited to the descendants of Nurgaci's father Taksi; all collateral branches derived from his grandfather Giocangga were simply "Gioro," and legal mechanisms were devised for the demotion of distant Aisin Gioro branches or miscreant members to Gioro status. Second, the name hinted at a direct historical link between the Aisin Gioro clan and the Jurchen Jin—or Golden—dynasty, an important element in Nurgaci's propaganda in his ongoing conflict with Ming China. Along with the new name came a very new and unique heritage. In their official lore, which was not refined until the Qianlong reign, the Aisin Gioro traced their roots to Bukuri Yungson of supernatural conception, who according to their tradition had risen to leadership of the amalgamated Jurchen peoples of Ilantumen, at the Songari-Amur confluence, in the thirteenth century.[9] It is possible that Möngke Temür's father or grandfather had been a headman of the Ilantumen Jurchens before their southward migration at the end of the fourteenth century to the region of modern Hunqun, verging both on the Korean border and the Changbai region. Whether more true or less true the myth was necessary, for it allowed the Aisin Gioro to subsume a good deal of Northeastern folk heritage under their own aegis and to lay ancestral claim to some strategic territory.

Aisin Gioro rhetoric on their own origins and the idealistic posture of the eighteenth-century court on the meaning of clan history for the origin and character of the dynasty may veil the fact that the very urgency of the court to systematize the documentation of clan origin was a response to actual irregularities in the origins and heritages of the peoples the court called Manchu after 1635. Jurchens had over the course of the Yuan and Ming periods shown great diversity, some forsaking the tribal territories for the acculturation of the Ming trading and administrative communities that dotted the northeastern frontier, others adhering to the more traditional Jurchen life of hunting, fishing, gathering and pelt production in the forests of the Northeast, and still others adopting the life and culture of the nomadic Mongols who then dominated North Asia and parts of Northeast Asia. Nurgaci created his khanate, the Later Jin, in

1616 after twenty years of wars of unification among antagonistic Jurchen federations, using the banners as a comprehensive military and social matrix to "unite the various peoples under one rule." By 1635, when the second Later Jin khan Hung Taiji declared that his incorporated, clan-affiliated military followers should be known, equally and individually, as "Manchu," a lasting political identity had been forged; divisions among the Manchus, Mongols and Chinese-martial within the banners, of which there were now eight, would henceforth be observed as a manifestation of the political relationship of the founding groups to the Qing rulers in the earliest dynastic period. The solidarity pretended to in Hung Taiji's state reformation was not entirely artificial. Plurality of cultural traditions in the middle seventeenth century did not preclude the presence of some very basic similarities in social organization and cultural themes among the Manchu ancestors. Clan organization and ritual, oral histories and genealogies, and shamanistic traditions were among the Northeast Asian elements that remained prominent in the family cultures of many of the peoples who became Manchu. For the minority whose ancestors had migrated to the Northeast from elsewhere, clan heritage was accepted as part of the new common culture; indeed, without the early Qing insistence upon the elementary importance of clan organization, the Eight Banners could hardly have been created. But the earlier clans had an importance that transcended the organizational and logistical needs of the Later Jin khanate, for they were the means through which each individual Manchu located himself within the socio-natural world, and through which he linked himself to his present as well as his past.

The post-conquest clans were, in short, primary political and cultural symbols. But the pre-conquest clans of the Northeast had fulfilled a radically different function. In the Jurchen homelands before and during Nurgaci's wars of unification, clans (*mukūn*) had been the organizations that governed hunting, gathering, farming and warfare. The clan had also been the medium through which all such activities were facilitated on the supernatural plane. The clan headman (*mukūnda*) in some cases was a shaman (*šaman*) himself, or moved close to the shaman, the better to invoke the needed communication with the spirits at the appropriate moment.[10] And the spiritual world had expanded in sympathy with the social and geographical extension of the people. In accord with a very ancient tradition, older sons were expected when grown to move downstream or over the hilltop, there to start a new homestead, initiate a new *mukūn*, and plant the new spirit pole (*šomo, shenzhu*) that would be the clan's— and each member's—point of communication with the clan spirits and the sacred features of the terrain.[11] Etymologically the word for clan, *mukūn*, suggests not kinship but a hunting or herding collective. Its Jurchen antecedent indicated a moving group; Qing glosses on "History of the

[Jurchen] Jin Dynasty" (*Jin shi*) cite the related Solon word *mouyouke*, "village."[12] The social conditions of the Northeast undoubtedly promoted a commingling of the realities of common residence and common kinship. All the same it is clear that even in the late sixteenth century biological kinship and clan association were not identical. Pre-Qing clans were not, as the clans of the dynastic period generally were, unexceptionally blood-bound. Migration to another region often necessitated adoption by another clan, as when Baindari's Ikderi ancestors managed to get themselves incorporated into the Nara clan.[13] According to folk history, inter-clan warfare also led to alterations in clan affiliation, as when Yangginu's Mongol ancestors annihilated a branch of the Ulanara clan and stole their name.[14] The sense of blood-relatedness was emergent but not triumphant in Nurgaci's time; the commission of oral genealogies to writing was encouraged, but individuals claiming no clan affiliation were assigned to functioning clans at the time of incorporation.[15] The companies, or *niru*, that formed the early banners drew their organizational principles from the traditional clan hunting group, and in many cases were merely registrations of existing or summarily reformed clan units.[16] In short, the formation of the banners by Nurgaci around 1601 depended upon an artful reshaping of many clan lines.

After the conquest of China, the walls that enclosed most garrisons excluded the clans from any sustained practical role in the economic or social life of the bannermen apart from company administration, and the consequence was a diminution in the importance of shamanism to the community. Bannermen no longer supported themselves by hunting, gathering or warfare with neighboring tribes, and in general they did not farm for a living. In short the clans were no longer work units, and when they did not work they communicated with their helping spirits much less frequently. Nor did the Manchus split their homesteads as they had once done; *mukūn* did not grow anew, and the spiritual universe did not expand. Younger sons moved no farther than down the lane or to a vacated house within the family compound. Those comparative few who were fortunate to be promoted into the mobile stratum of the banner command looked forward to brief sojourns of, commonly, three years or so in other garrisons; their families and their spirits were left behind, to be returned to during leaves, transfers, mourning or retirement. All Manchus belonged to *mukūn*, and most probably knew the name of the seventeenth-century ancestor who had come into China to found it; but to have actually seen the spirit pole planted by that ancestor, in Peking or in some other early-established garrison, was a point of pride.[17] In the later nineteenth century, being "of the same *mukūn*" (*tongzu*) would be a matter of great cultural and psychological importance, binding strangers together over the barriers of time and space. But the eighteenth century was a time of transition, when Hongli could see the clans and their religion receding from the daily lives of the bannermen, and he anticipated Manchu identity weakening apace.

The most famous learned definition of a Manchu clan comes from the work of Sergei Mikhailovich Shirokogoroff, who called it "a group of persons united by the consciousness of descent from a male ancestor and through male ancestors, also united by recognition of their blood relationship, having common clan spirits and recognizing a series of taboos, the principle of which is the interdiction of marriage between members of a clan, i.e. exogamy."[18] Shirokogoroff, who observed Manchus living in the Aigun region on the border between China and Russia in 1915, did not have access to relevant Qing records, or he would have modified at least one part of his definition: Not all Manchu clans traced their origins to a single ancestor. He stated, however, one ringing truth that is borne out by all evidence of Qing clan symbolism: *The clan cannot exist without a name and this is an important character of the clan.*[19] In the folk tradition, the clan name (*hala*), which was most often a toponym of ancient or recent vintage,[20] was the key to the origin of all *mukūn* sharing that name; it had no ritual function, but was assumed to encapsulate a history. To the Qing state, the names were ideologically indispensable. Names were the starting point for Nurgaci's revival of the clans in the early seventeenth century and were integral to his claim that his people were the direct descendants of the Jin Jurchens.[21] Around the names he organized registration, company structure, and integration into the khanate.

This presented problems for Nurgaci's descendants, particularly Hung Taiji, who wished to reorganize the polity into an imperium. The clans, which had been given hereditary control over a large portion of banner companies, were an impediment to centralization of control in the hands of the imperial clan and finally in the hands of the emperor himself. Once they had been a tool for state-building. Now they were a threat to completion of the emperorship. In the years of Hung Taiji's reigns (1627–1635; 1636–1643) the structure of the banners and of the companies below them was rearranged, a process that continued into the Shunzhi (1644–1661) and Kangxi (1662–1722) periods. The greatest and earliest change was that new companies were created while others were disbanded, progressively loosening clan association with certain companies or groups of companies. The second was that the company leaders, increasingly bureaucratic appointees, were not called by the ancient term "lord of the arrows" (*nirui ejen*) but were called by the neologism, "captain of the company" (*nirui janggin*); nor were they invariably clan headmen (*mukūnda, zuzhang*), though any officer's status as a headman would be noted in the banner records for the remainder of the Qing period. In

terminology as well as in administration, the banners were being transformed from socio-political organisms to bureaucratic units. Still later,
the Yongzheng emperor, determined to centralize political power in the
emperorship on a scale unprecedented in the regimes of his father and
grandfather, focused attention on the obstructions to imperial authority
present in the residual clan elements of banner organization. Ties of ownership to certain companies that some clans had enjoyed since Nurgaci's
time were abrogated, and the half-companies (*bange zuoling*) that had
allowed some tiny clans a claim to banner captaincies were abolished;
clan headmen were no longer recognized by the court as banner officials,
but were chosen according to the ostensibly meritocratic standards that
were permeating the banners as a professional institution.[22]

The strict limits placed upon the role of the clans in the banners by the
bureaucratic process were complemented with the excising of their cultural autonomy through the compilation of formal genealogies, while the
exigencies of life in the garrisons continued to undermine the social and
spiritual functions of the clans. The cultural dilemma created by the
court's shrinking of the autonomy of the many traditional elements of
Manchu life was becoming clear in Hongli's time. While addressing the
many faults he saw developing in the edifice of Manchu culture, he attempted to reestablish the spiritual and cultural functions of the clans by,
earliest of all, documenting them. He also made clear that the organization of "Researches on Manchu Origins" (*Manzhou yuanliu kao*), commissioned in 1741 and published in 1783, would reflect the fundamental
importance of the clans in the constitution of the Manchu people. "Tribes
and Clans" (*buzu*) is the first section of the work, and it is through the
clans that the earliest historically attested peoples of Northeast Asia, to
whom the Manchus linked their own heritage, are traced. The Yongzheng emperor had commissioned a standard authority on genealogical
matters, and in 1745 it was published as "Comprehensive Genealogies of
the Clans and Lineages of the Eight-Banner Manchus" (*Baqi manzhou
shizu tongpu*). It is apparent that the increasing tendency to see the clans
as the central feature of Manchu identity inspired the prominent inser-
tion of a rather detailed "Clans" section into the second edition of "General History of the Eight Banners" in 1799, during Hongli's tenure as
"Supreme Emperor" (*taishang huangdi*) and very shortly before his
death.[23]

In the absence of a function for the clans and under the limitations
imposed by the conditions of the forced urbanization of the Manchus, the
basic functioning social unit of the Manchus devolved from the clan to
the family. The boundaries of marriage, inheritance and authority
proved, after the passage of more than a century, to be best served by a
form of patrilineal household. There was no word for family in Manchu,

though as the need for such a word increased *boo*, or "household," was made to do. Overt expression of this fundamental social change disturbed the Qing emperors, who had begun to observe that some bannermen, in memorials to the throne written in Chinese, would prefix their personal names with a family name, in the manner of the Chinese *xing*. In some cases these were attempts at patronyms, taken from the first character of the personal name of the father, grandfather or some proximate male ancestor of the writer; this was a practice attested among urbanized Northeastern Jurchens well before the creation of the Manchus.[24] In other instances a single Chinese character would be used to represent an abbreviation of the traditional clan name. For instance, a man named Guanyinbao whose father had been named Sangge might sign himself with the patronym "Sang Guanyinbao;" a man named Jalangga who was a member of the Suwan Gūwalgiya clan might sign with a clan name marker, as "Gu Jalangga" or "Gua Jalangga" or "Guan Jalangga." In the late nineteenth and early twentieth centuries, many Manchus devised surnames by the still more remote practice of using the first character of their birth name (*ming*) followed by their bisyllabic adult name (*hao*). Thus the writer Dun Lichen (1855–1911) of the Fuča clan took the first character of his birth name Dunchang as a *xing* and used his adult name, Lichen, as his personal name. The same practice is attested in the necrologies compiled after the 1911/12 Revolution, and may have been a way to adopt a familial name without trespassing upon the particular interdictions of the court regarding the uses of clan names or their substitutes. In his own time Hongli had noticed the beginnings of this practice and registered varying degrees of objection. Manchu custom had never been to use anything other than personal names in public communications. The prefixing of the characters to the signatures looked like blatant imitation of the Chinese surname, and on these grounds, too, was offensive to the court. Avoidance of the use of clan names was the practice of Mongol bannermen, and of the members of the Chinese-martial banners who observed lineage-name omission as part of their cultural solidarity with the Manchus. Certainly, into the twentieth century the personal name was used singly by many bannermen as an expression of their cultural conservatism.[25] The elite, then, remained careful about the appearance of their names, moving rather slowly from traditional Manchu names to patterned personal names without surnames. But evidence abounds that in the garrisons the lineage names, all of which superficially resembled the Chinese surnames, were universally used—if not by a man himself certainly by his neighbors, his colleagues, and his daughters (the latter having, after a century or so of their lineage's habitation of a garrison, no other very useful way of indicating whom they could not marry).

Clan names as historical (rather than personal) signs, however, were the source of Manchu unity. Even the fabrication, or at least hyperbole, evident in official Aisin Gioro accounts of their own clan origins should not obscure the fact—for it was of supreme importance to the Qing and all who considered themselves loyal to them—that certain clans could claim that their ancestors were documented among the clans of the Jurchen Jin dynasty of the twelfth century. One was the Suwan Gūwalgiya. "While Gūwalgiya is a prominent Manchu name, the Gūwalgiya of the Suwan locality are the most prominent of all," states "Comprehensive Genealogies."[26] Indeed, they were the first of the "Eight Great Houses" (ba dajia) upon which the Manchu elite was founded. Members of the Gūwalgiya clans, many of whom began to use surnames such as Gu, Gua, Guan, Guang, and a variety of patronyms during the later eighteenth century, were extraordinarily numerous; today Guan remains a surname common among those of Manchu descent, and rare among those who do not trace their surname to a Manchu ancestor. The frequency of the surname is due both to the great number of Gūwalgiya tribes and lineages who were incorporated into Nurgaci's state during the wars of unification at the turn of the seventeenth century and to the failure to distinguish in the use of the Chinese surname Guan between the various subgroups of the clan. In Qing times, however, Manchus were not confused as to the identity of the subgroups or their social ranking. The Suwan Gūwalgiya traced their origins to the elite of the Manchu nobility, who in early times had supplied women to the palaces of Nurgaci and Hung Taiji. The only other Gūwalgiya lineage to gain prominence were the Hada Gūwalgiya, the clan of Yiliang (1791–1867) and Guiliang (1785–1862), who had the dubious honor of representing the Qing court in the negotiations connected with the Opium War (1842) and the Arrow War (1858). The cousins had commissioned the writing of a Hada Gūwalgiya genealogy that was published in 1849, the better to remind the court of their auspicious but previously under-appreciated lineage.[27] Other Gūwalgiya families, though numerous, were not considered to be truly elite. Outstanding men did, however, emerge from such lines; and certainly, there were many Suwan Gūwalgiya who lived lives not distinguished from those of the "average" bannerman. In sum the story of the Suwan Gūwalgiya offers an example of the early Qing argument for the importance of the clans in the Manchu relationship to the cultural past of the Northeast, and in the social traditions of the Manchu people.

The Suwan Gūwalgiya was one of the approximately thirty of the 645 clans represented in the genealogies that were considered ancient, or able to trace their pedigrees to documented clans of the Jin dynasty. The Gūwalgiya name can indeed be traced to the records of the earlier

Jurchen dynasty, to at least the time of Širon, who first came to prominence around 1212 and died in 1225.[28] He appears in the history as a
difficult man with a stormy political career, known mainly for his military
merit. Širon evidently was a favorite of the emperor Xuanzong (r. 1213–
1223). Of his family virtually nothing is known, other than that he was a
native of Longan, modern Nongan in Jilin province. In the twelfth century Longan, which was created a prefecture around 1213, was the center
of a tribal district that in earlier times had been part of the lands of the
Puyŏ, who established a state in northern Korea. First incorporated into
the Liao empire (907–1125) in the early tenth century as "Yellow
Dragon" prefecture, by the time of Širon's birth Longan was the only
town in Lishe county (xian), which was the only county in Longzhou (a
subdivision of Huining prefecture of the Shangjing circuit), and boasted
a population of just over 10,000 "households" (hu). The official history of
the Jin dynasty informs us that one of the landmarks of Longan in the
twelfth century was "Songari Hall," and that the Yellow Dragon prefecture had received its name after the sighting of a yellow dragon there at
the time of the town's founding. Nongan is now a city north of
Changchun, while Suwan (or Suwayan, "yellow")—the home of the
group of Gūwalgiya featured in this study—in all probability was modern
Shuangyang, southeast of Changchun.[29] In the sixteenth century, Suwan
was north territory of the Hoifa, the northernmost of the Haixi (later Hulun federation) of Jurchen tribes.

In Nurgaci's time there was still a concentration of Gūwalgiya in the
general vicinity of Changchun. But like virtually all the Jurchen clans of
the post-Jin period, the Gūwalgiya had been fragmented and scattered
from northern Liaodong to Changbaishan. Often, they were part of tribal
communities that seem to have ranged in population from a few dozen to
perhaps two thousand individuals. Gūwalgiya were to be found among
the Suwan, Yehe, Nayan, Hada, Ula, Anjulaku, Fio, Warka, Giyamuhu,
Nimaca and Hoifa tribes specifically, though this is clearly only a sampling of the affiliations that Gūwalgiya branches actually embraced.[30]
They had also settled in the villages and towns of Ming-governed Liaodong, including Guangning, Xintun, Shanfucheng, Fajicheng, Feng-
huangcheng and Shenyang, the provincial capital.[31] And they had moved
out among the non-Jurchen peoples; the name of a large Gūwalca Mongol
tribe, one of the "Nine Tribes" who attempted to obstruct Nurgaci's
movement westward, was a variant of the Gūwalgiya name, and it appears that some Gūwalgiya settled among the Dagurs.[32] Like the Mongol
Gūwalca, the earliest mentions of the Gūwalgiya make clear that Nurgaci
at first could not count the descendants of the clan among his friends. In
1585 he took the Antu Gūwalgiya village on the banks of the Suksuhu
(Suzi) River, and killed its headman Ruomouhun when he refused to ca-

pitulate. Not far to the northwest of the Antu Gūwalgiya village, Guala, the head of the Gūwalgiya clan in the Sarhu region, was an early follower of Nurgaci's rival Nikan Wailan.[33]

The Suwan branch of the Gūwalgiya could not have strayed far from their tribal home southwest of Changchun at the time of their alliance with Nurgaci in 1588.[34] The eighteenth-century genealogies described the Suwan Gūwalgiya as having sprung from three full brothers; unlike traditional Chinese genealogies, "Comprehensive Genealogies" of the Eight Banners frequently does not trace clans to a single individual. These brothers, Folgo, Niyagaci and Juca, lived as children at Suwan (Suwayan). But in accord with Jurchen practice, when Niyagaci and Juca reached adulthood they left the homestead. Only Folgo, the eldest, remained behind for a time, though eventually he also left. Niyagaci moved to the Sibo tribe, and Juca went to live among the Warka tribe.[35] It was Juca's line that came to be recognized as the Suwan branch of the clan. Beginning with his son Solda, the six generations after Juca may be sketched as follows:

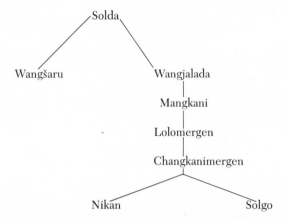

The source gives no dates for individuals before Solgo,[36] but Folgo, Niyagaci and Juca were probably alive at the end of the fourteenth century, which would make them roughly contemporaneous with (though far removed geographically from) the great Jurchen leader and Aisin Gioro progenitor Möngke Temür—and like Möngke Temür, the Suwan Gūwalgiya clansmen Lolomergen and Changkanimergen show distinct Mongolian influence in their names. Of Nikan, nothing is known. By the late sixteenth century, Solgo was leader of the Suwan tribe and his lineage was apparently recognized as most powerful. In 1588 Solgo decided to join Nurgaci's camp, and led more than eight hundred households of the tribe in capitulation. Nurgaci's base was not large at this time; the incorporation of the Suwan tribe was a major advance, and brought the Suwan

Gūwalgiya clan—led by Solgo and his twelve sons—into lasting esteem. As the chief of the Suwan tribe as well as the headman (*mukūnda*) of the Suwan Gūwalgiya, Solgo was the personal leader of more than five hundred households; Sando of the Suwan tribe brought three hundred more into Nurgaci's federation, and Zhading, also of Suwan, fewer than fifty.[37] Companies were soon established for the headmen. Sando was awarded several, led by himself and his sons. Zhading was given a single company, which he led personally. All these companies were later integrated with the Plain White Banner. Solgo was allowed to establish five companies, which were led by himself, his son Fiongdon, and others of his sons and nephews.[38] These companies were made hereditary companies in the Bordered Yellow, Plain Yellow and Plain White Banners after their establishment in 1615.[39]

Fiongdon (1564–1620), the second of Solgo's sons, was at this time about twenty-four years old, described as a good archer, exceptionally strong, unswervingly loyal and, like many Manchu heroes, "very frank in his speech."[40] The years 1588 and 1589 were those in which crucial alliances, not only with the Suwan headmen but also with the Donggo and Yargu tribes and the clansmen under [Tonggiya] Hulagu were consolidated, and rudimentary territorial control under Nurgaci was in the process of formation.[41] Almost immediately after his entry into the Jianzhou camp many of the major administrative tasks were entrusted to young Fiongdon by Nurgaci. In the middle 1590s, the daughter of Cuyen, Nurgaci's eldest son—and at that time his favorite—was affianced to Fiongdon. It was probably about this time that Fiongdon was able to cement the trust he was earning from Nurgaci: He learned that Tocin Bayan, the husband of one of his own nieces, was involved in a plot against Nurgaci, and had the conspirator executed. The incident is a vivid example of the values upon which the khanate that would eventually become the Qing empire was founded. Personal loyalty bound the headmen to Nurgaci, and when a breach of loyalty was detected within their families or clans, the headmen's reaction could be swift and ruthless. Murder of the suspected miscreant was sanctioned; Eidu of the Niohuru clan was reported to have strangled his son Daki during a clan banquet after becoming convinced that the young man was involved in a plot against the khan.[42] Fiongdon, as a maternal uncle to the wife of Tocin Bayan, was charged by tradition with the protection of his niece and nephew and, if necessary, with their punishment.[43] Nurgaci soon afterward appointed Fiongdon a "judge" (*jargūci*), making him not only a law-giver but also a policymaker within the tribal khanate.[44] Such recognition was crucial to Nurgaci's ability to make loyalty to himself, as khan, override all other kinship considerations. In 1612 Fiongdon was instrumental in the indictment of Cuyen—his father-in-law and Nurgaci's heir-apparent—for treason, specifically for attempts to hex Nurgaci and others in the family. The charges resulted in Cuyen's imprisonment and ultimate death, with concomitant rises in the status of Fiongdon together with Nurgaci's surviving, politically adept sons.

It had been soon after his exposure of Tocin Bayan and appointment as *jargūci* that Fiongdon was for the first time given a prominent role in the campaigns of conquest. In 1597 he led an attack upon part of the Warka tribe, capturing the Gejia region and killing the clan headman, then led the captured clansmen back to Nurgaci's base; the campaigns against the Warka were later continued under Cuyen, who took the Anjulaku district in 1598. In the ensuing eight years Fiongdon was primarily engaged in battles against the Hada and Yehe. But in the spring of 1607, as Fiongdon and Šurgaci (1564–1611)—Nurgaci's younger brother and rival for power[45]—were escorting the Fio clan of the Warka tribe to Nurgaci's base at Hetu Ala, their party was attacked by the Ula headman (*beile*) Bujantai with a very large force. It appears that Bujantai was a clandestine political ally of Šurgaci, and the latter took little active part in the ensuing fray. The Jianzhou Jurchens emerged victorious, and Fiongdon was given much of the credit by his two superiors, [Tonggiya] Hurgan and the chagrined Šurgaci.[46] Thereafter Fiongdon was assigned to assist Nurgaci's younger brother Bayara and seventh son Abatai in the various campaigns against the Ula in the north and west. When Nurgaci set up the banner system in 1615, Fiongdon was made a "lord" (*gūsa i ejen*) of the Bordered Yellow Banner; at least some of his brothers were registered in the Plain Yellow and Bordered White Banners.[47] In 1616, when Nurgaci declared the founding of the Later Jin state with himself as khan, Fiongdon, along with [Niohuru] Eidu (1562–1621), [Tonggiya] Hurgan (1576–1623), [Donggo] Hohori (1561–1624) and [Giolca] Anfiyanggū (1559–1622), was made one of the Five Councillors, or *amban*, the highest civil rank. Before his death Fiongdon took a leading role in two critical events in the military development of Nurgaci's state. In 1618, he led the attack upon the Ming town of Fushun, where cannon used by the Chinese startled his horse and his troops; Fiongdon's extraordinary poise put his forces back in order. The result was the kidnapping of most of the town's populace, acquisition of the cannon for Nurgaci's side, and initiation of full-scale war in Liaodong. In late 1620, only weeks before his death, Fiongdon defied Nurgaci's orders to retreat and succeeded in capturing Yehecheng, an event that drew to a close the twenty-five year effort to subdue the Jurchen Yehe tribe.

The same political order that demanded such fierce devotion to the khan also allowed a passionate devotion of the khan to his comrades. Fiongdon became one of Nurgaci's most trusted confidants, always among the first to be named to a civil honor, and a field commander who even when disobedient was invariably held blameless. In the spring of 1620 Fiongdon died, age fifty-six. The dynastic records state that as his illness took its fatal turn "the sun moved to the west, clouds came up, there was the sound of bells, thunder, there was lightning, rain and hail fell. And then it cleared up immediately;" Fiongdon, in other words, is honored with a death scene that is formulaic and strongly resembles other literary demises, including that of Gautama Buddha. A site at Zuling outside Shenyang, facing the tomb of Eidu and close to that of Yangguri, was chosen for Fiongdon's interment.[48] Nurgaci, now sixty-three, led the funeral himself, saying, "My indispensable councillor, my partner in joy and sorrow, today precedes me in death. How can I not be devastated?" The mourners all cried in sympathy, and stayed at the tomb until well into the night. In the fall, Nurgaci worshipped first at the tomb of Šurgaci (whom he had executed in 1611), then at Fiongdon's, where he personally poured the libationary wine three times, crying all the while.[49]

Fiongdon's career was the stuff of which legends were made, and in the event it proved to be suitable stuff for the making of a family fortune, too. His companies were passed to his sons Nagai, Sugai and Tulai—all of whom were given the seventh-rank hereditary rank of baronet (*adaha hafan, qingju duyu*).[50] In 1645, after the invasion of China, Fiongdon's son Guala was similarly entitled and awarded a captaincy in the Plain Yellow Banner.[51] For Suwayan, a new company was created in 1651, "in recognition of the accomplishments of his father Fiongdon Jargūci," and he was awarded the eighth-rank title *baitalabure hafan*, or *qidu yu*.[52] Many of Fiongdon's sons and grandsons entered the civil bureaucratic departments that developed under Hung Taiji. Sugai served in the Board of Punishments (*xingbu*),[53] and Tohui, Fiongdon's fourth son, was not a company captain but a non-heritable military adjutant (*sanzhai dachen*). Two of Tohui's sons, Jatai and Urgu, served as Imperial Bodyguards (*shiwei*). Guala's grandson Furdan (1683–1753) was a chamberlain of the Imperial Bodyguard (*shiwei nei dachen*) and later president of the Board of Appointments (*libu*).[54] But the fame of all was for a time overshadowed by their cousin Oboi, third son of Fiongdon's youngest brother Uici. From 1661 Oboi was regent to the Kangxi emperor, who deposed and then executed him in 1669.[55] The consequent abolishment of the ranks bestowed upon Oboi and eradication of the political influence of his immediate line left all Suwan Gūwalgiya prestige centered upon the descendants of Fiongdon.

Fiongdon's own posthumous career was as lively as it had been while he was quick. He was ennobled by Hung Taiji as the "Duke of Unswerving Righteousness" (*zhiyi gong*) in 1632 and his tablet was erected in the Tai Miao, the imperial clan temple at Mukden; as "Duke Who Aids the Imperial Mandate" (*zuoming gong*) with heritable rank in 1670; as "Duke of Trustworthy Valiance" (*xinyong gong*) by the Yongzheng emperor in 1731; and was raised to a duke of the first class by the Qianlong emperor, Hongli, in 1778, two years before the court reaffirmed the permanent exclusion of Oboi's descendants from the entitled nobility.[56] In 1743, the emperor had already paid homage to Fiongdon's undying fame among the Qing founding companions, naming Fiongdon only with [Niohuru] Eidu and [Hešeri] Khife (d. 1652) as those "whose merit aided our Way" (*doro de aisilaha gungge*)[57]; their virtue, Hongli went on, surpassed that of Xiao He and Zhang Liang, two worthies who had served the Han dynastic founder Liu Bang in his campaigns of conquest nearly two thousand years before.[58] Beginning as outsider to both the Aisin Gioro clan and the Jianzhou tribe, Fiongdon had risen as high as was possible under the conditions of the Later Jin state and his memory was venerated by the Qing court until its end. For his recognized descendants Fiongdon's name was the touchstone of noble affiliation and court recognition. Each posthumous rank, and its privileges, was awarded to a living member of his lineage, and if lost passed to another member. After Fiongdon's time, the Gūwalgiya clan name was associated primarily with the Suwan branch, which he had represented. By the time the Qing armies passed through the Shanhai Pass in 1644, Fiongdon was already well represented among their ranks, since the vast majority of his ten sons and more than thirty grandsons accompanied the Manchu armies into China and were eventually settled there.

"Among the Gūwalgiya," Fiongdon's tenth-generation descendant Jinliang wrote in the 1929 introduction to selected biographies of his clansmen: "A distinction is made between the old and the new. Those who live in the Northeast are the old clan, and those who live in China proper are the new clan. When the new clan entered China, there were altogether nine lineages (*zu*), one lineage being about 100 households. The main clan (*dazong*) was registered among the banners at Peking, and the remaining eight were sent separately to the garrisons. Those who were sent to Zhejiang are three lineages of the lesser clan (*xiao zong*), and those in Hunan are four lineages of the lesser clan. Now when you look into the Gūwalgiya at Hangzhou, you find that we have two main branches: those sent to Hangzhou from the capital and those sent here from Hunan. My own lineage is one of the three lineages of the lesser clan. Originally we were sent from Peking to Hangzhou, and afterwards were transferred to Zhapu. Still later we were transferred back to Hangzhou. That is more than two hundred years, over nine unbroken generations, and in one compound we had over seventy people, from ageds to infants."[59] For many twentieth-century Manchus, clan lore remained as vivid as Jinliang's recitation suggests. Like other clans, their *mukūn* were ossified after the immigration to China; "greater" and "lesser" distinctions between lineage branches became the innovative means of identifying the unprecedented fragmentations caused by the rapid transfers of the garrisoning process. New *mukūn* were no longer generated after dispersal to the garrisons, but all members in China functioned as a giant, invisible *mukūn*, spiritually centered on the clan mansion in Peking.

Fiongdon was literally the dividing point between the "old" and the "new;" the new Suwan Gūwalgiya lineages were thereafter those descended directly from him, while the old ones of the Northeast descended from his brothers, uncles or cousins. He was the source of all the clan's prestige, since he represented the early clan alliances under Nurgaci (which the state symbolically venerated as it proceeded to dismantle all political vestiges of clan influence) and the pre-eminent place of the Suwan Gūwalgiya among them. His titles descended to the end of the dynasty, and until the early years of the twentieth century the lineage's spirit pole stood in the courtyard of their mansion in Peking. In the nineteenth century, Wenxiang, a native of Mukden; Dingchang, a nobleman of Peking who inherited Fiongdon's dukedom; and Fengrui, a bannerman of Hangzhou who followed his father into a profitable printing trade, considered themselves "of the same *mukūn*" (*tongzu*) because of their common descent from Fiongdon. In 1898 it was also the link between Ronglu, the ally of the Empress Dowager Xiaoqin, and Jinliang, an energetic if naive supporter of the Guangxu emperor. Even as the empire was dismantled in 1912 and bannermen sought patronage among the warlords of North China and the Northeast, Suwan Gūwalgiya connections were a thing to be mentioned advantageously.[60] And as the remnant court struggled to survive in its confinement to the Forbidden City after 1911, loyalists clung all the more intensely to the symbolism of the great clans and the world of heroes and power they had represented.

CHAPTER III

The Hangzhou Garrisons

IMMURATION of the Manchus following the conquest of China not only disrupted their relationship to their putative culture and the traditional Northeastern social structure, but also transformed the nature of wealth and its distribution. The old Jin khanate under Nurgaci had been to large degree a booty state. In exchange for loyalty and service, the khan had divided his booty with the princes, who divided it with their unit leaders, who in turn divided it with their kinsmen and colleagues who composed the early banners. Even slaves were rewarded with booty and enthusiastically followed their captors into battle against a neighboring village, tribe or nation. The eighteenth-century Qing empire, no longer booty-based and now saddled with a complex of financial responsibilities, rewarded its followers in more prosaic manner with rice and silver stipends derived primarily from the empire's tax and rice tribute base. As the stipendiary values fell further and further below the actual cost of sustenance, accoutrement and entertainment, a new pattern of distribution emerged. Princes extorted from their officers in exchange for a promise of more glamorous or more remunerative assignments, officers extorted from their bannermen in exchange for recommendation to the princes, while bannermen concealed deaths of males in the family in order to continue drawing stipends, concocted injuries to seek remuneration, falsely reported births, weddings and deaths which would have made extraordinary demands upon their finances, and broke nearly all the laws established by the state to prevent them from engaging in the urban trades by which they might supplement their small incomes. Hongli's father, the Yongzheng emperor, had found the increasing indictments of Manchu princes and their underlings for malfeasance convenient to his general program of destroying the last vestiges of noble control of the Eight Banners. "The enumeration of their extortions of every description would be endless. This state of things has led to the officers under their control exhausting their means to send in gifts, and rendered them unable to keep themselves pure and good; and from this the cashiering of officers on account of their having fallen into the crime of embezzling the national revenue has all arisen."[1] The garrisoning of the Manchus, though imperative for the security needs of the early state, appeared to be their undoing; from the beginning of the dynasty to the end, emperors exhorted their bannermen, with little effect, to resist the temptations of city life and to preserve their Manchu purity of identity and purpose.

Though it would seem to have been inevitable in the wake of the conquest, the establishment of Manchu garrison communities in China was in fact a tentative, gradual, regionally unsynchronized process that did not reach full development until the Qianlong period. Many garrisons were firmly established within only a few years of the conquest, when the dynastic finances were precarious and their hold over China tenuous; in some cases almost a decade passed before the garrison was made permanent by the government. They were assigned commanders, permission was given for the soldiers' families to immigrate from the Northeast, banners not represented among the founding population were ordered to supply troops to the community, transfers between banners were mandated in order to equalize the membership of each of the Eight Banners within each particular garrison, and mechanisms were established for the wresting of necessary supports from the local resources. Where possible, the lands and estates of the former Ming nobility were appropriated for the sheltering of the garrison population; where none were available, the lands were carved from the holdings of Chinese residents, some of whom exchanged their land rights for banner incorporation as "land-bringing capitulators" (daidi touchong).[2] Within the first two decades of the conquest, it is evident that subsequent enclosure orders augmenting the size of some garrisons were issued in response to demands from the bannermen—possibly underscored by instances of marauding or other violence—for increased land.[3] Besides area for each garrison proper and its attendant training grounds, fields sufficient to allow agricultural support of the garrison population, grazing lands, and burial ground for banner dependents were appropriated. Finally, provincial and local taxes for support of the garrison and its facilities were instituted. Long-term provisioning of bannermen in China demanded massive innovation from the court. At first the question of supporting the bannermen (baqi shengji) was a matter of restructuring local landholding and taxation policies; in later times it would become the hinge upon which turned a series of financial and social crises.

By 1661 the infrastructure of the garrison system in China proper was established, as the Capital Garrisons of Peking were put in place, nine large garrisons were chartered in provincial capitals, and ten smaller installations were ordered created at strategic points. Until 1669 the process of land seizure was intense. Within a 170-mile circumference of Peking alone, which was protected by an enormous internal garrison and a ring of eighteen external compounds, more than seventy sites were appropriated for the use of "those who have come from the East" (dongliu); Chinese displaced in this process would find that, if the garrison commanders became dissatisfied with the condition or location of their lands, new removals could be summarily ordered.[4] There is some slight disagreement in the records regarding the amount of land enclosed in this period, but in total it seems to have been slightly in excess of 2.12 million acres (about 14 million *mou*), the vast majority of which was concentrated in the control of garrison officers, with only a small fraction to be shared by the bulk of garrison soldiers and their families.[5] By the end of the dynasty there were over 106 garrisons in existence (some occupying more than one site of land); three garrisons are reported to have been abolished in the late dynastic period due to the attenuation of their populations.[6] The earliest garrisons to be commissioned were Xi'an and Nanjing in 1645, Jinjiang and Dezhou in 1654, and Hangzhou in 1658, while the last garrisons included Qingzhou and Zhapu in 1729, Suiyuan, Liangzhou and Zhuanglang in 1737. A perceived need to continue the defense of the Northeast kept nearly half of the banner forces at home. Peking was of course heavily fortified from the time of its conquest by the Manchus in the summer of 1644. As the Qing armies moved over the Chinese provinces, temporary encampments were established and abandoned as strategic needs changed. Territorial expansion continued well into the eighteenth century, requiring major transfers of banner personnel via northwest China into Xinjiang and via southwest China into Tibet. At the same time, interior provinces such as Anhui and Henan, once occupied during the period of actual conquest, lost their garrisons by the middle eighteenth century. Precariously pacified and isolated provinces such as Guangxi, Guizhou and Yunnan were controlled by large consolidated garrisons in nearby provinces.[7]

A visible geographical division between the bannermen left in the Northeast and those in China proper emerged in the early Qing years. Pre-conquest bannermen in Liaodong and Jilin had been regarded as agricultural producers, and their land grants had been taxed. In the home garrisons of the Northeast, bannermen lived in small villages, many of them ancestral, and continued to pursue agriculture; increases in population were in many situations alleviated by the opening of new lands, still a possibility in this frontier region.[8] In China, where bannermen were occupiers and not producers, the sustenance of the soldiery was originally planned to have two components: land grants, provided for in the ways outlined above; and regular stipendiary installments of rice and silver. During the first century after the conquest, the lands of many garrisons were alienated through legal or illegal means, while the dependent population grew. Stipends were not, however, increased proportionately. The result was a visible impoverishment of the bannermen, beginning with the dense garrison populations of Peking, which had already become a cause for concern in the Kangxi and Yongzheng periods. In the Qianlong era the provisioning of the bannermen became a problem for intense debate and memorializing.[9]

The garrison process also had a profound impact upon the administrative mechanisms by which the banner population was governed and the patterns of careers dependent upon that administration. The establishment of the garrisons across China meant a significant increase in the number of military officers, and qualitative changes in the existing ranks. In general, the tendency was toward a ceremonial character for the banner ranks instituted by Nurgaci and Hung Taiji. Bureaucratic military careers for individual Manchus developed; where previously company (*niru*) rank had derived from one's clan status or elevation to high rank by virtue of imperial favor and outstanding military accomplishment, one could now take tests and receive good service reports. Part of the impact that settlement in the garrisons had upon Manchu social structure is told by the "brigade-general" (*fudutong*) rank. Prior to the conquest, when enclosure within rigid compounds not defined by lineage was still unimagined, the *meiren i janggin*, predecessor to the *fudutong*, was exclusively a banner rank; his title identified him literally as the commander of a "wing" ("shoulder"), a major subdivision of the banner. As such he was second in command after the *gūsa i ejen*, the banner "lord." The latter rank subsequently became *dutong*, "lieutenant-general," in Chinese, and *meirin i janggin* became, logically, the "assistant" *dutong*—the *fudutong*. Thus, during the Shunzhi period, the sequence of banner command was fixed as: "lieutenant-general," or *dutong* (of which there was one for each banner, or altogether eight for each of the three national divisions, making a total of twenty-four); "brigade-general," or *fudutong* (twenty-four, divided among eight banners in each of the national divisions); "colonel," or *xiaoqi canling* (altogether 320—these are the old *jalan i janggin*);[10] "lieutenant-colonel," or *fuxiaoqi canling* (320); "captain," or *zuoling* (681 for each of the eight banners in each of the three national divisions, altogether 5,448—these are the old *niru i janggin*), and "lieutenant," or *xiaoqi xiao* (5,448).[11]

The effect of the blending of banner hierarchy with the demands for garrison leadership was first of all to behead this sequence; by the early eighteenth century *dutong* were banner commanders exclusively, and were rapidly becoming ceremonial fixtures. Their assistants of old—the "brigades-general"—now served the "generals-in-chief" (*jiangjun*), the commanders of their respective garrisons, and ranked above the "colonel of the regiment" (*xieling*), another new garrison rank. The identification of certain clans with certain banners through the hereditary companies diminished but did not disappear; the ranks once associated with the splitting of companies to accommodate small clans evaporated as companies became somewhat more uniform in size and soldiers sought promotion through the garrison ranks, commonly moving from banner to banner to do so. The mobility between regions that often marked the careers of officers above a certain rank, however, did not apply to the Manchu garrison populations in general or to the non-officer ranks of "corporal" (*bosoku, lingcui*) and "private" (*uksin, xiaoqi*), the latter divided between the cavalry (*majia*) and infantry (*bujun*) divisions.

Under the Later Jin khanate, bannermen had lived in villages and were self-sufficient, farming when not campaigning and storing what they had produced. As a rule one man in three was required to work the officer's fields each day, and one out of twenty was subject to corvée requirements.[12] The pre-conquest empire of Hung Taiji left this policy basically unchanged. When mobilized, the troops were provided grain (or money to buy grain) from the government stores; when demobilized, they were expected to support themselves. After the conquest, bannermen in the Northeast continued this general way of life, but those garrisoned in China were considered to be in perpetual full-time mobilization. It was not required that actively serving bannermen do agricultural labor. Banner staple lands were tended by *zidi*, by cadets, by domestic slaves, by Chinese soldiers of the Green Standard Armies, by indentured Chinese, by Manchu women or by paid laborers.[13] Each actively serving bannerman was awarded a monthly silver stipend and annual rice allotment consonant with his rank, a horse-maintenance allowance supposed to be sufficient for three to six horses (in actuality few bannermen kept more than one horse, and in the late dynastic period many had no horse at all), and occasional grants intended as rewards or compensation for extraordinary expenses. The court never declared an intention to support the garrison populations indefinitely. The absolute number of banner stipends was fixed in the later seventeenth century, when it was not at all clear that the Qing would be occupying China permanently. After the suppression of the Rebellion of the Three Feudatories in 1681, the Kangxi emperor and his court began to be more certain about the stability of the Manchu regime in China; even though the banner population had grown considerably, there was not a correlative increase in the number of banner stipends, for the evident reason that a new professional army drawn from the Chinese population—the Green Standard (*lüying*)—had been formed and effectively utilized. Nor, paradoxically, were statutory regulations banning Manchus from civil employment lifted. In Peking, an official reported, "Weapons are insufficient [to supply all the available men], but the subjects may not become literati, or farmers, or workers, or merchants, or regular soldiers, or commoners, but must remain clustered within a few hundred *li* of the capital. On account of this their livelihoods decline day by day, with no means of alleviation. Those who are not appointed [active] bannermen have no means at all of livelihood."[14]

The amount of silver, rice and other supplementary payments established for each bannerman in the early post-conquest period was more than ample to meet the needs of the time. In addition to the measures taken to provide independent local sustenance for the bannermen (which in practice left land exploitation exclusively to the discretion of the garrison officers), the court provided hulled rice (*mi*), along with beans and hay for the support of horses. Dispensation varied tremendously with rank, from over twenty piculs (*shi*) per month of hulled rice for a general-in-chief to one picul for an infantry private. In principle the allowances were based upon the mobilization provisions of the pre-conquest period, and upon a very general equation of .25 picul (two *dou*, five *sheng*) per individual per month.[15] The assumption was that a private might supply rice for a household of four from his monthly provision, and a general-in-chief a household of eighty or more—in the latter case, this would include slaves, bodyguards, adjutants and staff in addition to actual family members. Finally, bannermen received monthly silver allotments, again graduated according to rank, ranging in the years just after the conquest from two taels (*liang*) for an infantryman to fifteen for a general-in-chief. The court's intention in the early period seems to have been to steadily decrease the stipend, perhaps to shift the burden of support to local mechanisms. The corporal stipend at Peking, for instance, dropped from three taels in 1649 to 1.5 taels in 1655. The Three Feudatories Rebellion, which demanded massive remobilization of the Eight Banner forces as well as critical deployment of the Green Standard Armies, forced the government to elevate salaries temporarily. Over the long term the trend in banner stipends was to consolidate the commodity stipends with the silver stipend, in most cases by increasing the silver payments in partial compensation for the loss of staple supplies. Some provinces had fixed ratios of taels to measures of commodities for the supply of additional silver; others had no fixed ratio but depended upon current price information (much of which was unreliable) to determine how much compensatory silver the bannermen should be supplied. In general, a non-commissioned bannerman's silver stipend through the eighteenth and nineteenth centuries stood at 1.5 taels to three taels, and officers' compensation ranged upward from this.

The effects of the court's economic retrenchment in the eighteenth and nineteenth centuries were not distributed evenly among the segments of the banner population, but fell disproportionately upon the rigid divisions that had been rather arbitrarily created in pre-conquest times. After the middle eighteenth century, Chinese-martial bannermen—a large segment of whom the court was steadily alienating from Manchu and Mongol bannermen—were expected to bear the brunt of the economizing measures. In 1761 non-commissioned Chinese-martial bannermen were no longer given rice stipends or any increased silver compensation for the lack. During the same period garrisons with Chinese-martial contingents received orders to force at least a portion of their Chinese-martial bannermen to "quit the banners and become commoners," after which their stipends and in some cases their housing were assumed by Manchus.[16] Through the seventeenth and possibly most of the eighteenth century, the bannermen may have enjoyed the residual benefits of deflation of silver in the middle seventeenth century; the rather generous silver stipend fixed at the time of the conquest and reestablished during the Three Feudatories Rebellion was unchanged in later decades, though the purchasing power of silver may have increased during the late Kangxi and Yongzheng years. While the value of silver was relatively inelastic in the eighteenth century and its ratio to copper eventually grew much more favorable in the later Qing period, inflation in other sectors may have been such that the ability of the garrison populations to buy their necessities—even if the bannermen had continued to receive their wages on time and in full—declined in the early nineteenth century.[17] Two taels of silver could be counted upon to purchase two to 2.5 piculs (very roughly 370–460 pounds) of rice well into the nineteenth century in many localities.[18] But apart from this staple, the cost of other items increased steeply.[19]

The generals-in-chief, not the central government, were the first to confront problems in the support of their communities, and a few were exemplary in their response to the widening shortfall in banner compensation. Most garrisons had charitable funds for the support of widows and orphans, as well as reserves to which bannermen might apply for relief in meeting the expenses of funerals, weddings, and loan payments. Some of these funds remained healthy, being managed in increasingly innovative ways. Many garrison commanders rented unused banner land and fed the charities from the proceeds. Some speculated in rice, using garrison funds to purchase when the price was low, and selling it back to their own bannermen at undermarket cost when the price escalated. Others were more sophisticated, using the money from rented land to make loans at 2 or 3 percent interest to local merchants, then rolling over the interest to establish funds for loans of 1 percent to their own bannermen. Garrison commanders took the initiative in austerity as well. Their attention was directed to their greatest expense: weapons and ammunition, which any garrison was expected to supply and maintain from its own budget.[20] In the later eighteenth century many garrisons abandoned musketry and artillery practice because of the expense of ammunition, and in the nineteenth century the commanders began being sparing in the use of paper and ink.

Despite the fact that the austerity measures of the garrison command-

ers were obviating the very purpose of the banner forces, the state devised no master policy for the improvement of garrison economies. Sev-
enteenth- and eighteenth-century emperors did attempt adjustments.
The Kangxi emperor raised the budget for payments to the bannermen
for settlement of obligations from 541,000 taels to 655,000 taels, which
still fell short of the contemporary banner debt.[21] The Yongzheng court
made two gift dispensations, each of 3.56 million taels, yet the court
noted at the same time that such acts did nothing to alter the permanent
indebtedness of the bannermen.[22] The Qianlong court supplemented the
practice of occasional dispensations with the regular payments of thirteen
months' stipends during the normal year. Such intercalary strategies had
once rectified the Qing calendar; they did little, however, to solve the
problem of a growing, forcedly unemployed population. A special fund
was established in 1729 to make low-interest loans to bannermen, but
was abolished in 1761 when the Qianlong emperor discovered that the
garrison commanders actually were using it to make high-interest loans
to local merchants.[23] The problem of land dearth was also addressed.
During the Qianlong period, four redemptions of mortgaged banner land
were made at a total cost of nearly four million taels and returned to their
garrisons; the records do not make clear the immediate effects, though in
the long term it appears that lands repurchased dearly by the state were
later sold cheaply by the bannermen to whom they were entrusted.[24]
More effectively, after 1763 the Qianlong emperor no longer required
bannermen to serve exclusively as soldiers. With the permission of their
company commander, they could enter a profession (other than acting)
or receive license to live outside the garrison compound.[25] In fact, bannermen below officer rank were no longer barred from owning property
after this time, and could buy homes and fields for themselves if they had
the means.[26]

At length the Qing took the obvious though financially ruinous step of
enlarging the number of banner appointments. The Shunzhi total of approximately 80,000 was increased to 120,000 during the Kangxi years.
The Yongzheng emperor added 4,800 cadet (*yangyu*) appointments after
being advised that silver allowances were insufficient for the support of
banner dependents, and the Qianlong emperor added 25,000 auxiliary
cadet appointments, at a monthly allowance of 1.5 taels. There is evidence of dramatic growth in these auxiliaries to the end of the dynasty.[27]
The impact of the increased enrollments upon the treasury was softened
somewhat by an attempt to reduce the stipends proportionally for new
appointments. In 1738, for instance, garrisons were authorized to make
three appointments for each of two vacancies, though compensation
would be not the three taels enjoyed by existing posts, but two taels.
Similarly, a 1753 regulation allowed the creation of five new positions in

the event of four regular vacancies, but with a decreased stipend of 1.5 taels for each new appointment.[28] It was understood at the time that such measures would only slow, not prevent, the burden of banner support from outstripping imperial reserves. In the end, the court continued to rely upon the austerity measures that had begun with the garrison commanders. In 1822 it set a limit of five hundred taels (still an enormous sum) on wedding and funeral expenditures, in 1855 abolished all means of providing aid to bannermen for the financing of weddings, and in 1859 drastically limited the legal limits of garrison expenditures for ink and paper.[29]

There seems to have been an awareness in the early eighteenth century that the urbanization and immuration of the bannermen might be the cause of their problems. Certain elements of traditional economic and social life had been preserved in the plantations (*zhuangyuan*) run by the Imperial Household Department in the Northeast, where self-sufficiency was still a possibility for bannermen.[30] The Yongzheng emperor attempted to move a hundred households of unemployed bannermen out of the Peking area to state farms (*guanzhuang*) under the control of the Board of Revenue (*hubu*) and the Imperial Household Department (*neiwufu*); the experiment failed, and within ten years ninety of the households had returned to Peking. A similar Qianlong plan to transfer three thousand households to Lalin in Jilin province to farm resulted in all the participants illegally returning to Peking within four years.[31] Few bannermen in China proper had an interest in farming and by this time none had direct experience; attempts to instruct them were without effect. In practice, the state farm policies eventually were seen as multiply disadvantageous. Bannermen sent down in this way almost inevitably became vagabonds or bandits, and the government lands entrusted to them were purchased by the local Chinese at bargain prices.[32] Hongli's successor, the Jiaqing emperor Yongyan (r. 1796–1820), also saw grave security risks in the thinning of the banner ranks at Peking, since in his time civil unrest no longer spared the capital or even the imperial compound.[33] In the early nineteenth century a slightly more successful strategy was happened upon, one that parallelled the education programs of the Yongzheng and Qianlong years: Volunteers were sought from among the unemployed or underemployed of the garrisons. A state farm plan called for the dispatch of three thousand households from Peking to farm at Shuangchengbao in the Lalin region of western Jilin, and volunteers from the ranks of *zidi* and cadets were solicited with the promise of tax-free working of the land for five years; 698 volunteer households were reregistered under the plan. Within a short time, others were enticed to the project from rustic settlements in Jilin and from elsewhere in Fengtian, so that by 1825 there were nearly a thousand households in the community. Using a conventional reckoning of fifteen persons per Manchu household in this period, it appears that roughly 15,000 people were relocated successfully under this voluntary program, which was later repeated at Petuna and Hulan.[34] A significant number of bannermen's lives had been improved, but at very considerable expense while the effect upon the urban garrisons, whose populations had little intention of volunteering themselves for transport to the Northeast, was negligible.

These schemes had been devised in response to manifestations of intensifying unrest in the garrisons. Most incidents were related to grievances concerning the inadequacy of the silver stipends, but this was associated with a host of economic difficulties. Against the court's design, by the early eighteenth century the majority of bannermen were attempting to live off the silver allowance exclusively, the land granted to them from the post-conquest appropriations having been gradually lost through indebtedness or opportunism of the garrison officers. The bannermen of China proper, in contrast to those who had remained in or returned to the Northeast, were not inclined to farm either their own land or land on which they might be relocated. And banner appointments through which one "earned" the silver stipend were becoming difficult to obtain. As early as the Kangxi period, bannermen began gathering outside their commanders' offices and demanding silver increases. In 1692, a demonstration protesting the inadequacy of the stipend was held by four to five thousand bannermen in the Imperial City (*huangcheng*) itself. In 1725, a crowd of several hundred bannermen of the Imperial Household Department vandalized the homes of Prince Lian[35] and Li Yanxi, not far from the Forbidden City (*zijincheng*). Later the same year, at the Fuzhou garrison, soldiers and sailors refused to drill unless given silver rewards.[36] By the Qianlong period, strikes and riots on the state farms by agricultural workers (many of whom were disenfranchised bannermen and *zidi*) were epidemic.[37]

Before liberalization of the residence laws in the middle eighteenth century, an unknown number of bannermen fled the garrisons to which they were legally bound rather than continue to live within the narrow economic confines there.[38] In 1741 the Ningguta general-in-chief reported that many of the Manchu bannermen of Ula in Jilin province had absconded because of their poverty. Within the single year 1745 there were more than 250 reports of fugitive bannermen in the Shanhaiguan region, the borderland between China proper and the Northeast. The superiors of fugitives were frequently cashiered, and if captured a deserter's punishment was severe. The Qing codes provided for execution, though it was possible for this to be commuted to "being returned to his native place to serve as a slave, and never be allowed to return to the capital."[39] In effect, "native place" is to be construed here as the Northeast, and indeed many captured bannermen were sent to Heilongjiang as agricultural and mining slaves in the middle eighteenth century. If uncaptured, the fugitive was still punished with being struck off the clan registers, and effectively excommunicated from his clan spirits; the frequency of the "absconded" (*tao*) notation in the genealogies is an index of the magnitude of the problem.[40] In a society in need of manpower for the colonization and mining of frontier regions in Xinjiang and Heilongjiang, the very frequency of the crime worked to lower the punishment from decapitation to forced servitude. By the middle eighteenth century the rule was that after an absence of a month, regardless of whether the offender returned voluntarily or was captured, he was to be expunged from banner (and clan) registration and sent to Heilongjiang as a slave. In the nineteenth century, surrenderers might retain their clan and banner registration, but were still forced into servitude. By the same period the government had appreciated the importance of flexibility in dealing with the bannermen. Peking bannermen were given the right to farm for a living should that be their choice, and officers from provincial garrisons were more frequently given permission to make the coveted transfer to the capital. In 1825 [Socolo] Yinghe (1771–1839)[41] recommended to the court that should unemployed bannermen of the Capital Garrisons ask for a leave of absence, the garrison officers receiving these requests should be advised generally to grant permission to work outside of the garrison.[42] The law already provided for this, but bannermen may have found it hard to have the regulations observed without financial enticement for their superiors.

Despite the powerful cultural, social and scenic traits of the Hangzhou and West Lake vicinity in Zhejiang, the Eight Banners communities established there were in many ways affected profoundly by the pressures and problems that permeated the world of the provincial garrisons. The large garrison inside the Hangzhou city walls was established in 1645, in the wake of the Manchu conquest of eastern Zhejiang, but was not made permanent until 1651. The naval garrison at Zhapu was one of the last established, in 1729. Together they formed a double-garrison system in the eighteenth and nineteenth centuries. On balance, the middle Qing period was a comparatively happy time for the Hangzhou garrisons. It was, however, preceded by a bloody conquest of the region by Qing troops in the seventeenth century, and succeeded by equally bloody incursions by the British and the Taipings in the nineteenth century. The Hangzhou bannermen would often claim that they were adopted by the province where they were settled, just as they had adopted it as a second home. They gave up their language early, and did not pride themselves overmuch on their martial skills. Their links to the court, however, were strong. Over the course of their history they were in some ways less affected by chronic problems of destitution and desertion than were the Capital Garrisons, though in the nineteenth century they bore extraordinary and repeated war losses. In both the earlier and the later dramas, the Suwan Gūwalgiya descendants of Fiongdon played prominent roles.

When Hung Taiji died in 1643, his armies were already set for a move into China. His ninth son Fulin (1638–1661) succeeded him as the Shunzhi emperor, and his younger brother Dorgon (1612–1650) was appointed regent. In the last days of May 1644, Dorgon agreed to combine forces with the Chinese general Wu Sangui in order to drive the rebel troops of Li Zicheng out of Peking.[43] Soon, in betrayal of apparent Ming expectations, the Manchus occupied the city, and by autumn Fulin and the entire Qing government had been moved from Shenyang (Mukden) to Peking. Ming resistance to the Qing incursion, however, continued. Zhu Yousong, a cousin of the late Ming emperor,[44] set up a base in Nanjing and proclaimed himself the Hongguang emperor.[45] The Qing first turned their attention to consolidating their position in the north by pursuing Li Zicheng through Henan and Shaanxi provinces, ultimately defeating him near Xi'an in the spring of 1645.[46] In early April, a Qing army under Nurgaci's fifteenth son Dodo set southward, to conquer the Jiangnan region.[47]

The key to much of Qing success in these campaigns was its cavalry, and one of the fiercest leaders of the cavalry units was [Suwan Gūwalgiya] Tulai (1600–1646), the seventh and most prominent of the sons of Fiongdon.[48] The invasion of China offered Tulai, as it did his fellow officers, unprecedented opportunities for promotion and ennoblement. He had come to fame in the 1629 raid on Peking early in Hung Taiji's reign; for his valor in the first attack upon the Chinese capital he had been awarded minor hereditary rank. Later he distinguished himself in the battle at Lushunkou in 1643, where his elder brother Nagai died, and in the capture of Datong in 1644. When, in the autumn of 1644, the Qing made their full-scale attack upon North China, Tulai was rewarded with promotion to third-class "wing commander" (*meiren i janggin*). Shortly afterward, he commanded the Chinese-martial banners in western Liaodong and northern Hebei, receiving successive promotion to first-class wing commander and to "grand adjutant" (*amba janggin*). While serving under Dorgon, Tulai participated in the routing of Li Zicheng, becoming a third-class "duke" (*gong*) in the process; in very early 1645 he aided Nurgaci's son Dodo in the securing of Shaanxi province, and then followed him into Jiangnan.[49]

The Qing army under Dodo entered Jiangnan in May, and found the remnant Ming forces engaged in a bitter factional dispute that had seriously weakened the defense organizations for Nanjing, resulting in the expulsion of the Grand Secretary Shi Kefa, who removed himself to Yangzhou, north of Nanjing and on the Grand Canal.[50] The Qing armies moved toward Nanjing in early May, and en route reached Yangzhou on the 10th of May. At Dodo's orders Tulai, Nurgaci's nephew Bayintu and [Irgen Gioro] Ašan surrounded Yangzhou with their forces on May 13.[51] By the time the invaders reached Yangzhou, bannermen were a minority within their force. A great number of the Ming soldiers and local militia had joined the Qing forces during the campaign against Li Zicheng in spring and summer of 1644 and stayed with them afterward.[52] Many others began to follow the Manchu standard after the conquest of Peking and initiation of the southern campaigns. It has been estimated that by the time of the descent upon Yangzhou, former Ming servicemen in Dodo's units alone may have numbered as many of 138,000, more than the total of Manchus mobilized in all the Qing armies of conquest; the capture of Nanjing would bring another monumental addition of 100,000 deserters.[53] On May 20 the Qing army entered Yangzhou, which they plundered for ten days before continuing their campaign.[54] A contemporary account by Wang Xiuchou describes the terror of the Yangzhou populace who attempted to conceal their presence from the swarm of invaders in order to avoid murder, rape or bondage. Houses were pillaged and then burned by the conquerors to destroy the people's hiding places, and there was general conflagration in the city for longer than a week. It was reported that more than 800,000 corpses were cremated after the seige, which according to Wang "does not include those who had drowned themselves by jumping into wells or into the river, who had hanged themselves, who had been burned to death behind closed doors, or who had been carried away by the soldiers."[55] After a week's warfare the city was lost, and Qing troops captured the Grand Secretary Shi Kefa as he was attempting to leave through the city gate. When the invaders had surrounded Yangzhou, Shi had apparently attempted suicide but failed; now he refused to collaborate with them, and they killed him. His corpse was never recovered, but his clothing was later buried in the Meihua hills, north of Yangzhou.[56]

Dodo next advanced on Nanjing. Once again, the attack was put under the joint command of Tulai, Bayintu and Ašan. The city was taken on June 8 with relative ease, but Zhu Yousong—the erstwhile Prince of Fu and now the Ming Hongguang emperor of Nanjing—whom the two Chinese apostates Tian Xiong and Ma Degong had promised to deliver into Qing hands, escaped through some fault of Tulai's.[57] Nurgaci's grandson Nikan, along with Tulai, chased the fleeing prince as far as Lake Wu, where he jumped into a boat and tried to cross the water.[58] Tulai also took a boat and attempted unsuccessfully to cut off the prince's escape; in the end Zhu was taken only because of the intervention of Tian and

Ma. Forced to accept most of the blame for the prince's initial escape, Tulai visited Peking to apologize to Dorgon in person. Possibly Tulai had inherited both his father's frankness of speech and his political resourcefulness, for while in Peking he became involved in a harsh exchange of words with Dorgon, and in the end avoided grave troubles only by exposing two conspirators, who were eventually executed.[59]

In the summer of 1645 Nurgaci's grandson Bolo led more than three thousand soldiers into Zhejiang, intending to broaden the Manchu conquest southward through the province into Fujian, where Ming resistance was beginning to coalesce.[60] Tulai had been assigned as one of Bolo's commanders, having recently improved his standing by suggesting a plan for the suppression of roving bandits in Henan and Jiangnan and receiving in turn a promotion to first-class duke. One of their objects, as they moved into the Hangzhou region from the west, was the capture of a second Ming pretender, Zhu Yihai (the Ming Prince of Lu), who intended to establish a new court in Shaoxing.[61] The Ming general Fang Guo'an had positioned his troops along the eastern bank of the Qiantang River; in this way his forces faced the oncoming Manchus across a broad expanse of water. Fang's forces were equipped with boats, apparently intending to meet the Manchus somewhere near the west bank. The Manchus had prepared no boats. They waited until the tide fell, which narrowed the drought-shrivelled river to about a two-mile stretch of shallow water, and then rode across, "there being not a man or horse left that was not soaked through."[62] Fang, shocked at this tactic, attempted to withdraw to Shaoxing, the Manchus in pursuit. The Ming pretender in the meantime fled first to Jinhua, then to Taizhou.[63] Hangzhou fell almost immediately in the general blanketing of the region by invading forces. In a brief battle fought partly on boats—for the city was then heavily crossed by canals—and partly on foot, the invaders captured the Ming garrison by West Lake on June 14 and began preparations for establishment of an Eight Banners garrison in its stead. The Prince of Lu had now fled eastward to the Zhoushan Islands, off Hangzhou Bay; when rebels there refused to shelter him, he moved further south to Fujian province. After only a few days, Bolo moved on to Fujian in pursuit of the Prince of Lu, and Tulai accompanied him; they ultimately were unsuccessful in their attempts to capture the pretender. Tian Xiong, the Ming deserter, was appointed brigade-general at Hangzhou in 1646, which made him commander of all forces in Zhejiang. Eight years of campaigning under Tian's leadership would be required to gain initial control of the province and of the Zhoushan Islands off the coast; and for more than fifteen years sporadic rebellions would challenge that control. The Prince of Lu himself collaborated with the eastern Zhejiang underground resistance until his arrest in 1651.[64]

The bloody pattern of the Qing incursion into Jiangnan was not entirely characteristic of the conquest. Indeed there is more evidence that the misery common to many parts of China in the years subsequent to the conquest was due more to climatic, epidemiological, agrologic, and economic aftereffects of events of the late Ming period than to the immediate effects of the Qing invasion. The troops under Dorgon who took Peking—like those who had conquered Liaodong for Nurgaci—were generally orderly, strictly instructed not to disrupt the routines of the people or to loot; even in Nanjing those convicted of looting were put to death.[65] The pacification of Jiangsu, Jiangxi and Zhejiang was undoubtedly the most ruthless chapter in the Qing conquest of China, and the reasons are complex.[66] Dodo and Bolo, who oversaw much of the southern campaign, were evidently less sensitive to the problems of the Manchu image and the way it was affected by violence than was Dorgon, who himself was not above blood-letting and desecration when he thought it the most effective means to his ends. Their lack of care on this point may have been due to the increase in absolute strength for the Qing, while the large number of mercenaries and Ming deserters they had taken on contributed in its own right to the escalating problems of control. Certain cities in Jiangnan—such as Jiangyin, Yangzhou, and Jiading—had committed themselves to resistance, and the Qing found many fewer there than in the north who, whether opportunistically or philosophically, were prepared to join their cause. The region was also very densely populated, which only increased its vulnerability to the secondary misfortunes of war. Whatever the cause of the special suffering in Jiangnan, the ugliness of the conquest there made a deep impression upon both the local population and upon the Qing court. Though the Kangxi and Qianlong emperors remained wary of the literati circles of the region, they were attentive in sponsoring monumental architecture in Hangzhou, particularly; in attempting to entice many of the Zhejiang scholars to participate in the special (*boxue hongru*) examinations of 1679; and in making the nationalist icon of the West Lake district, Yue Fei, the center of an imperially endorsed cult. But the scars of the Jiangnan conquest never healed completely. In the last decades of the Qing, as Chinese nationalist sentiment arose, the massacre at Yangzhou would be remembered as manifestation of a deep brutality in the nature of the Manchus. Liang Qichao (1873–1929) spoke for many—and far more delicately than some: "Whenever I read the 'Ten Days' Diary of Yang-chow' and the 'Massacre of the City of Chia-ting' by the Manchu Conquerors, my eyes overflow with warm tears. . . . If there were a way to save the nation and at the same time help us to take revenge against the Manchus, I would certainly be delighted to follow it."[67]

These very Jiangnan campaigns consolidated the careers of Fiongdon's descendants, particularly Tulai, who was honorarily appointed the first banner lord (*gusai ejen*) at Hangzhou but never served; he died in 1646 on his way back to Peking,[68] and his ranks and company passed to his son Hoise.[69] Besides Tulai and his nephew Gusu,[70] there were many others of Fiongdon's descendants involved in the southern campaigns, and at least two Gūwalgiya companies figured prominently in the conquest of Zhejiang province. In the Manchu Bordered Yellow Banner, the Suwan Gūwalgiya company was led by Zhaobutai, its hereditary leader (*niru i janggin*). Hele led the Gūwalgiya (probably Suwan) company of the Bordered White Banner. Both were part of Bolo's troops at Hangzhou, and Hele also fought afterward at Jiaxing. Fiongdon's grandson Wage, who would later succeed to captaincy of the Plain Yellow Banner Suwan Gūwalgiya company that had been established for his father Guala, helped to capture Hangzhou. Shakexi died in the 1651 attack upon the Zhoushan Islands, and Gente fought in all the Zhejiang battles, eventually being awarded the rank of third-class baron (*nan*).[71] Many other Gūwalgiya clansmen were part of Bolo's campaigns, in the Plain White and Bordered Red Banners particularly.[72] Salantai, who was killed defending Jinhua against an assault by the troops of the rebellious Fujian satrap Geng Jingzhong in 1674, was among the Fiongdon descendants serving the court in suppression of the Three Feudatories Rebellion.[73]

Immediately after the fall of Hangzhou in June 1645 the garrison was established, and the bannermen found themselves in an ancient Chinese capital of pleasure. The dense urban development of the lower Yangzi was unlike anything the Manchus had encountered before; eastern Zhejiang was regarded as so crowded that the garrison there was given no agricultural land—the only garrison in the country to be not so endowed—while a tiny drill field was provided inside the garrison and one of adequate size could be found only in the northwestern suburbs of Hangzhou.[74] The change in climate, too, must have affected the bannermen. In Liaodong, winter temperatures were normally below 20 degrees Fahrenheit, and summer temperatures rarely reached 80. It was unusual for eastern Zhejiang to have winter temperatures below freezing, and the summer heat often ran into the 90s and higher.[75] Hangzhou itself could trace its history back to the Sui dynasty (589–618), who made it the termination point of the Grand Canal; later it served as the capital of the Wuyue kingdom (893–975). The very landscape had been civilized: West Lake, renowned then and now as perhaps the single most scenic urban spot in China, was virtually man-made; the island and dikes intersecting it are all equally artificial, and without periodic reinforcement of the bank that separates the lake from the Qiantang, its waters would quickly merge with the sprawling river as it flows into Hangzhou Bay.[76] The engineering of West Lake had first been accomplished by the early Tang (698–906) and the Wuyue. It was later improved upon by the Song, who moved their capital here after north China was captured by the Jin Jurchens in 1227. The bridge network marking the "Inner" from the "Outer" lake had been begun in the seventh century, and repaired and elaborated almost every century since. Several medieval figures—most notably the poets Bai Juyi of the Tang dynasty and Su Dongpo of the Song—had been credited with contributing to the engineering of the lake, but perhaps the greatest individual influence upon the West Lake in late imperial times was Ruan Yuan (1764–1849), who in his various official capacities founded the Gujing Academy and the Lingyin Library not far from the shores of the lake, oversaw the dredging of the lake and the clearing of the Yongjinmen River that feeds it, and created the small artificial mound that is now called "Duke Ruan's Island."[77]

In the refinement of its cultural life and the diversity of its architecture, the Hangzhou and West Lake district gave evidence of the delight taken in it by the rulers of the successive dynasties. During the very late years of the Ming dynasty, however, West Lake and parts of the city had been allowed to fall into some disrepair. The lake and the Yongjinmen river were thickly silted, and the lake perimeter was overgrown with weeds. Most of the pagodas and deserted monasteries around it were in poor condition. The city walls had not been expanded or significantly overhauled since the Song period.[78] Hangzhou itself, which in the thirteenth century already had a population of well over a million, was not equipped for the logistical rigors of warfare; it was particularly vulnerable to fire, because of its overcrowding and its partially wooden architecture, and to disease because of its stagnating canals. West Lake's aspect changed as the interest shown in it by the Qing emperors and officials deepened. Upon a site on the northern shore where a Tang pavilion once stood, the Kangxi emperor ordered the construction of the "placid lake, autumn moon" (pinghu qiuyue) pavilion; from Qiantang Gate, which opened into the Eight Banners garrison, this was in clear view at the Orphan Hill end of the Bai Juyi dike. Beyond it, after the 1780s, rose the Wenlan Palace constructed on the order of the Qianlong emperor to house copies of the Imperial Encyclopedia (Gujin tushu jicheng) and the Four Treasuries (Siku quanshu) collections.

Both the Kangxi and the Qianlong emperors were fond of Hangzhou and West Lake; the garrison there received six visits (yingluan) from each during their "southern tours" (nanxun). On his first visit to Hangzhou, in 1684, the Kangxi emperor had been accompanied by the renowned Manchu poet and avatar of elite cultural intimacy between Manchus and Chinese, [Yehe Nara] Singde,[79] who despite his ill health (he would die the next year at the age of thirty) dutifully requited his ritual obligations as an imperial bodyguard. The visits took place in February or March, before the advent of Hangzhou's oppressive summer heat; both the Kangxi and Qianlong emperors came repeatedly in the company of their aged mothers, and Hongli's mother Xiaosheng (1693–1777) on occasion came without her imperial son.[80] Changes in conditions, however, were reflected in the differing tempers and programs of the two emperor's visits. The Kangxi emperor noted during his sojourn in 1689 that the bannermen and civilians of Hangzhou lived peaceably together, which he said pleased him greatly; he only regretted that Hangzhou townsmen were so "contentious and litigious" (zhengsong), to which qualities he attributed a great number of social ills. All imperial visits featured demonstrations of horsemanship and archery by the bannermen, and on occasion the Kangxi emperor would himself join the exhibitions; in 1699 he was reported to have shot two arrows, both of which hit the mark, and to have shown his skills not only in shooting from horseback but also by doing it left-handed (zuoshe). The emperor was modest in assessing his showing, and in what may have been a gesture of paternal indulgence he complemented the Hangzhou bannermen first on their horsemanship and archery and then on their "great accomplishment" in spoken Manchu. At this time, exhibitions were followed by banquets for all bannermen, at which the emperor gave gifts of gold to elderly men and women of the garrison. In 1684 and 1689, men and women over the age of sixty were so rewarded; by 1699, the age had been raised to seventy, and the banquet was held only for bannermen below the ranks of "general-in-chief" (jiangjun) and "brigade-general" (fudutong).

With the coming of the eighteenth century, the tightening of military finances and the strain between the court and the garrison commanders may have taken a certain toll on the festivities associated with imperial visits. Military demonstrations, which after 1728 included exhibitions by the sailing bannermen of Zhapu, rarely provoked imperial comment, and no praise for the spoken Manchu of the locals came forth. The truth was that by the middle eighteenth century the Hangzhou garrisons had figured prominently in the reports by military inspectors citing deficiencies in military preparedness and manjurarengge among the provincial garrisons, and Hongli had bitterly rebuked Hangzhou commanders for their apparent complacency. In 1762, the year that a large number of Chinese-martial bannermen had been expelled from the garrison and at the request of the Fujian-Zhejiang governor-general enrolled in the Green Standard Armies,[81] the Eight Banners and Green Standard soldiers of Hangzhou and Zhapu were ordered to simplify the imperial schedule by giving joint military exhibitions. At about the same time, the economic discrimination against the Chinese-martial bannermen remaining in the garrison found expression in the imperial banquets, as only Manchu non-commissioned bannermen were invited; the invitation list was further shortened to garrison officers above the rank of "lieutenant" (*xiaoqi xiao*) and below the rank of "brigade-general." As military inspections became more perfunctory, the largesse of the court during the visits became more ritual and perhaps more demeaning. All the visits of the Qianlong emperor, the last of which occurred in 1784, resulted in the distribution of an extra months' wages to the bannermen, in a transparent effort to prop up the failing garrison economy and to forestall further complaints from the bannermen.[82] Yet before, during, and after the visits of this period, the Qianlong court never ceased to carp on the physical, cultural and spiritual indolence of the provincial bannermen.

The Eight Banners garrison was built into the northwestern corner of the Hangzhou walls. By 1648 the inner walls were completed, rendering a garrison enclosure about two miles in circumference and about 240 acres in area. This was far in excess of the area occupied by the former Ming garrison, and the acting commander in 1661, Kedo, memorialized the Privy Council (*neige*) that since its founding the garrison had followed instructions to appropriate necessary housing from the residents of Hangzhou, and to date had acquired 1,452 buildings of various sizes and uses. The displaced were now in great misery, yet the garrison's requirements had not been met; Kedo was in the position of attempting to deal with homelessness and disorder among both the conquered civilians of Hangzhou and the conquering Eight Banner soldiers. His request that monies be provided for the construction of new buildings was rejected, and he was instead ordered to follow the cheaper option of compensating those whose shelters had been or would shortly be seized.[83] Originally the garrison had five gates, at irregular intervals; in 1674 a sixth was added and the garrison area was augmented by enclosure of the massive Qiantang Gate, facing West Lake.[84] The Manchu soldiers were settled into the garrison first; in the spring of 1646 their wives, children and parents began arriving from the Northeast.[85] Those of the banner forces who fought in Zhejiang and eventually resided there were part of the approximately 20 percent of the Manchu population located south of the Yangzi.[86] The number of bannermen settled at Hangzhou immediately after the conquest is unclear, primarily due to the chaotic conditions of housing, resettlement and constant transfers to and from Hangzhou in these years. An order of 1646 transferred 4,540 soldiers to Hangzhou along with 119 "mechanics"—smiths, fletchers, bowyers, coopers, cartwrights, saddlers and so on—but the number of soldiers they were joining at Hangzhou is undetermined. Three years later an order to transfer 3,920 soldiers to Hangzhou reveals more about the structure of the community than about the total number of bannermen there, since it stipulates ranks and specialties as follows: 240 corporals, 1,750 mounted privates (*majia*), 1,770 infantry privates (*bujun*), 190 mechanics, and 764 cadets (*yangyu*). For nearly three decades the Hangzhou banner population fluctuated as transfers to and from the installation were necessitated by the exigencies of the ongoing conquest of the south: 500 bannermen were transferred from Hangzhou to Fujian in 1652; nearly 1,900 Chinese-martial sojourned in Hangzhou en route from Fujian back to the north in 1660; 1,000 soldiers were transferred to Hangzhou from Baoding, Dezhou and others of the Capital Garrisons in 1668; 200 arrived from Guangzhou in 1671; 300 from Taiyuan in 1674; and for the ensuing period of the Three Feudatories Rebellion Hangzhou received and dispatched groups of a thousand soldiers or more on an irregular but frequent basis.[87] It is probable that the goal was to keep the population of actively enrolled bannermen at Hangzhou somewhere between 6,000 and 8,000 in the later eighteenth century, which would make it one of the larger provincial garrisons. Certainly, the garrison community embraced not fewer than 20,000 individuals during the Kangxi period.

The bannermen could reach West Lake by walking out of the Qiantang Gate, where a small pier had been built at the lake's eastern shore;[88] a footpath continued over the Bai Juyi dike to Orphan Hill Island, another led to the inconveniently distant banners drill field (*jiaochang*) three miles to the northwest. Like Hangzhou city and West Lake, the garrison was artificially pretty. The houses were for the most part the traditional houses of Hangzhou, narrow two-storied structures of white-washed brick below and lacquered wood above, crowded into the slender, twisting streets of the ancient town. A long canal, over which arched nine stone bridges, ran north and south across the enclosure, between "Well-Letter Tower" (*jingzi lou*) in the northern wall, whose two cross-pieces gave it the appearance of a stylized ideograph for a "well," and the Yanling Gate on the southern. Unlike the remainder of the city, the garrison had some open spaces; a drill field was cleared near the Qiantang Gate,[89] and there was a relatively large open area near the center of the garrison town, where the long canal was met by a shorter one that entered near "Little Gate" (Hongzhen) in the northeast curve of the wall.[90] The general-in-chief's residence, a complex of 164 buildings on an area of over seventy acres, stood near the southwest corner of the garrison,[91] on grounds of a family estate dating to the Song period. North of and adjacent to the general-in-chief's residence were the Meiqing Academy and the temple to Guan Di, who because of his identification with Nurgaci was regarded with special affection by the Manchus.[92] Also located within the garrison were civil adminstrative offices, most important among them the residence for the governor-general (*zongdu*) of Zhejiang and Fujian, for the Zhejiang financial commissioner (*buzhengsi*), and the government offices for Hangzhou prefecture (*Hangzhou fu*), where the Qianlong emperor started and ended his West Lake tours during his visits.[93]

At the time of its creation, the Hangzhou garrison was commanded by Tian Xiong as "wing commander" (*meiren i janggin*—soon to be "brigade-general," *fudutong*),[94] the city having no standing as an independent military jurisdiction in its early period. In 1660 the "controller" (*zongguan*) was established.[95] Three years later the command rank at Hangzhou was raised to general-in-chief (*jiangjun*), whom westerners would call "Tartar General."[96] The rank was one of seven to ten such officers stationed in the provinces; during the final decades of the dynasty, the number of generals-in-chief was fixed at eight. These officers, designated as military officials of the first rank (*pin*), second class (*cong*), were part of the very mobile, elite stratum of the military world. Generals-in-chief of some provinces, notably Shanxi and, at certain times, the Northeast, were responsible for the coordination of entire military sectors. In other provinces (including Zhejiang), they acted as the heads of the garrisons in the provincial capitals and the various branches; in such cases, they were directly responsible to the governor-general (*zongdu*) with jurisdiction over their provinces. Generals-in-chief stationed in provincial capitals were granted the right to keep the keys to the city gates, and the general-in-chief could be of great importance in cases in which the loyalty or competence of the governor-general was in question. In secure areas the general-in-chief office was a sinecure, and in economically developed, scenic regions it was a plum.

During the seventeenth and early eighteenth centuries the garrison at Hangzhou remained of critical strategic importance. Its commanders, normally given the title "Great General Who Pacifies the South" (*pingnan da jiangjun*), were chosen from the ranks of active officers, and in the eighteenth century had a fixed salary of fifteen hundred taels of "honesty-incentive" (*yanglian yin*) together with ten piculs of hulled rice and supplies for forty-four horses (raised to fifty-four horses in 1777).[97] In time, command of the garrison at Hangzhou took on a genteel quality. This center of literary accomplishment in a scenic and wealthy region was often a reward at the end of a lengthy and distinguished career. Assignment as the Hangzhou general-in-chief became a last step before retirement; indeed, in many cases, it was itself a retirement in very sheer disguise. In an ironic instance, Nian Gengyao—then in the process of removal from official life that preceded his death in 1726—was first appointed general-in-chief at Hangzhou.[98] More usually, the post was intended as a reward for the overworked and the elderly. In many instances the rest was probably well earned. With increasing frequency during this period, men who had spent a good part of their careers in busy commands in Mongolia, Xinjiang and the southwest came to Hangzhou to pass their final years.[99] Others probably were deemed deserving merely on the basis of family and clan connections. Of the nineteen generals-in-chief during this time, six were members of the imperial clan and Yuji (d. 1818), one of the three Chinese-martial commanders, was a son of the official Li Shiyao.[100] During the Jiaqing (1796–1820) and Daoguang (1821–1850) periods, the commanders of Hangzhou died on the average less than a year-and-a-half after retiring from the post, and fifteen of these men (about 62 percent) actually died in office or within a few months of retirement. On the other hand, the Hangzhou general-in-chief enjoyed an average stay that was, compared to the dynastic average of tenure for that rank, on the long side at about 2.25 years, which suggests that the appointees were on the whole left to die in office or retire willingly.

In 1674, the year the garrison area was marginally increased, the Chinese-martial banners were introduced into the garrison; a brigade-general (*fudutong*) was established for the Chinese-martial exclusively, while two additional brigades-general were created to administer the Manchu troops.[101] At the time of the creation of the Zhapu garrison in 1728, the number of brigades-general in the Hangzhou system was regularized to two. Like Hangzhou, Canton, Xi'an and Jingzhou were garrisons with more than one brigade-general. At Canton they represented the ethnic components of the garrison after the middle eighteenth century, and at Xi'an and Jingzhou they commanded separate "wings (*yi*)." But at Hangzhou, they were manifestations of the actual physical division of this peculiar garrison: Hangzhou, the mother garrison, faced westward onto West Lake, while Zhapu was the eastward-facing coastal installation in Pinghu county. It is difficult to assess the extent to which the unmartial character of the general-in-chief affected the brigade-general ranks of the Hangzhou garrisons in the early nineteenth century. Certainly the brigades-general at Hangzhou were, as in most garrisons, very different in profile and responsibility from the general-in-chief, and at five hundred taels of honesty-incentive at Hangzhou (a thousand at Zhapu) together with 8.75 piculs of hulled rice and supplies for thirty-four horses, were subsisting on a salary that was a fraction of that of their superiors. They were much younger than the generals-in-chief; it was not unusual in many garrisons for there to be a generation's difference between the general-in-chief and his brigade(s)-general. Indeed, most successful military officers spent the better part of their careers as brigade-general, hoping to spend a few years at the end as general-in-chief—or more likely acting general-in-chief for an ailing or absent commander. The brigades-general of Hangzhou and Zhapu averaged nearly five years in length of service, normal in comparison with other garrisons. Overall, it appears that the Hangzhou garrison population was more stable than those affected by the eighteenth-century mobilizations associated with the conquest of Xinjiang. At Hangzhou, the last major changes in the constitution of the garrison occurred during mobilization of a thousand troops dispatched to Yunnan in 1720 to join the invasion of Tibet, and the removal of over eight hundred Hangzhou bannermen to the newly created Zhapu branch garrison in 1728.

In that year the large Hangzhou garrison was subdivided when a Left Wing (*zuo yi*) brigade-general was created at Zhapu to oversee the naval garrison on the shores of Pinghu County. Zhapu was the port of Hangzhou. It was connected to the greater city a day's journey away by inland canals and by a series of guard stations behind a palisade that ran along the northern bank of the Qiantang, then continued along the northern coast of Hangzhou Bay. The Qing had authorized Zhapu as the only port for the trade to Japan and Korea, which made it busy and rich; by the middle nineteenth century it was a leisure and shopping center for eastern Zhejiang, and with Hangzhou was the central depot point for grain transported southward from Peking via the Grand Canal. From the sea Zhapu appeared nestled against the heights of Mount Guanyin and its surrounding hills on the east. These hills were part of a chain stretching about eight miles along the coast, remarkable protuberances at the edge of the enormous inland alluvial plain of Jiangnan. In the nineteenth century the hills, not naturally hospitable to agriculture, had been carefully terraced; on the sides facing Zhapu, they were studded with grave monuments.[102] The city itself, which in Ming times had been vulnerable to raiding by Japanese and Chinese pirate fleets, was a mile from the water and fortified by high walls about three miles in circumference, externally bounded with a shallow moat; its suburbs stretched not only as far as the beach but also east and west of the city walls to a distance of four or five miles.[103]

Against the featureless inland Zhejiang plain, Zhapu was an oasis of comfort, pleasure and wealth. The garrison was well planned in advance, with all construction taking place before the new population was imported in 1728—a contrast to the perpetual chaos of the crowded Hangzhou installation, and perhaps a better reflection of the bannermen's housing preferences.[104] Within the garrison, the families lived in small houses, surrounded by yards, gardens and outbuildings, many of the plots bordered by bamboo fences; to the outsider, accustomed to the tight residential rows common to both Chinese and European cities, the arrangement seemed haphazard.[105] The houses themselves were whitewashed like those of Hangzhou, and adorned with black trim, those of officers bearing insignia of the appropriate rank. G. Tradescant Lay described the interior of a common bannerman's home in the middle nineteenth century: "Some have merely a bench for reclining at night, a table, a few stools, and perchance a solitary cupboard for the bestowment of some spare garments; others, though unpromising in outward show, are well stored with the necessaries, the comforts, and not in a paucity of instances, with the elegancies of life."[106]

Of the 1,600 bannermen assigned to Zhapu, about 800 had moved from Hangzhou, 400 from Jiangning, and 400 from Peking, all drawn from among *zidi*, cadet and other unemployed classes of those garrisons.[107] By the early nineteenth century there were between 1,200 and 1,500 bannermen living at Zhapu at any one time; with their dependents, the population of the banner quarter was probably around 8,000 people. The Qing maintained no navy, but only a series of coastal installations under the control of provincial garrisons. Moreover, despite the fact that some of their Jurchen ancestors had manned the boats of Khubilai Khan during his two sea campaigns against Kamakura Japan, the Manchus were considered by no one to be natural sailors. Chinese officers of the Green Standard Army were brought in to instruct the new Zhapu bannermen on the arts of navigation. Because the Zhapu naval bannermen were drawn from the poorest class of the garrison and because they had to undergo a prolonged period of instruction, their wages were lower than those of their brethren in Hangzhou. Following the example of the naval garrison at Tianjin, they drew two taels, one picul a month until Hongli announced during his visit of 1751 that he would raise their salary to equal that of the Hangzhou non-commissioned men—two taels, 2.5 piculs a month.[108]

The change did not make the Zhapu bannermen wealthy, but only made their destitution comparable to that of Hangzhou. As early as 1694 Hangzhou bannermen were demanding tolls from those travelling through the garrison gates, claiming that their wages were insufficient for their expenses. The eighteenth-century generals-in-chief at Hangzhou were among the more sophisticated in their attempts to augment garrison income by leveraging funds, being known at various times to sell their rice at a slightly inflated price in order to cover their paper and ink costs, to run pawn shops and usury operations that attempted to profit from the local need for commercial investment, and to operate garrison workshops designed to capitalize upon local tastes. Though the garrison was without agricultural land, enclosed pasture land for its horses amounted to over 14,000 acres (84,000 *mou*) in the suburbs of Hangzhou; since 1782 half of that had been sold or rented with the permission of the government, and the proceeds collected for a widows and orphans' fund, to cover costs of transporting grain to the garrison, and other incidental fees. By the turn of the century, land was reported being rented or sold not only for the support of widows, orphans and the destitute of the two garrisons, but also to cover the normal operating expenditures of the garrison. By the middle nineteenth century it was revealed that the scarcity of grazing

land had led the bannermen to cease letting their horses out to pasture—
there were, by this time, presumably few or no horses in the garrison, in
spite of which the horse-raising allowance (three horses per banner private at Hangzhou) continued.[109] Though there is no incontrovertible evidence of it, it is probable that the economic condition of the Hangzhou-
Zhapu bannermen, fragile as it evidently was, surpassed in some degree
the national average for garrisons. Total government expenditures for the
support of the Hangzhou-Zhapu bannermen, reported at 99,866 taels,
1,293 piculs of hulled rice, and 15,622 piculs of unhulled rice in 1778,
may well have represented only a little less than 10 percent of the budget
for all garrisons, a disproportionate allotment that may have been related
to the garrison's inability to provide its own food staples.[110] Well into the
Daoguang period (1820–1850) the income from rented land and the management of government grants to the garrison supported not only the
charities for the needy and many of the incidental operating expenditures, but also the supply of wedding and funeral expenses no longer
provided by the government, maintenance and heating costs for the
Meiqing Academy and travel funds to Peking for garrison examination
candidates for both the military and the civilian national (jinshi) degrees.[111]

Despite the fact that a good number of Manchu bannermen lived outside the garrison until the middle eighteenth century (when the purging
of the Chinese-martial banners from the quarter finally assured a place
for every Manchu inside the walls), they were a recognizable community—though they did not rely upon alien speech or customs to make
themselves so. It is clear that a certain identification with local interests,
many of which had now become the bannermen's own, affected some
garrison policies. In 1795, for instance, the general-in-chief Chengde memorialized the Board of War for permission to carry out cannon practice
in the fall only. Previously the garrison had followed the national policy
of artillery drilling both in the spring and in the fall, but it seemed that
the spring practice disturbed the silk worms, which were reaching the
height of their industry at that time; in the interests of the local economy,
Chengde explained, it was necessary to leave the silk worms in peace.[112]
An eighteenth-century inspector in Hangzhou remarked that a century
after the invasion, "Spoken Manchu has declined and the Manchus speak
the same as the local Han Chinese. Local customs have corrupted their
manners, and there are none among them to be emulated. Somehow it
must be ordered that spoken Manchu not be forgotten."[113] Zu Zhizhen,
sent to review the military skills of the Hangzhou garrison at roughly the
same time, reported that preparedness at Hangzhou was in a shocking
state of neglect, particularly as it affected the most expensive areas of
artillery maintenance and training. He stridently recommended rigorous

monitoring of the garrison, but warned, "This will not be settled easily."[114] Little wonder that the Qianlong emperor, obsessed with the myth
of Manchu martiality, could not bring himself to the indulgent but empty
praises with which his grandfather had graced the seventeenth-century
bannermen of Hangzhou.

Native bannermen of Hangzhou and its sister naval garrison at Zhapu had
come to cherish expert knowledge of local history, ancient ruins and rel-
ics, literature inspired by the beauty of West Lake, and had themselves
begun to generate no small amount of poetry and painting celebrating
the local landscape. The works of the Hangzhou bannerman later became
part of the collection of documents on the garrison community there collated by the Chinese-martial bannerman Zhang Dachang in 1893 and
published with a preface by the local luminary Yu Yue. They were enthusiastic in their formation of literary and charitable societies, and on occasion seem to have invited their Chinese neighbors to join them. Certainly by the early nineteenth century the bannermen of Hangzhou had
formed closer and more casual ties with their surroundings than was the
case for the provincial garrisons in general, and the cultural environment
had a great effect on them. The proportion of Hangzhou-Zhapu bannermen who successfully sat for the civil degree examinations was higher
than for most other garrisons, which mirrors the outstanding achievement of Zhejiang civilian candidates in the competitions. In violation of
the wishes of the court, Manchus of the Zhejiang garrisons found fortune
as well as diversion in the literary industries of Hangzhou and the West
Lake district. As illustrators, as printers, and as booksellers some bannermen supplemented their hereditary stipends, securing their finances
and, they imagined, their local status.

Such a banner family, the Suwan Gūwalgiya household of the bannerman Jalangga, became well established among the literary world of Hangzhou and Zhapu. Jalangga's ancestor Ubahai, a grandson of Fiongdon,
had been among the bannermen sent from the Capital Garrisons outside
Peking to Hangzhou (*via* Jinjiang) in 1668. How long he lived afterward
is not known, but he apparently died at Hangzhou; his body was transported back to Peking, as was required for active bannermen before the
middle eighteenth century, and a tablet was set up in his honor on the
grounds of the Lingyin temple, part way up the mountainside to the west
of West Lake.[115] His sons Jigantai and Shutongga were born in the Hangzhou garrison. Jigantai married a woman of the Chinese-martial banners,
surnamed Wen. They were the parents of Jalangga, who when grown
served as a corporal of the Plain White banner at Zhapu.[116] Shutongga,
who eventually served as lieutenant-general of the Chinese-martial banners at Zhapu, had two sons, Guanji and Jingcheng.[117] Jalangga accom-

panied his uncle and cousins as a portion of the Hangzhou bannermen were transferred to Zhapu in 1728. His first son Tuwohana, probably born around 1762, had been hopeful of a career within the command ranks of the garrison system. But when Tuwohana died young, Jalangga and his widowed daughter-in-law were left with the prospects of the family dying out. Through luck and perseverance, and with the help of a virtuous young woman of the Chinese-martial banners, the family eventually continued with the boy Guancheng, who in his later career as printer, writer and magistrate assured the place of his family's story in the local histories, literature and popular entertainments.

PART TWO

The extraordinary shocks China sustained in the nineteenth century profoundly altered the conditions of life in the garrisons. Economic and social conditions made devotion to martial skills a marginal consideration, at best, for most bannermen. But the intrusion of the Opium War into Zhejiang forced residents of the garrisons to fight virtually in their own doorways for the protection of their families, and when engagements were lost, to hang themselves in their own sheds or drown their wives and children in their own wells. They had, moreover, to answer to the court for their inability to drive out the foreign invaders. Before recovery was possible, assaults by Taiping rebels, who used a particularly vivid racial rhetoric against the Manchus, had ended in massive slaughters of whole garrison communities. In the aftermath of the struggle against the Taipings, the Qing court was financially and politically devastated. It could not or would not supply the resources necessary to restore the garrison communities of Jiangnan, and gradually removed the restrictions, as well as the supports, that had defined garrison life throughout China for two hundred years. Now, the Manchus themselves would or would not sustain their communities and forge an identity. Through the Hundred Days' Reforms, the Boxer Rebellion, the Revolution of 1911/12, Manchus found various paths toward political, cultural, and historical integrity.

The Suwan Gūwalgiya lineage of the Hangzhou garrison saw the process from the inside out, and left a record.

CHAPTER IV

Guancheng

SIR NANCHUAN

GUANCHENG, who came to adulthood in the Jiaqing reign (1796–1820), was known to his home community as Guan Weitong. His two names are a reminder that under the strictures of garrison life Northeastern folk culture was given two metamorphoses with the Manchus of China. On the official level, it became an institutionalized, formal cultural system, symbolic of Qing belief in the legitimacy of their provenance and the universality of their rule. On the popular level, the Manchus gradually came to see themselves as what they had not been before: a race. Concepts of race that had once been foreign to Jurchen or Manchu thinking were endorsed by the Qianlong court, which propagated both informational works and new educational systems to revive *manjurarengge*, or the behavior that in its view would have accorded with Manchu racial identity. But popular logic seems to have followed another tack: Since race is heritable and indelible, the precise cultural inclinations (or the naming practices) of an individual of a certain race do not much affect that racial identity. Early nineteenth-century Manchus who could acquire the proper education aspired to careers in the civilian bureaucracy, which in comparison to those in the military bureaucracy or in the garrisons were lucrative and leisurely. Those with some capital preferred to use it to acquire land, and so to live as landlords. Those with no money and no prospects, which was the great majority, abandoned themselves to passive poverty (sometimes reinforced by opium addiction) or begging and even banditry.

Within the garrisons, a culture derived from the specific conditions of the garrisons—rather than from the expectations of the court which had created the garrisons—arose. It embraced a mixture of romantic pride in a martial (but increasingly distant) heritage, a continued pleasure in the folk arts of the Northeast, an emotional attachment to the orally transmitted history of the clans and the emperors, a fascination with the aesthetics of Chinese culture, and the taste for trivia that can best be fostered by those who neither reap nor sow, and have few cares in life beyond the acceptance of permanent communal indebtedness. Kites, praying mantises, birds and bird cages, tops, folk songs, classical poetry, opera and tea house entertainments were all avidly pursued by the bannermen of the early nineteenth century. The court worried about the condition of the garrison populations, but it was a different concern from that of Qianlong times. Hongli had wished the bannermen to speak Manchu, ride well, shoot straight, and drill regularly. His son Yongyan, the Jiaqing emperor, and grandson Minning, the Daoguang emperor (r. 1821–1851), were more occupied with keeping the bannermen out of the black market and extortion trades, off opium, away from banditry and in the garrison compounds. Less rhetoric was directed in the early nineteenth century to the question of whether or not the Manchus *manjurarengge* or were abiding by the Old Way (*fe doro*). But in the aftermath of the Opium War a curious thing began to happen. The bannermen of Zhapu, whose martial spirit blazed bright enough once ignited, experienced a certain estrangement from the court. And with that estrangement came the impulse, at least in [Suwan Gūwalgiya] Guancheng, to call himself not a slave (*aha, nucai*) but a "Manchu."

Guancheng was a product and a producer of a colorful episode in local lore. Sources on the history of Hangzhou and its surrounding regions preserve the story of Jalangga, Shao-shi, Wanggi-shi and the salvation of the Gūwalgiya lineage by luck and virtue.[1] Jalangga was among the Hangzhou banner population transferred to Zhapu in 1728, at which time he was certainly an infant or small child, and later served as his ancestors had in the Manchu Plain Yellow Banner.[2] His rank of corporal (*bosoku, lingcui*) indicates that he must have been literate in Manchu, at a minimum; he owned books, we know, which his widow often aired on the windowsill to prevent mildew. About 1762 his first wife gave birth to a son, Tuwohana. She died shortly afterward, leaving the boy the only child of the marriage. At an early age Tuwohana showed literary abilities; he took the style name (*zi*) of Yanyu, was accomplished in Manchu and at about twenty years of age began to serve as a "clerk" (*bithesi, bitieshi*) of the Bordered Blue Banner at Zhapu. Tuwohana was himself registered in the Manchu Plain Yellow Banner, but in his professional capacity served another banner—a normal feature of garrison careers.[3] Soon he was preparing for the local licentiate (*gongsheng*) examination. But around 1787, at the age of twenty-four, he died. Tuwohana had married a Manchu woman of the Wanggi clan. His young widow and his father Jalangga were now left to fend for themselves. If they followed the law and reported Tuwohana dead, they would have received from the court a compensation payment and their monthly income would thereafter have been calculated according to Jalangga's old corporal's salary. Many bannermen simply neglected (which might have involved a substantial payment to the local officers) to report deaths and continued to receive the deceased's stipend, but in the case of Jalangga such a ruse would have been pointless—Tuwohana's clerk's salary and Jalangga's corporal's salary were the same, four taels per month. The elderly Jalangga was disconsolate, for his wife had died earlier and he was left without descendants or aid in his old age. He considered adopting a child from another family, but at Wanggi-shi's insistence he consented to marry again. Before long the widowed daughter-in-law had effected a marriage between Jalangga and a young woman only one year her senior of the Chinese-martial banners, surnamed Shao. In time Shao-shi did produce a child, but it was a girl. A year later, she gave birth to a boy, Guancheng.

Our view of Wanggi-shi and her role in this drama comes from the hagiographies of her published years later at Guancheng's expense. The Confucian conventions of these accounts are patent, but some palpable sense of Wanggi-shi's personality and viewpoint emerge. Her clan, the biographies assure us, was one of the old clans of the Changbai region; charity and service lists for the garrison suggest that her clan was numerous (which is not to say prominent) at Hangzhou and Zhapu. Wanggi-shi herself was not literate, but is reported as a child to have spent her time listening to her father and older brothers talking of "the pure officials of old, filial children, righteous scholars, and chaste women." She grasped great ideas quickly, and what she heard "immediately shaped her mind, never to be forgotten" (*shi che zhi yu xin bu wang*).[4] At twelve years (*nian*) of age, she married Tuwohana, then aged fifteen, and went to live in his household. The young man's achievements brought some financial security and much hope to the family, but when he died Wanggi-shi was widowed at the age of twenty-two, childless and with a father-in-law aged well over sixty to care for. "She preserved her chastity through bitter determination," a local history later remarked.[5]

After some time Jalangga announced his wish to adopt a son from one of the other three Suwan Gūwalgiya lineages in the garrison. An outburst is attributed to Wanggi-shi that (assuming for a moment that it is not apochryphal) must have sounded strange to the ears of a man of Jalangga's generation: "Filiality does not find its great part in having descendants to look after one's self. We, who are ourselves descendants, must continue the blood. To raise someone else's son is in no sense to raise one's own bone and flesh, and will not be sufficient to honor the greater lineage (*dazong*)."[6] Jalangga understood that only his own household and not the great Suwan Gūwalgiya clan as an entity was in jeopardy; he was interested in the practicalities of having a young man to help with the firewood and finances. To him, Wanggi-shi's concerns must have appeared decidedly new, for they centered upon the families and bloodlines that had emerged as important social forms only within the lifetime of Jalangga himself. When, however, Wanggi-shi had arranged a second marriage, Jalangga consented, and the child Guancheng, who would grow to be prosperous and father four sons to survive infancy, was born. "Gracious and generous Heaven did not end the Gūwalgiya clan," the local history jubilates. "The Gūwalgiya generations are firmly established, their days are rich, and when performing their sacrifices they fill the doorways."[7] Wanggi-shi, a childless widow, lived as the senior woman in Guancheng's household.[8] In 1820 she died at the age of 54, after a period of anxiety, then grief, over the illness and death of Guancheng's first infant son. Guancheng fasted in mourning for her, and later spent the early part of his career promoting her in the local chaste-and-filial-woman cult.

The status of Manchu women in comparison to Chinese women has often been a subject of conjecture. The question may be generalized to the non-Han dynasties. Cases of usurping woman rulers, the most infamous being the Empress Dowager Xiaoqin [Yehenara-shi, Cixi (1835–1908)], seem limited to dynasties of alien origin, as in the instance of the Liao Empress Dowager Chengtian [Ruizhi (d. 1009)] or to dynasties in which alien influence was strong, as in the instance of the Tang "woman emperor" Wu Zhao [Zitian (624–705)]. Something in these cultures, the reasoning runs, must have encouraged women to seek control, or have encouraged men to yield to them. The possible explanations are perhaps too numerous to be meaningful. The weakness or absence of Confucianism is usually observable in these situations; the social structures of the North and Northeast Asian peoples often emphasized female roles as the interfaces between lineage segments, and in some cases there is evidence of matrilineality or, less probably, matriarchy in the very early societies from which such peoples sprang; shamanism in many Northeast Asian forms may originally have depended upon female shamans; and the economic life of the steppes and the forests often lacked the impetus to confine and isolate women and their labors. Certainly, among the Qing emperors—as among the Mongolian khans before them—a tendency to depend upon the counsel of older women (whether mothers, grandmothers, stepmothers or wet-nurses) was marked, and Hongli surprised his Jesuit courtiers by demanding to know whether France had ever had a woman ruler. But it is dangerous, particularly in the Qing case, to make assumptions about the general population on the basis of the predilections of the court. Equally it is unwise to rely upon Shirokogoroff's observations of Aigun Manchus in 1915, where women were free to sleep with younger men without benefit of marriage and controlled a good portion of clan property and clan decisions.[9]

The garrisoned Manchus of China did not bind the feet of their girls, which made Manchu women appear uncouth to many Chinese, and unfettered to many Western observers of the later nineteenth and twentieth centuries. Popular entertainments (such as that presented below) spoke of men preparing food and families being marginally grateful for the births of female children. But in an urban setting the Manchus felt the same pressure as did the population as a whole to proscribe female legal and physical freedoms. If Manchu men suffered the limitations of employment in only one profession, Manchu women suffered exclusion from all occupations; as a consequence every Manchu woman of China proper was dependent upon the incomes of her husband or sons. As the locus of property management devolved from the clan to the family, it became more important to excise those traditional rights that women had enjoyed over property disposal; belongings, or wealth if there should be any, now proceeded from father to son, a straightening of the zigzags between brothers or collateral branches that had frequently occurred in the old society. In such circumstances, sons took on the critical importance they had among the Chinese, and the cult of the chaste widow was as vigorously promoted among the Manchus in China as it was in the society at large, which nicely eliminated the levirate—attested among many Manchus in preconquest and early postconquest times—that would have transferred property rights between collateral lines. A chaste widow, it should be emphasized, was a living widow; the court sternly reminded women that self-slaughter on the occasion of a husband's death was considered the path of least effort, and was not condoned: "After her husband dies, a wife's responsibilities become even greater, " the Yongzheng emperor instructed in 1728. "She must serve and care for her parents-in-law, taking the part of their son; she must guide and instruct her offspring, taking the part of their father."[10] It is evident in the story of Wanggi-shi that such considerations were uppermost, though there seems to have been some question of her returning to her own family, for Jalangga is reported to have requested permission for her to stay with him. The court, looking for ways to supplement banner support in the early and middle eighteenth century, offered to grant the expenses incurred by a garrison family wishing to publicize the virtues of its widows. Survivors hoping to construct memorial arches for such women (as Guancheng did for Wanggi-shi) could apply for subsidies, compensatory gifts of silver, as well as silk and commodities for sacrifice.[11]

Such monuments were for the benefit of the survivors, who could use the occasion to notify the court of the existence of a worthy family and to receive remuneration in exchange; the publicization of female virtue together with the fondness for the production of genealogies was part of the vogue for family and lineage glorification that enveloped much of the elite, both Manchu and Chinese, in the nineteenth century.[12] Indeed Wanggi-shi's family-by-marriage as late as 1880 was still requesting, under the leadership of Guancheng's son Fengrui, that the court promote Wanggi-shi in status and finance an entitlement ceremony for her at Hangzhou.[13] Local histories and even institutional histories such as "General History of the Eight Banners" (*Baqi tongzhi*) are glutted with stereotyped "biographies" of chaste women, considerable in volume but not very informative in content; Wanggi-shi herself was the topic of at least six instructive biographies in the Qing period or shortly after.[14] It is perhaps more significant that few women of the Qing period (including Wanggi-shi) have their personal names recorded, and in many family histories it is impossible to guess how many daughters a family may have raised, since their existence is mentioned only in passing if at all. In the case of Jalangga's family, no woman's personal name is known until Hualiang (born around 1875), whose father Fengrui seems to have been affected by the progressive ideas of the day. Of Guancheng's older sister there is absolutely no mention in any of the family materials, apart from much lamenting over her birth; in view of the family's poverty at the time, she may have been a victim of infanticide.

The story of Shao-shi and Wanggi-shi, at Guancheng's instigation, became the subject of a nineteenth-century "zidi tale" (zidi shu). The texts of these tales, which were recited to a seven-word rhythm, do not do much to communicate the spirit of the entertainment, but since the text of the Shao-shi and Wanggi-shi tale survives, it is worth considering here. By local tradition the composition was attributed to Guancheng; his sons were later credited with talent in both writing and performing zidi tales and other drum songs, and it is possible that he was indeed the originator of it. The text begins with Guancheng's memories of a sorrowful childhood, then uses the voice of Shao-shi to go back in time to the death of Tuwohana, to describe the lonely life of Jalangga and Wanggi-shi afterward, Wanggi-shi's determination that the Gūwalgiya line be perpetuated, Jalangga's new marriage to Shao-shi, the drama of Guancheng's birth, Jalangga's death, the selflessness of Wanggi-shi in raising young Guancheng, and ends with Shao-shi's instruction that, if her son should achieve the national degree (jinshi)—an honorary bestowal of which he was probably angling for at the time of the tale's composition—he should ask the emperor to honor not only his mother but his sister-in-law as well:

> I remember, when I was a child, playing with the other boys, one of whose father had prepared a snack for him to eat. Later I returned home, and I asked Mother and Auntie where my own father was. Mother wept silently and Auntie cried too. Then mother said:

> When your elder brother was still a child, his mother was taken. At the age of only fifteen he was married to your Auntie. With extra help in the kitchen, your brother had time to read your father's books. But he died just after his first academic success. Auntie shed tears of blood. The old patriarch was devastated. To comfort him, Auntie hid her own tears, working all alone in the kitchen, separating the rice from the husk for him. The house was cold and lonely; tearful, Auntie begged the old man to marry again. Moved by her

heartfelt tears, he consented; and the young widow prepared to welcome a new mother-in-law.

When I came into this household, I was immediately in sympathy with your Auntie. By the rite, we are mother and daughter-in-law; but in fact we are as sisters. When we discovered our ages, she was one year younger than I.

A boy—I wanted to have a boy. But the well-wishers who came into the courtyard were repulsed by girlish cries, and the old man swallowed his tears. Auntie sighed in despair, and said, "When you wish for rice, you get gruel. Yet it is better than an empty stomach."

But there was a bud within me that flowered. I was about to give birth again. The old man felt your hands quiver, and his own heart was racing. He burned incense and prayed to Heaven that this time I would give birth to a boy, to perpetuate his lineage. He had no hope of seeing you grow up or become famous. You were a red-skinned baby, your father a white-haired old man.

The next year, he lay dying. The infant laughed and chattered beside his pillow, clinging to his father as if it were his mother, with no knowledge of his illness. The father grieved to know that only a few moments remained before the parting.

I held to a life of struggle only because of my infant son. What can be compared to my tears? Only the crystal raindrops frozen on the plums. Only the thousand *li* waters of the River Xiang.

Mother-in-law and sister-in-law, we struggled together to raise you. We aired out your father's books each year, hoping that you would one day be learned. For Auntie, it was like caring for an orphan. When she had no little brother-in-law, she prayed for one; when she got him, she nursed him from the tenderest age. Now that young sprout has grown strong. Without arduous cultivation, how do you imagine there could have been such a late crop? In olden days, Han Yu mourned his older sister-in-law as his mother. In our time, Hu Yunpo petitioned the court on behalf of his elder sister-in-law. If you should receive the honor of the Five Flowers, you must, my son, beg the Emperor to honor your Auntie. Only a mother's love, it is true, is a mother's love; but your obligation to Auntie is no less.

The charm of such recitations, which were one of the focal points of garrison life, lay not in the moral issue but in the characterizations, pathos and humor that were evinced in the production. With its improving theme of triumph over tragedy through clan loyalty (transmuted here into filial piety), hard work, and perseverance, the story of Wanggi-shi and Shao-shi was perhaps well-suited to propagation in the local press. Its actual popularity, however, was probably more closely related to its redaction in the form of a *zidi* tale. Like other drum songs, it was acted to the accompaniment of a small hand-drum and, perhaps, a two-stringed violin, or *erhu*. The Jiaqing period in which Guancheng lived out his adolescence and early adulthood was a high point in the dissemination of this form of entertainment among the garrison populations. The style of the Shao-shi and Wanggi-shi tale, it should be noted, is not representative of the *zidi* tales in general; the text attributed to Guancheng is altogether elegant in comparison to the language generally found in these popular ditties. More interestingly, it avoids (for Guancheng in his shrewd way may have assessed well the tastes of those he wanted to impress) the Chinese-Manchu argot that is preserved in many of the texts and which probably reflects the early nineteenth-century speech of the uneducated majority in many garrison communities. A fair number of Qianlong-Jiaqing songs are preserved in Manchu with Chinese gloss to remind the performer of the meaning of difficult or arcane passages, others are in Chinese with Manchu gloss, and others in a demi-language, Chinese in grammar but laced with Manchu and a small number of Mongol words.[15] Certain terms, such as *sula* (unemployed) and *inenggidari baitakū* (never having anything to do) showed a great durability in garrison discourse. The small-scale retention of Manchu political and social terminology in the vocabulary of the bureaucracy was clearly dwarfed by the massive survival of Manchu words in the speech of garrison inhabitants of the late Qianlong, Jiaqing and early Daoguang periods, and which at Peking continued into the last years of the dynasty.[16] It is not likely, however, that the Qianlong emperor, so distressed at the imperfect Manchu of the garrison elite sent to court, would have been comforted by the nineteenth-century vitality Manchu had gained from its uninhibited interbreeding with the sundry dialects of China.

Eighteenth- and nineteenth-century Chinese society generally was obsessed with popular theater, and the Manchus could rightfully claim the deepest fanaticism in this regard. Dramatic recitation was an ancient tradition of the Manchus, and through the Qing period continued to be an indispensable element in court shamanism, as bannermen would spend the pre-dawn hours of specified days treating the emperors to magical reenactments of the hunting adventures of Nurgaci, or the emperors themselves would attempt to charm the gods with the singing of potent songs.[17] The patronage of the Qing court was undoubtedly the greatest catalyst in the refinement of "Peking opera" (*jingju*), which emerged in its mature form during the Daoguang years (1820–1850) when Zhang Nenggui dominated the stages of the capital. Theaters were forbidden within the Inner City in Peking, which meant they were outside the precincts of the banner habitat. The result was not only uninhibited breaking of the curfews by bannermen eager to attend performances in the Outer

City but also the increasingly popular practice among the nobility of maintaining private theatrical troupes. It was usual to hire independent or semi-professional companies for performances, but the extravagance of private patronage of troupes was the ruin of many a nobleman's precarious finances; the imperial clansman Zhaolian (1780–1843), for instance, contributed to his own financial debacle by maintaining an acting troupe in his household, for which he commissioned original works of music and drama.[18] In the late Qing dynasty and in the Republican period, many Manchus actually made their living performing in the streets and tea houses, although it was strictly forbidden by statute before 1912 and they risked losing their stipends by doing so. In the very late Qing period some of the most famous performers of opera, street theatrics, and "drum songs" (gurci) were Manchus, perhaps foremost among them Dejunru (said to be a grandson of Mujangga). Well into the twentieth century, the fascination of the Manchus with theater and street performing was well known.[19] Certainly, the Hangzhou bannermen were not immune to the charm that chanting, clapping, drum pounding and acrobatics held for their colleagues elsewhere. In the garrison at Hangzhou, for instance, the gate of the Guan Di Temple inside the grounds of the Commander's Residence had an opera stage built into it, and it was apparently in very frequent use.[20] Lao She later attributed the mania of the bannermen for opera and street performance to the fondness for the arts that permeated Qing Manchu garrison culture in the absence, as it were, of more pressing concerns:

> In the last decades of the Qing dynasty, the life of the bannermen, apart from consuming the grain and spending the silver supplied by the Chinese, was completely immersed, day to day, in the life of the arts. From the emperor and the aristocracy above to the banner soldiers below, everybody knew how to sing arias from the classical opera, play the one-stringed accompaniment, perform recitations with the drum, and chant the popular tunes of the day. They raised fish, birds, dogs, plants and flowers, and held cricket fights. Among them were many with outstanding calligraphy, or some talent at landscape painting, or writing poetry of some kind—and those without such talents could at the very least make up some reasonably humorous and melodious drum song. They didn't have the strength to defend the borderlands or maintain their political power, but they developed a very intimate relationship with their pets and their culture.[21]

The pastimes of the garrison dwellers may have affected Guancheng earlier than the tastes of the West Lake literary world that surrounded the banner community. Like Hangzhou, Zhapu was a wealthy city, but the bannermen inhabited their own small paradise of straitened circumstances within it. Though Zhapu was officially regarded as a naval garrison, it was not the case that Guancheng's family were at all accustomed to seafaring; offshore maneuvers were very rare in the nineteenth century, the junks were not in good repair, and a sea-transport grain scheme that might have solved the decades-old problem of moving grain along the silted Grand Canal and created new demand for the services of the Zhapu sailing bannermen was finally quashed by local officials in 1824. Guancheng's family owned no land, and in Jalangga's youth could not have enjoyed the support of an active bannerman in the household, since the portion of the Hangzhou population transferred to Zhapu were drawn from the unemployed or underemployed of the mother garrison. Until Guancheng was ten or so (at which point he would have become eligible for a cadet's appointment), the family lived off the remnants of Jalangga's old corporal's salary and the institutionalized charity of the garrison community. It is unlikely, however, that they experienced the sort of hopeless poverty that was by this time endemic in the garrison world. Few garrisons made even a pretense of being able to arm their actively enrolled bannermen adequately. Visitors to the Canton garrison, for instance, were greeted by half-naked bannermen dragging rusted swords and old bows.[22]

Unlike the emperors of the eighteenth century, the nineteenth-century emperors showed little willingness or ability to aid the garrison populations. While population growth disproportionate to the available banner appointments, the loss of banner lands, and inflation of commodity prices in the nineteenth century had bankrupted the family economies of the bannermen, the imperial treasury had been dissipated by Heshen and his vast network of bureaucratic plunderers. The Jiaqing emperor had rid himself of Heshen, but had not made the absent silver reappear in his treasury storehouses; the 70 million taels reported for the treasury in 1781 had declined to 12.4 million in 1814, and by the end of the Daoguang period in 1850 would be all but gone, while the state collected about a tenth of what it was spending.[23] In Zhejiang and other parts of mid-coastal China, even grain prices were beginning to outstrip the spending margins allowed bannermen by the inflation of silver's value caused by the opium trade. Rice production in Zhejiang was continuing a long slide; in the 1820s the quota for Hangzhou's tribute circuit was partially remitted, and by mid-century the quotas would be lowered further while transport surcharges were reduced. Hangzhou and its neighboring regions were in no sense capable of supplying themselves with staple; grain was imported from Jiangxi and Hunan, and soon the residents of Hangzhou would seek their rice from as far away as Sichuan in central China.

By the beginning of the nineteenth century the court had begun a more serious approach to controlling garrison expenditures than had previously been in evidence. Growth in the cadet and auxiliary appointments that had been improvised by the eighteenth-century court to alleviate some of the garrison distress was allowed to continue; indeed between the Qianlong and Jiaqing reigns alone the numbers of cadets (*yangyu*) doubled. The ranks of garrison officers, however, where the bulk of remuneration had always been concentrated, were reduced rather drastically. Normal garrison officer ranks, whose numbers had peaked in the Qianlong reign, were slashed by 40 percent by the end of the Jiaqing period, compared to a rough 10-percent drop in non-commissioned active ranks among the land forces; the total number of banner companies, which in 1644 had numbered over 500, had declined during the turn from the eighteenth to the nineteenth century from 446 to 325.[24] As the discipline of many garrison communities disintegrated and the stipends from the court attenuated in direct proportion to the coming bankruptcy of the government, many bannermen took up the search for sustenance or, if possible, profit. Some operated tea or noodle carts, many dealt in drugs, those who could sold heirlooms from their own homes or stolen from the nobility. For certain of the bannermen at Zhejiang, opportunities for investment may have been very real; because the garrisons lacked endowments of agricultural lands, their supplementary compensation was higher than that received by the bannermen in other provinces. Some bannermen of the early nineteenth century were clearly landholders and landlords. The favorable economic circumstances for this group translated into favorable cultural circumstances, a factor markedly affecting the fate of Guancheng.

Thanks to the efforts of Wanggi-shi and Shao-shi, the child Guancheng was provided an education. He attended the banner schools, where he was educated in both Manchu and Chinese, though there is no indication that he excelled at the former. Elementary education within the garrisons dated from the conquest and was generally financed and administered by boards representing clan or banner organizations. The curriculum after the Qianlong period seems to have been influenced by study fields established within the banner officers' schools: Manchu, classical Chinese, mathematics and astronomy (*tianwen*). The higher schools had themselves been chartered in 1791, on the basis of an edict reiterating Hongli's demands that written Manchu be revived among the bannermen. "Every single man has a responsibility to study written Manchu," the emperor had continued his endless and largely unheeded sermon. "This is the root of his mission!" By 1796 officers' schools had been chartered in all garrisons. Instructors' salaries as well as student expenses were covered partly by government grants, partly by the banner and clan charities, and when possible from personal expenditures.[25] At Hangzhou, the banner officers' school occupied grounds of the Meiqing Academy, where the twenty-two old "arrow halls" had been razed and eight new ones built, one for each banner, while some of the old buildings were consolidated as a department of Manchu language study. There is no evidence that students were graduated from the academy before 1800, the year that the general-in-chief, the Chinese-martial bannerman Fan Jianzhong, reported selecting new officers from among the candidates of the Hangzhou garrison officers' school.[26]

By the age of twenty, Guancheng was serving as a tutor within the garrison, and in 1818, at the age of twenty-seven, he qualified for the provincial (*juren*) degree; he thereby entered into the patronage relationships that brought him into close contact with the West Lake literary community and stimulated his interest in printing and publishing. As a provincial degree recipient and aspirant to the national degree, it was necessary that Guancheng should have at least one style name (*zi*). His given name, Guancheng, was typical for a garrison Manchu—the Guan element, which was homonymous with the character already established as the family name used by many Gūwalgiya, played the same part in his personal name that Guala, also a diminutive of the clan name, had played in the personal names of seventeenth- and early eighteenth-century Gūwalgiya clansmen.[27] It was characteristically formulaic. As the Chinese transliterations of traditional Manchu personal names were dying out in the nineteenth century, a cascade of two-character names, large numbers of which relied upon the favored elements Wen, Kui, Bin, Cheng, Xi, Lin, and Rui, began to appear. While Chinese names are often described as having a small selection of surnames and an unlimited range of personal names, the opposite was true for Manchus, who because of the large number of clan names, patronymics, and their permutations tended to produce nearly unlimited surnames, while the choices for personal names were less varied, clearly guided by sound rather than meaning. For a Manchu who no longer used a traditional Manchu name, being mistaken for a Chinese on the basis of name alone would have taken an effort. There is no evidence that Guancheng made such an effort. His adult name (*hao*) was Weitong, and it is clear from the garrison records that he often—perhaps normally, at least in his youth—referred to himself as Guan Weitong, using the surname so despised by the emperors and avoided by the nobility. His first chosen literary name was Guating, "melon pavilion." Later his son Fengrui occasionally used the name Guashan, "melon mountain," and his grandson Jinliang's most famous literary name was "old man of the melon patch" (*Guapu laoren*). In 1933 Jinliang's son Guandong commented that these epithets were all part of a family joke, for although Jinliang did indeed raise melons in Hangzhou and later in Shenyang, the practice of using melons in their literary names was "solely on account of our Gūwalgiya clan name."[28]

Not much of Guancheng's writing survived. One poetry collection was still extant at Hangzhou in the late nineteenth century, and a selection of works was later reprinted by Jinliang as "Miscellaneous Writings from the Melon Pavilion" (*Guating zalu*).[29] The dates for most of Guancheng's compositions are unknown, but from the beginning his literary work seems to have been connected to his printing. One of his earliest efforts, for instance, was an introduction to a collection of memorial essays to Shao-shi and Wanggi-shi, which he gathered from Wang Yinzhi and others of his acquaintances among the local literati;[30] he also contributed an introduction to his own edition of an imperial prince's commentaries on the "East Gate Chronicles" (*Donghua lu*). The blocks for this original collection were later burned when the family property was sacked during the Taiping invasion of the Hangzhou and Zhapu garrisons in 1861. Jinliang found some of the original essays reprinted in "History of Pinghu County" (*Pinghuxian zhi*), "History of Hangzhou Prefecture" (*Hangzhoufu zhi*), and "Annotated History of Zhapu" (*Zhapu beizhi*), and combined them together with some essays solicited in Shao-shi's and Wanggi-shi's honor by Fengrui into a volume called "Topical Offerings on Biographies of the Chaste and Filial" (*Jiexiao zhuan tici shu*).

How Guancheng learned his printing skill—which if he wrought by his own hands would have involved some expertise in calligraphy, wood carving and possibly paper-making—is not clear.[31] There is no evidence that either his father or his deceased brother knew printing. It was, however, a wisely chosen occupation. Hangzhou was not only an ancient habitat of China's poets and painters, but in the century of their occupation of the city the bannermen, too, had developed their avid literary interests. "Sketch History of the Hangzhou Eight-Banner Garrison" gives titles and synopses of fifty-five extant (in 1893) works by the Hangzhou bannermen, and this is clearly only a fraction of their output.[32] By 1830 Guancheng had attracted the business of many of the literati of eastern Zhejiang, and after the death of Wang Yinzhi in 1834, he was selected to print the eulogies for Wang written by Tao Zhu (1779–1839), then governor-general of Jiangsu, Jiangxi and Anhui; Dai Xi (1801–1860), a Zhejiang provincial degree holder of 1819 and national degree holder of 1832; Tang Yifen (1787–1860), a painter and poet disciple of Dai Xi; Zhang Tingji (1768–1848), who had considerable local fame as a graduate of Ruan Yuan's Gujing Academy on West Lake; and the legendary Lin Zixu (1785–1850).[33] His business depended upon exploitation of academic contacts, and Guancheng had made it his first ambition to participate in the higher literary examinations, for which he seems to have had little aptitude.

Manchu and Mongol bannermen participated in the regular examination system on the Manchu quota, or *manzi hao*; the Chinese-martial also had their own quota, the "allied category" (*hezi hao*). Prior to 1816, bannermen were required to take the provincial examination in Peking, their legal home; after 1816 they were permitted to participate in the examinations of the provinces in which they were garrisoned, though the quota still pertained.[34] Guancheng had probably begun his formal preparation in expectation of taking the provincial examination during the 1816 administration, the first he would have been eligible to take in his "home" province. Gong Zizhen (1792–1841) and Yu Hongjian (1781–1846), both acquaintances of Guancheng's, were among the successful Zhejiang candidates of that year.[35] As it happened, Guancheng sat for the special "grace examination" (*enke*) of 1818 (for which all quotas were doubled), and won his provincial degree (*juren*). Of the three Hangzhou bannermen who passed the examination, Guancheng ranked the lowest, being eighty-second on the list of successful candidates.[36] Wang Yinzhi (1766–1834), a dominant figure in the Jiangnan intellectual world,[37] was the provincial examiner in both the 1816 and 1818 administrations, and success in getting the provincial degree was more than a matter of prestige for Guancheng. It gave him a formal connection that he manipulated to the benefit of both his publishing and his bureaucratic careers.

In the later 1820s, Guancheng decided to take up the challenge of the preliminary examination in Peking leading to the national degree (*jinshi*), an undertaking possibly directly encouraged by the establishment in 1820 of a fund to support Hangzhou garrison candidates travelling to Peking.[38] For all bannermen Peking, where the emperors dwelt in their Forbidden City (*zijincheng*) within the Imperial City (*gugong*) within the great walled capital first laid out by Khubilai Khan, was literally at the heart of the Qing cultural map. Barely more than the Great Wall separated it from the ancestral homelands of the Northeast; the Mongolian khans, to whom the Qing emperors indirectly traced their mandate to rule and much of their methods too, had made the city the enduring capital of the Chinese empire. Since the summer of 1644, when the invaders had cleared the Chinese inhabitants from the central city because of a fear that contact with them would result in contamination with smallpox, the capital had belonged to the Manchus.[39] It was endowed with its own garrisons, the Capital System (*jifu*), which were administered separately from the network of provincial garrisons (*zhufang*) that serviced the rest of the empire. Peking's Manchu City was by far the single largest urban preserve of the Manchus, sheltering as many as 150,000 individuals. It was only the heart of the Capital Garrisons, and communicated with a series of eighteen smaller garrisons, located in a roughly circular pattern around Peking.[40] In all, the Capital Garrisons incorporated, by the middle nineteenth century, something much more than 200,000 souls;[41] the imperial clan itself, or at least those branches that the court elected to support with its imperial plantations (*huangzhuang*) in the Northeast and elsewhere, had grown from 2,000 at the time of the conquest of Peking to more than 30,000 in Guancheng's time, and would increase to over 50,000 by the dynasty's end.[42]

Peking showed the marks of domination by the sizeable, powerful, and assertive Manchu minority. The local Chinese dialect, the theater and drum songs that were the centerpieces of tea house entertainments, the children's pastimes, all gave clear evidence of the profound influence upon Peking culture of its occupation by the Manchus, even as its architectural landmarks were founded upon the mansions and gardens of the Manchu nobility. Through the entry ways into many private compounds in the capital, one could glimpse the temporary sheds built for the shamanist rites that accompanied weddings, funerals, or seasonal sacrifices; in the Inner City crowds of young men milled around in the customary *san shuang*, pushing invitation cards into their friends' sleeves with mock surreption to hide their "embarrassment" (perhaps only symbolic) at the solicitation of gifts on the occasion of a wedding or birthday.[43] Pastry shops catered to the Manchu taste for *shaqima* cakes and *guandong* and *shuiwuta* candies; furriers stood ready to provide sable jackets to those licensed to wear them. Horse racing had become the show sport of the city's wealthier young men on horseback and Manchu women driving carts, who flocked at the appropriate times to the Great Bell Temple (*Dazhong si*) north of the city, the Fishing Terrace (*Diaoyu tai*) to the west, or Sandy Mouth (*Shazikou*) in the Outer City to try their skill.[44] Manchu speech survived not only in the street language of the banner quarter but also in the *zidi* tales of Peking, which had developed at least two distinctive styles in the drawling, artificial tones of the "west side" (*xicheng*) school and the livelier pace of the "east side" (*dongcheng*). Bannermen entertainers in the street, beating the Manchu eight-cornered drum, were also ready with "victory songs" (*desheng ge*), supposedly folk renditions of the exploits of the bannermen who conquered the country in the seventeenth century.[45] Such performances were often featured in the dark, steamy, smoke-filled tea houses of the southern and eastern quarters of the city, where nineteenth-century observers estimated that half of all customers were bannermen—all out of uniform, of course. They were also a major part of the clientele of the legitimate theaters concentrated in the district south of Zhengyang Gate, in the Outer City, which verged on the "dancing and prostitution" quarter outside Qianmen. Private dinner theaters—the alternative of choice for Qing officials forbidden to frequent the public theaters—were dominated by well-off Manchus and their wives, the only women in the capital permitted formal public socializing.[46]

For Guancheng, as for many bannermen never lucky enough to see the capital in their lifetime, Peking was the center that integrated the political, cultural and spiritual elements that were the Qing empire. It was, perhaps, the only universally recognized central point in a Manchu world that by the beginning of the Daoguang period was profoundly diverse. At the same time, signs of decline were present for Guancheng to see. The Inner City, where the Peking bannermen were concentrated, was shabby, its narrow streets crowded all day by unemployed, poorly clothed and sometimes visibly decrepit men. The effects of opium addiction were detectable, to those willing to see, among the literati and the nobility. Horse racing, which in both equipage and wagering demanded a high price from participants, was not what it had been twenty years before. And the gossip of the days of Guancheng's arrival was the disgraceful ruin of the elephant grounds inside the Xuanwu Gate of the southwest Inner City. The animals had been a feature of Peking life since the Ming dynasty, always present in imperial pageants, their grounds sometimes accessible in between times to the public at large. Quite beyond the traditional mystique of the elephant because of its association with Chinese pharmacological practices, the Manchus had a special interest. The high, rigid hairstyles of Manchu women required an effective lacquering agent, and the premium source among the Peking elite was the dung from the elephant grounds inside the Xuanwu Gate. More the grief, then, when it was learned that the elephants, including a bronze-tusked denizen that was believed to have arrived during the Tang dynasty, were dying of neglect and starvation because their keepers were diverting the elephant funds to themselves.[47]

Guancheng supported himself by working as a private tutor, in a cooperative effort with his fellow Zhejiang provincial graduates Gong Zizhen and Dai Xi (1800–1860), the latter a Hangzhou native and Zhejiang provincial degree holder of 1819. In these early Daoguang years, Peking was the center of serious discussion of the problems—real and foreseen—of the empire. The White Lotus Rebellion and the corrupt outrages of Heshen were more than twenty years in the past; the political confrontations leading to China's disastrous defeat in the Opium War were less than fifteen years in the future. The treasury was bankrupt, public works were in disarray all over the country, and the hints of widespread opium use suggested ominous consequences to those who thought seriously of state strengthening and reform. At the same time, [Guogiya] Mujangga (1782–1856) seemed to be gaining a dominance at the court that was too reminiscent of Heshen before him. Yet intellectuals remained generally hopeful that Minning, the Daoguang emperor, would prove a strong and wise leader. Rightly or wrongly, he was credited as a prince with having rushed from his classroom and driven the Eight Trigrams rebels from the Forbidden City during their incursion of 1813.

Certainly, he had shown himself willing to experiment in his efforts to deal with the country's increasingly evident financial crisis, certainly perceived by serious thinkers as the most frightening public issue of the day. Minning was tireless in exhorting capital and provincial bureaucrats to curtail expenditures, and he did not demur to set a good example: the imperial robes were retained to be worn another day, and it was rumored that they were even mended on occasion. In 1831, when spectacular revelations concerning the degree of opium addiction among the nobility and the Eight Banners were revealed, Minning was able to stem dismay by seeming to take swift and effective action. For their part Gong Zizhen and Dai Xi, Guancheng's fellow tutors, were outspoken critics of the spreading use of opium among both the privileged and the common classes; Gong in particular abjured the latitude given to the foreign importers of the drug in Canton and opposed the advocates of partial legalization who were gaining ground in the capital.

Like his colleagues, Guancheng was invigorated by his proximity to great affairs, and superficially his life resembled theirs. He supported himself as they supported themselves, and shared their concerns over the widespread use of opium, though there is no evidence that he exerted himself to speak out as they did. He may have often socialized with them and their circle, too, but there was a dimension to his life that they could not share. In fundamental contrast to Hangzhou, Peking was a Manchu world, from the glamor of the court to the pastimes of the street. For Guancheng, the local terminology of "Inner City" (*neicheng*) for the Manchu quarter and imperial compounds and "Outer City" (*waicheng*) for the Chinese precincts had a precision that his colleagues Gong and Dai could hardly (and might not have cared to) appreciate.

Guancheng had not been in Peking very long before he found the mansion, in East Sipailou Road in the northeast section of the city, built for the descendants of Fiongdon. The four *pailou*, or wooden memorial arches, for which the district was named, framed the busy intersection of Chaoyang Gate Street and East Market (*dashi*) Street (the northern extension of Hatamen Street) east of the enormous Longfu Temple, then one of the busiest and best known intersections of the city.[48] The gates of the Fiongdon compound opened onto the major thoroughfare of the eastern quarter of the Inner City, leading to the Chaoyang Gate in the eastern Peking walls. Not far away were the residences of the imperial princes Heng and Yi. The mansion was then inhabited by the family of [Suwan Gūwalgiya] Shenggui, who had also inherited Fiongdon's honorary rank of "Duke of Trustworthy Valor." At the time of the rank's creation in 1731, it had gone to Shenggui's great-grandfather, the hapless Furdan (1683–1753), a great-grandson of Fiongdon. Manchus were in the habit of introducing themselves to strangers whom they learned shared their clan name (*hala*), particularly, one suspects, if that stranger was of higher rank. Shenggui—whose great-great-grandfather Wage had helped conquer Hangzhou—seems to have welcomed Guancheng into his social circle, and the provincial visitor soon found himself sharing the same table with other descendants of the great legendary figures of the early dynastic period. Imperial princes and near-princes were numerous in Peking, and Guancheng met many of them. He shared their fondness for imperial lore, spending many evenings among them mulling over the origins of this tradition or that, the reason for such-and-such a phrase, and gossip. It was at Shenggui's that he met Yigeng, a descendant of the Kangxi emperor's sixteenth son, Yinlu (1675–1767), and younger brother of the current Prince Zhuang, Yimai. Guancheng later received an invitation to attend a gathering at Yigeng's house. Like Guancheng, Yigeng was a *zidi* tale enthusiast, and had composed a number of ditties, albeit on rather erudite themes; like several members of the nobility Yigeng was also an accomplished historian.[49] Guancheng waxed enthusiastic on the knowledge and skills of both the imperial prince and the Suwan Gūwalgiya kinsman: "Every question that Yigeng was asked, he answered, and every answer was complete, inspiring and elegant; everybody there was filled with admiration for him. . . . It was an extremely congenial gathering, and I made a point of praising both the erudition of Shenggui's remarks and the fact that he had brought up so many subjects touching on our dynastic history. When I got home I wrote down all that he had said."

For Guancheng's new friends, "dynastic history" was literally that—not an account of the Qing regime, but an exploration of the lore of the court and the imperial clan. What had caught Guancheng's fancy was the fact that the entire circle gathered at Yigeng's shared his passion for the minutiae of Qing court culture. The group was riveted by Yigeng's recitation of imperial symbolism, which Guancheng knew was often a source of debate among the uncertain populations of the provincial garrisons. Now such questions would be resolved by an authority from the imperial line. Someone asked Yigeng the meaning of being admitted or not being admitted into the "Eight Notables" (*ba fen gong*)—who were themselves the subject of an entire cycle of drum songs.[50] Yigeng answered by saying, "In the beginning of the dynastic period there was established a Council of Princes (*yizheng chu*), consisting of eight men, and the princes and dukes were eligible to join. Those who participated in this Council were called the Eight Notables, and those who were outside it were called 'those who were not among the Eight Notables' (*bu ru ba fen gong*)." Having satisfied the group's curiosity on this matter, he was asked to proceed to the differences between the yellow belts, red belts and purple belts worn among the various degrees of Aisin Gioro and Gioro

bannermen. He said, "Yuan, Xing, Jing and Xian were the Four Ancestors.[51] Only the direct descendants of Xian are called the Inner Clan
(*zongshi*), and all wear yellow belts. Descendants of the other three are
called the Gioro, and they all wear red belts. Now, if members of the
Inner Clan commit some offense, they are demoted to wearing red belts,
and, like all those who wear red belts, would be called by the simple
name of Gioro. If those Gioro of the red belts commit some offense, they
they are demoted to wearing purple belts." The questions continued in a
sartorial vein, as someone asked about the significance of having buttons
on top of officials' caps. "In the early dynastic period," Yigeng explained,
"it was only the hats that were worn at court which had a sort of jewel
embedded in them; there was no decoration on the top of the hat. Then,
in the fourth year of the Yongzheng reign [1726], it was stipulated that
there should be six brands of feather decorations and hat buttons, with
the princes and dukes using a ruby, and the first through ninth grades
(*pin*) being marked, for those both within the court and without it, according to color. This was how the whole sumptuary system was refined."[52]

Yigeng at one point interrupted his dissertation to turn and address his
visitor from the provinces. He said to Guancheng, "The noble Gūwalgiya
clan has served our dynasty for many generations. In the early period,
people had a saying, '*Guan man chao*,' which they used together with
'*Tong ban chao*.' Now [the Gūwalgiya] glory is even greater." Yigeng was
referring to a doubleness of the Tong (the maternal lineage of the Kangxi
emperor) and Gūwalgiya lineages that was often celebrated by Suwan
Gūwalgiya clansmen.[53] *Tong ban chao guan man chao* was a well-known
pun of uncertain origin. *Tong ban chao* meant both "the Tong who fill up
half the court," referring to the ubiquity of the Tong surname in the
Kangxi years, and also "the Tong who are half the court," an allusion to
the fact that the mother of the Kangxi emperor was of the Tong lineage.
Guan man chao, on the other hand, meant both "those who are connected to the Manchu court," a clear enough reference to the early association between Nurgaci and Fiongdon, and also "the Guan [Gūwal-
giya] who fill the court," a reference to the many women of the Suwan
Gūwalgiya line imported to the palace, and probably a pun for punning's
sake. The fates of the Gūwalgiya and Tong lineages were linked in 1688
when [Shi] Huwašan, claiming Suwan Gūwalgiya descent, joined the
brothers Tong Guogang and Tong Guowei in petitioning the Kangxi emperor to alter their registration from the Chinese-martial to the Manchu
banners.[54] Also, the Tong lineage mansion was located in Lantern Market
Street (*Dengshi kou*), a short walk from the Suwan Gūwalgiya mansion
on Chaoyang Gate Street. Guancheng was undoubtedly gratified to hear

that imperial clansmen had not lost interest in the lore connecting the Suwan Gūwalgiya and Tong lineages.

Neither his general delight at being included in the company of nobles and near-nobles nor his enjoyment of their salons overrode Guancheng's natural inclination to look after his business interests. Yigeng, he knew, had written a commentary to Jiang Liangqi's "East Gate Chronicles" (*Donghua lu*). Jiang's work had been banned by the Qianlong emperor's Four Treasuries (*siku quanshu*) censors soon after its composition in the later eighteenth century, but was now enjoying a vogue among the Peking elite.[55] Guancheng later proposed to the nobleman that they publish the work together with a biography of Jiang. Yigeng agreed, and in 1838—the year that his (Yigeng's) elder brother Yimai was banished from the capital for opium smoking—the completed work, *Donghua lu zhui-yan*, was distributed with introductions by Yigeng and Guancheng.

The connections Guancheng forged in Peking became useful to him in another way. Unlike his fellow tutor Gong Zizhen, who received the national degree in 1829, Guancheng was unsuccessful in his academic quest. Eventually he was granted honorary national degree status "by selection" (*datiao*), which made him eligible for a magistracy "on probation."[56] In 1833 he set out for Sichuan province with at least part of his family, including his sons Xirui, aged about eleven, and Fengrui, aged nine. His wife and two youngest sons he sent to the home he had purchased in the Zhapu suburb of Longchuo. In Sichuan, Guancheng served briefly as magistrate (*zhixian*) of Bishan, Changle, Longhua and Dayou counties (*xian*) successively, and then in 1834 settled in for a seven-year tenure as the magistrate of Nanchuan. Now forty-five years old, Guancheng may have expected that Nanchuan would be a pleasant place to pass a year or two—the normal length of tenure in the county, which was an agricultural and tea-producing region about thirty miles southwest of Wulong. The countryside, only about thirty miles south of the Yangzi but elevated enough to be cooler in summer than humid Zhejiang, was green and dramatic, with rushing streams, sharply rising mountainsides, and an architecture showing the distinctive local style. Chongqing (Chunking), fifty miles away, was close enough for the book-collecting expeditions that Guancheng seems to have indulged himself in when opportunity permitted. He had never before travelled to central China, nor south of Hangzhou. Sichuan he would have known by reputation as one of the fertile places supplying rice to his home and a number of localities that were no longer capable of supplying themselves.[57] Guancheng may even have heard particulars of Nanchuan before arriving, since he was preceded in the post by many other men of Zhejiang, like him all provincial licentiates or lower in academic rank; there were no regular national degrees (*jinshi*) among them, and a minority of them seem never to have achieved the provincial degree (*juren*) either.[58] It must have been the case that the magistrates at Nanchuan were often chosen in the "great selection." Guancheng was the second bannerman to serve as magistrate in Nanchuan, but he would be followed, before the end of the dynasty, by four more, a rate slightly less than the national average of bannermen serving as county magistrates.[59]

The magistracy of Nanchuan was a moderately ancient one, having been established at the end of the fourteenth century, and it was not particularly important. In fact, prior to the late eighteenth century there was no independent annual record-keeping in the county, since such duties were normally subsumed by the prefectural office in Chongqing.[60] Moreover, the tax system at this time was still the simple "single-whip" method.[61] The Qing government had fixed the magistracy of Nanchuan at its normal seventh grade (out of nine grades), with an annual salary of forty-five taels (the lowest possible), supplemented by an "honesty incentive" (*yanglian*) of six hundred taels, a considerable addition but a comparatively low incentive rate allowed for a county magistrate—in fact, the lowest allowed in Sichuan province. His yamen staff, too, was relatively small, at thirty-one regular members.[62] For all that, Guancheng had reason to be pleased with his setting; the remuneration he was receiving (before augmenting it in the various ways magistrates were wont to do) was small by bureaucratic standards but big by the measure of the garrison, where he would have had to enter the ranks of the garrison lieutenancy, *fangyu* (of which the number available nationwide was 335 and falling), before being able to make a similar monthly salary.

The press of Guancheng's responsibilities may well have outstripped the resources at his disposal on many an occasion. Figures from a census completed less than ten years after Guancheng's departure record a population of slightly less than 150,000, composed of 33,538 households (*hu*), or 149,562 individuals.[63] He was charged with the governance of one of the more densely populated regions of the province—more than twice as dense, in fact, as those nearer to the provincial capital of Chengdu.[64] Southern Sichuan was in the early stage of the rapid developments in settlement and resource exploitation that characterized it in the later nineteenth century. Such factors worked to make Guancheng's stay in Nanchuan eventful. It was auspiciously inaugurated in late autumn of 1834 with the sighting of "a comet visible in the night sky for more than thirty days," which we now call "Halley's."[65] In 1837 the peace was interrupted by the incursion of two rebel bands from western Sichuan, the first led by Mu Yuhong, and the second by his kinsman Mu Duanxin. In the latter invasion a portion of the Nanchuan town walls was knocked down, and peace was restored only after the arrival of a contingent of the provincial army dispatched by the Manchu governor-general of Sichuan

and general-in-chief of the Chengdu garrison, Oushan. These were abo-
riginal rebellions of the sort Yang Fang was attempting to suppress in
southwest Sichuan in 1834 and 1835;[66] but no child of the Jiaqing era
could have failed to note that the violence was a bequest of Heshen and
his network, who had prolonged the late eighteenth-century Miao rebellions of the region (while claiming to suppress them) for the purpose of
draining the last bit of military appropriations out of the treasury. Guancheng repaired the town walls and survived the embarrassment of the
attack; but when he left Nanchuan to return to Zhejiang in 1842, the
crops had been devastated by locusts and the taxes for the county were
forgiven, a measure that did not prevent famine conditions during the
next two years.[67]

From the perspective of himself and his sons, Guancheng's years in
Sichuan seem to have been happy ones, on balance. As local life went,
the rebellions and famines of his tenure in Nanchuan may not have been
particularly grave affairs, and he did manage to have the taxes reduced at
the critical time. The local history of Nanchuan county praises him for
"being reluctant to prosecute casually," and the residents of Longhua
county evidently erected a memorial to him while he was still alive,
called "Little Guan Temple (xiao guan miao)" in honor of his informal surname.[68] Certainly, his son Fengrui had pleasant memories of his father's
interaction with the local people at various localities in Sichuan, likening
him to "a white bamboo phoenix around which the other birds love to
flock and chatter."[69] For the friends and relatives to whom Guancheng
and his sons returned in 1842, his exotic sojourn in Sichuan—and the
comparative wealth and prestige it represented—was the definitive element in his adult reputation. He was called "Sir Nanchuan" (Nanchuan
gong) in honor of his great standing in the outside world. Any reference
to the Suwan Gūwalgiya within the Hangzhou-Zhapu garrison was likely
to be prefaced with a reference to Sir Nanchuan, son of Sir Chaste Abode
(Jiezhai gong) Jalangga, and son-in-law of the Chaste and Filial Lady
(Jiexiao nu) Wanggi-shi.

These titles, which had no official standing but were supported purely
by local custom, suggest that Guancheng was held in genuine respect and
affection by his home garrison community. His experiences with the nobles of Peking and his ability to set himself up as Yigeng's publisher appear to characterize a man to whom social betters had a positive response. He seems, too, to have made himself a popular magistrate in
what to him was the almost foreign country of Sichuan—the suggestion
in the records, of course, is that he did so by a certain benevolent neglect
of his prosecutorial duties and evident unwillingness to collect taxes
when times were bad. Overall Guancheng's profile seems that of a genial,
energetic, even public-spirited fellow with few overt pretensions. But

there is another side to Guancheng that highlights him against the Jia-qing-Daoguang world in which he lived. He was, first of all, the nearest an early nineteenth-century Manchu could come to being a self-made man. Though it is unlikely that the home kept by Wanggi-shi and Shao-shi after Jalangga's death was truly desperately poor, it is clear that Guan-cheng—very possibly as a result of the extraordinary qualities of Wanggi-shi herself—made the most of such talents as he possessed and of his opportunities for study. It should be noted that such opportunities would not have been available to a civilian youth of Guancheng's economic class; unlike Chinese, Manchus of the late eighteenth century did not generally feel that studying would deprive them of the chance to earn a living. It was moreover possible to be paid for attending school under the government's incentive programs for bannermen; indeed, the less quali-fied the student, the greater the blandishments.

Guancheng's success in the provincial examinations was not stunning, but it was sufficient to allow him to introduce himself to the Hangzhou literati community and to inspire him to seek greater academic and bu-reaucratic heights in Peking. He showed a very striking ability to com-bine what may have been his true filial inclinations with acumen in ex-ploiting new opportunities for self-advertisement and advancement. Certainly, his arrangements to publish essays by Wang Yinzhi and others extolling the virtues of Wanggi-shi and Shao-shi was a milestone in his career. Similarly, the intensity of his interest in imperial lore must have been in some part nurtured by his sense that Yigeng may have been look-ing for a competent and sympathetic printer for both his historical essays and his *zidi* tales. Guancheng's keen sense of self-interest may also have been connected to the apparent thinness of his social relationships; unlike his son and grandson, there is little hint of who his intimate friends might have been, on which side of the garrison wall they resided, or what they may have thought of him. His education and tastes clearly made him comfortable with Gong Zizhen and Dai Xi; but as the son of a very tra-ditional bannerman and a member of a proud clan, he was impressed by and understood the terms of the Manchu circles as easily in Peking as in Hangzhou. Either the Chinese or the Manchu world would do, and in their turn both allowed Guancheng to advance his status and create fi-nancial security for his family. There is, in fact, very little evidence of a conscious choice made by Guancheng regarding his social or cultural af-filiations before his return to Zhapu in 1842. In that year Guancheng was fifty-three years old, regarded by the Hangzhou-Zhapu bannermen as rich and famous. He learned that disaster had visited his home commu-nity at Zhapu, and the fate suffered by childhood friends and family as-sociates could not have failed to impress upon him the good fortune of the path he had chosen out of the garrisons. At no conceivable profit to himself he expended his money and reputation in an attempt to preserve the honor of the Zhapu bannermen, and signed himself, "Guancheng, a Manchu."

THE HONOR OF ZHAPU

While Guancheng pursued his self-advancement in Peking and worked his magisterial stints in Sichuan, the country moved unwittingly toward its disastrous confrontation with foreign opium traders and, ultimately, the British Navy. During 1831, the year in which the Daoguang emperor was shocked into taking a more positive stance against the drug, Guancheng had been in Peking and had been acquainted with many of the Manchu nobility implicated in the scandals. The movement toward confrontation quickened very steeply in the 1830s, and it is fair to say that the Chinese government roused itself in an unprecedented way against opium use. For centuries the court had tried through various sorts of legislation to discourage the use and distribution first of tobacco, then of *madak* (a tobacco and opium mix), and finally of unadulterated opium itself after its introduction in the eighteenth century.[70] Such campaigns had not been effective, and the court evidently declined to pursue strictly prohibitive policies. Nor did it attempt to grapple with the more fundamental problem of opium importation, which was accomplished by a complex network of foreign coastal smugglers and Chinese underground distribution gangs; although the drug and its effects were considered undesirable, it was not clear that there was no medicinal benefit in occasional use of opium, and the crime of dealing in the drug was not considered felonious.[71] The Jiaqing emperor Yongyan, who was in the unhappy position of confronting much that was rotten in the Qing state after his succession, suspected that addiction had permeated the court, the armies, and even his own band of bodyguards. But it was his son Minning who as the Daoguang emperor conducted a relatively systematic investigation of the problem. The year of his accession, 1821, brought mass arrests by Ruan Yuan of dealers in Canton; during the 1820s the court added to existing prohibitive legislation, but the efficacy of the program was in question.

Finally in 1831 officials from all over the country were instructed to write informing the court of the methods of distribution and sale in their localities, and most had something of which to unburden themselves. From Guangdong, Fujian, Sichuan, Zhejiang, Hubei, Hunan, Yunnan, Guizhou and other provinces came convincing reports of vigorous underground traffic and huge fortunes amassed by vendors. Local magistrates were reported to be blackmailing known users within their jurisdictions, and padding their tax collections with payments from sellers and growers hoping to avoid exposure to higher authorities; the wealthy were spending their silver fortunes (most of which found their way outside the country) on the drug; soldiers were found to be unfit for duty because of the debilities caused by their addiction; Manchu noblemen and court eunuchs bought, sold and used the drug together; and perhaps most frightening, the highest levels of the bureaucracy were clearly penetrated by the silver-eating weevil. The numbers of users and addicts were unknown, but an estimate by Lin Zixu later in the decade put the number at one percent of the population; considering that at this time opium use was not common among the peasants the indication was that the official population was very heavily involved; a foreign estimate of 1836 put the number at 12.5 million. "At the present time there are opium smokers in all the provinces," Lu Yinpu advised the emperor in his report of 1831, "with special concentration in the various yamens; we estimate that among governors-general and their subordinates, and at every level of both civil and military officialdom, those who do *not* smoke opium are few indeed."[72]

Laws were elaborated against users, those who provided space for opium dens and those who manufactured pipes and other paraphernalia; officials were instructed to make greater effort to see that existing laws were enforced. A debate at the capital ensued over the possible suspension of prosecution against smokers or purchasers in order to concentrate effort upon the seizure of primary distributors and their suppliers; in addition, it was suggested, the government could assuage some of its own troubles by taxing opium. The statecraft circle including Gong Zizhen, Wei Yuan and Lin Zixu advocated very strict prosecution of importers and growers, but greater leniency toward users; Lin Zixu even went so far, in 1838, as to propose a detailed plan for rehabilitation of addicts, complete with a graduated timetable of punishments in the event that rehabilitation should be resisted or recidivism evident. The Manchu elite at court, it should be noted, was—in contrast to their later outspokenness on the conduct of the war against Britain—quiet on the problem of opium and opium addiction. It was clear that Minning was unlikely to brook opposition on the issue of opium's eradication. Quite aside from the moral issue, on which the emperor had pronounced himself unswervable, was opium's relationship to the economic crisis. Silver flowed out of the country in exchange for opium, and copper was minted to attempt to keep up the flow of specie.[73]

The emperor resolved to "radically sever the trunk from the roots"[74] of the opium weed. He commissioned Lin Zixu to go to Canton and dissuade the foreign importers and their compradors from pursuing the trade. Lin was energetic, incorruptible and ruthless in his duty. In March of 1839 he demanded the surrender of all foreign opium supplies in port, and had the foreign "factories" (the residences, offices and warehouses) blockaded. Captain Charles Elliot, charged with protection of the British traders at Canton, persuaded the merchants to give up their opium; the local market had temporarily dried up, the commodity was rotting in the warehouses. Elliot assured the merchants that the British government would recompense them for the value of their losses, a measure which made the contraband surrendered to Lin property of the British government and its destruction possible grounds for war. The impasse was not, however, resolved, for having destroyed the opium delivered to him Lin demanded written guarantees from the British that they would import no more opium in the future. As a body the merchants refused, though some remitted the bonds in order to continue trading. Before the question of guarantees could be addressed after consultation with their respective governments, Lin and Elliot had a new problem. Drunken British sailors mortally wounded a Chinese resident on the mainland facing Hong Kong island. Lin demanded surrender of the responsible party for punishment under Chinese law; Elliot, acting in accord with his government's horror at its previous experiences with Chinese justice, refused. In September, when Guan Tianpei (d. 1841)[75] approached Elliot's fleet to attempt to seize hostages in order to secure the surrender of the guilty man, a chance encounter with a bonded British vessel headed for Canton provoked the British ships to fire warning shots, to which Guan responded with cannon fire and was quickly routed by the British. The Opium War had begun, and the Qing had lost their first engagement.

For the British, the war in its early stage consisted largely of roaming northward along the coast, firing at will upon the impotent Qing batteries and fortifications, then passing on with little care for the Chinese response. Elliot's rather logical idea was to shortcut the geographical distance and layers of bureaucracy separating him from the court by travelling directly to Tianjin, the port of Peking, to make the emperor see the light of reason. "With our feet upon the threshold of the Inner Chamber, they will be ready to compound with us," he advised Prime Minister Palmerston.[76] Even better, his northward voyage would bring him closer to what he considered a worthy trophy of conquest: the Zhoushan Islands off the coast of Zhejiang, which the Qing had fought six years in the seventeenth century to secure for themselves. The islands would be a valuable acquisition, but at present they had a strategic appeal, too, for British strategists had contemplated an invasion of the Chinese mainland in the area of Hangzhou ever since the outbreak of the hostilities.[77] As early as April 3 of that year Elliot, had urged Prime Minister Palmerston to order the occupation of the Zhoushan Islands; ultimately, Elliot suggested, Britain could demand their permanent cession. For more than a year, the Zhoushan Islands became the center of a debate at the British

Foreign Office. Palmerston resisted the idea of occupying any Chinese territory, whether the Zhoushan Islands, as Elliot suggested, or elsewhere. Such a move, he felt, would destroy any possibility of developing a commercial treaty with the Chinese. But Elliot and George Eden advocated a permanent territorial acquisition, and they specifically desired the Zhoushan chain, whose principal island was the site of the walled city of Dinghai.[78] According to Elliot, it was beautiful, habitable, was strategically located to control the estuaries of both the Qiantang and the Yangzi, and was close enough to the heart of the Chinese empire to make the court tractable.

In the late spring of 1840 Elliot got his way, and on July 3 a British fleet reached Dinghai harbor. In their first attempt at landing, they were chased off by militiamen with arrows and firearms. On the morning of July 4, they found that a barrier of fishing nets had been strung around the island. When the smaller of the British craft, the *Atalanta* and the *Wellesley*, attempted to negotiate their way through the nets, they found a flotilla of Chinese war junks from Zhapu in the harbor; the ships exchanged cannon fire, and the British temporarily withdrew. In the evening the invading fleet was visited by a group of Chinese officials, who boarded the *Wellesley* and stated, through the British interpreter Robert Thom, that they had no way to defend Dinghai against a full-scale attack. Commodore James Gordon Bremer, in charge of the British fleet, agreed to wait until 2 p.m. of the next day for a peaceful surrender. But when no more was heard from the Chinese, the British attacked. Slightly before 3 p.m. on July 5, Bremer's forces occupied a hill overlooking the city, and in the night the Chinese population—nearly a million people—began mass desertion of the island. Dinghai harbor had the distinction of being "the first Military Position in the Chinese Empire captured by Her Majesty's forces."[79] Elliot arrived on July 7, and immediately set about exploiting the new gain. At Zhenhai, on the mainland coast, he made an attempt to deliver a letter from Palmerston to the Chinese court, but was rebuffed. On the 15th of July he attempted to disrupt the thriving trade at Zhapu by ordering a blockade from Zhenhai to the mouth of the Yangzi; and on July 28 he set off for Beihe, near Tianjin and much nearer to the capital, where he hoped to confront high officials of the Chinese government directly.[80] This was all to little avail, and when Elliot returned to Dinghai on September 28, he faced the end of his Zhoushan expedition. Of the 4,000 British troops garrisoned at Dinghai, 1,300 had fallen victim to an "epidemic,"[81] and 150 had died. Elliot returned to Macao in defeat, and the Foreign Office for the moment turned its thoughts away from acquisition of the Zhoushan Islands.

The local officials along the coast, like those at Zhapu, were not kept well apprised of the situation as it had developed in Canton. They were issued sketchy bulletins of the likelihood that foreign "pirates" (*fei*) would appear in their vicinity. In June of 1840, before Elliot's arrival, [Ujala] Qimingbao,[82] the general-in-chief at Hangzhou, reported to the court that, in his opinion, Turtle Head Cove (Yenzi tan) on Hangzhou Bay was the key position for the defense of the regional waterways, and he recommended stationing troops in Chaoshen ("God of Waves") Temple there. He also reported that the area was being swept for "Chinese traitors" (*hanjian*). His concern on this point may have been a response to rumors of treachery circulated by dispirited soldiers and commanders anxious to divert blame from themselves for defeat; certainly the court had heard enough about the ubiquitous traitors in their midst by now to expect Qimingbao to show proper wariness on this count, and after the engagement at Zhapu claims of native abetting of the enemy would arise.[83] But like so many aspects of the bannermen's military encounters in the middle nineteenth century, the Qing fears were directed very much against their own history of conquest. Once, in extending their rule through the Northeast and China, the Qing armies had depended upon internal helpers (*neiying*) to throw open city gates to the conquerors, either because they had been bribed or because they were not prepared to face the consequences of resistance. Now, the Qing feared the new invaders would pull similar strings inside the walled cities of Zhapu or Hangzhou, or even within the garrison communities. Qimingbao passed the word along to Changxi, the brigade-general at Zhapu, that those of whom he was suspicious should be rounded up and expelled from the city or imprisoned.[84] When, in July, the British made a brief and to them inconsequential foray against Zhapu as part of their move to blockade Hangzhou Bay, the garrison there suffered the shock of six deaths from enemy shell-fire.[85] For his part, Qimingbao may have had grave (and probably very realistic) doubts about the ability of the Zhapu contingent to defend themselves against an attack. The eighteenth-century strength at Zhapu had grown to 3,600 occupying soldiers, but by 1840 had declined to about 2,500 active bannermen. Like all garrisons, Zhapu had also been affected by the drastic reduction of officers' stipends and the consequent rise in ratios of soldiers, cadets and *zidi* to officers. The resulting weakness in organization was fatally compounded by the garrison's abandonment of drilling in either land or sea maneuvers and its inability to purchase adequate arms for itself.

Qimingbao selected troops in advance and planned to send them to Zhapu under cover of night; when he heard of the alarm raised in Zhapu in anticipation of the attack, he personally led his troops from Hangzhou to come to the aid of Changxi, but received an order from the court to stay in Hangzhou and send his own brigade-general, Hengxing, in his stead.[86] As it happened the British withdrew from the Zhapu environs after some perfunctory shelling, and Qimingbao then engaged in a bit of the exaggerated narrative that contributed to the court's undoing: "Our troops advanced, fought bravely, and drove the British out of Zhapu."[87] The local commanders were chastened by their unhappy first experience with the invaders, and Changxi memorialized the court on what he considered the serious inadequacies in weapons and defensive works at Zhapu. His appeal was acknowledged by the court, which ordered that troops from neighboring garrisons should be sent to Zhapu to augment the contingent there. Only Hangzhou complied with the initial order, and the emperor expressed his displeasure at the evident foot-dragging of the soldiers and officers in other garrisons. In the meantime, Hengxing and his troops were ordered to remain at Zhapu, and [Aisin Gioro] Yilibu (1761–1843) was appointed, on August 2, as special military intendant at Zhejiang, to oversee the strengthening of defenses.[88] Qimingbao reported another brief attack on August 8, before Yilibu's arrival, and stated that he had immediately begun assembling a force and drilling so that they should be prepared to defend Hangzhou if the pirate ships should reappear. Minning approved, and warned, "Although the pirate ships have withdrawn there is still danger."[89]

Indeed the emperor knew, but did not inform Qimingbao, that the British ships had moved from Zhapu and Dinghai in order to continue their move northward. Though the British had been rebuffed at Tianjin and momentarily abandoned Dinghai, Minning had been alarmed by Elliot's approach to Peking, and the entire war effort—which had begun as a social amelioration policy—was reconsidered. Manchu counselors, foremost [Guogiya] Mujangga (d. 1857), now pressed Minning hard for a negotiated settlement to the war and won him to their point of view, despite the existence of a formidable war party led by Qi Junzao (1793–1866) and others.[90] [Borjigit] Qishan, who was in Tianjin to oversee the preparation of defenses there, was authorized by the emperor to treat with Elliot, and Lin Zixu was dismissed from his commissionership, ordered first to Zhejiang to serve in a minor military post, then to banishment in Xinjiang. It was rumored that Mujangga suppressed protests from provincial officials over the treatment of Lin;[91] in fact Lin may have retained some influence even after his dismissal and in any case returned to government service within a few years. Qishan, for his part, reported that on the basis of promises to Elliot that a reasonable solution could be reached, the British had left Tianjin to return to Canton. Zhapu was stripped of its Hangzhou reinforcements, including those temporarily stationed at Chaoshen Temple, and left again in the charge of Changxi. Qishan himself was dispatched to Canton to serve as imperial commissioner, and his reports for months after his arrival worked to discredit the conduct of Lin Zixu at Canton.

By January of 1841 the promised negotiations had not begun, and the British shelled and captured the forts at Quanbi, east of Canton; after more delay the British seized the forts at the Bogue (Humen), the water entry to Canton itself. Qishan evidently took it upon himself to listen to British demands, which as formulated at the time provided for cession of Hong Kong Island (then a rocky and sparsely populated outcropping at the mouth of the Pearl River) in perpetuity, reopening of Canton to foreign trade, payment of Mex$6 million in reparations, making good the debts of Canton merchants to the British traders, and allowing diplomatic intercourse between the British government and the Qing court.[92] As time passed and the agenda did not turn into a treaty (for Qishan was understandably reluctant to make the court fully aware of its contents), British assaults continued against the fortifications on the waterways of Canton. Of the "Chuenpi Convention" all other Qing officials initially claimed ignorance, but [Hada Gūwalgiya] Yiliang eventually reported Qishan's dealings with Elliot to Peking. On February 26 a furious emperor fired Qishan from his commissioner's post, rescinded his titles and ranks, confiscated his fortune and had him dragged in chains to Peking. He was sentenced to death but, as often happened in those days, had his sentence commuted to banishment in Xinjiang. In Qishan's place, the imperial clansman Yishan (1798–1878) was assigned with two elderly helpmates, the Manchu [Irgen Gioro] Longwen (d. 1841) and the Chinese Yang Fang, a hero of the White Lotus wars forty years before.[93] Yilibu was ordered to work with the Mongol [Boluoqin] Yuqian (1793–1841), governor of Jiangsu, to dislodge the remaining British troops from the Zhejiang coast.[94] On January 26, he was ordered to attack and secure Dinghai, to which he responded that an immediate attack was not feasible, but he would proceed with plans for the campaign. On February 6 he was ordered again to take Dinghai, and when on February 10 he was still making explanations he was dismissed as military intendant.[95] Yuqian took his place, but before he had to face the prospects of attacking Dinghai, the British had left the island as part of the negotiating process at Canton.

For his part, Elliot had also disappointed his government by failing to demand cession of the Zhoushans in his negotiations, and the Foreign Office made plans to replace him with Sir Henry Pottinger. But Elliot was still in charge of the British water forces at the time that Yishan and his fellows decided to attempt to drive the foreign warships out of the mouth of the Pearl River. Hugh Gough, the general in command of the land troops, wanted to seize Canton immediately; Elliot persuaded him to wait, and at the end of May got the Qing commissioners to agree to pay a ransom of Mex$6 million to stave off a sack of the city. Gough's bellicose mood was soon complemented by that of Pottinger, who arrived in August and began assembling a fleet for the retaking of the Zhoushan Islands by force. In late August of 1841 Xiamen (Amoy) in Fujian province was captured, and the British fleet turned northward, intending to move into Hangzhou Bay again. The court was frantically alerting local governors to the danger, and when possible dispatching military commissioners to oversee defense preparations. On September 26 the British fleet assembled in Dinghai harbor, where they found that some changes had been made: The entire waterfront had been fortified, though there were still no cannons in place. The ships shelled the fortifications, while a British and Indian infantry and artillery force attacked the city walls. On October 5 Dinghai was captured again, and a British garrison of four hundred troops was established there. Next the British turned their attention to Ningbo on the Zhejiang mainland, where they hoped to spend the winter. On October 10 the *Wellesley* and the *Blenheim*, each equipped with seventy-four guns, were directed against Zhenhai, where Yuqian temporarily had his headquarters; the shelling demolished the seaward bulwark, the line of defenders broke, Yuqian tried to drown himself, and the invaders took the city by two in the afternoon. On October 12, Ningbo was taken without resistance.

Again Mujangga and his group petitioned the emperor to negotiate for a settlement; the complete unpreparedness of the Qing forces had, in their eyes, been demonstrated, and only abject defeat could be expected if resistance were to continue. Minning, however, had grown if anything more ferocious in his determination to fight back. The present emperor had been fourteen at the time of the death of his grandfather, Hongli, and had vivid memories of the days when the court had been at the height of its confidence and evident power. He was not personally inclined to surrender or to negotiate; as a prince he had taken a musket and killed two rebels who had broken into the imperial compound during his studies, and as an emperor, he had been adamant, if not imaginative, in his attempts to bring drug and money problems under control. Moreover, Minning was evidently shocked by the rapaciousness of the terms demanded by the British at Quanbi. If Qishan's misadventure had provided any insight into the cost of negotiating with the British, it may well have seemed to Minning that the consequences of carrying the war to its conclusion could hardly be greater than those of early surrender. In a high fury he demanded investigation and punishment of Yuqian, but was informed that the Mongol governor had died of the effects of his attempted suicide the day after the attack. Needing new leadership in Zhejiang, Minning entrusted to his favorite cousin Yijing (d. 1853) the task of driving the British from Ningbo, where they were encamped until they could begin their spring campaigns. [Feimo] Wenwei (d. 1856), a Manchu president of the Board of Revenue, was appointed his second in command. On October 22, they were joined by [Tatara] Teyishun (d. 1849), as a second assistant.[96]

Hangzhou was made the center of the military operations in Zhejiang, and Qimingbao got a good look at the new leaders sent down from Peking. It is possible that he did not like what he saw. Wenwei, at least, was an opium addict. Yijing had no real military experience. Together with the Zhejiang governor Liu Yunke (d. 1853), Qimingbao and his Hangzhou brigade-general Hengxing requested and received a mandate to proceed with their own plans for defense of the city and for provisioning Qing troops in the area; in December, they followed up with a specific request that the Hangzhou garrison be reinforced with troops from other provinces.[97] At Zhapu, anxiety over the plans of the British ran high. The troops of the invaders had begun foraging through outlying towns and villages around Ningbo as early as October for their winter supplies, being seen at various times at Yuyao, Fenghua, and Xiji. On January 24, 1842, Changxi reported a British fleet off Zhapu, and on January 29 they returned; [Xiangdashan] Yingdengbu, a colonel at Zhapu, ordered his cannoneers to open fire on the ships, and reported an improbable double hit, one ship being smitten in the "head" and one in the "tail."[98]

Yijing, Wenwei and Teyishun were otherwise engrossed in a scheme to dislodge the British from Ningbo, Zhenhai and Dinghai.[99] They had organized a "grand battalion" (da ying), or composite army of over five thousand banner troops, Green Standard troops, gentry-led militia and mercenaries, in which they evidently had serious problems attempting to establish chains of command and response. Once formed, their plans to reinforce military strength in Zhejiang by addition of soldiers from Sichuan, Shaanxi and Gansu provinces became hostage to the normal means of Qing troop transfer: walking. It took between seventy-four and 110 days for the additional (exhausted) units to arrive.[100] March 10, the day chosen at length by supernatural consultation for the attack, proved to be one of the rainiest of the rainy season; the Northwestern troops prodded into the vanguard at Ningbo could not follow the battle plans because of an inability to understand orders in standard Chinese;[101] Wenwei, who was supposed to be leading the attack on Zhenhai, collapsed into opium stupor at the crucial moment, and his men dispersed, eventually drawing back to Jiaxing "to defend it"; the troops dispatched to Dinghai embarked but did not sail for the island, instead roaming along the coast for more than two weeks before finally owning up to the truth of their failed venture. Little disturbed by the aborted onslaught, the British commenced a mopping-up operation in the surrounding countryside. At first Minning himself took the blame for the failure, noting Yijing's inexperience in military affairs; by April, however, when it was clear—contrary to Yijing's initial reports—that even the Dinghai expedition had come to naught, the emperor began to feel less indulgent toward Yijing, who was allowed to retain his titles and his ostensible functions in Zhejiang for the time being. Qiying (d. 1858) temporarily had taken over Qimingbao's post of general-in-chief at Hangzhou, and it was he who now assumed primary authority for the defense of the Zhejiang coast. Yilibu, whose profile was brightened considerably by the performance of his successors in Zhejiang, was also assigned to the Hangzhou garrison in late March, but did not arrive for several months.

At Zhapu, a nervous eye was kept out for British activity in the aftermath of the Ningbo debacle. Enemy ships were spotted not far from Zhapu on April 5, and on April 6 Zhapu scouts saw British ships ferrying troops from Ningbo to Dinghai. The long-requested reinforcements for the Hangzhou-Zhapu garrisons finally arrived in the form of the same Northwestern natives who had participated in the Yijing campaign against Ningbo, and in order to afford a second line of defense for the garrison itself a company under the command of [Xurxu] Longfu was stationed in the Tianzun ("Reverence for Heaven") Temple, on Mount Guanyin a little over a mile outside the southeastern walls of Zhapu.[102] During early May, the British commanders decided to withdraw their troops from Ningbo and concentrate all forces at Zhenhai; this was the final stage in the preparations for an attack upon Zhapu. On May 16 Zhapu scouts saw two steamships and more than twenty other ocean-going vessels near Mount Huangpan, on the coast very close to Zhapu. By May 17 the force had been assembled. Qimingbao immediately ordered Changxi and Yilibu to supply troops for the defense of the coast, moving at night to avoid detection. The massing of British troops may have struck even Minning as ominous; he instructed Yilibu to submit plans for the institution of a "loose rein" (jimi)—that is, lenient and remote—policy for dealing with the British "barbarians."[103]

This was irrelevant, since on the morning of May 18 the British were already moving across the bay toward Zhapu. The attack, long feared at Zhapu and never adequately prepared for, had begun. Seven warships, four steamships, several dozen transport and sampans brought the British toward shore. The Qing battery was shelled, and 2,200 British and Indian troops were landed below Mount Huangpan and Mount Tangwan, both of which they had been reconnoitering a few days earlier. They divided at the hills along the coast, below the Qing batteries and battle line. The Qing forces had arranged themselves on the hills above. In the first assault by the British, members of the vanguard Xiangyin, Xiangcheng, Jirha, Qunsuo, Longwu, Sufan, and Xianggui all received serious wounds and died; Changxi reported enemy casualties of sixteen. The British ships opened fire on the inner fortifications; only a small number of troops were within the city, most having been arranged in anticipation of the attack on the hillsides outside the Zhapu suburbs. Again the British divided their ranks; a unit moved on Mount Longchuo, east of the garrison itself, and attacked the Green Standard division there. The Qing troops fell in comparatively large numbers. Their cannon, which were fixed in position and could not be deployed against the advancing ground troops, were useless, and their weapons—matchlocks that in accuracy, reloading and firing capability were no equal to the flintlocks of the British—were crude and dangerous to themselves. Nevertheless Qiying later claimed that the more hopeless the struggle, the more ferocious (*jinghan*) the soldiers became.[104] The impotent cannon were abandoned as the British scrambled up from the beach, and the banner troops began running for the Zhapu walls and the garrison within as darkness fell. The British halted the attack for the day, and the next morning began shelling Zhapu and its suburbs with mortar fire from their position on Mount Dengguang. Changxi apparently was wounded in the subsequent attempt to prevent the push of ground troops toward Zhapu, and his colonel Yingdengbu was bayonetted not far away. Changxi's wound was mortal; he threw himself into the large canal leading to Hangzhou in an apparent suicide attempt, but was dragged out by his aide, Shangabu, who carried him into the garrison. Now, only the Manchus inside the Tianzun Temple stood between the advancing British and the Zhapu garrison. The temple grounds were surrounded by a low brick wall pierced by a single gate. Captain Longfu,[105] together with his lieutenants [Tuokelu] Guishun and the Mongol [Tukejiding] Etehe, arranged their troops in the upper walkway of the central temple building, with full vantage of the small gate, while the monks and novices waited in the background.

In two initial attempts to enter the temple grounds, the British lost two of their men, killed by fire from Longfu's soldiers' matchlocks. At length the compound was entered and the central hall surrounded by two companies of the Eighteenth Royal Irish, who fired a small cannon against the walls, killing Guishun, among others.[106] The bannermen still could not be driven from the building, and the British troops began to explode bags of gunpowder against the walls. Several times, the British attempted to enter the temple itself by different routes, and each time were picked off or blocked by Manchu sharpshooters on the upper story. It was in this way that Colonel Tomlinson of the Royal Irish, the only British participant mentioned by name in the Chinese accounts, met his demise; he overheard a remark from one of his colleagues of the Hertfordshire regiments (who had arrived to help) which he thought reflected on the fortitude of the Royal Irish, and rushed the door of the temple. "Scarcely a second had elapsed when he fell a corpse into the arms of his men, having received two balls in the neck."[107] Three or four soldiers as well as most of the monks and novices made a running escape into the nearby Ren forest shortly afterward, and after more futile attempts to blow in a portion of the walls, the British decided to burn the temple down. A bag of gunpowder was pressed against the foundation and ignited. The explosion tore away a portion of the wooden temple wall, exposing a number of bannermen crouched inside, some of whom were shot immediately and some of whom managed to find cover. Those bannermen attempting to gain vantage points thereafter had difficulty. "Whenever a Tartar shewed himself at a window in any part of the building, several muskets were levelled at him; and on the other hand, so well did the Tartars take aim with their matchlocks, that one of the Royal Irish, who *would* persist in merely peeping round the doorway, 'just to see if he couldn't pick off a Tartar,' received a shot in his knee just before he had himself time to fire."[108]

The British troops collected the ruined wood from the building and set a fire that they hoped, still, would engulf the entire temple. Gunpower in the weapons of dead and wounded bannermen as well as what they customarily carried in a bag strapped to their bodies began to explode, and the entire building was finally ablaze.[109] To avoid catching fire themselves the remaining Manchus stripped off their tunics, but they were eventually forced out of the temple into the yard. Those who attempted to run away were shot, and those who were captured were tied together by their queues and marched off to Zhapu. The British seem to have imagined that the blood-letting had ceased for the day. They might have realized otherwise when, as the fighting was dying down, an elderly Manchu approached the line of bayonets with his group and was severely wounded. Through an interpreter he was informed that he was now a prisoner and would be treated with "kindness and mercy," to which he replied that kindness and mercy on the part of his captors would consist in memorializing the emperor that he had fallen "in the front fighting to the last."[110] The remark failed to prepare the invaders for the scenes that were to follow:

> The high spirit of the Tartar soldiers, the descendants of the conquerors of China, and soldiers by birthright, could not brook a total defeat; and when they were further stimulated by the excitement of opium, their self-devotion and stubbornness tended to increase their loss. When they could no longer fight, they could die; and the instances of mad self-destruction, both within the city and without, were truly horrible. Many of the Tartars were with difficulty prevented from cutting their throats, which they attempted to do with apparent indifference. On visiting the large building or joss-house [i.e. the Tianzun Temple], which had resisted so long, and had cost so many lives, a number of dead and wounded men were found huddled together in a horrible manner, in

one of the out-buildings attached to it. The ruins of the house were still smoking, and Captain Hall's object was to drag out the wounded and put them under cover until they could be properly attended to, for, on all occasions, the Chinese wounded received every attention that could be shewn them from our medical officers. Just as the men began to move aside the dead bodies, a Tartar soldier, who had until now concealed himself among them, literally rising from the dead, stood up and suddenly drew his sword. But instead of making a dash for his life, or giving himself up as a prisoner, he began deliberately to hack his own throat with the rusty weapon, and inflicted two wounds upon himself before his hand could be stopped.[111]

Among those who killed themselves in the aftermath of the loss of the Tianzun Temple was Longfu. Of the 276 bannermen who had been in the temple, 233 died.

The British advanced on Zhapu city, at which point the magistrate Wei Fengjia led militiamen to the banks of the canal to oppose the invaders, where he was killed by rifle fire. Colonel Gairhanga was with those attempting to defend the eastern gate, the point at which the British entered the garrison, and was presumed killed; his cap and button were later mourned, in the absence of a corpse, in burial. Changxi was spirited out of the garrison to a safe spot near the coast by his retainers and died of his wounds in the evening. The British entered a garrison that was quiet except for the moans and screams of those in the process of murdering or being murdered by their families. Whole households, having killed themselves or been killed by the family elders, were piled in the yards and alleys of the enclosure, or stuffed into the wells. Some of the suicides had not yet been completed as the troops entered the garrison, and the British watched in frank horror "the women destroying their children, drowning them in wells, and throwing themselves in afterwards; the husbands hanging and poisoning their own wives, and deliberately cutting their own throats. . . ." An observer of a later, similar scene in the lost garrison at Jinjiang wrote, "The hardest heart of the oldest man who ever lived a life of rapine and slaughter could not have gazed upon this scene of woe unchanged."[112] For the few Manchus who survived, the terror had not ended. Ming loyalist accounts of the Qing conquest of Zhejiang once were mesmerized by the horror of the alien sifting of the local women for abduction and abuse; now Qing accounts of the loss of Zhejiang were riveted by the determination of the new barbarians to commit the same atrocities. Chinese sources accused the invaders of systematically dividing up the surviving young women of the garrison and the town and distributing them to British or Indian soldiers (according to degrees of desirability) for rape.[113] And just as the invading Qing troops under Dodo and Tulai had been followed by hordes of looting, ravishing vandals in their sweep through Zhejiang, the British victory gave such elements their first access to the Manchu garrison at Zhapu. "As the greater part of the Tartar population had abandoned the Tartar portion of the city, the Chinese rabble set about plundering it, and frightened the few who remained, even more than our own troops."[114] General Gough, commenting specifically on the rampant looting which the British command had tried in vain to control at Ningbo, Xiamen and their other sites of conquest on the coast, later wrote in his journal, "When I look at this I am sick of war."[115]

After establishing themselves at Zhapu, the British moved on to attack Wusong, Yushan, Yangzhou and Shanghai, finally descending upon Jinjiang with a force of 15,000 on July 21. The brigade-general [Gorolo] Hailing led 1,600 bannermen in defense, armed with spears, swords, bows and arrows.[116] The effectiveness of the resistence at Jinjiang and the bloodshed in the garrison afterward shocked the invaders nearly as much as that at Zhapu had.[117] Hailing burnt himself and his entire family to death in their home and nearly five hundred others killed themselves or attempted to as flames spread through the garrison.[118] With the province of Zhejiang lost, Minning had no choice but to acquiesce in Mujangga's insistence that negotiations with the British were inevitable, and rehabilitated Yilibu, whom he understood to be respected by the British, or at least by Elliot. As the British drew closer to Nanjing the court hastened its preparations for negotiation, assigning Yilibu as imperial commissioner to Canton in July of 1842. Yilibu died in the south before he could complete his role in the formalization of the Treaty of Nanking, at which Qiying finally presided as the Chinese representative. The disastrous provisions of the treaty were hardly different from those of the "Chuenpi Convention," with the exceptions of a huge Mex$21 million indemnity (more than three times what Qishan had negotiated at Quanbi) and the opening of four additional trade ports besides Canton.

In the aftermath of the loss of Zhejiang and of the war, the search for scapegoats commenced. Lin Zixu and Qishan had been punished early on, and many of the principals, such as Yuqian and Yilibu, were dead. Yijing, who in the last weeks of the war simply ignored such orders as he received from Peking, was ordered to appear at court after the signing of the treaty and sentenced to death along with Wenwei and Yishan. Blame for the disasters in Zhejiang in 1841 and 1842 was posthumously fixed on Yuqian, but the court evidently wished a blood debt to be paid: Yu Buyun, the commander of the Green Standard forces in Zhejiang who had made little attempt to prevent the British capture of Zhenhai and Ningbo, was ordered beheaded in late 1842. And court disapproval sought lower depths, probing the conduct of men and officers at Zhapu who had shown, or could be reported to have shown, cowardice. Qi-

mingbao, who was very ill, died of natural causes but with no state enco-
miums soon after the Zhapu debacle; Changxi was rumored, after his
death, to have been a deserter, and Hengxing was cashiered from his post
as brigade-general at Hangzhou.

It was at this point, in the autumn of 1842, that Guancheng returned
to Zhapu to find his childhood friends from the garrison dead, wounded
or nerve-ridden over their ordeal. His home was intact, for he had used
his official salary to purchase an estate for himself in the Longchuo district, outside the garrison proper and in a neighborhood little disturbed
by the skirmishing. His mother, Shao–shi, his wife and his four sons were
safe, but Guancheng, who was fifty-three years old and very ill, was well
aware of the damage—physical, psychological and political—done to the
Zhapu garrison community. Now under the command of Teyishun, the
garrison was traumatized by its first contact with a foreign invader and
paralyzed by the paperwork necessary to document the identities of those
dead in battle. Widows, parents and orphans were anxious to receive
their compensation payments and to see the proper memorials erected
to the fallen. It was necessary that the name and banner affiliation of each
decedent be ascertained, and that as much anecdotal evidence as possible
attesting to the valiant demises of the soldiers be supplied; like the bannerman who asked to be remembered as having fallen fighting to the last,
such descriptions as having shown "ferocity" (jinghan), or "fighting vigorously to the death" (lizhan zhenwang) were valued, and appear frequently in the necrologies published at this time by Guancheng and,
later, his son Xirui. The official toll counted 279 bannermen dead, including the 233 men who died in the defense of the Tianzun Temple; 400
soldiers of the Green Standard, including the 50 men dead in skirmishes
on Mount Guanyin; 267 men fallen in defense of the garrison itself; 56
women and children dead within the garrison, and enough civilians to
bring the total death tally at Zhapu to between 1,200 and 1,500 individuals. In memorials to the court, Teyishun requested compensation and
public recognition for the brave men and chaste dependents. He addi-
tionally requested compensation for the burials of and memorials to
Changxi, Yingdengbu and various captains who had fallen in battle.[119] In
view of the decimation of the garrison population, Teyishun hinted, it
might be best for the garrison to be abolished, and its fifty remaining
sailors incorporated into the Green Standard Army of the region.

The publication of Guancheng's "Record of Martyrs from the Zhapu
Manchu Garrison in the Years 1840 and 1842 of the Daoguang Reign"
(Daoguang gengzi renyin Zhapu manzhou zhufang xunnan lu) aided in
the effort to publicize to the court and to officialdom the valor and wor-
thiness of compensation that had in his opinion characterized the deaths
of the mass of soldiers fallen in defense of Zhapu.[120] Unspoken in his

introduction to the piece was the rage of many at Zhapu over the inconstancy of the central military bureaucracy who had assigned a series of incompetent intendants, and at some periods tandems of incompetents, to oversee and override the conduct of the local banner officers; the incomprehensible string of orders to attack and then not to attack, then to attack again; the indifference of neighboring garrisons—with the exception of the mother garrison at Hangzhou—who failed to comply with repeated requests from Qimingbao and even orders from the court to supply troops to aid in the defense of the Zhejiang coast; and the present rumor campaign to discredit the Zhapu garrison in order to divert blame from other quarters. But Guancheng did allow hints of local frustration to surface. The families of the six who had died in the first British cannoning of Zhapu in 1840, he noted, had received prompt compensation. But even now, after his own return to Zhapu months after the disaster, the dead had been buried, many had been ennobled, but many families of Zhapu were still left without aid.[121] He reminded the court of the local sacrifice: "In the twenty-second year, renyin [1842], fourth month, the British again invaded the city. Rallying to the defense, civil and military officials took to the streets, while soldiers and volunteers assumed positions at each wall. It has not been precisely calculated how many of these men and women died at that point. One high-ranking Manchu garrison officer was killed, and seven others perished later in the fighting. Two hundred and seventy regular soldiers died in battle, six others died later of their wounds. Fifty-six men, women, boys and girls were martyred. Five sailors who were in training at the garrison were also killed, along with one soldier assigned to the Manchu garrison from elsewhere for the purpose of defending it." He suggested the psychological pain of a community that had been at peace for two hundred years, and suddenly found itself confronted with the necessity of recovering the corpses of family and friends from its own wells, alleys, gardens, stables and houses: "The officers, soldiers, men and women of our garrison were ill-prepared for this, the corpses having been found piled against buildings and even suspended from the battlements. In mourning our nation's dead, how could we bear to allow these loyal clansmen to be buried without benefit of ceremony?" He signed himself in an uncharacteristic and, for the times, peculiar way: "Guancheng, a Manchu,"[122] underscoring his identity with the "Manchu garrison" where he did not live or work, but with which he had an indelible bond.

Official compensatory ranks, encomia, and remuneration for widows and orphans were eventually forthcoming, but the court was too busy with the furor over the first Opium War and the ensuing unequal treaties to be able to expend much wonder on either the reported heroism of the banner troops who attempted to defend the port or the inherent vulnerabilities of the region to attack. The news of the fall of Zhapu, for many, was not the numbers who had turned to fight the enemy, but the numbers who had run away. Guancheng's account of the attempted suicide and subsequent death of Changxi, the Zhapu commander, was disbelieved by many, who claimed instead that Changxi had been a deserter.[123] While the questions lingered, Guancheng died, in February or March of 1843. Xirui printed a new "Record of Martyrs" shortly after his father's death, and in his preface addressed those doubts, which he evidently felt struck at his father's reputation as well as that of the garrison at large. The commander Changxi, Xirui insisted, had not deserted; on the contrary he had stood on the ramparts and killed with his own hands those who were trying to desert. After the fall of the garrison Changxi had tried to kill himself and had been prevented by his officers several times before finally taking poison. But more than anything, Xirui reminded his readers, the issue was the despoiling of Zhejiang by the foreign invaders, and its meaning; this was more important than the issue of the manner of a single commander's death.[124] Xirui claimed to echo his father's sentiments in feeling that the devastation of the Zhapu garrison was deeply inauspicious. "One can only worry about Zhapu: From the time of the piracy in the Ming period, there have been more than two centuries passed here without military disaster, and now we have been twice violated by the British."[125]

The meaning of the Zhapu disaster for the bannermen there and for the court could hardly have been expected to coincide. For the court, the loss had opened the way to the domination of Zhejiang by the British and the approach to Nanjing that had finally ended the war. An unprecedented loss had been inflicted upon the empire, probably due to local incompetence or cowardice, and for the moment the barbarians seemed to have the upper hand. Military solutions to the country's problems were not on the agenda for the 1840s; political solutions were explored instead, as the court and local governors simply refused to comply with the provisions of the post-war treaties, attempting to buy time for a more efficacious strategy. Since a military response was not considered by the court, the plight of the bannermen was of little immediate concern, particularly since regular troops, local militia and composite armies would probably be the court's resources in the event of another confrontation. To the bannermen, however, measures for military defense were now, suddenly, of paramount importance. For the first time the vulnerabilities of the garrison system had been graphically demonstrated. It was in accord with their ancient customs that the soldiers lived together with their kinsmen; the majority of garrison residents were unable to defend themselves, and those charged with their defense were inadequately armed and poorly trained to do so. For their part, the Manchus of Zhapu were clearly shocked by the necessity of defending themselves within their own garrison; since taking up the peculiar life within the walls, this was the first time they had been forced to fight there. Their world out of the world had become, if only briefly, a slaughter pen.

The bannermen of Zhapu did not know, and the court did not note, that the opinion of the British commanders was that the Zhapu engagement had confronted them with the stiffest and most surprising resistance of the war. Landed engagements had been few before Zhapu, and while the Qing artillery had been incapable of doing real damage to British warships, it was clear that the British expectation that the bannermen would be so enervated by opium addiction and chronic poverty as to be disinclined to or incapable of resistance had been overdrawn. After their nearly effortless conquests along the southern Chinese coast, the invaders took their own nine dead (whose bodies were reported to be grotesquely mutilated) and fifty wounded at Zhapu rather seriously. At least at Tianzun Temple, it was the weapons and not the men that had been defective. "If the loss of the Chinese was great that day," Hall later commented, "so was it on our side much greater than on any previous occasion." In light of the decades of well-attested and well-justified government anxiety over the neglect of preparedness in the garrisons, British comments on the skill shown by bannermen may be taken as reflection of the magnitude of the abilities of the conquering forces of the seventeenth and eighteenth centuries. At the same time, the "Tartar spirit" celebrated by the British after Zhapu and Jinjiang may have been due more than anything else to the fact that bannermen were defending, as best they possibly could, their homes and loved ones. From the British point of view, the causes of the Chinese defeat hardly required sustained inquiry. Despite the relatively large number of troops on the rolls— about 200,000 bannermen and over 600,000 Green Standard soldiers— the Qing had no means of mobilizing and coordinating the placement of their forces; unlike the British, the Qing no longer engaged in offensive military maneuvers, and had dispersed and localized military control for purposes of policing and defense. Also in contrast to Britain, which was the world's greatest sea power and which could coordinate and supply its operations from Singapore, China had no navy, only a series of naval garrisons attached to provincial garrisons, as the garrison at Zhapu had been attached to Hangzhou. The empire had never experienced a coordinated naval threat, and indeed did not construe their problems with Captain Elliot and General Gough to be a confrontation with a sea power. The war was regarded as a rather large and stubborn outbreak of piracy, and was dealt with as piracy had been dealt with in the past: warning shots fired from shore batteries, followed by sallies of armored junks. Beyond questions of communications and transportation, the disparity in technological levels was gross. Shallow-draft armored ships like the *Nemesis* could reach riverine ports, like Jinjiang, that would have been inaccessible a decade before. To the British troops serving in China, their flintlocks were old-fashioned, soon to be replaced by new rifles and repeating guns; but they more than served against the sticks, stones, rusted swords and wick-fired matchlocks used against them by furious peasants and desperate bannermen.[126] With such advantages, it would have been irrational for the British and other foreign nations not to press the Chinese for more and more concessions.[127] And with such demonstrated weakness on the part of the court and its internal defenses, it would have been irrational for domestic forces of discontent to remain in awe of the poor, idle, tale-spinning, song-singing, cricket-fighting and now loftily impugned Eight Banners.

CHAPTER V

Fengrui

THE VOLUNTEER

MOST OF THOSE who had suffered the wrath of the emperor over their failures in attempts to deal with the British were brought back in good public standing by the middle 1840s. Yilibu had been praised at the time of his death in 1843. Lin Zixu was once again governor-general of Hu-Guang. Qishan and Qiying were restored to grace. Except for those, like Yu Buyun, who had actually suffered execution in the period of Minning's rage, most bureaucrats appeared to be returning to normal life. Indeed this was the official posture in the 1840s, as China resisted the provisions of the Treaties of Nanking and Wanghsia (except for the cession of Hong Kong, which they were hardly in a position to prevent). As late as 1848, Governor Ye Mingchen (1807–1859) was continuing the local policy of keeping the foreigners out of Canton, and the governors of Fujian, Zhejiang and Jiangsu steadfastly refused to open their designated "treaty ports" to trade.[1] For its part the court dwelt no more upon the issue of whether the bannermen at Zhapu had been brave or cowardly. To the satisfaction of Xirui and his younger brother Fengrui, both of whom were now responsible for the maintenance of the family printing business and interested in seeing their father's defense of the Zhapu bannermen justified, there were occasional reports of banner valor and even banner victories in other regions through the 1840s and into the early 1850s. In the latter period, particularly, when the rest of the nation was engrossed in the question of whether the dynasty would survive the challenge of the Taiping rebels, banner communities vibrated with reports of Manchu success in beating off Russian encroachment in the Northeast. In 1850, and again in 1852, Manchus together with Feiyaka tribesmen had prevented incursion by a small Russian force into Heilongjiang, while in 1857 the Jilin general-in-chief Jingheng (d. 1875), leading a combined force of Manchus and Golds, had turned the Russians back at the Amur River.[2] Whatever glory was garnered by Northeastern bannermen, the years after the Opium War were acutely uncomfortable for the Manchus of China. The military mission of the seventeenth century had been superseded by the ideological mission of the Qianlong period, which in turn had been abandoned by a court laboring under burdens of insolvency, military humiliation and political disorientation. In few ways did the surviving garrisons resemble military institutions. Officers were few in number, supernumeraries were increasing in droves. A small elite possessed education, skill and status. For the others, the garrisons were subsistence-level holding camps, where the government detained a population unprepared for competiton in China's merciless urban economy, too volatile for sudden disenfranchisement, and with peculiar claims upon the dynastic bounty.

Changes in the economic conditions within the garrisons were the more palpable for the change in court attitudes under the Xianfeng (1851–1861) emperor, Yizhu. Now the contraction of banner resources was integrated with and accelerated by the general disarray of the national economy. In 1844, for instance, a rent strike by tenants working the Imperial Household lands in Fengtian had minimized the moneys collected there; in 1854 there was a similar strike at Niuzhuang. In 1852 Manchu tenants joined Chinese in a strike at Fushun, and the same thing happened at Liaoyang in 1854. By 1851 the Imperial Household Department had confirmed a dramatic increase in fugitives and declared itself incapable of sustaining the state farms that had been founded in the Northeast. When, in the 1850s, the Xianfeng government faced total financial collapse under the manifold pressures of fighting the Taipings, resisting the West in a second opium war and finally rendering reparations due from the forced Treaty of Nanking, it took measures to sever its economic obligations to some garrisons—first by delay of rice stipends, and finally in the outright ceasing of support, particularly grain deliveries. The immediate impact was intended to be softened by a scheme that allowed the Board of Revenue (*hubu*) to charter minting operations in the garrisons from 1853 to 1859 and to issue salaries to officers in certificates drawn against the mints. Some garrisons, including Hangzhou, enjoyed moderate success with the plan, but most communities were devoid of the resources to operate mints; the substitution of the valueless certificates for the specie stipends resulted in the rapid impoverishment of the officer class as well as the non-commissioned soldiers, and the government was forced to renew specie payments.[3] In many areas the response to the deprivations was violence: banner soldiers staged a demonstrative assembly protesting the rice delay at Zunhua in the Northeast in 1857, a riot broke out over the failure to distribute rice in Liaoning in 1859, soldiers protested the stoppage at Canton and at Urumqi in the Northwest in 1862, and the Imperial Household Department reported the same year that twelve officers and 138 soldiers from a contingent of bannermen posted from Jilin to Fengtian had absconded, apparently in dissatisfaction over the suspension of wages.[4] Contrary to Zhapu general-in-chief Teyishun's suggestion in the aftermath of the British invasion, the garrison there was not disbanded. Nor was it, however, the object of concentrated rebuilding, which may have been his hope in hinting that the community was on the verge of extinction. The 1840s were economically more difficult for Hangzhou and Zhapu than had ever previously been the case. Provisions for the Hangzhou garrison were delayed in 1843, and then cut by 20 percent for non-commissioned men (from 2.5 taels for a corporal to two taels); the same happened at Zhapu.

There is little to suggest that the general economic difficulties of the 1840s and 1850s had much effect upon the survivors of Guancheng. As the law permitted, Guancheng had sought and received from his banner superiors license to reside outside the garrison. Hangzhou and Zhapu bannermen below officer rank had been permitted to purchase land since 1740, and Guancheng had apparently taken advantage of the provision. His young sons owned some land in the Zhapu vicinity, probably inherited from him, and drew rent money from it.[5] His sons and their families all continued to live in or near his old house in the Longchuo ("waterfall") district of Zhapu, to the east of the garrison proper. In the center of the family compound stood the "Dear Harmony Hall" (*Guihe tang*) with the name, carved by Guancheng, displayed on the traditional placard above the entrance, and not far from the hall was a pool stocked with goldfish. Within the compound dwelt Guancheng's eldest son Xirui—a local licentiate (*shengyuan*), and clerk (*bithesi, bitieshi*) of the Manchu Plain White Banner at Zhapu—and his family, along with Fengrui (Guancheng's second son, eighteen at the time of his father's death) and the youngest sons Yunrui and Dingrui. In the Zhapu garrison lived their cousins Wenrui and Binrui, the grandsons of Guancheng's cousins Guanji and Jingcheng respectively.[6] During the 1840s and 1850s, the family apparently lived well. They had their normal rice and silver stipends—in the case of Xirui and Fengrui, four taels each per month when paid—which the males appointed to banner service were eligible to draw from ages fifteen to sixty. And they had their family printing business, which Fengrui in particular continued after Xirui's assumption of his banner duties in the garrison.

During the 1850s, Fengrui himself had little involvement in garrison administration aside from a Zhapu appointment as a Manchu Bordered Yellow Banner clerk (*bithesi*), which required him to demonstrate some ability in Manchu as well as in Chinese.[7] As a young child with his father in Sichuan, Fengrui had evidently shown considerable literary talent; by the age of seven he was reported to have been a voracious reader and to have demonstrated a great aptitude in memorizing, reciting and writing poetry.[8] When grown, he took the style name Tongshan, and produced a considerable volume of verse and prose. Nevertheless, he avowed no interest in the examinations that led to an official career. Nor did he tend to submerse himself in the composition or performance of drum songs or operas, though the household was full of enthusiasm for such things. Both Xirui and, later, Fengrui's eldest son Chunliang were reported to be fond of "Eight Notables tales" (*ba fen shu*), a type of *zidi* tale celebrating the adventures of the princes who had aided Nurgaci and Hung Taiji in the founding of the empire.[9] Yu Yue (1821–1907), apparently an appreciator of the genre, praised Chunliang most lavishly.[10] But Fengrui had no great love of or talent for drum songs, possibly because one's reserve would be quickly shed in their performance. In middle age Yu Yue described Fengrui as having "a very broad face and forehead, a thick beard, and a rather stiff and ponderous manner,"[11] hardly the mien of a born performer.

In contrast to his brother and his sons, Fengrui was a quiet man, who jealously preserved his moments of privacy. As a youth he developed a deep interest in Buddhism and esoteric Daoism, spending many hours in meditation. Later in life he became averse to things he regarded as empty and ostentatious, showing a preference for the metaphysical and mysterious, and a reverence for things of the past. When young he was an enthusiastic traveller. He had a great interest in walking tours (then and now a pastime of Hangzhou residents), and while away from the garrison and while living there was known for his ability to absorb and dispense details of the history and legends associated with each inlet, bridge or rock of the West Lake. Fengrui returned to Sichuan four times to climb Mount Omei, saw the sunrise from Mount Tai twice, and at least once went to Peking, seeking out the mansion of Fiongdon's descendants in East Sipailou Road where his father had spent so many congenial evenings.[12] He was also an expert collector, particularly of jade carvings and stone inscriptions, and had both the opportunities and the means to indulge his interests. Unlike his father, Fengrui did not spend much money or time acquiring books, which he frankly found lacking in antiquarian mystique: "So-called ancient books and paintings are usually less than three hundred years old. But metals and stone might go all the way back to the legendary Three Dynasties, or earlier. And of them all, only jade can really be considered ancient." Eventually his collection grew to contain more than two thousand items, including "at least something" from each of the reign periods of the Qing dynasty.[13] With rather more money (though considerably less leisure) than most bannermen his age, it is probable that Fengrui would have spent his entire life looking after his estate, his business, his collections and—in later life—his children, had circumstances permitted.

In his twenties, still unmarried and with more travelling planned, Fengrui began to assume more responsibility for the family printing business, and stayed for lengthy periods at Hangzhou to solicit commissions. The

Hangzhou literary community had long had a reputation as one of the most tight-knit, and the friendships forged by Guancheng among his fellow licentiates and bureaucrats stood Xirui and Fengrui in good stead. Fengrui himself was acquainted with Yu Yue and in later life would count him among his closest friends; the two men's connections went back to the late Jiaqing period, when their fathers had passed the Zhejiang provincial examinations in close succession.[14] Dai Xi, one of Guancheng's former tutoring partners from Peking, who took his provincial degree the year after Guancheng spent most of the 1850s in Hangzhou and continued to recommend Guancheng's sons to those scholars and poets in search of printers for their works. It helped that Dai himself was the center of a large circle of painters and poets, including Tang Yifen.

Like other literati of the West Lake region, Fengrui was a frequent visitor to the Wenlan Palace (*Wenlan ge*), the imperially commissioned library on the island where Orphan Hill stood. From the garrison he walked out the Qiantang Gate, and then either took a small ferry from the pier there to the landing west of the "Still Lake, Autumn Moon" teahouses, or might have walked over the Bai Juyi Dike to the road that passed directly in front of the Wenlan Palace compound.[15] The Wenlan was a commanding edifice inside high-walled garden grounds, looking south across the narrow street to the lake and its islands. It was one of the eight "palaces" built in the 1780s as repositories for the editions of the Four Treasuries, the massive collection of reprinted—and in some cases amended—literature that resulted from twenty years of court-sponsored review of the great libraries of the land.[16] Since Ming times the mercantile wealth of the Jiangnan region had been exploited for cultural development, as local merchants and mercantile associations were expected to underwrite the building and curatorial cost of institutions such as the Wenlan Palace, as well as the actual production of the library to be housed there.[17] The Wenlan Palace was one of the "Three Southern Repositories," together with the Wenhui Palace in Yangzhou and the Wenzong Palace in Jinjiang, built with donations from local merchants and literati, totalling more than 300,000 taels each.[18] The *Four Treasuries* edition, also purchased at local expense, consisted of 36,500 volumes (*juan*) in four divisions—classics (*jing*), histories (*shi*), philosophy (*zi*) and "belles-lettres" (*ji*), each division bound in boxes covered with brocade of a seasonal color: spring green for the classics, summer crimson for the histories, autumn white for the philosophies, and winter black for belles-lettres.[19] But the Wenlan Palace was not exclusively dedicated to the Four Treasuries collection; the first story and most of the third were reserved for it, but on the second was found a copy of the Imperial Encyclopedia (*Gujin tushu jicheng*), as well as special editions of noteworthy local books.[20]

In Fengrui's time the Qing emperors no longer had the inclination or the extra funds for the "southern tours" (*nanxun*) that had brought the Kangxi and Qianlong emperors to Hangzhou; the bannermen, however, continued to frequent the Wenlan Palace, far closer to the garrison than the drill field three miles away. Those who were interested could enter the first floor and view the book cupboards where the Four Treasuries was held, but it was very difficult—for many, impossible—to actually handle the books. In the 1890s, when Fengrui's son Jinliang attempted to get permission to read a volume or two, he had to ask an official from the garrison general-in-chief's staff to intercede. After more than a month he received an appointment to meet with a Wenlan librarian, a procedure that could not have varied greatly from that of his father's time: "A curator came out dressed in a very elegant fashion and bid me welcome. He then told me I would have to wait until I was summoned, and abruptly bustled out. It was later in the afternoon before he returned and instructed me to come upstairs with him. He made a great show of gazing at all the books for a time, and then asked me which one I would like to read. . . . The curator had just handed the book to me, and I had begun to read a few characters, when he announced that the library was now closing. He had an appointment in town, he said, and was afraid that he wouldn't make it in time; and besides, he hadn't eaten all day. We went downstairs together, and I asked to make an arrangement to return the next day, to which the curator replied that it would be necessary to make another application. . . ."[21]

The literary enthusiasm of the local educated, whether civilians or bannermen, could not have made them insensible to the deepening problem of local control, which by the time of Fengrui's early adulthood had become a national concern, and had affected the life of Hangzhou's intellectuals. During the 1850s the poets and bureaucrats of Hangzhou began to take on a paramilitary role, a reflection of the nationwide militarization of the literati class that had begun almost sixty years before. As the banner forces and then the Green Standard forces successively faltered in their abilities to quell local disorder, the gentry—whether rank-holders or merely large property holders—began to organize their own localities into militia, or "drill groups" (*tuanlian*) for defense.[22] In the Hangzhou region, such groups, combined with the banner and Green Standard forces to form the composite "grand battalion" (*da ying*), had attempted hastily and unsuccessfully to fend off the British attack of the Zhejiang coast in 1842. Two grand battalions—the Southern (Jiangnan), for the recapture of Nanjing, and the Northern (Jiangbei), based in Yangzhou— would be fielded in the prolonged struggle against the Taipings, but neither would prove to be a successful vehicle for suppression of the rebel forces. Like the composite army created to fight the British, the anti-

Taiping grand battalions were beset by rivalries for power and unclear lines of command, both of which contributed to the debacle at Nanjing under the Manchu Hechun (d. 1860) and the former Chinese rebel Zhang Guoliang (1823–1860) in 1860. The loyalist armies organized by provincial governors, following the example set by Zeng Guofan (1811–1812) in the early 1850s, were more effective. Dai Xi, Guancheng's old associate, was himself a leader in the organization of local defense for Hangzhou; in 1854 he, Li Pinfeng, Zhu Lan and Lu Feiquan were installed as local officers in the Hangzhou drill groups that were incorporated into Zeng's Xiang (Hunan) Army, which grew to encompass units from the provinces of Hunan (Zeng's base), Anhui, Jiangsu, Zhili, Henan, Shandong, Zhejiang, Jiangxi, Guizhou and Fujian.[23] In 1859, as Hangzhou began to experience its first skirmishes with the rebel vanguard and successfully defended itself against attack, Dai Xi was among those awarded rank for his service.[24]

The Taiping rebellion, though striking enough in its own right as the world's most destructive civil war and the bloodiest armed conflict before the twentieth century, was part of a complex of revolts that might well have shattered Qing rule in the middle nineteenth century had it not been for the government's willingness to allow the creation of special armies under the command of Chinese civil officials and the acceptance of military and financial aid provided by Western nations to whom the Qing had become indebted. The disorders of which the Taiping conflict was a part sometimes shared links with secret societies, many of which claimed to champion the racial dignity of the Chinese and to prophesy the return of the Ming dynasty, an underground catch-phrase dating from the first days of the Qing. Many, though not all, were influenced by heterodox religion—White Lotus millenarian Buddhism or, as in the case of the Taipings, Protestant Christianity. The causes of some can be traced, albeit indirectly, to the economic difficulties of the nineteenth century and the necessity of self-defense among communities in superficially governed regions. Most rebels claimed at one point or another that their rebellious passions had been incited by the spectacle of China's humiliation by foreigners in the Opium War. In many ways, the rebellions were not new. It remains a question whether the Qing authorities saw anything unprecedented in the early rise of the Taipings in Guangxi province in the very late 1840s.

The "God-Worshipping Society" (baishangdi hui) founded by Hong Xiuquan (1813–1864), a failed examination candidate, began unpromisingly but grew rather rapidly among the Hakka minority and economic demimonde of Guangxi between 1844 and 1847, thanks less to the efforts of Hong himself—who was frequently absent—than to a cousin who proselytized in his stead. In ensuing years there was some competitive ecstacy among the more ambitious members of the community, who seem to have manifested trances, visions and fits in efforts to displace Hong as leader of the movement. Ethnic rivalries, leadership contests and possibly some doctrinal schisms were finally resolved in Hong's announcement, on January 11, 1851, of the Heavenly Kingdom of Great Peace (*taiping tianguo*) which he, as the younger brother of Jesus, would henceforth lead with the aid of his military supporters. As many as ten thousand believers may have been mobilized by the Taipings at that time, and when the government attempted in February to break up the Taipings, they met with the first of what would be a long series of defeats. As the movement grew in momentum, the danger quickly took on a startling and terrifying face. Huge numbers of people and broad spans of territory were incorporated and effectively administered by the Taiping organization. Technology was no significant advantage to either side, since the Qing had limited access to money and the Taipings had limited access to armories; weapons moved quickly from one side of the conflict to the other, the balance of technology being most nearly threatened by Taiping acquisition of western weapons after defeat of international units fighting for the Qing. But armies of a size not seen since the Qing conquest of Jiangnan were on the march, many hundreds of thousands of men being mobilized by both sides, with the inevitable looters and camp followers swarming in their wake. Many battles were actually lengthy provisioning matches, in which commanders were willing to dig in for months in order to attempt to pinch off the supply lines of their opponent while sustaining their own, hoping that starvation and intramural strife would accomplish their ends for them. As the rebellion outgrew its base in southern China and spread to the middle of the country, refugees flooded eastward and northward, and with them rumors of the strange doings of the rebels who cut the queues imposed by the court upon its subjects, let their women go about with unbound feet in contravention of Chinese tradition, and spouted a weird religion of a heavenly elder brother and a holy ghost. In the garrison communities, tales of Manchu slaughter by the Taipings arrived early and with graphic details. Weapons, provisions and officers, though requested, did not arrive. The luxuries of ignorance and surprise that had been afforded the bannermen in the confrontation with the British was gone; they were left helpless and anxious behind their walls.

Taiping capture of Nanjing in March of 1853 brought hundreds of thousands of refugees into Jiangsu and Zhejiang and threatened to carry the civil war to that region as well. The symbolism of the taking of the erstwhile imperial capital electrified the Chinese official world, which feared that Peking would fall next and began to prepare itself. Manchus were more disturbed by the news that the population of the huge garrison community of Nanjing had been systematically exterminated in the course of the siege. Though individual Taiping leaders, particularly Li Xiucheng (1824–1864), would sometimes modify their rhetoric, rebel polemicists had from their earliest days identified the Manchus as the root of most evil in China, labelling them devils (*yao*), or—marking their ritually servile status—devil slaves (*yaonu*), and in their theology associating them with Satan. The coming war, in Taiping eyes, was to decide whether China would belong to God or to the Manchus; indeed the Heavenly Lord had already condemned the Manchus to destruction and to hell, and the Chinese people had nothing to lose by joining the holy cause.[25] "Extermination of devils (*yao*)" was the Taiping program for the elimination of the Manchus, and for good measure, those surrendering Manchu heads to the Taiping leaders would be granted rank and rewards.[26] At Nanjing, general-in-chief [Aisin Gioro] Xianghou and most of his officers had been killed in battle.[27] After the taking of the garrison, thousands of Manchu women and children had been driven through the main gate and slaughtered as they emerged. The government later estimated that more than thirty thousand residents of the garrison had been killed; virtually the entire community had perished.[28] The Taipings had proven the sincerity of their pledge to rid China of its Manchu conquerors.

By the summer of 1853 it appeared that the rebels had the momentum and the intention to continue their conquest northward to Peking, which the Heavenly King, Hong Xiuquan, had rechristened "Devil's Lair" (*yaoxue*). The Manchu fear of Chinese traitors and informers revived with a new intensity at the capital. Chinese who had previously been permitted to reside in the Manchu Inner City because of their rank or their trade were expelled; homeless people and beggars were swept from the streets in and around the garrison and the imperial compound; and the gendarmerie was put on the alert for spies and infiltrators. Chinese families with the means began leaving the capital. The Xianfeng emperor, Yizhu, made every effort to publicize the fact that he was frequently visiting the Temple of Heaven to beg divine protection,[29] a pitiable contrast to the days when Hongli had ordered his attendants to don waterproofs as he strutted to the same temple to demand rain. For reasons that are not entirely clear, the Taipings decided in the end to base themselves at Nanjing, and sent only a small force of 25,000 soldiers northward against Peking, an expedition foiled by regional forces before the capital was endangered. For the time being the Taipings appeared to be consolidating their position in Nanjing, and few special preparations were made for the defense of Hangzhou and Zhapu before the very late 1850s, when Hangzhou had become a major nexus of command and supply in the campaign to contain the growth of the Taiping "Heavenly Kingdom" and the defenses were numerically reinforced by the addition of nearly four thousand militia.[30] By the time this measure was taken, however, the Taipings were already preparing to move against Hangzhou; as early as 1856 they were seen scouting the environs.[31]

In March of 1860, when Nanjing had been surrounded by the Southern Grand Battalion under the joint command of [Hešeri] Hechun (d. 1860) and Zhang Guoliang, the charismatic peasant general of the Taiping forces Li Xiucheng decided to attack Hangzhou, from which he knew the Southern Grand Battalion was being supplied. During the early months of 1860, Li had cut a swathe through southwestern Jiangsu, controlling Lake Wu in January and taking the strategic point Guangdezhou in early March, then passing on to Huzhou at the southern end of Lake Tai. He left his cousin, Li Shixian, to capture the town, and himself pushed on toward Hangzhou.[32] On the evening of March 11, leading a force of seven thousand men, he reached Hangzhou, which with his small force he hoped to harry just long enough to draw the troops of the Southern Grand Battalion away from Nanjing. He first moved through the suburbs, destroying the outlying guardposts and working round to a southerly advance on the city. The general-in-chief of the Hangzhou garrison, [Niohuru] Ruichang, dispatched two hundred men under command of his colonel Saishatu together with a unit of local militiamen to attempt to drive Li's raiders off, while ordering four hundred riflemen from Zhapu to Hangzhou to aid in the larger city's defense.[33]

The first major confrontation between Li Xiucheng and the Hangzhou forces occurred at Huochao Gate, on the city's southern perimeter, on March 17. Ruichang feared for the Qiantang and Wulin Gates on the lake side of the city, which he knew Li had reconnoitered soon after arriving in the Hangzhou locality; both gates gave onto dense northern sectors of the city and were dangerously close to the garrison, which Ruichang feared was Li's primary target. He ordered his brigade-general Laicun to take his units and secure the Wulin Gate, while Ruichang himself undertook to guard the Qiantang Gate, outside which the rebels were encamped on the night of March 17.[34] At dawn of the next day, the Taipings broke open several feet of wall and entered the city through Qingbo Gate, on West Lake and well to the south of the banner positions at Wulin and Qiantang. Militiamen charged with defending the city deserted their posts, allowed the Taipings through the remaining gates, and joined in the general pillage.[35] The townspeople were enraged. Even before the Taipings could enter in force the citizenry had turned on the militiamen, rushing from their houses to meet them in street fighting, then hunting down and sometimes lynching those who attempted to run.[36] Ruichang ordered the gates of the garrison quarter opened, and together with his brigades-general, the Manchu Laicun and the Mongol [Jahasu] Xilingga[37] of Zhapu (the latter of whom had accompanied his four hundred riflemen from the coastal garrison) led banner soldiers into the city proper to attempt to quell the rebellion of the militia and turn the Taipings back.

In the ensuing days the combat engulfed nearly every individual in the city. Townsmen were pressed into service by both sides, while Manchu women and girls were seen resisting the invaders with spears and short swords, and aiding in the defense of barricades by lighting mortar fuses.[38] The bannermen at Zhapu had not been attacked, and were able to supply grain and weapons to the Qing forces in some areas of northern Hangzhou via the canal, transported by a troop of boatmen from Ningbo. The southern portion of the city belonged to the Taipings, who attempted to tunnel under the interior walls that still prevented them from moving northward into the garrison. Li's small army made little progress, however, against the combined civilian, remaining militia and banner defenders. For six days the impasse endured. The time was long enough for Zhang Guoliang's younger brother Zhang Yuliang and a portion of the troops of the Southern Grand Battalion to arrive on March 24. Zhejiang governor Wang Youling and Ruichang, fearful that Zhang's forces harbored Taiping spies, hesitated to open the gates to him, but finally realized the hopelessness of doing without Zhang's aid.[39] Leaving Taiping flags waving from the ramparts to delude Zhang Yuliang into thinking that they still occupied a portion of the Hangzhou precincts, Li Xiucheng withdrew through Yongjin Gate on West Lake and set off for Anhui, whence he made his way back to Nanjing and handily beat off the remnant Southern Grand Battalion forces still encircling the Heavenly Capital. At length the troops of Zhang Yuliang entered Hangzhou, and upon discovering that its Taiping occupiers had gone, began to plunder for themselves what was left.[40]

The "defeat" of the Taipings was the subject of much self-congratulation by the Qing commanders involved, who continued to report sightings and exterminations of rebels in the Hangzhou region for weeks afterward. Ruichang for his service was awarded a second grade hereditary rank and would later be appointed temporary superintendant of the Southern Grand Batallion after the humiliation of Hechun at Suzhou; Laicun (who died later in the year) was made a "protecting hero" (*karman baturu*), while ranks and honors were distributed to many other officers from the Hangzhou and Zhapu garrisons.[41] The success in Zhejiang— which, it was not pointed out at the time, made possible Li Xiucheng's rout of Qing forces at Nanjing—was gained at grotesque cost to the residents of Hangzhou. The siege had been brief, by Taiping War standards, but bloody. Dai Xi, responsible for a portion of the local militia, had drowned himself together with Tang Yifen when he learned of the Taiping entry into the city. Officials estimated that in the first onslaught, between 60,000 and 100,000 people had died, something over 10 percent of the population. Of these, over 2,500 were bannermen and women, probably about 20 percent of the garrison population. Had the fighting actually reached the garrison quarter, the banner toll would undoubtedly have been much higher.[42] Sporadic raids by the Taipings continued in Jiangsu and Zhejiang through the fall and winter, and it was clear that the region was still at grave risk of Taiping assault.[43] Ruichang, probably on the basis of a sober assessment of the situation, made what must have seemed like the lavish request of two to three thousand troops from Peking as reinforcements. The request was denied. Governor Wang Youling began to work closely with Ruichang to raise local donations for the repair of the city walls and gates.[44] By the spring the intensity of Taiping raids in Jiangsu increased, and in late April of 1861 the Zhapu garrison was hit by the forces of Li Xiucheng's cousin Li Shixian, who was actually retreating from Anhui under pressure of the loyalist forces.

Fengrui's family were damaged severely in this surprise engagement. Xirui, as an active officer, had been harried since the December attack upon Hangzhou, when he had helped organize the supply operations along the canal and the coast. He had also been mobilized in defense of the eastern Zhejiang region all fall and winter, including boat patrols of the Qiantang and canals since the August 31, 1860 capture of nearby Pinghu, whose recovery by banner troops under Xilingga had been rapid but, again, costly. Before dawn on April 18, 1861, Xirui ordered Fengrui to assemble the family in "Dear Harmony Hall" at the family compound at Longchuo, and told them that the Zhapu garrison was being attacked; the colonels Guifu, Shende and Darana had been killed attempting to defend the western approaches to Zhapu, and it was clear that the city would soon come under full-scale assault.[45] He, Fengrui and Yunrui, who was now of service age, would have to report together with their cousin Boliang to the garrison to aid in its defense.[46] Dingrui and two young cousins who were in temporary residence at the estate, Wenrui and Binrui, were ordered to stay at home. Xirui mounted a horse and rode to the garrison, while Fengrui, Yunrui, and Boliang, who evidently had no horses and access to none, ran in the same direction. Yunrui was an enlisted man, and was enrolled in the same company as Xirui; Boliang, a junior officer, reported to his own unit while Fengrui reported to the company he had been assigned to as a clerk within the Bordered Yellow Banner. Their orders, Fengrui learned as he assembled with his company in the garrison's chaotic inner grounds, were to defend the northern gate, and Fengrui took up a command placard to display for the troops' information. It was at this moment, evidently, that the garrison brigade-general, Xilingga, rode across the compound toward the southern gate, with

Xirui close behind him. "My elder brother and I were so startled to see one another," Fengrui later wrote, "that we could not speak. But we understood that this was the final goodbye."

The word spread among the bannermen gathered in the middle of the garrison that the northern gate had been attacked. Fengrui ran with the crowd of bannermen to the northern gate where artillerymen under the command of Chinese-martial lieutenant Cheng Yunling were able to turn the invaders back. Then, again following the crowd, Fengrui ran toward the southern gate, where it was reported that a second attack was in progress. By the time he arrived, however, the southern gate had already been broken; Xilingga was ordering his vanguard to fall back to defend the inner garrison. Fengrui frantically asked the whereabouts of Xirui from the soldiers of Xilingga's units as they retreated, but he could only learn that the southern garrison had been lost while Xirui's company remained within it, battling the rebels. Fires broke out in the garrison as a result of Taiping shelling, and hopes for the defense of the garrison community dwindled quickly. Suddenly the inner garrison was vacated. Xilingga had turned and gone to his own house. The signal was understood by all. The brigade-general drowned his wife and children in a well, then with his elderly father and teenaged son led the family's servants back into the streets to fight. Other officers and soldiers were following suit; Fengrui's family in Longchuo was out of reach. The fighting and the chaos within the garrison lasted only a few hours, until the forces of the Southern Grand Battalion were able to surround the city and drive off the raiders.

Fengrui began to search for his kinsmen. Boliang was safe. In the vicinity of the south gate Fengrui found the bodies of Xirui and Yunrui; that of the older brother had been stabbed at least ten times, and witnesses assured Fengrui that even when hacked and bleeding profusely his brother had continued to fight the rebels relentlessly. His elderly cousins Guanji and Jingcheng were also dead within the garrison. When Fengrui returned to Dear Harmony Hall within the family compound at Longchuo, he found the bodies of the children Dingrui, Wenrui and Binrui; Dingrui had evidently drowned his two younger cousins in the goldfish pool, then poisoned himself.[47] Like the garrison community generally, Fengrui set about the task of burying and honoring the dead; a public funeral was held for Xilingga, who had finally been felled by a massive chest wound from a rifle blast, and for the military intendant Yinghui, whose body could not be identified, his cap and robe being buried in its place.[48] Fengrui and other garrison clerks shouldered the documentary task before the garrison, as once again it faced the necessity of identifying and justifying the dead.

The rebels continued to maintain a presence in the Hangzhou region throughout the winter of 1860–1861. In November they raided the guard station on Orphan Hill, and in December it was necessary for Gachun, the new brigade-general at Zhapu, to lead his "West Lake Water Forces" to use boats and rifles to cut off rebels attempting to cross Yudai Bridge into the south suburbs. At the same time, the regional defense forces were in decline, particularly after Zhang Yuliang was shot to death at Hangzhou on November 17.[49] In May of 1861 Li Xiucheng's cousin Li Shixian was decisively defeated by Zuo Zongtang in Jiangxi, and he retreated again toward Zhejiang. Under his command were approximately 100,000 troops, and his intention was to link up with Li Xiucheng—then commanding over 700,000 soldiers—in order to conquer the entire province. In late September the cousins were united, and it was decided that Li Xiucheng would lead the expedition north to Hangzhou. The next month the combined Taiping army closed in upon the city, taking up a strategic position outside the Wulin Gate, on the north of the city wall and with nearly direct access to the garrison. In middle October, the siege began. Li Xiucheng, mindful of the massacres of the Manchus that had followed the occupation of Nanjing, sent a message to Ruichang in which he attempted to assure the commander-in-chief that Manchu lives would be protected. His overtures were, however, rejected. Ruichang and Wang Youling had conferred together and determined to attempt to wait out the Taiping seige. Ruichang ordered the ten gates of Hangzhou city locked, which bought time for the civil authorities to plan the provisioning of Hangzhou from Shanghai in anticipation of a prolonged siege. Wang Youling himself sent a messenger to Shanghai to request aid from the foreign legations. More than a month later the Southern Grand Battalion arrived, as before, to repulse the invaders. This time it was they who were repulsed, a defeat that effectively marked the end of the Southern Grand Battalion.[50]

Like many others of the major engagements of the long Taiping War, the second battle of Hangzhou was as much a strategy of provisioning and logistics as of men and weapons. Wang's census at the time revealed that the normal Hangzhou population of about 600,000 had been swollen by refugees, soldiers and militiamen to 2.3 million. The fall of Shaoxing, Ningbo and other points of grain transport to Hangzhou in late October and early November cut off the last lines of supply, and attempts to move staples over water from Shanghai failed repeatedly.[51] In one notable cooperative effort worked out by Zeng Guofan, 20,000 piculs of rice and a quantity of firearms were secretly transported to Hangzhou by ship, but they were wholly insufficient to support the city.[52] After more than two months of siege—which was in effect a blockade—the food supplies of Hangzhou were completely exhausted, and Wang estimated that 30,000 to 40,000 had died at Hangzhou of starvation. The survivors were reported to be eating roots, dogs, horses, grass, leather and human flesh, the former of which at least one foreigner reported selling "at so much as a catty in the streets, or twopence per pound."[53]

Li Xiucheng's own supplies had run low, and he considered lifting the siege until informed of conditions inside Hangzhou by spies or by people driven out of the city by its officials. During the night of December 28 the Hangzhou militia guard again deserted, and in the early morning of the 29th the Taipings climbed the walls and opened the Huochao, Fengshan and Qingbo gates for themselves. Li Xiucheng stormed the outer city. Wang Youling hanged himself in his garden, and Li later buried him with honors.[54] The gates of the Manchu garrison remained locked. Ruichang once again rejected assurances—shot into the garrison on arrow shafts—that a slaughter of the Manchus was not imminent; in response to one entreaty Ruichang's marksmen opened fire, felling 1,100 Taipings. Li began a fervent propaganda campaign to persuade Ruichang to open the garrison gates. He claimed to have nothing against the Manchus, other than that they happened to be in the wrong place; the Taipings would be happy to let them go home again, and would even supply travelling money for them to "return to their own country."[55] Manchus and their property would be safe, Li averred, if Ruichang would only open the gates. Each time Li's offer was rejected. In an intense and very bloody forty-eight-hour assault, the Taipings finally succeeded in capturing the Hangzhou garrison, which was in the process of being entirely consumed by a fire that was probably of accidental origin. Ruichang, his brigade-general Guanfu who had just arrived from Xinjiang, and most of his officers died in the fighting. More than ten thousand men and women killed themselves as the garrison was lost.[56]

The campaign by loyalist and international forces for the reconquest of Jiangnan was on. The Southern Grand Battalion had been virtually dismantled, and hope for Qing control of the coast lay with the Anhui, or Huai Army, under the command of Li Hongzhang. Foreign advisors, foreign weapons and foreign guns had been incorporated into the effort by Li, who followed the paths pioneered by Zeng Guofan. In the aftermath of the attack on Zhapu both Fengrui and Boliang petitioned the court to allow them what in other times would have been an unusual favor: To put their hereditary banner status in abeyance long enough for them to join the irregular forces under Li Hongzhang for the suppression of the Taipings. Fengrui, who published a hasty necrology of those fallen in the defense of Zhapu, prefaced it with a memorial to the court in which he described the obliteration of his family. Possibly remembering the reaction to the claims of his father regarding the behavior of the bannermen in 1842, he was careful to make the obligatory comments regarding the tenacity of the troops, emphasizing that at the time of Xilingga's death in the April raid on Zhapu, "Those who were with him fought to the death, to the very last man, and none ran away."[57] He ended with his own brief but direct testament. "On account of this calamity I have lost my entire family, and I swear death to the rebels. I will kill rebels in Jiangnan until I die myself."[58]

Fengrui's decision should be placed rather precisely in the context of the times. The Xiang and Huai armies, although irregular in the manner of their command by civilian officials and in their uncharacteristic forms of command and remuneration, were nevertheless commissioned by the court, which kept itself closely apprised of their actions. They in no important sense shared in the autonomous character of the militia units upon which, paradoxically, they were based.[59] Moreover, bannermen had been prominent in the creation of the Grand Battalions, which had been the first of the irregular institutions deployed on a provincial basis against the British and against the Taipings. [Borjigit] Senggerinqin (d. 1865), a Mongolian prince, had overseen several innovations in military structure in his defeat of the Taipings' "northern expedition" in 1855 (one of his subordinates there had been Ruichang), and led the court's struggle against the Nian rebels until his assassination by them in 1865; Zeng Guofan and Li Hongzhang (1823–1901) later continued his campaigns. Hechun, as co-commander of the Southern Grand Battalion with Zhang Guoliang, had set a precedent, though not an unproblematic one, for Manchu roles in the growth of military structures superseding the Eight Banners. Dexinga, Tuominga and other Manchus had also played critical roles in the creation and command of the composite forces. Fengrui thus saw himself as willing to participate in an innovative force directed against the Taipings and fully sanctioned by the emperor. On the other hand, the request to be temporarily removed from the garrison duty carried with it a consciousness of stepping out of the glorified servitude to which as a Manchu Fengrui was destined, and from which he had no personal economic motive for being exempted; he now volunteered himself—a bannerman, poet, property owner and recluse—for what he saw as patriotic service. He was not unique. Within the Xiang Army, Dolungga (1817–1864), who eventually hunted down the Taiping leader Chen Yucheng, and [Tuorgiya] Tacibu (1817–1855), one of the most dramatic figures in the war against the Taipings, had already taken early roles as intermediaries between the traditional and the reorganized military.[60] After joining a unit of Li Hongzhang's Huai Army, Fengrui himself was assigned to a cavalry unit composed entirely of Manchu and Mongol volunteers, whose equestrian skills were considered to be more advanced than those of the Chinese irregulars.

Fengrui's unit was commanded by a Mongolian bannerman named

Hualianbu, who was given the rank of commander (*tongling*) by his Chinese superiors. Fengrui himself, whose horsemanship could have been serviceable at best, was made second in command (*bangling*). The unit was under the supervision of Li Hongzhang's younger brother Li Hezhang, whom the cavalrymen referred to as "Number Three" (*San daren*) since he was the third man in their command chain after Li Hongzhang and Xue Huan.[61] For some time Fengrui was on only distant terms with the younger Li. Number Three was not a dazzling commander, and often had trouble with his unit leaders breaking ranks and retreating without orders, leaving other troops to advance unsupported into the fray. Such violation of discipline, Fengrui was well aware, had once been punished among the banners by death, enslavement or exile. But for the new loyalist forces, such authoritarian policies were impracticable; wage delays and unpleasant encounters with Western mercenaries in the service of the court had the militiamen constantly on the verge of desertion or rebellion, and an officer of Number Three's rank could rarely punish disobedience swiftly or harshly. The battle of Hanshan, Henan, part of a northward push by the Taipings in early 1862, was a rout for the loyalist forces. As Hualianbu led the cavalry unit into the fight, his head was blown off by a cannon ball and hit Fengrui, riding by his side, squarely in the chest. The latter nevertheless continued riding forward, and when he later turned saw the loyalist forces leaving the field. At Fengrui's order the cavalrymen finally scrambled to retreat, too. After regrouping at the camp, Number Three convened a haranguing session in which he furiously demanded that the company leaders confess where they had stopped the attack and where they had withdrawn. Fengrui stood in for the dead Hualianbu, covered with the Mongolian commander's blood, and when he in turn was questioned said simply, "I did not retreat. I advanced." The younger Li, who could be excitable, was evidently impressed with the calmness of the Manchu *bangling*, and on the spot promoted him to Hualianbu's command.[62]

Fengrui did not stay a cavalry officer long; during the Shanghai campaigns in December 1862 he served as an aide to Li Hezhang (duties more closely resembling his clerk's job in the Zhapu garrison), and next distinguished himself as a sort of heroic bursar during the attempts by the Huai Army to recapture Taicang, Jiangsu province, in February of 1863. Taicang had become a sore point for the loyalists, who had lost it not once but twice to the Taipings, the second time in a poorly planned allied action that incited mutual recriminations between Li Hongzhang and his foreign commanders. Li was now in command of a multi-national force incorporating the "reorganized" Ever Victorious Army under the command of J. Y. Holland. But Li was in danger of losing control of his forces because he could not, or would not, distribute pay and rations to the troops. Henry Burgevine, the erstwhile commander of the EVA, had already brought the situation to crisis once in December by threatening to take his troops over to the Taipings if they were not paid; in the end Burgevine forcibly took the money from an unfortunate merchant in Shanghai, which led to the American's dismissal. In January of 1863, with the EVA remobilized under Holland, Li ordered Cheng Xueqi and Guo Songlin to begin the campaign for the recapture of Taicang.[63] The Taipings were at first inclined to surrender the city as they had other points in Jiangsu, but when reinforcements arrived led by Li Xiucheng, they determined to fight. On February 14 Fengrui joined the assault upon Taicang when Li Hezhang—Number Three—and Holland cooperatively led a force of over nine thousand men in an attack upon the city. They worked five hours with a battery of twenty-two cannons to make a breach in the wall; but when their troops entered the city, Taiping rifle fire felled nearly two thousand of their number, and the international army left off the attack. More than two months passed before they were able to recoup, during which Holland was forced out of command by threats of desertion from his mercenaries and Charles Gordon assumed his position.[64] The Taipings again indicated their willingness to surrender the city to Li Hezhang, but when he and Cheng Xueqi entered the city they were nearly killed by sniper fire.[65] In the meantime rations ran very low. Number Three was faced with the possibility of desertion by his troops. Aides, including Fengrui, were instructed to forage the locality for grain. By some means Fengrui made contact with a former grain merchant of his acquaintance, now dealing in the black market, named He Guoxian.[66] The latter was indebted to Fengrui, and through him Fengrui was able to lay hold of more than 100,000 taels, which he used to purchase supplies for the troops. Thus replenished, Li's forces went about the reconquest of Taicang; Fengrui was on his way to his only rank reward for his war service and He Guoxian was on his way to legal rehabilitation.[67] The loyalists finally managed to retake Taicang on May 2, part of the shift of momentum to the Qing forces in Jiangsu.

While the Huai Army and the EVA worked to dislodge the Taipings from Jiangsu and Anhui, Qing forces under Zuo Zongtang, the new governor of Zhejiang, were attempting to recapture Hangzhou. Zuo tried and failed many times to make headway into Li Xiucheng's territories in central Zhejiang; for most of 1862 his troops were debilitated by an epidemic, probably malaria.[68] In September of 1863 Zuo's troops engaged the Taipings at Mantou mountain, Fenghuang mountain, and the Leifeng pagoda, all within about a mile of the Wulin gate. Once they used mortar fire on the Fengshen Gate, destroying several feet of wall; but as they stepped through the breach into the city, a mob of Taiping defenders forced them back out again. At about the same time, banner troops from

Zhapu and Jinjiang began a long battle for Yuhang, north of Hangzhou, a battle that after nearly eight months would be decided in their favor.[69] A Franco-Chinese force under D'Aiquebelle arrived at Hangzhou in February of 1864 and encamped in the hills south of West Lake, planning a spring attack when reinforcements from Zuo would arrive. By early March a detachment of Zuo Zongtang's troops had in fact joined them, and the government finally decided to first make an assault upon Hangzhou from the water; on March 3, they began a month of bombardments that destroyed the Qiantang river bank defenses of the Taipings and a portion of the city wall; and on March 4 the land troops commenced their move on Hangzhou. Nearly a week later the loyalists succeeded in breaching the rebel battery at Qingbo Gate, but sharpshooters from within prevented them from entering the city. A second attempt was made on March 20, in which an officer and eight men were killed and six wounded.[70] Zuo Zongtang in the meantime cut off Taiping communications and supply lines to the north, and stationed himself at Haining. On midnight of March 30, 1864, the Taipings withdrew through the Wulin Gate, and a combined Chinese and French force entered and sacked the city.[71] An army under Zeng Guofan's younger brother Zeng Guoquan moved against Nanjing soon afterward, and the "Heavenly Capital" was retaken on July 19, 1864. The war against the Taipings was essentially concluded with the capture of Li Xiucheng in the autumn of the same year.

The death toll in the Taiping War has been estimated at 30 million, most from disease and starvation. Whole sections of the country were depopulated in the fourteen-year war, and many areas had not experienced an agricultural recovery even by the turn of the twentieth century. But the war was also the foundation upon which the late Qing political structure was built. Not since the conquest of China in the seventeenth century had so many men of modest background had new opportunities to lay the foundation for bureaucratic careers. When the last of the Taipings were suppressed in 1864, the commanders and sub-commanders of the loyalist forces found degrees and appointments showered upon them. Fengrui himself was granted an honorary provincial degree (*juren*) and offered a magistracy, like his good friend Number Three.[72] Unlike Number Three, Fengrui declined the offer. He professed no desire for further government service, and may have been rather cynical about the pattern of rewards; he often said afterward that glory for the effort had been appropriated by the higher-ranking commanders, particularly Li Hongzhang, who Fengrui felt had exploited Number Three's achievements for his own benefit.[73] He may also have sensed that, despite his special pleading for the recognition and rewarding of bannermen who had aided in the loyalist effort, the coming era was not to be one in which Manchus would prosper. New military forms had proven their merit, and the crushing expense of the maintenance of the garrisons was not likely to be a burden the emperors would be willing to bear much longer. Some communities, like that at Nanjing, would never reappear. Others, like those at Hangzhou and Zhapu, had been physically destroyed, though a malnourished and dispirited community remained. Fengrui returned to Hangzhou expecting to have little leisure to contemplate any ambitions beyond rebuilding his business, his home and his family. To his Chinese comrades, his rejection of the court's rewards seemed strange, even heroic. At Number Three's request, Li Hongzhang later wrote a poem for Fengrui, which he prefaced with the observation, "In Jiangnan they have somebody of outstanding character: He killed rebels all over, swearing to continue to the death, and when he had accomplished his service, he suddenly gave up his posts and returned to his home—such a very extraordinary fellow surprises me greatly."[74]

The Enclave of Gods and Ghosts

Fengrui spent the rest of his life in awe of his survival of the Taiping attack on Zhapu and of his war to "kill rebels all over Jiangnan." He might have marvelled equally at the ability of the Qing regime to muddle on indefinitely after the shattering of its economy and much of its society in the internal and external conflicts of the middle nineteenth century. The Taiping Rebellion may have been the only real threat to the survival of the dynasty in the middle nineteenth century, but the magnitude of that menace was due to the multitude of other pressures on the government, both from within and without. Since the seventeenth century, there had been very few and very brief periods of near total peace; even the glory days of Qianlong had been marked by large military expenditures for the consolidation of Qing control over Xinjiang and the pacification of perennially festering minority rebellions in the interior of the country. But from the White Lotus Rebellion of 1796 to 1804 the appearance of large, challenging disturbances accelerated; the Eight Trigrams of 1813, the Yao rebellions of 1836 to 1849, the Taipings from 1850 to 1864 (1866 if one considers the action against rebel holdouts in Fujian), the Nian (1853–1868), the Miao (1854–1872), the Muslim rebellions in Shanxi, Gansu (1863–1873) and in Xinjiang (1862–1878) presented a nearly overwhelming aggregate challenge to a government whose traditional military resources had proved inadequate long before and whose financial reserves were exhausted.

Nor was this the full extent of Qing worries in these years. British impatience with the intransigence of Guangdong governor Ye Mingchen, who was as good at keeping the British out of Canton as he had been at keeping the Taipings out from 1850 to 1852, was wearing thin, and the Chinese arrest in 1856 of the Chinese crew of the lorcha *Arrow*, flying the British flag, was seized upon as an occasion to renew hostilities. Very early in 1857 an allied Anglo-French force captured Canton, deported Ye to Calcutta (where he died the next year), sailed north to Dagu near Tianjin, and by April was demanding negotiations of the Chinese. The Treaty of Tientsin, signed with Britain, France, Russia and the United States, called for the opening of ten new treaty ports, a four-million-tael indemnity to be paid to Britain and a two-million-tael indemnity to be paid to France; the Chinese were mute about the fact that the British had installed a governor of their own liking in Canton and virtually governed the city until 1861. Britain continued to insist upon full diplomatic exchange. In June of 1859 when Sir Frederick Bruce attempted to proceed through Dagu to Peking, his group was fired upon by Senggerinqin's troops and seriously damaged. Brimming with premature confidence, the Xianfeng court abrogated all provisions of the Treaty of Tientsin except for the American version, which demanded no diplomatic representation, no freedom of travel for foreigners or foreign ships, and no indemnity. In response an Anglo-French force of more than two hundred ships carrying more than 20,000 troops descended upon Dagu; in their attempt to resist, the troops there accidentally exploded their own powder magazine, and the fort was to all purposes destroyed. The foreign allied force continued on to Peking, where they burnt and sacked the emperor's Summer Palace (*Yuanming yuan*), and Yizhu fled to Rihe. The Qing government agreed to the Treaty of Peking: The mainland facing Hong Kong island was ceded to Britain, British textiles were exempted from customs duties, foreign ships were allowed unlimited access to Chinese waterways, and the Chinese government was saddled with a new 16-million-tael indemnity. The inability of the Chinese government to pay such an indemnity contributed to the impetus behind the creation of a synarchic maritime customs agency to aid in the reorganization of Qing finances and to allow direct foreign management of a portion of the revenues.

The survival of the government in such extraordinary times was testament to the improbable durability of the Qing regime. This resilience was due in part to a happy ability to approximate the interests of foreign powers, which led the West to intercede on behalf of the Qing against the rebels when it finally seemed necessary to do so; the Taipings had failed after a time to secure the confidence of the West in regard to their ability to rule the country and to live up to existing treaty obligations. Britain and France contributed to the anti-Taiping effort, particularly after the conclusion of their own hostilities with China in the Treaty of Peking, and after the civil war their relationship with the Qing bloomed into the "period of cooperation." The Western powers involved in China cooperated with each other, or purported to, and seemed to aid in China's self-strengthening movement, which proceeded apace after the war under the guidance of court statesmen and provincial governors. Technological advisors and language teachers were supplied by Britain, France and the United States, while Westerners such as Thomas Wade, S. Wells Williams, Anson Burlingame and Sir Robert Hart became functionaries of the Chinese government and worked very effectively to safeguard Chinese interests in the critical post-war period; indeed Lord Elgin, his younger brother Frederick Bruce and Rutherford Alcock were accused by their fellow nationals of amalgamating British and Chinese interests in the diplomacy they shaped in the late 1860s and 1870s.[75]

A second element in the resilience of the Qing government in the middle nineteenth century was the ability of a new stratum of leadership to reconstitute the court after the death of the Xianfeng emperor Yizhu, in 1861. In retrospect Yizhu must be credited with a willingness to give greater authority to those who demonstrated their abilities to be successful in the war against the Taipings, regardless of their background or status. When funds ran so low that salaries and basic military needs could not be met in 1853, he forced the Peking elite (particularly Mujangga, for whom he had a very remarkable dislike) to subsidize the treasury. The daily need to develop and reinforce reliable methods of reconquest and defense created new power classes both at the local and capital levels, while the bankruptcy of the central government led the court to devalue traditional symbols of elite status, indulging on a massive scale in the ancient but once circumscribed practice of selling bureaucratic degrees. In the provinces, new patterns of power and wealth emerged. At court, on the other hand, the last years of the 1850s saw the emergence of a powerful faction under the leadership of [Aisin Gioro] Sushun and [Aisin Gioro] Zaiyuan. When Yizhu died at Rihe in 1861, his only son Zaichun, aged five, was named as the Tongzhi (1862–1874) emperor, and Sushun headed the regency that oversaw the government. But Yizhu's widow Xiaozhen, and Xiaoqin, the mother of the infant emperor, were wary of Sushun's group and by the end of the year had, in cooperation with Yizhu's younger brothers Yixin (1833–1898)—Prince Gong, the sixth son of Minning—and Yihuan (1840–1891)—Prince Chun, the seventh son of Minning, overthrown the regency and had Sushun executed.

During the 1860s, the empresses allowed foreign and internal affairs to be managed by Yixin and [Suwan Gūwalgiya] Wenxiang, the most liberal forces at court, and under them the preeminent power Zeng Guofan had achieved during the war was institutionalized. He was the first Chinese to be enfeoffed by the throne, and in 1870 was made Northern Intendant (*Beiyang dachen*) at Tianjin, the incipient stage in the development of an independent power zone which at his death in 1872 he passed on to Li

Hongzhang. Partly thanks to the patronage of Zeng, Li, Zuo Zongtang, Hu Linyi and Luo Bingzhang, a new generation of provincial governors arose that included Zhang Zhidong and Sheng Xuanhuai. In their industrial, communications and educational projects they routinely sought the imprimatur of the court, and thanks to the efforts of the progressive party that included Wenxiang, Yixin, Yihuan and Hengqi (1802–1867), usually received it.

The man regarded as the most able of the post-war statesmen was [Suwan Gūwalgiya] Wenxiang (1818–1875), a ninth-generation descendant of Fiongdon who was born and raised in the Northeast.[76] It is worth considering for a moment why Wenxiang, the most famous and best regarded court bureaucrat of his day, often appears as only a minor figure in modern narratives of the later nineteenth century. The most obvious reason is a matter of circumstance. Wenxiang was partially incapacitated by a stroke in 1870, at the age of fifty-two, and died on the eve of the accession of the Guangxu (1875–1908) emperor; thereafter, the absence of leadership such as Wenxiang's contributed to the rapid accumulation of power in the hands of the Dowager Empress Xiaoqin. A more fundamental reason may be his association with the central government. The profoundest impact of the Taiping War was its role in catalyzing the shift in political and economic development away from Peking and toward the regions under the control of the great governors of the period. Yet the Western nations attempting to restructure relations with China continued to view Peking as the point of central authority, and it is certainly true that the decisive loss of control by Peking was still decades in the future. Another factor is Wenxiang's association with failed institutions, most notably the new Foreign Office (*zongli yamen*), the Foreign Language College (*Tongwen guan*) and Peking Field Force (*Shenji ying*).[77] The nominal head of the first two, Yixin (Prince Gong) got the lion's share of credit for the creation of and blame for the ultimate failure of these innovations, though the contemporary record indicates that the most dynamic role in both belonged to Wenxiang. A final factor is that as a Manchu he has often been considered by historians as backwash; the wave of the future, our retrospective wisdom often goes, was actually Zeng Guofan and the governors he trained to exercise personal control over large portions of the country. In fact, Wenxiang represented the role played by the Manchus as the pivot upon which the early self-strengthening movement turned. He was also the progenitor of a progressive Manchu leadership that remained active and developing to the end of the century.

Despite his illustrious ancestor, Wenxiang was not a member of the nobility. Nevertheless he could hardly have come from a destitute household; he received the national degree in 1844 and purchased a berth in the lower Peking bureaucracy, a frequent enough practice in the period after the Opium War and even more common thereafter. He distinguished himself in the eyes of the Xianfeng emperor who was looking for new talent, because of his calmness in the face of general panic. In 1853 and again in 1858, when the capital feared invasion first by the Taipings and then by the British and French, Wenxiang did not join the general exodus from Peking but remained at his post, cool and regularly communicating to the court his various suggestions for restoration of public confidence. Together with Yixin and [Hada Gūwalgiya] Guiliang, Wenxiang was sent to negotiate the Treaty of Peking. The impression he made upon the foreign representatives, particularly Thomas Wade who became a great admirer, was vivid. Wade claimed he had "never encountered a more powerful intellect," and others described Wenxiang as the most able, most advanced, most patriotic, most prepossessing in appearance, most honest, most modest, or simply best man in China. [78]

The foreign appraisal of Wenxiang is perhaps no surprise. Foreign visitors and scholars of the nineteenth century approved of the relatively high rate of bannerman interest in Christianity (and Christian charity), and were often sympathetic to Manchus, whom they regarded as being rather like themselves in appearance, unencumbered by such unfathomable customs as the binding of women's feet, having had the good sense to use a phonetic script in the writing of their language (which many Westerners learned as an aid to learning Chinese), free of the purported Chinese inclinations to circumlocution and deception, and retaining (at least in the noble class) "an expression of force and energy, the signs of which can still be met in Manchu, but never in Chinese, faces."[79] The English, proclaimed Thomas Meadows while advocating foreign study of the Manchu language, had now encountered the Manchus "both as foes and as friends, and found [them] by no means despicable in either character."[80] The nineteenth-century West accepted—perhaps even applauded—the efficiency and ruthlessness of the Manchu conquest of China two centuries before, and regretted only whatever emasculation the Manchus' ascribed racial character might have suffered as a consequence of their submersion in China. Such an appraisal, it should be obvious, has as much or more to do with Western denigration of the Chinese as it had to do with their actual knowledge of the Manchus. In the Manchu difficulties in guiding the Chinese and in the evident dangers under which the Manchu people continued their habitation of the country, many Western observers saw a mirror of their own frustrations in dealing with a people they regarded as greedy, insular, arrogant, ignorant, and xenophobic.

Wenxiang was often praised and rarely criticized by those in China as well. But it did occasionally happen that he would be an object of criticism, particularly by the conservative party led by the Mongol [Uqigeri]

Woren (d. 1871), which opposed virtually every reform advocated or enacted by Wenxiang, Yixin, Guiliang or Hengqi. Wenxiang, the group contended, was a traitor in Qing garb, who pandered to the ambitions of the West while pretending to protect the national interests. In actuality, Wenxiang was not enthusiastic about foreigners, even when he worked hard to create joint policies with them. In a frank moment he is reported to have told Robert Hart that the empire would gladly recompense all the revenue created by the Imperial Maritime Customs Service under Hart's control if the British would only go home and leave China in peace.[81] Cooperation was to him a painful necessity in a period of transition from the ruinous warfare of the last twenty years to a period in which a militarily strong and financially sound China would be able to hold her own against the agressive nations who were surrounding her. But his willed openness to limited foreign ideas and practices did not spare him criticism from their quarter either. However impressed foreign envoys may have been with Wenxiang's personal qualities, they were never moved to see him as anything other than a reactionary and an obstructionist.[82] Thomas Wade, probably to serve his own interpretation of events, claimed that the massacre at Tianjin of thirteen foreigners by a furious crowd in 1870 had been the result of Wenxiang's "thirsting for revenge" because of Western rejection of his attempts at treaty revision in the Alcock Convention of 1869.[83]

Whether or not Wenxiang thirsted for revenge in 1870, he was acute enough to see, as the leaders of Meiji Japan saw, that treaty revision was an indispensable component in restructuring Sino-Western relations, though his attempts to achieve equality in the treaties were all unsuccessful. The Foreign Affairs Office (zongli yamen) was authorized in 1861 and opened its doors in 1862. It was a forced provision of the Treaty of Peking—fulfillment of Western demands that the Chinese create a foreign office to handle diplomatic affairs on the Western model, and not as part of the traditional border management process. In its early period, the institution was almost exclusively staffed by Manchus. It is possible that the court was more trusting of the Manchu elite than of the Chinese, upon whom its new dependence in the aftermath of the Taiping War was perhaps seen as a liability. But it was also true that Yixin and Wenxiang, in particular, represented an emerging, talented, reform-bent element of the Manchu elite; even if other alternatives had been available, the emperor could have done far worse than to appeal to this group to create the institutions now imposed upon China by circumstance and by treaty.

As a corollary of his position at the Foreign Office, Wenxiang was concurrently appointed overseer of the Foreign Language College (Tongwen guan). The association with the Foreign Office gave a superficially novel and professional aura to the school. It was originally commissioned to administer instruction in English, but by the end of the century French, German and Japanese would be added, and the old Russian school in the Imperial City had been absorbed and reformed by the Foreign Language College. An expanded curriculum ultimately included mathematics, astronomy, and chemistry, so that the Foreign Language College and its provincial branches took on the appearance of the forerunners of the modern university in China.[84] But languages, mathematics and astronomy had also been customary subjects of instruction in the Eight Banners officers' schools, and it is not surprising that the Foreign Language College has been seen as an extension of the banner school tradition.[85] The ultimate authority for the colleges resided with the generals-in-chief (*jiangjun*) of their respective regions. Administrators were officers of colonel (*xieling*) and lieutenant (*fangyu*) rank from the garrisons, and language teachers were foreigners recruited by the Foreign Affairs Office, closely watched for any signs of religious proselytizing. Students for the early colleges were all bannermen, and though Chinese were admitted in small numbers for a short time, the policy was eventually changed to again allow only bannermen to enroll. They were paid stipends, as they were in the banner schools, and assigned proportionately to the languages to be studied.

The choice of Manchus as students in these colleges was logically elegant, and the progressive aims of the institutions were not irreconcilable with their intimate banner ties. The traditions of banner education, in which the study of at least documentary Manchu was emphasized along with Chinese, guaranteed that the students would have some experience with language learning, and a few might even have some talent for it; indeed certain banner schools began to add instruction in European languages to their curricula in imitation of the Foreign Language Colleges and perhaps as defense against the possible loss of students to the new schools.[86] At the same time, recruitment of bannermen appeared to guarantee a stable enrollment. For the period in which Chinese were allowed to attend the college, it was claimed that problems developed with students who would learn enough English to make a good living as a translator or comprador in one or another of the treaty ports, and then leave the program. Poor bannermen, on the other hand, in the 1860s were still largely people without a place to go, who could be counted on to complete their studies in the hope of receiving a comfortable bureaucratic assignment. The colleges were shaped to a certain extent by the hope of preparing bannermen for the new opportunities being envisioned by Wenxiang and his colleagues; armaments factories, in particular, hired graduates to oversee some of their operations in the 1890s. Finally, the prospect of opening up a new opportunity for bannermen helped in a very small way to alleviate the sharpened distress of the Manchus in the later nineteenth century. Indeed banner officials became more jealous of diplomatic studentships and appointments for bannermen in the ensuing years; Wenxiang may well have appreciated the possibilities of creating a diplomatic bureaucracy of bannermen, as the sometime military slaves of the empire would become its diplomatic slaves.

In addition, Wenxiang took primary responsibility for military reforms. At the conclusion of the war against the Taipings in 1865 he was appointed head of the Peking gendarmerie, and as a military man he distinguished himself as much as he had in civil roles up to that time. He personally created and drilled an elite modern fighting force, the Peking Field Force, and led it in the quelling of an inchoate bandit problem in the Northeast. Though in time a very small number of civilians would be admitted to the administrative and technical departments of the Peking Field Force, it was primarily reserved for bannermen, on the 2:1:1 Manchu/Mongol/ Chinese-martial ratio that characterized banner officer appointment policies after the eighteenth century.[87] Wenxiang, having dramatically demonstrated the efficacy of his proposed military reforms with the defeat of 30,000 local rebels by his 2,500 troops,[88] argued that in future a well-trained, well-armed, comparatively small number of bannermen would suffice for the empire's defensive needs. His thinking was parallelled by other counselors of the time; Robert Hart, for instance, suggested in 1865 that an army of 90,000 would suffice.[89]

Few of Wenxiang's proposed reforms for self-strengthening or modernization were ultimately successful. The factors in the defeat of his programs are instructive. The Foreign Affairs Office, though serviceable in time as a communications and information bureau, never became an instrument through which China was able to pursue her own interests in her interaction with foreign powers; the major change it effected in China's foreign relations was that its overseers were and remained strong proponents of adherence to the provisions of treaties from the Treaty of Peking onward. Lawful treaty revision remained quite outside the scope of the Foreign Affairs Office's powers, despite Wenxiang's attempts to pursue it. Instruction at the Foreign Language Colleges, meanwhile, was not effective, and the Foreign Affairs Office did not expand rapidly enough to absorb the graduates; as the foundation of a new professional role for Manchus and as a hope for a new livelihood for the students individually, the colleges were a disappointment, and their failure only led to greater problems in the recruitment and retention of students.

Military reforms, upon which turned so much of the self-strengthening programs, were also overwhelmed by the inability to integrate developments in such a way that innovative institutions might reinforce each other rather than impede each other. Technologically it was impossible, regardless of the measures that China might have taken, to bridge the gap with the West. Even as the Chinese attempted the manufacture and utilization of more "modern" weapons, the West was undergoing its technological leap as the result of the the Crimean War and American Civil War. The court was wary of the rapid or careless dissemination of technological information among the troops outside the Eight Banners or the Peking Field Force. Percussion caps, for instance, had been introduced before the end of the Taiping War, and their use was intended to prevent the tragedies of accidental self-combustion that resulted from the use of wick-fired matchlocks. Only banner officers, however, were allowed to know the production technique; and they were so jealous of the privilege that they unsuccessfully petitioned the court to coin a secret Manchu word for "percussion cap."[90] In the small factories they oversaw they were regarded by their Chinese workmen as having been taught the skill "by the devil."[91] The secrecy contributed to many irregularities in application of the technology; the caps were unreliable, and the technology failed until breech-loading rifles were produced in the armories founded by the provincial governors in the 1880s.

But better rifles did not significantly improve military performance. Ever since the founding of the Green Standard Armies it had been the policy in non-banner units that all artillery and rifles be kept in a locked arsenal, and soldiers selected a weapon anew each time its use was called for; drills could consist of soldiers lining up and firing a single rifle, one after another. Given the irregularities that often entered into the manufacture of rifles even in the late nineteenth and twentieth centuries, the policy was disastrous. Soldiers often did not know how to load or fire the weapons they were issued on any particular day, and could not adjust to the peculiarities of individual weapons. Probably with reason, the court was unwilling to allow the mercenaries and militia troops that had formed in the years of the Taiping War to maintain weapons. As a consequence, its demands for technological expertise and manpower in the 1860s fell disproportionately upon the Manchus in a fraction of whom the court may have felt some real confidence in light of the fighting spirit shown at Zhapu in 1842, the tenacity of many bannermen in their struggle against the Taipings and against the Russians in the Northeast, and the reportedly swift and decisive success of Wenxiang in his suppression of the disorders in the Northeast. But the court was unwilling to make its financial and political support for the Manchus commensurate with its hope for them in the military and diplomatic realms. Just as, in the Tongzhi years, more opportunities seemed to open for Manchus, the Manchus themselves were finding it necessary to actually forsake banner registration in order to be physically safer and economically more secure. Of those who remained, few in the 1860s and 1870s possessed the elementary education necessary to take advantage of the new roles offered. With time, those opportunities faded away for all but a very select stratum of Manchus, as the momentum for development moved away from the court to the provinces.

The specific conditions of Manchu life in the 1860s and 1870s are difficult to generalize about; for years after the retaking of Nanjing in 1864 the Jiangnan Manchus, particularly, were in transit and in conflict, unsure whether to return to their garrisons and to the life they had lived there before the Taiping War. Only a minority of bannermen throughout the nation's garrisons understood the implications of Wenxiang's reforms and the new opportunities the Foreign Language Colleges and the Foreign Affairs Office seemed to promise. Most were more directly affected by what appeared to be a ruthless policy of alienation which, they may or may not have known, was also designed in part by Wenxiang. In 1852 the sale of banner land to Chinese was legalized everywhere in the empire except for the Northeast. The policy was suspended between 1859 and 1863, but remained in place thereafter; even the Northeast was included in the provision after 1905. The long term result would be the aggregate loss of nearly 80 percent of banner lands by the turn of the century.[92] In 1860, the court began selective discontinuation of stipends and grants to garrison officers. At the same time, the banner administration began to reform registration procedures in an attempt to ascertain the actual number of people, and their respective statuses, within the garrison.

By law, population figures were supposed to be revised every three years, but from the earliest period after the conquest it was well-known that corruption and incompetence had made the figures unreliable. The rules prescribing the reporting of children over one month of age to the company captains (zuoling), boys of the age of ten to the banner commanders (dutong), and adolescent males of service age to the captains were reinforced by the requirement that all registration papers be signed by the captain, the banner lieutenant (xiaoqi xiao) and the recording corporal (lingcui), after which the documents were to be bound by the corporal, affixed with the seal of the banner commander and forwarded to the Board of War. Yet this system of mutual guarantees was not considered adequate to ensure accurate reporting of the garrison census, and spies were sent out by the court to observe the population, the records, and the activities of the garrison officers responsible for the birth and age reports. Concurrently, it was determined that the only real measure to prevent over-reporting was to remove the incentive. Beginning in 1862, the normal banner stipend was lowered to whatever was deemed necessary to support only a man and one wife (the absolute amount varied according to local prices); children received no support at all until boys reached the age of ten, at which time they would become eligible for the plentiful (but not generous) cadet stipends.[93] The long-standing poverty of the bannermen quickly turned to desperation, as it was reported that the populations first pawned everything they owned to buy food, and when even these funds ran out they walked the streets with "clothing worn thin, shoes shredded away, and their bodies in much the same condition as their attire."[94] Hunger drove adults and children out of the garrisons into the countryside in search of food, and after the first frost many died in the cold night temperatures. By 1864 the government was willing to admit its inability to arm or support the bannermen, and allowed garrison residents to apply directly to the central government for permission to enter trades while retaining their registration; within a few years, bannermen and former bannermen would be found in carpentry, weaving, pottery, mechanics and many other skilled trades.

Bannermen—or more precisely that portion of the banner officer population who remained comfortable on the returns of land and commercial investments—were also found as managers and investors in government enterprises. In 1864 selected bannermen were sent to Suzhou to study foreign armaments, including machines and machine tools. In 1866 [Wanggiya] Chonghou (1826–1893) was commissioned by the court to open a machine tool factory in Tianjin—this is what took him to that city, where he later was shot at by M. Fontanier in the imbroglio that led to the "Tientsin Massacre" of 1870—and took along a cohort of bannermen to be his students and managers; Wu Dahui at Jilin did the same in 1881, as did Yihuan at Peking in 1883.[95] Those who participated in these and other approved projects, it should be noted, remained bannermen in every legal sense. It is a fair estimate that on the eve of the revolution that destroyed the empire in 1911/12, one of every twenty registered bannermen was still attempting to support himself as a soldier. Others who had not entered the skilled trades or the government armories were tenant farmers, day laborers, noodle vendors, entertainers, teachers or independent small business owners.[96] Throughout China, economic circumstances were harsh, and unemployment was a problem in a period when prolonged, widespread warfare had destroyed so much agricultural land and so many sites of industry in the cities. Many bannermen turned readily to labor and factory work when it was available, but in China proper the resources for reconstruction were still limited and the opportunities did not meet the real needs of the garrison populations. The effect was to attenuate the few resources remaining to the banner population generally, while creating limited opportunities in which a comparative few (many of whom were already well off) might prosper.

In other ways the court continued cutting the ribbons that had bound the Manchu communities to it. The traditional concern with the written Manchu language was abandoned with the 1862 decree abolishing the former requirement that banner degree candidates translate portions of the Chinese classics into Manchu. The differential legal treatment to which they had once been subjected was partially rescinded. They could now live as common people, requesting residence in the region of their choice and employment in civil professions; offenses would be dealt with as severely as they would for the common Chinese. As institutions, of course, the banners survived, and the legal and cultural impediments to intermarriage with the Chinese remained. The result, however, was to foment a crisis of affiliation, in which some bannermen left the garrisons and to all intents after a generation were no longer Manchu, others left the garrisons but retained banner registration and Manchu identity, and others remained in the garrisons, on the rolls, and firmly Manchu—the choice, in practice, was left to the individual.

Government motivations on this point have been probed.[97] The most penetrating and comprehensive interpretation has been that of Mary Wright, who explained the policies in terms of the identification of the Qing court with Confucian values. The Manchus as a people and the Manchu traditions they represented were, according to her thesis, no longer of great importance; and in any case the sinicization of the Manchus had progressed so far as to make indiscernable any signficant differences that might really exist between Manchus and Chinese. Other interpretations might be described as having a political foundation, asserting that the government was so dependent upon the support of the Chinese provincial governors and the foreign synarchists that it was actually anxious to dissociate itself from the bannermen. Certainly, any treatment of government objectives in offering the Manchus freedom from immuration must consider the economic crisis in which the government was perpetually embroiled in the middle nineteenth century, when troubles were magnified by the government policy of minting money to meet its war expenses. The Taiping War ended with a million soldiers on the Qing service rolls, of whom only a fraction could be confirmed to exist or to have participated in campaigns. Over half that number were putative bannermen. Wenxiang was one of many in the government who felt that a fundamental priority must be rapid demobilization and derollment of the troops on record, on a literal scale of 10 to 1. He feared violence from the irregulars, particularly, under Zeng's control, and it was probably for this reason that the Xiang Army units were permitted to remain partially intact following the conclusion of the war. The bannermen, he knew, would be violent, too, as they had been in the past when unhappy over their economic situation. But all in all the threat posed by unfed, insecure Manchus in their scattered communities could hardly be weighed against that of concentrated mercenary forces, many of whom had themselves quite a history of rebellious and anti-social behavior. In short the Manchus were the biggest expense—the mercenaries were supported by the *lijin* and other indirect revenues—and may have represented the easiest strike-off for the government's financial managers. There were also secondary financial benefits to the legal dissolution of the communities. Banner land, which in China proper was tax exempt, would become taxable at the moment it was sold; this was indeed one of the earliest of the reform provisions, and in accord with the government's expectations banner land sold briskly. These were powerful arguments, regardless of Wenxiang's opinion of the cultural and social condition of the bannermen themselves.

The motivations of the Manchus in making the various choices they made are much more difficult to understand if we accept Wright's thesis that in this period all barriers between Chinese and Manchus were artificial and that the government was only legislating in response to its self-identification with all things Confucian (which should not be taken as identical with "Chinese"). With legal privileges stripped away, the garrisons without the financial support they had enjoyed in the past, the special relationship to the court all but disowned, it would seem improbable that bannermen would continue to adhere to their banner status. Yet a majority, particularly in Peking and North China, did. The possible explanations are numerous. Inertia, a fear of change, an uncertainty about the likelihood of competing with the Chinese for a living may all have been significant factors. But it is also possible that individual factors were less important than the fact that circumstances of the preceding two centuries had molded the garrisons into communities with an internal coherence that was no longer dependent upon the sponsorship of the court.

Certainly, under the legal and economic conditions of the time Fengrui was one of those who would have had many opportunities, indeed incentives, for severing his ties there and beginning life under new circumstances. His family had been nearly destroyed in the Taiping onslaught of Zhapu, and he had little in the way of attachments to keep him there. At the time he returned to the garrison, he had not yet married, and had no reason to give consideration to family circumstances of a wife or children. Moreover, whatever remnant salary he might have drawn from his banner registration was neglible compared to what he was soon earning from his business and his rented land. Yet he seems to have given little thought to the possibility of not returning to the Hangzhou garrisons. When first demobilized Fengrui went first to Shanghai, like hundreds of thousands of other refugees and soldiers. There the problem of homeless and starving people, refugees from the fighting, was particularly pressing; the city's continuing problems in absorbing those displaced by the warfare were now compounded by an influx of demobilized soldiers. Fengrui worked with other Huai Army veterans to set up a charitable dispensary, distributing food and clothing, and arranging temporary lodging until the refugees could be returned to their home districts. He also petitioned the court to give special recognition to the bannermen who had volunteered to serve in the irregular forces. Specifically he advocated the speedy return of demobilized bannermen to their home garrisons, where they should be rewarded with positions of responsibility.[98]

When he returned to his own home a few months later, he found terrible devastation in Zhapu and Hangzhou. Both cities had been sacked by defenders, sacked by invaders, sacked by liberators. Dead bannermen and their families from Hangzhou and Zhapu had been buried in mass graves; it was years later that Fengrui began to attempt a complete necrology of those who had perished from the two garrisons.[99] In his house at Longchuo, he found that his father's books, many of which had been painstakingly acquired in Sichuan, and the few volumes that had belonged to Jalangga had all been destroyed. The woodblocks that had been used for the printing business, including the prototypes, were gone; throughout China, the literary loss as a result of the Taiping War was incalculable and unrecoverable.[100] The Hangzhou garrison community—fewer than two thousand individuals, returned from various regions to which they had fled in 1861—began to rebuild, mostly on the basis of charitable contributions from financially capable Manchus, like Fengrui, and from a small number of sympathetic literati in the West Lake area. Under the general-in-chief Liancheng,[101] the Qiantang Gate was repaired; the General-in-chief's Residence was partially restored, together with the Meiqing Academy and the Guan Di Temple within its grounds. New temples were built (with government compensation grants), in the "Twin Wells" (shuangjing) section of the garrison, to the bannermen who had died during the sieges of the city.[102]

Hangzhou and other parts of Zhejiang were noteworthy as places scarred to an extreme extent by the prolonged violence of the Taiping War. The legendary overcrowding of the West Lake and surrounding regions dissipated in the criss-crossing campaigns, and for decades afterward the Hangzhou delta was an invitation to peasants who had been crowded off their ancestral plots elsewhere or were simply in search of fertile ground. Labor, particularly skilled labor, remained under demand in the region. For all that, economic recovery was stalled. Tenancy and ownership practices did not smooth the way for immigrants, Shanghai lured away much of the development capital that was available, and whole areas of northern Zhejiang remained overgrown and impassable. The truth, which was not grasped by many who saw only new opportunities for expansion in the depopulation of portions of Jiangnan, was that most of the major cities, including Hangzhou and Nanjing, were not going to recover, but would settle into permanent subordination to Shanghai and other centers of development in the post-Taiping age.[103] For the moment Zhejiang was expected, like the country at large, to reconstruct itself on the basis of the financial reserves and organizational energies of its officials, property owners and merchants.[104]

By 1870 West Lake elites had turned their attention to the wrecked Wenlan Palace, a fact basic to Fengrui's ability to establish himself in Hangzhou. The shuttered upper floors were gutted and open to the elements, its collections either burned or rotted. Zeng Guofan, who was now the governor-general of Jiangxi and Jiangsu, had issued regulations in 1864 for printing offices to be established at Nanjing, Suzhou, Yangzhou, Wuchang and Hangzhou in order to attempt a recovery of the literary losses of the lower Yangzi region; his demobilized officers were employed as proofreaders.[105] In the meantime, local scholars and merchants attempted reacquisition of the Wenlan's Four Treasuries collection. Many of the books had been stolen, and a good number had been removed to other places by literati attempting to preserve them from the ravages of the militia and the Taipings. Some local families who had taken shelter in Shanghai and other places had been on the alert for signs that the Wenlan collection was being dismantled during the Taiping occupation of Hangzhou, and had attempted to take some curatorial measures. Ding Bing (1832–1899), who was later the publisher of the loyalist record of the Taiping attack, *Geng Xin qi Hang lu*, and his brother Ding Shen were among the most resourceful of the regional literati who attempted to preserve the materials of the Wenlan. They came from a locally prominent family of scholars and printers, their ancestors being among the local literati who donated volumes to the Four Treasuries project in the eighteenth century.[106] After the fall of Hangzhou in 1861 the brothers fled north to Jiangsu province. Early in 1862, while visiting northern Zhejiang, Ding Bing discovered some papers from the Wenlan being used as wrapping materials, and guessed that the repository had been sacked. He and his brother later hired a man to sneak into Hangzhou in an attempt to recover Wenlan materials and transport them to Shanghai; he returned with two hundred bundles of materials, which altogether comprised about 6,600 volumes from the Four Treasuries collection. When the brothers returned to Hangzhou in 1864 the materials were temporarily kept at the prefectural school in Hangzhou city.[107] Bit by bit, attempts went forward by the local residents and the government to restore the Wenlan Palace itself. In 1880, funds were collected for repair of the edifice, and during the ensuing ten years officials recollected and reprinted the missing volumes. The Ding brothers supplied the materials they had recovered while in Shanghai, and the Bao family of Tongxiang donated their entire private collection, which had been spared from destruction during the Taiping occupation of the area. Between 1867 and 1888 the printers of the region, including Fengrui, reprinted more than 2,800 titles.[108]

Fengrui's employment in the Wenlan restoration projects created a frame and the financial beginnings for his invention of a post-war life for himself. "Dear Harmony Hall" and the rest of the estate outside Zhapu was ruined. His printing business would have to be restarted, and Hangzhou was a more central location. In addition, his cousin Boliang had been assigned, for his service against the Taipings, as a banner lieutenant general (*dutong*) at Hangzhou, and had taken up residence near the confluence of the two canals, at Wooden Bridge.[109] Ignoring the registration statutes that would have kept him in the former garrison at Zhapu, Fengrui found temporary residence at Hangzhou; his transfer there was officially granted later, in 1877.[110] He took with him a wife, a Chinese woman from Zhapu, surnamed Qian, whose family also lived in the Longchuo suburbs not far from Guancheng's estate.[111] In "New Dragon Lane," close to the General-in-Chief's Bridge at the southern wall within the Hangzhou garrison, Fengrui began renovation of a compound for his family, which by 1881 included five children. The final building of the new home was completed in 1878, shortly before the birth of Jinliang, his third son. Fengrui retained the grounds of the old family home in Zhapu, including the remains of Dear Harmony Hall and its pool; he later kept a garden there and rented a portion of it to others seeking garden plots.

Both at Hangzhou and at Zhapu, Fengrui retained close ties with the Manchu communities. At Hangzhou he was active in relief and education projects, and he made a special plea to his Taiping War superior Xue Huan (then a regional commercial liaison) for relief for the dead Zhapu brigade-general Xilingga's son, who was being raised by his late father's servant, surnamed Shi.[112] The walls and houses of the Hangzhou garrison were destroyed, the populations had died, deserted or fled. Fengrui began to work with the other returned bannermen to feed, house and clothe themselves, on the land to which the court still retained title on their behalf. But Fengrui's involvement with the garrison did not prevent him from renewing and creating friendships among the West Lake literati. Yu Yue had returned to Hangzhou in 1867 to head the Zhejiang Provincial Printing Office (*Zhejiang guanshuju*) chartered by Zeng Guofan and to take over the administraiton of the Gujing Academy on West Lake. It was partly due to his personal connection with Yu that Fengrui received many commissions from the Printing Office. Fengrui was also recommended to Peng Yulin (1816–1890), who had served in the Xiang Army under Zeng Guofan and retired to Hangzhou in 1869.[113] Peng and

Yu were close, and their grandchildren eventually married; they were the center of a post-war literary circle that grew quickly and included Feng-rui.[114] Seeking to right his finances in the early 1870s, Fengrui fell back on the tried and true; in the early 1870s he solicited and received poems from Yu Yue and Peng Yulin for a new memorial collection for Shao-shi and Wanggi-shi. Through Yu's and Peng's influence as well as that of some of his other old war acquaintances, Fengrui was able to include short poems on the subject of the two women from Li Hongzhang and Zeng Guofan, as well as his Suwan Gūwalgiya kinsmen Wenxiang and Dingchang (the latter had inherited Fiongdon's ranks from Guancheng's old host in Peking, Shenggui, and briefly inhabited the lineage mansion).[115]

Fengrui took not only his printing but his own writing seriously. Besides his style name Tongshan he also adopted the literary names Gua-shan and Ruru laoren (the latter because of his cultivation of the art of "stillness" as a result of his intense interest in Buddhism), which he used in signing his collection of poetry, "The Old Man of Stillness Dreams of the Flowered Hall" (*Ruru laoren meng Hua Guan shi*). Yu Yue wrote a long introduction to this volume (published the year a small house was completed for him by his students at the foot of Orphan Hill), signing it "stupid little brother Yu Yue."[116] He took the opportunity to write a short memoir of his old friend, and it sheds a little light on Fengrui's frame of mind in these years. He described Fengrui's literary precocity, his youthful love of travel, his enrollment in Li Hongzhang's army to fight the Taipings, his honors, his return to his home afterward. In old age, he noted (Fengrui was fifty-six in 1880), his friend was very much as he had been in youth: physically strong, mentally quick. By nature he was loyal, kind and generous to a fault. He was acclaimed a "good man" (*shanshi*) by all in the region who knew him. During his late years he lived "as a hermit"—that is, accepting no official positions—but took great pride in his breadth of experience, in his detailed knowledge of the history of Hangzhou and West Lake, and in his jade collection. Most revealing, he thought, was Fengrui's study, where over a clutter of books and artifacts hung two scrolls, Fengrui's copy of the lines:

> When you love learning, you will be almost wise.
> When you have made the utmost effort, you will be almost compassionate.
> When you know shame, you will be almost courageous.

> He whose goals are wisdom, compassion and courage
> cannot be corrupted by wealth,
> nor weakened by poverty,
> nor bent by force.

> He is a genuine man.

"The righteous energy of these scrolls was enough to move anyone," Yu Yue added, "and those who saw them without exception exclaimed that Fengrui had realized these very virtues in himself."[117]

Nevertheless the poem was for others, not Fengrui. When Jinliang, Fengrui's third son, was middle-aged himself, he recalled, "After the [Taiping] war was over, my father lived as a hermit, and did not serve [in a public capacity]. He called himself 'Mr. Whole Tile.' Once he sighed and said, 'It is hateful that I, too, was not a corpse wrapped in horsehide, for I had just the same wish to die for the Empire that my elder brother Xirui had.' " Fengrui had also called himself "whole tile" when he signed his first memorial on the death of his family, in which he lamented, "It would have been so much better to be smashed jade than to be a whole [clay] tile."[118] Jade and clay were traditionally the qualities of male and female, respectively; the imagery had been used in Guancheng's bannerman tale on the sufferings of Jalangga, Shao-shi and Wanggi-shi, and was in any case a cliché that Fengrui would have been familiar with from an early age.[119] His fascination with jade was founded on the qualities he associated with it. It was the most ancient of materials, and for this reason he collected it avidly. It had the miraculous ability to sacrifice itself for the protection of others, and he often told the story of how he had been saved by his jade talisman when he fell into a ravine while out for a walk: The jade had been smashed to bits, and he had been saved.[120] But finally and repeatedly jade served as his contrast to the surviving and unworthy: Xirui and the others were the smashed jade to his whole clay tile. His lament was for the cheapness, the literal unmanliness of his life as a survivor.

Fengrui made his life after the war a life, primarily, of thought and imagination. He was a competent manager of his lands and his business, and regularly participated in the design and support of charitable projects within the garrison; but the center of his life was his writing and the tutoring of his children and of his nephews. Fengrui and his children were inseparable. He was their teacher, their supervisor and their entertainer. In his classroom he included his daughter Hualiang, born around 1875; when grown she achieved some distinction as a painter and poet.[121] Yu Yue had earlier educated his own daughters, the second of whom, Yu Xiusun (1849–1883) was a poet; and Zeng Guofan, whom Fengrui admired, had also educated his daughters, the youngest of whom, Zeng Jifen, was a well-known writer.[122] The education of the daughters of the wealthy was not new or unusual, and the publication of women's works occurred from time to time. It was not, however, universally accepted that the education of common women was worth the trouble or the expense; much later, Jinliang would play a part very like his father's in the Hangzhou garrison debate over girls' education.

Fengrui's eldest son Chunliang was, like the late Xirui and quite unlike

Fengrui himself, a vivacious singer of arias and drum songs. Equally like his uncle and unlike his father, Chunliang pursued a military career within the Eight Banners; he grew up to be a high-ranking banner officer and achieved the coveted transfer to Peking.[123] The second son, Xingliang, was more inclined to private life and the management of the family's business affairs. In the 1880s Fengrui's classroom also included his younger sons Jinliang and Wenliang, his grandsons Xiongwen (son of his oldest son Chunliang), Xiongfei (son of his second son Xingliang) and [Irgen Gioro] Naigeng (son of his daughter Hualiang). They memorized small portions of the Confucian classics and read often from the works of Wang Wei, Tao Qian and others of Fengrui's favorites. They were also tutored in Manchu; the family had at this time an unbroken tradition of Manchu literacy back at least to Jalangga, who as corporal (*bosoku, lingcui*) had been required to be literate in the language. Tuwohana had learned Manchu in the Zhapu banner school and later qualified as a clerk (*bithesi, bitieshi*), and Guancheng had likewise learned his Manchu in the banner school. Fengrui had evidently been tutored by his father, in Sichuan, and his own appointment as clerk at Zhapu suggests that he was considered by some objective standard to perform adequately in Manchu. His children heard much from him on his theories of language. Some of Fengrui's ideas sprang rather directly from Qing scholarship on etymologies and cognition; through Guancheng, Fengrui insisted, the family were adherents to the interpretive school of Wang Yinzhi.[124] Others of his ideas were inspired by his own comparisons of Manchu and Chinese. Jinliang's imagination was fired by his father's recitations on the form, sound, and meaning of Chinese characters, on the ancient origins of the writing, and on the early connections between Manchu and the dialects of the Northeast, particularly Solon (Evenk). He considered himself a philology (*xiaoxue*) specialist when grown, and made a living for a time from his knowledge of Manchu, all inspired by his studies with his father in Hangzhou.[125]

For all the fondness and respect he seems to have commanded from his friends and the community at large, Fengrui was a man with a powerful and morbid imagination, and it greatly affected the world he built for his younger children. Jinliang absorbed his father's love of augury, prognostication, ghostly presences and clan spirits; in middle age he would draw upon his father's tales for the supernatural vignettes which he depended upon for part of his living and part of his reputation. The war against the Taipings, the history of the garrison, the city, West Lake, were all made vivid by Fengrui's recitation. Ghostly otters lived in the canals of Hangzhou; martyred heroes walked the hills around West Lake; dreams foretold tragedies and joys; disembodied voices, unfortunate glimpses of forbidden scenes, a clumsy trip along a footpath were all signs of impending deaths or births; miraculous healings and dramatic escapes punctuated the family history.[126] The boys Jinliang, born in 1878, and Wenliang, born in 1881, lived in a world of clan glory, traced from the illustrious Fiongdon to Wenxiang, at whose tomb Fengrui had worshipped and whose sterling character and devotion to public service Fengrui venerated from his private, shaded nest in Hangzhou.[127] They knew, too, the goriest details of the deaths of their clansmen in the Taiping onslaught.

Fengrui was not a particularist in his story-telling. Like all locals he took great pride in the cult of the patriotic hero Yue Fei, and like all bannermen he understood and venerated the Qing imperial ethos of absolute loyalty to which that cult was tied. The boys heard from him the story of Yue Fei's execution for his inflexible opposition to the Jurchen occupiers of North China, and they heard of his supernatural link to Jinliang. On the strength of several of Fengrui's recitations, Jinliang and Wenliang developed an obsession with "Dear Harmony Pool" (*Guihe chi*), as they called the dry goldfish pond on the grounds of the ruined family estate in Zhapu. There, they knew, their uncle Dingrui and cousins Wenrui and Binrui—all children roughly their own ages—had met their deaths. There, too, they had heard that two Ming loyalists, Li Zhenyuan and Xu Shizhai, had starved themselves to death in protest of the Manchu conquest. When they were a little older the boys read the accounts of the two martyrs in the local histories, and back in Hangzhou, Fengrui (who may well have associated the suicides of Li and Xu with those of Dai Xi and Tang Yifen in 1860) showed them an ink-stick that he kept in his study, reputedly carved by one of the Ming martyrs. Jinliang and Wenliang were so impressed with the story that they began to act it out; they would refuse to eat during family visits to Longchuo and would pretend to be starving themselves by the pool. One day this entertainment made both of them ill, and when their mother Qian-shi found out what they had been doing she was violently angry. Both their illness and their mother's reaction frightened the two boys, but, as Jinliang later remembered, "Although we were in awe of the moral conviction of the ancients, we still did not understand the significance behind their self-deprivation."[128]

Fengrui's own birth, according to his telling, had had an omen. The poet Jin Nong had entered the dreams of family members on the night before Fengrui's birth, and as the boy grew up everybody said he not only looked like Jin Nong, but that his calligraphy resembled the poet's very much.[129] Inevitably, the conclusion was voiced that Fengrui was a reincarnation of Jin Nong. Jinliang, not surprisingly, also had a birth omen for Fengrui to tell. As he was being born, their neighborhood of New Dragon Lane was filled with the sounds of rushing chariots, "like a thousand armies and ten thousand horses." The neighbors were all awakened and rushed out to see where the noise was coming from. Some people came from outside the garrison, from as far as Yongjin Gate on West Lake. They said that the sound came from the Jinhua Temple (dedicated to General Cao Gao of Jinhua), which had long been noted as a place where eerie things happened; Fengrui accordingly gave his son the name-character Jin. But the next day it was reported that the sound had actually come from the grounds of a temple, south of the city, that was dedicated to the hero Yue Fei. So Fengrui gave his son the nickname "Little Loyal One," in honor of Yue Fei. The boy was very pleased that as he grew up, people remarked that his aspect was indeed very like Yue Fei.[130] When Peng Yulin heard the story of the signs that accompanied Jinliang's birth, he wrote a placard for a new hall on Fengrui's grounds that read "Loyal Yue Fei Hall." Soon after Jinliang's birth there came a prediction from Fengrui's old friend Number Three (Li Hezhang), who on the basis of the date of Jinliang's birth foresaw a great future for the child: "This boy has the potential for being a general or a great minister." As a child Jinliang was perhaps overly proud of the auspicious circumstances of his birth; in old age, he lamented, "I smashed all his hopes and wasted my life. Of a hundred opportunities, not one has come to anything. He spoke of a general or a minister. So this is how I fulfilled Number Three's hopes for me!"[131]

The Suwan Gūwaligya clan, too, was part of the children's imaginary realm. Walking tours of West Lake with Fengrui included trips to the tablet in honor of Ubahai, founder of the Hangzhou branch of the Suwan Gūwalgiya, on the grounds of the sprawling Lingyin temple, deep within the forests to the west of the lake. The tale of Shao-shi and Wanggi-shi they heard repeatedly, both from their father and from the local storytellers. Fengrui told many stories of the children's grandfather Guancheng, and his experiences as the magistrate of Nanchuan; in fact they referred to their grandfather, as did the rest of the garrison community, as "Sir Nanchuan" and Fengrui told them of his own childhood in Sichuan, vividly describing the love the local people had for Sir Nanchuan and how somewhere in Longhua County there stood a small temple to him, built while he was still alive.[132] He told them of the clan mansion in Peking, where the main branch of the clan lived and performed the sacrifices for them all (though he undoubtedly knew that the lineage had lately lost the estate), and how he and his father before him visited the mansion built in honor of their great ancestor Fiongdon.

For the child Wenliang, a meeting with a Suwan Gūwalgiya clansman became the fulfillment of a dream. Fengrui had a kinsman of the Fiongdon *mukūn* named Songjun, who lived outside the province but was in close enough contact with the Suwan Gūwalgiya lineage at Hangzhou to share generation markers in their style names (*zi*). When in Zhejiang, Songjun and his brothers, if they should be accompanying him, would stop to see Fengrui and his family. One of the younger brothers, Songfan, had a style name—Xihou—that was identical to Jinliang's, and when together Songfan and Jinliang amused themselves by pretending the rituals of older and younger brother.[133] The north-south canal running under the General's Bridge was not far from Fengrui's house in New Dragon Lane, and the children often played along the canal's embankment. During these games, it happened one day that Wenliang lost his footing and fell into the filthy water. Xiongwen tried to help him out, and then fell in himself. At this time Songjun and two attendants arrived for a visit with Fengrui, and Songjun quickly realized that the two boys were in terrible trouble. He ordered his attendants to fish them out, and delivered them to Fengrui's courtyard. Jinliang was, according to his account, astounded to hear their story, for just days before Wenliang had told him of a dream in which a mountain god (Songjun's name contained the character for pine, combined with the radical for mountain) had saved him from a deep ravine.[134]

Despite Wenliang's miraculous rescue on this occasion, it seems that his fascination with superstition did eventually prove fatal. When he was thirteen, he died in a medical misadventure. In his family he often heard stories of people being cured by eating a bit of the flesh of a healthy relative; this folk-cure was widely known (which is not to say it was definitely widely practiced) throughout China, and usually involved cooking a bit of the child's flesh or boiling it in soup for feeding the sick parent. His elder sister Hualiang had once tried this method when her father was ill, and was later commended by the court for it. When his mother became ill, Wenliang apparently attempted to cut open his heart; his mother recovered, but he died.[135] Jinliang later compared the two boys' imaginary flirtations with death beside Dear Harmony Pool to Wenliang's confrontation with the real thing. "It was only after my little brother's death that I came to realize what the substance of death and life is. A person has a few decades of life, and then it is a question of whether one's death will be as heavy with significance as Mt. Tai, or as light as a feather; it is only I who can decide this for myself."[136]

Jinliang was fully aware of the fact that it was Fengrui's imagination that had instilled in him his own sensitivity toward the past, the unseen, the predestined. He later wrote of his father's death in 1906 in an essay entitled "Telepathy" (*linggan*):

Most people have some telepathic power, but it is especially strong between those of the same flesh and blood. When I was little I always stayed by the side of my father Tongshan. Now, it is our custom in Hangzhou to love good tea, and when I was grown a little they all liked to go to a place near West Lake and have tea. One day it happened that I did not go with them, and in the afternoon I decided to join them. But as you go down to the lake there, the road takes three branches, and I had no idea which one to follow. So I found a little shrine, and in front of it I began to meditate on how my father must have gone. Then I got up and went down the path that had come into my mind, and I never made a wrong turn all the way there. My father thought this was very intriguing. One time he deliberately went by a very circuitous route, to see if I could really find it later. But I was able to follow the path without error. Now if it wasn't telepathy, how do you imagine I could have done it?

When I was just grown, I took a trip, not too far from home. My father experienced some pain, and I immediately sensed this and returned. One day Father's illness took a turn for the worse. He instructed the others not to tell me; but even though I was away from the house at the time I could feel it, and in the middle of the night I hurried back. There Father was, groaning in pain on his sick bed.

After I came to Peking to work, I tried to find the time to go back and visit, but could not. One day on some business I approached Liuqiao on my way to the capital, and looked for a hotel to spend the night. Suddenly I saw my father. I immediately felt extremely agitated in my mind. I could not sit or stand quietly. My maternal relative Kang Jiangxiang was with me, and tried to reassure me. But a telegram found me there, from my family. I was so alarmed I could not speak, for I knew this must be the end. It took me three days and nights to get back, by boat and by carriage. I went a thousand miles before I reached Hangzhou. And it was a pity, my father had died three days before.[137]

The supernatural overtones that Fengrui's death had for Jinliang were undoubtedly increased by the morbidity of Jinliang's attitudes in that year, as he found himself in an imperial capital afflicted by a hungry cancer and haunted by the ghosts of past glories. The historical importance of Fengrui's life and his choices rarely intruded upon the speculations of Jinliang. But the fact was that Fengrui's choice to remain Manchu was a conscious one, and the choice confronted all bannermen and their families—who in total may have numbered a little over four million—who survived the Taiping War, whether or not they lived in the Jiangnan garrisons most directly affected. The government was all but indifferent to the choice, and was offering little in the way of encouragement to those who might wish to remain in or return to their communities. Many left. In the case of Fengrui, neither his close association with the Chinese literati community of Hangzhou nor his own service in the regional armies commanded by Chinese civil officials, nor his father's decades of civil service had weakened his identification of himself as a Manchu. On the contrary, his and his family's experiences in the Taiping War intensified his association with his Manchu community and its traditions. Unlike his father's time, the events of Fengrui's life had exposed powers in Chinese society that were capable of forcing the Manchu label upon those who might otherwise have been indifferent or even hostile to it. And unlike his father personally, Fengrui lived in circumstances in which it was no longer possible to be comfortably poised between the garrison and the civil milieux, which is paradoxically in conflict with both the supposed fusion of these two worlds in the "restoration" thesis and with the apparent affinities between garrison and civil reconstruction efforts. Guancheng pursued his civil career in a time in which it presented no threat to his status as a bannerman, which still appeared to be a thing genealogically ordained. The legislative reforms of the 1850s and 1860s forced all bannermen to examine the real costs and benefits of banner status, and to choose to remain a registered bannerman or to strike out into Chinese society. It is quite true that for Fengrui, who had a well-established alternate livelihood to draw upon, retention of banner status represented no real economic sacrifice, but under the new terms of banner affiliation this was true for all. For the garrison stratum with the least prospects, continued banner registration represented a possibility, not a guarantee, of at least a modest monthly income. For the economic and social elite of the garrison, however, the choice was more clearly a choice of identity, not merely of registration—identity with their native community, with the symbolism of the clans, with banner tradition, with the history of Manchu servitude to the Qing court.

CHAPTER VI

Jinliang

BODY AND SOUL

ONE DAY in his late teens Jinliang and two other young men sat by the West Lake and began discourse upon the relationship of the soul to the body. Each of the three had developed a slightly different interpretation. The first, Yue Gongge, was of the opinion that the soul, once engendered, was immortal; the body could be destroyed but the soul could not. The second, Zhang Binglin, pronounced the soul and body to be blended during the lifetime of the individual, the soul being drawn from an undifferentiated state at birth and returning there at death. Jinliang's notion (he was much younger than the other two) was perhaps unsophisticated by comparison. "I said the body and soul are inseparable. Heaven and Man can communicate. Everything is without birth and without death."[1] Later, Jinliang would look back with irony upon his youthful pronouncements regarding birth and death, and upon his lifelong connection with Zhang Binglin.

Jinliang had early been singled out as the most academically talented of Fengrui's surviving sons, and in his teens was already preparing for the provincial examination. There is a hint, in his account of his conversation on body and soul with Zhang Binglin and in others of his remembrances of his youth, that his tendency to self-dramatization and perhaps a certain amount of pomposity was already evident. From his childhood he accompanied his father around West Lake, visiting friends and overseeing business. Jinliang gloried in the attention of "uncles" whom he later discovered were scholars, poets and war heroes of note. It was at Yu Yue's Gujing Academy on the shores of West Lake that he discovered Zhang Binglin (1868–1936), ten years his elder.[2] Zhang was Yu Yue's star pupil, a young man of powerful and complex scholarly abilities. He saw his study at the Gujing as more or less placing him within the line of academic descent from Dai Zhen (1724–1777); he later acclaimed Dai, together with Wang Yinzhi and his son Wang Niansun (two former patrons of Guancheng), as the most crucial scholars in the development of his fields of philology and hermeneutics.[3] This was, as Jinliang saw it, precisely his own intellectual genealogy. Jinliang was fascinated by the intelligence and learning of Yu Yue's disciple, and he determined to remain Zhang's friend. How Zhang Binglin may have felt about this is not clear. At the time, it is true, he was a student of the classically oriented reformism of his teacher Yu Yue. In ensuing years he would become sympathetic to the ideas of Kang Youwei, but would eventually break with Kang and Liang Qichao over the issue of the acceptability of the Qing dynasts as constitutional monarchs. Zhang would in fact become one of the most individualistic spokesmen not only for the Chinese nationalist revolution, but also for a policy that would explicitly exclude Manchus and Mongols from full participation in Chinese society after the fall of the Qing dynasty. It appears that Jinliang already understood something of Zhang's "reputation for wanting to get rid of the Manchus" during their acquaintance in the late 1890s; despite this, he would claim in his old age that "the first time I saw [Zhang Binglin] we became fast friends, and we continued ever afterward to get along very well."[4]

To understand Jinliang's opinion of Zhang it must be remembered, first, that the revolutionary rhetoric for which Zhang would later become famous had not been well developed by him or by anybody else at the time of Jinliang's youthful meeting with him; second, it is necessary to look closely at the variety of Manchu political opinions and options at the end of the nineteenth century. Certainly Jinliang saw his own political activism, such as it was in this period, as consonant with the reformism of Zhang Binglin and of the generation of Fengrui and Yu Yue before them. For both Jinliang and Zhang, the proximate inspiration for their politicization was the intensification of China's humiliation at the hands of militarily powerful foreigners. The number of treaty ports had multiplied exponentially; virtually all coastal cities of any significant size and many important interior cities had come under the partial jurisdiction of Westerners, who within their own enclaves lived by their own laws, promulgated their own religions, and wrote the economic and some of the political rules for the Chinese populations of their vicinities. Military defeats did not cease; in 1885 the Chinese concluded a peace with France that renounced traditional Chinese influence over Annam, the event that Sun Yatsen later claimed galvanized his own opposition to the dynasty. Moreover, Japan, after working for over a decade to alienate the traditional Qing suzerain region of Korea, had now entered the skirmish for treaty rights in China itself. China's disastrous first war with Japan ended in April of 1895 with Li Hongzhang's signing the accord at Shimonoseki that ceded Taiwan, the Pescadores (Penghu) and the Liaodong Peninsula to Japan, imposed upon the Qing government an indemnity of two million taels and accorded the Japanese unprecedented financial, commercial and industrial privileges. Russia and Western nations with interests in China were alarmed. International competition for territorial privileges in China's coastal and Northeastern regions was accelerated by the Shimonoseki agreement. Students and intellectuals in China were outraged by the humiliating terms exacted by the Japanese. Their formal protests to the court and its officials continued through 1896, as the implications of the treaty became more immediate.

Out of the general consternation of the educated classes and the chagrin of the court arose the forces that swept Kang Youwei and his associates to prominence for a time. Kang, a national degree recipient of 1896, had tried in various ways to make a name for himself in scholarly and bureaucratic circles, finally succeeding with a memorial to the throne that was approved by the imperial tutor Weng Tonghe (1830–1904) and eventually circulated to the provincial governors. The ideas in the work appealed to a fair number of influential members of the court, and in early 1898 Kang and his group of academic reformers were summoned for an imperial interview; as a result, Zaitian retained them as his special advisors and initiated the so-called Hundred Days of Reform. In essence it was a program for the restructuring of the educational system, the pruning of the ceremonial bodies of the government and all sinecure appointments, the establishment of ministries for trade, industrialization and agriculture, and institutionalization of a consultative body.

A great deal has been written on Kang Youwei and the fate of the Hundred Days' Reforms. Comparatively little has been said about the interaction between the new reformers and Manchu reformism. Perhaps more than any other single event of the post-Taiping era, the Hundred Days exposed the ambiguities and contradictions of Manchu reformist elements. What emerges from a consideration of these questions is that late nineteenth-century progressivism among the Manchu elite at the capital shared roots with the reactionary Manchu resurgence that marked the dynasty's last years. The Hundred Days was a polarizing field for the many fluid, ambivalent elements within the central and provincial Manchu elites.

Public reaction against the Treaty of Shimonoseki discredited Li Hongzhang. The Empress Dowager for more than ten years had regarded Li as the prime servant of the court, after the dismissal of Yixin (Prince Gong) from the Grand Council and Foreign Office presidency following China's loss of Annam to the French in 1884. Yixin's fall had marked a shift away from the policies of the Tongzhi period, when he and Yihuan (Prince Chun) had worked with Wenxiang and Hengqi to create the institutional and diplomatic innovations of the period following the Treaty of Peking in 1860. Now, in the aftermath of Shimonoseki, it was Li who was dismissed as president of the Foreign Office, and Yixin was restored to his former responsibilities in the imperial bureaucracy. On the surface it appeared that power had slipped, after almost two decades of steady increase, away from Li Hongzhang and back to the Manchu courtiers led by Yixin. Even though neither of the brothers harbored any friendly feelings for the West, Yixin and to a lesser extent Yihuan had continued to exert a moderating influence over the court after the death of Wenxiang in 1875. Yihuan, the father of Zaitian who by Xiaoqin's machinations had been selected the Guangxu emperor, was among a number of imperial princes who continued Yixin's consultative role after 1884, and would continue to do so until his own death in 1891. Their position was one committed to observation of treaty provisions, development of a limited diplomatic and commercial relationship with the West and gradual modernization of the defense forces; as China failed to gain ground by these means, Yixin (perceived by his peers as the more arrogant and wrongheaded of the two) was visibly chastised by the Empress Dowager through the 1870s and ultimately lost influence to Li Hongzhang. It would be a mistake, however, to assume that Li's position on matters such as military reform, armament industries and education were opposed to those advocated by the Yixin-Yihuan group. Both the court and the governors were in agreement on the bundle of programs associated with "self-strengthening" in the 1870s and 1880s; their differences arose over how, by whom and from what locality the programs should be controlled. Even as Manchu moderates appeared to recoup their position in the months following the signing of the Shimonoseki agreement, Li was carrying on with the consolidation of his own power and that of his subordinates; the return of Yixin meant the widening of the split between the court and the maturing centers of provincial control.

On the eve of Kang Youwei's famous memorial of 1896 the court reformers had moved somewhat beyond the tradition of Wenxiang, who had emphasized economy, technological modernization in the military and in education, and some prophylactic knowledge of Western legal and social traditions. Military development had proceeded very much along the lines laid down by the Tongzhi reformers in the period between Wenxiang's death and the Sino-Japanese War. The Peking Field Force had been imitated in the creation of new modernized units, including the Tiger Spirit Corps (*Hushen ying*) based in Peking. Attempts to spread Western weaponry and training among the bannermen generally were pressed by [Wanggiya] Chonghou, but restrained by Yihuan, who provided a last echo of the Qianlong emperor by expressing the fear that bannermen would forget the "fundamental arts" of riding and shooting.[5] The attention of the central government was curiously limited, whether by default or by design is unclear, to the Eight Banners and the new units carved from them. Reform of the Green Standard Army was left to Zeng Guofan until his death in 1872, and the development of naval defenses fell to Li Hongzhang and Zhang Zhidong, though Yihuan, in particular, was a consistent supporter of their innovations. The shock of the loss to Japan in 1895 led the provincial governors to call for a complete reworking of the military reform strategies. Sheng Xuanhuai and Zhang Zhidong called early for abolishment of the Green Standard Army; this recommendation would be realized in 1901, as the court attempted a late show of interest in fundamental restructuring. The Eight Banners, however, remained untouchable; their numbers had reduced markedly since the early nineteenth century, they could be shorted on salaries and supplies as necessary, they remained an exploitable pool of candidates for the modern military units and the new academies and, as Yihuan had implied, no matter how poor or few they were, the Eight Banners performed a symbolic function that the court had no intention of parting with. It would take the parvenu vision of Kang Youwei and his followers to suggest, in 1898, that the garrisons be abolished and the bannermen be given "useful occupations."

In the civil sphere, the Foreign Language College in Peking had become an outlet for some of the reform programs of the years after Wenxiang's death. A press had already been established there in 1873, more languages were added in the ensuing years, a large circulating library was created and a chemical laboratory built. In 1896 state educational reforms were advanced markedly with the chartering of the Peking Imperial University (jingshi daxuetang), built on the grounds of the former estate of [Fuča] Fulung'an (1743–1784). Sun Jianai (1827–1909), who with Weng Tonghe had been encouraging the Guangxu emperor to assume greater control of the government, was made president, and the American W.A.P. Martin, who had formerly been associated with the Foreign Language College, was made head of the faculty. Planning proceeded for eighteen months, as the emperor moved closer to the more radical reform programs of Kang and his followers. The staff of the college was mixed between conservatives, moderates and progressives, but progressives certainly dominated the program in the early stages, and it is not too much to say that the Peking Imperial University was seen as the vanguard of the emperor's aspiring forces of reform. One of the most vocal progressives was [Aisin Gioro] Shoufu (1865–1900), son of a former Hanlin academician, Baoting (1840–1890), and son-in-law of a well-known political moderate, Lianyuan (1838–1900).[6] At the time of the Sino-Japanese War Shoufu had been a member, as his father had before him, of what has been called the "disinterested demeanor faction" (qingliu dang), who criticized corruption in power.[7] But Shoufu soon went far beyond what his father's generation had envisioned. In 1898, the year he attained the national degree and was appointed to the faculty of the Peking Imperial College, Shoufu travelled to Japan—like many other curious, dissatisfied and apprehensive intellectuals of the time—and returned advocating a modernization program modelled on that of the Meiji oligarchs; specifically, he claimed that constitutions were the source of the political strength of both Japan and the West, and called upon the court to promulgate a constitution for China. The dynamics of the Hundred Days were complicated by these groups' resentment of the sudden appearance of Kang Youwei, and most were probably disturbed by the anti-dynastic accent of some of his proposals: Years were to be numbered consecutively from the date of Confucius's birth, and it was proposed that the name of the state become Zhonghua (based upon a racial designation for the Chinese), rather than the dynastic designation of Da Qing (Great Qing [Empire]).[8] Even more disturbing, perhaps, was the overt anti-Manchu sentiment of some of Kang's associates, notably Tan Sitong.

Political programs such as that advocated by Shoufu depended upon an estimation of the personality and prospects of Zaitian, the Guangxu emperor, that may have been too optimistic. For diverse groups including not only Kang and his reforming scholars but also Shoufu and progressive court Manchus, as well as Jinliang and aspiring Manchus of the provinces, the hope was that Zaitian would play a role like that of the Meiji emperor, Mutsuhito: a monarch dynamic enough to use his legitimacy to sweep away the influence of corrupt obstructionists, but self-effacing enough to leave policymaking in the hands of an enlightened oligarchy. Such hopes elided the young emperor's murky legitimacy; at the time of the Tongzhi emperor's death in 1875, Zaitian, a four-year-old child of the same generation as the deceased Zaichun who was not the son of an emperor, had been chosen successor over a handful of other prospectives, including the son of Yixin. As the son of Yihuan and the nephew of Xiaoqin, Zaitian was a candidate capable of consolidating the interests the Empress Dowager and the prince who had once helped her eliminate her son Zaichun's regents, but he was certainly not the candidate of unanimity for the imperial clan. The two empresses dowagers, Xiaoqin and Xiaozhen (Yizhu's widow), formed a *de facto* regency for Zaitian, as they had for the Tongzhi emperor, Zaichun, before him; following Xiaozhen's death in 1881 Xiaoqin played the primary parental role for the adolescent.

In 1889 Zaitian, aged eighteen, married Xiaoqin's niece, after which Xiaoqin recognized the emperor's majority but continued until 1891 to wield despotic power. The signs of Zaitian's assumption of actual authority that began to surface in 1891 had a marked effect upon the attitude of educated, young, self-styled progressive Manchus like Jinliang and his cousin Naigeng. Exploiting Xiaoqin's summers away from the Forbidden City, Zaitian repudiated the interferences of eunuchs in his affairs and demanded with convincing determination that the Imperial Household Department sharply decrease its expenditures. With every step Zaitian took on his own he appeared to pull away from the noxious influence of Xiaoqin, who as a woman, as a former sub-concubine and as the apparent promoter of an extraordinary range of unsavory government practices was despised by many Manchu statesman. Zaitian himself seems to have aspired to the heights of glory enjoyed by the Qianlong emperor, and often retraced the steps of Hongli through the Forbidden City; beyond the walls waited ambitious reformers, both Manchu and Chinese, whose hopes to restore Zaitian to his rightful place of power or to use his prestige for modernization conflicted not only with each other but with the interests of Xiaoqin and all those who, in crisis, would identify their interests with hers.[9]

The question of distillation of interests between Zaitian and Xiaoqin throws additional light upon the problem of the ambiguities of the reformist tradition among the Manchus prior to the conflict of 1898. In the later stages of the struggle between the Hundred Days' reformers and Xiaoqin, the former turned for aid to Yuan Shikai, who was then commandant of a modernized army unit in addition to his bureaucratic appointments in the capital. This seems a curious (in the event it was fatal) notion on their part, until it is considered that Yuan was the protegé of [Suwan Gūwalgiya] Ronglu (1836–1903), whose career in the years prior to 1898 strongly suggested to many that he was the personification of Wenxiang's reform hopes. Like Wenxiang, Ronglu was a ninth-generation descendant of Fiongdon. He had been awarded the provincial degree and minor noble rank in honor of his father, Changshou, who died fighting the Taipings in 1852. In the early 1860s Ronglu had served under Wenxiang and Yixin in the formation of the Peking Field Force and a few years later served closely with Wenxiang again, both in the Peking gendarmerie and in the campaigns against banditry in the Northeast. At the same time he held in rapid succession a series of very high civil posts. He was instrumental in Xiaoqin's securing of the emperorship for Zaitian in 1875 (the year of Wenxiang's death), but from 1879 to 1885 was not active in the central government, possibly because of friction between himself and Yixin. In any event he was highly ranked again in banner administration after 1885 and in 1895 returned to Peking at Xiaoqin's request, to serve concurrently as head of the Peking gendarmerie (Wenxiang's old post), a member of the Foreign Affairs Office, of the Board of War, and of the Grand Council. Ronglu was an important patron of the Peking Imperial University after its chartering in 1896, and he continued his keen interest, once shared with Wenxiang, in the creation of modern military and police forces. It was he who recommended Yuan Shikai, a protege of Li Hongzhang, as a likely commander of the Zhili provincial units.[10] In other provinces, Ronglu also encouraged the growth of such armies under Song Qing, Dong Fuxiang and Nie Shicheng.

The permanent alienation of Ronglu from the reformers in 1898 and his exclusive alliance with Xiaoqin thereafter extends this question of the ambiguities of early court reformism to the Empress Dowager Xiaoqin herself. By the end of the dynasty Manchus of most political persuasions were regretting the peculiar hold Xiaoqin gained and maintained over the government; they liked to repeat the legend of the Ming emperor Chongzhen, who as he was hanging himself from Coal Hill pronounced a curse upon the first Manchu invader he glimpsed—a member, as it happened, of the Yehe Nara clan. And, in fulfilment, Xiaoqin of the Yehe Nara clan had descended upon the Manchus. Few, in the final years, were blind to the ineptness of the imperial regimes over which Xiaoqin gained control. Major military needs went unmet while she diverted funds for her own use, most flagrant being the Yihe Summer Palace (including marble boat and opulent opera house) she built for herself near Peking during the years prior to the Sino-Japanese War with funds appropriated from the new naval program. Her taste for corruption seemed to expand to fill the possibilities. Certainly Jinliang, in writing later of his horror of the political, financial and sexual corruption of her court at the turn of the century, was speaking for his entire class of educated, politically aware Manchus. Yet Jinliang was less than ingenuous on this point. As late as 1903, when he was preparing himself for a career in the Peking bureaucracy, his family was inviting and accepting the favors of Xiaoqin: In that year his older sister Hualiang and another bannerwoman of Hangzhou, Wang Shao, were granted the rare privilege of an audience with the Empress Dowager, who bestowed honorary rank upon them in recognition of their literary merits.[11] Indeed, Xiaoqin seems to have assumed and continued well beyond Zaitian's majority an imperial role that no bannerman would be willing to dispense with: She was the imperial patron, the personification of the court's bounty and expectations. This went quite beyond the symbolism implied; in the years after the Shimonoseki agreement, it was Xiaoqin and her associates who stood between the bannermen and the provincial governors seeking to pare away military inadequacy and economic waste. The public roles of the court she played very well, too, and was enthusiastic in her adaptation of photography and Western social styles to such purposes. While most Manchus shared some degree of distaste for Xiaoqin's usurpation of the emperor's role, it remains a question how many, how early, were able to look through her very successful facade to the disorder beyond.

This problem is compounded by the fact that Xiaoqin's remarkable career was due largely to her acute talent for handling the subtleties of court business, and that in her early years of power she supported the reformist group headed by Yixin. It is common to dismiss Xiaoqin for her naive understanding of industrialization, her complete lack of interest in any matter not related to the Qing court, her apparent enthusiasm for bureaucratic corruption on a grand scale, and her frequent duplicity in dealing with foreign powers. But she established herself by her keen understanding of the political tensions of the 1860s, and thereafter was kept at the center of politics in the capital by the acquiescence of the provincial governors, particularly Li Hongzhang and Zhang Zhidong, who preferred to follow their regional agenda rather than attempt to collaborate with the progressive court faction in order to restructure the political order from the center out. Xiaoqin's father, Huizheng of the Yehe Nara clan, had been a minor official before being prosecuted for deserting his post in the Taiping War. Xiaoqin first entered the palace through the normal channels of concubine—in her case, sub-concubine—recruitment for the Xianfeng emperor. She was exceptionally well-educated for a woman of her rank and early on developed a taste for having her fingers in the policy process; Yizhu allowed her to organize the memorials that he was expected to peruse each day. In 1854 she gave birth to Yizhu's first son, Zaichun, and was promoted to concubinal rank; a second imperial son by another woman died in infancy, and when Yizhu died prematurely in 1861, Zaichun succeeded to the Tongzhi (1862–1874) emperorship. Xiaoqin never attained highest rank while Yizhu lived; after his death she shared consentual authority over the new child emperor with Xiaozhen, Yizhu's first consort. Xiaozhen and Xiaoqin persuaded the regency of eight men created for Zaichun to recognize them as empresses in name and to require their seals on all edicts. Together, the two women used the invasion of Peking in 1860 by British and French forces and the subsequent burning of the Summer Palace (*Yuanming yuan*) outside Peking to precipitate the dissolution of the regency. With the aid of the brothers Yixin and Yihuan they effected the arrest of the regents as a group and the execution of the head regent, Sushun. Thereafter, Xiaoqin seems to have battled Xiaozhen and the imperial princes for exclusive power, manipulating officials, eunuchs and often Zaichun himself in a game that was sometimes deadly for the pawns involved. Challengers to her power had an improbably high extinction rate. At one time or another, she was rumored to be instrumental in the deaths of Zaitian (who predeceased her by something less than twenty-four hours in 1908); Xiaozhen; Zaichun; and Yizhu's second infant son. She was clearly responsible for the death of Sushun, and it was also suspected that by one means or another she had prevented Zaichun from conceiving an heir, leaving the successor to be chosen at her own convenience. Indeed nearly a month before Zaichun's demise in January of 1875, Xiaoqin had already arranged for Zaitian to be named the heir apparent.

Until the 1890s Xiaoqin kept the court on the path it had plowed for thirty years. "Self-strengthening" in armaments and education should progress far enough to appease the literati and reinforce the ambitions (and coffers) of the regional governors; it should stop short of undermining the status or what remained of the wealth of the nobility. Progressive programs were rarely rejected out of hand by her; a nod may have been enough to assuage the ego of the reformer, and the perpetual delay in implementation that often resulted protected any significant interests involved. Xiaoqin managed, in this way, to gather the threads of diverse interest groups in her hands; until Zaitian began to show signs of willfulness in the early 1890s she was unchallenged in her supreme position at court. When the revolt did come in 1898, actions by Xiaoqin to contain Zaitian's overzealousness were swift. In September of 1898 she and Ronglu moved to suppress the reformers and their sympathizers.[12] Kang Youwei and his young disciple Liang Qichao fled to Shanghai. The other reformers, including Kang's younger brother Guangren, either refused to flee or were unsuccessful in the attempt, and on September 27 the government executed the "Six Exemplars" of the movement. Xiaoqin promoted Ronglu to governor-general of Zhili and Yuan Shikai, who had betrayed the emperor's plan for a restoration coup, assumed Ronglu's military posts in Peking. By the end of October, Zaitian himself was literally a prisoner of his enemies at court. During the ensuing year, moderates or progressives in many provincial positions were replaced by conservative Manchus.[13]

The reaction was also felt among Manchu moderates who had not been directly involved in the Kang Youwei party; the staff of the Peking Imperial University was swept for undesirables, and Shoufu and Kuoputongwu, among others, were dismissed. Newspapers in Peking were forced to suspend publication and a strict prohibition on the assemblies of students and intellectuals who had gathered in the capital over the previous weeks to learn of the changes in progress. In the milling crowds was Jinliang, who had trailed after his friend Zhang Binglin to Peking and was lodging at the home of his eldest brother, Chunliang, now an officer in the Peking garrison. Jinliang, now twenty years old, was a late-coming Manchu to the reform movement. The political clubs formed during the Sino-Japanese War had included many Manchu participants. Naigeng, the son of Jinliang's older sister Hualiang and his former fellow student in Fengrui's classroom, was prominent in the "National Protection Society" (Baoguo hui) founded by Kang Youwei at Peking in April of 1898. Demao, Deshan, Wenyuan, Tongshu and others were signers of the "Ten-Thousand Word Memorial" submitted to the throne by Kang and his followers.[14] Many Manchus of Jinliang's and Naigeng's background and economic standing were enthusiastic about reform programs that promised to vest rulership in Zaitian instead of the Dowager Empress, and to strengthen the national defenses while undercutting the wasteful privileges of Manchu aristocrats and Chinese bureaucrats. Jinliang had a particular objection to the conduct of the government by a small and corrupt group who obstructed the Guangxu emperor's right to govern. He flung himself before the gates of the Forbidden City (which had been closed) and made a scene by demanding the death of Li Lianying, Xiaoqin's favorite eunuch and the individual whom Jinliang and his group were now indicting as a major villain in the reaction.[15] Jinliang was dragged away by gendarmes as the crowd shouted its approval of him—indeed one of the observers, Tang Shouqian, soon made Jinliang celebrated in the progressive press in Shanghai for his deeds.[16] Upon hearing of his brother's arrest Chunliang hurried to beg an audience with Ronglu. When admitted, Chunliang explained that Ronglu and Jinliang were fellow clansmen—both direct descendants of Fiongdon.[17] Ronglu suggested that a position in the government might be found for the young prisoner, but only, he added, after he had a chance to talk face to face with his relative. The time for the interview was fixed and Jinliang was released from jail. But instead of keeping his appointment with Ronglu, Jinliang—probably wisely—left the capital and went back to Hangzhou.[18] Zhang Binglin, for whom the first of many arrest orders had been issued, had already fled to Hangzhou and was in the process of moving on to Taiwan, where he would find haven under Japanese rule.[19]

Ronglu could not have known that Jinliang would later have the power to undermine his historical reputation; what was clear was that he could well afford failed experiments in the cooptation of boy intellectuals from the Manchu middle class. He had effectively destroyed all true reformist energy within the central government, a significant achievement given the depth of feeling among many bureaucrats in the years following the Treaty of Shimonoseki, and an achievement due more to the terror inspired by the deaths of the detained reformers than to anything else. More germane to the present discussion, the Hundred Days and its aftermath exposed divisions of outlook, ambition and expectation among the Manchus. The young emperor had been the cynosure of the centrist, reformist faction. But the events of 1898 only alienated the reformist Manchu middle class more sharply from the court. A critical portion of the higher nobility including Ronglu, Zaiyi, and Zaifeng, had thrown in their lot with Xiaoqin in an attempt to maintain their own position; they moved closer to the ultra-conservatives of the court who had always categorically opposed reform, like Gangyi (d. 1900), whose byword was "Reform harms the Manchus and benefits only the Chinese." The tensions between loyalism and reformism that appeared and intensified after 1898 were further aggravated by persistent foreign pressure aimed at protection and if possible elevation of Zaitian's position (and consequent diminution of Xiaoqin's), a congruence of native reformist and foreign interests that did nothing to help enhance the standing of reformist Manchus between 1898 and 1900. For the poorer people among the garrison pop-

ulations as well as for the Manchu aristocrats, the death of court reformism in 1898 was in all probability a relief; the former were deeply fearful
that a fundamental reform would lead to absolute abolishment of remaining silver and grain stipends while the latter would have had all major
sinecures cancelled. But for Manchu moderates and progressives, the
middle road of reform from within was constricting sharply in the years
after 1898; capitulation to the controlling faction or support of radical alternatives were looming as the only choices for educated, propertied, yet
politically weak elements of the Manchu elite.

The promise and the failure of the Hundred Days' Reforms has been a
central problem in modern Chinese historical interpretation, and the
perspective of Manchu political and indeed economic divisions in this
period helps to sharpen the importance of some recent treatments of the
events of 1898. The received interpretation of the reforms and their aftermath has tended to focus upon the roles played by Kang Youwei and
Liang Qichao. It was they, in this scenario, who brought the progressive
program to Zaitian. Their nemesis was the empress dowager, Xiaoqin,
who quickly marshalled the most reactionary forces in the government to
suppress the reforms. Inevitably, such an interpretation posits the nationalism of Kang and Liang against the selfish exploitativeness of Manchus, led by the Empress Dowager and her faction. More recently, structural interpretations have seen the aspirations of a young, ambitious but
displaced social stratum behind the reform movement.[20] And still more
recently, court factional politics have again been emphasized, to the diminution of the role formerly imputed to Kang Youwei.[21]

It is clear that a discussion of a "Manchu" role in the development or
the dismantling of the reform program is not useful. Manchus were in
evidence on both sides of the struggle, but their divisions were not haphazard. Jinliang, Naigeng, Shoufu, Kuoputongwu and the other young
Manchus who supported Zaitian (and this may have come before their
support for the reforms particularly) were representative of a particular
stratum of the Manchu world: affluent, educated, committed to reform,
expecting to assume leadership in their home communities, and opposed
to the continued prominence of the Empress Dowager's faction, which
they may well have feared would block the few opportunities to the
higher bureaucracy that existed for them. At the same time, the reformist
faction among the Manchus was not new, and Jinliang may have represented the general view of this group in seeing the reform program of
1898 as a continuation of the post-Taiping reform programs sponsored by
Wenxiang, Hengqi and others. Indeed the Tongzhi and the Guangxu reforms shared the same themes of streamlining the military and civilian
bureaucracies while increasing their efficiency, of centralizing (at Peking)
planning for industrialization and communications, and of retention of

the Qing traditions of collegial rule. Because Kang's group made few serious attempts to integrate progressive Manchu energies with their program, the real possibilities for reform in 1898 may forever remain elusive. Less mysterious is the probability of a successful political coup by Zaitian and the "Six Exemplars." Xiaoqin had built around her a fortress that was nearly unable to be toppled. Before and after 1898, she on occasion became convinced of the advantages to herself of sponsoring reform. In the case of the aborted "restoration" of 1898, her advantages all lay in easy destruction of the upstart group.

The crushing of the internal impetus to reform in 1898 did not solve the failing government's problems or ease the anxieties about foreign penetration of the society. No progress had been made in reversing the apparently rising tide of national weakness and humiliation. In many areas resentment of repeated defeats combined with local economic malaise to spark outbreaks of violence. Manchus no less than Chinese were profoundly distressed at the sharp increase in the foreign presence and the apparently rising degree of foreign control over certain aspects of daily life. The anti-foreign sentiments of the Manchus took much the same forms as they did among the Chinese, among them membership in secret societies. Manchus in China had a long, if minor, history of mixing in some localities with heterodox religious groups, from the White Lotus to the Taipings. In Peking, Manchus shared membership with Chinese in guilds, religious organizations and some economic cooperatives. Xiaoqin liked to sponsor the creation of and Manchu participation in martial skills clubs (*wu hui*), many of which could hardly be distinguished from the Boxer (*yihe tuan*) cells that began to foment rebellion in Shandong as early as 1897. In fact it became clear that during 1898 and 1899 the Boxers had a large number of sympathizers among the bannermen of Peking, who wore red belts as the emblem of membership in the movement.[22] The usual appeal of secret societies may have been enhanced for bannermen by the slogans of the Boxers, which indicated as early as 1897 a wish on the part of some cells not to exterminate the Qing (as earlier cults had sworn) but to rescue them: "Support the Qing and Purge the Foreigners" (*fu Qing mie yang*) was the cry that was heard, and attempts by Zhang Zhidong to suppress the growing movement may have been subverted by Xiaoqin and her reactionary ministers at an early point.[23]

By the time the Boxers swept into Peking in June of 1900, Xiaoqin and her court were barely making a pretense of attempting to keep the rioting Boxers and their sympathizers under control. Indeed Zaiyi and Zaifeng were among the Manchu nobles who took to the streets themselves to oversee Boxer assaults on foreign religious and diplomatic establishments, and the Manchu Enčun of the modernized Tiger Spirit Corps (*hushen ying*) sparked the uprising at Peking by assassinating the German ambassador von Ketteler on June 20, 1900. In the ensuing pandemonium foreigners amalgamated their supplies and guards behind the walls of their legation compounds in central Peking, while their governments planned a landed invasion of north China. By August the allied army had reached Peking, and the next day Xiaoqin, with Zaitian in tow and escorted by the Peking Field Force and the Tiger Spirit Corps, fled the city. Fearing the demands for punishment that would inevitably issue from the foreign occupiers, noblemen who had incited or abetted the Boxer riots hustled to eradicate the evidence of their complicity. Yet Manchu moderates who had opposed the Boxers had already paid the ultimate price. Lianyuan, who, like his son-in-law Shoufu, had lost his university post in the reactionary wave following suppression of the Hundred Days' Reforms, was executed before the arrival of foreign troops for his advice to Ronglu to purge Dong Fuxiang from leadership of the modern army units, and for his plea to the court to abandon the Boxer cause and surrender Peking to the foreign forces. Shoufu himself committed suicide as the Western occupiers moved into his quarter of the capital. It may have been Xiaoqin's hope that in encouraging the concatenation of riots that constituted the Boxer "rebellion" she would drive the foreign powers from north China. Instead, Russia took advantage of the opportunity to increase its influence in Mongolia and the upper Northeast, Japan became entrenched in Liaoning and Jilin. The debacle resulted not only in the military occupation of the capital and the expulsion of the court, but also the imposition of a massive 470-million-tael indemnity with a payment schedule that meant the eternal mortgaging of major sectors of the Chinese financial apparatus.

The Boxer disorders left the garrison populations of Peking and north China poorer and more dispirited than had ever been the case. Young Jinliang, provided with plenty, had been aware, because of his father's concerns, of the rapidly deteriorating condition of most of the residents of Hangzhou's ruined garrison in the years before 1898. It was a time when the deprivations of the post-war period had lowered living conditions for the Manchu populations in general from desperate poverty to true misery. While the nobility and wealthier strata thrived on a combination of official salaries, rent incomes and often the accumulated spoils of generations of graft, the poorer bannermen were expected to subsist on the irregular dispensation of one or two taels of silver or the counterfeits that, in Lao She's words, "found their way in there;" the new appellations of bannermen as "eating" (shi) or "not eating" (fei shi) differentiated those receiving this modest support from those no longer entitled to any income at all. Even at the lowest economic level of the garrison, income continued to skew toward those with a surplus, and the banner rolls were undoubtedly laden with an excess of those who could not possibly have done military service.

Now conditions were worsening sharply, particularly in Peking. The reform and education programs that opened new opportunities to bannermen in the Tongzhi and early Guangxu years had been discredited in 1895 and many had been discontinued; Boxer and anti-Boxer violence in 1900 had levelled whole portions of the Inner City at Peking, large (but at this date undeterminable) numbers of bannermen had been killed or seriously wounded in the fighting, and the bannermen's great protector, Xiaoqin, was in apparent retirement at remote Xi'an in Shaanxi province. Poverty, illness, opium addiction and in many areas social alienation had left the remaining garrison populations with little to draw their attention to the capital other than fears that the trickle of silver, grain and cloth from the government would finally cease. For those who still enjoyed support, the transition to a world without the emperor's bounty was as daunting a proposition as it had appeared to be forty years before. It is reasonable to surmise that many bannermen were deprived of any sense of self-respect and that an ironic derision of their condition was instilled in their children. Jinliang's contemporary, Lao She (whose father was killed in the Boxer fighting), later looked back at the state of the garrison Manchus in the nineteenth century. "No wonder the French and English Allied Armies broke through the gates of Peking and burnt the Summer Palace," he commented. "With an army composed of widows, hunchbacks and cripples living off the defence budget along with the captains and cavalrymen of the likes of Eldest Sister's father-in-law and his son, how could China possibly have fended off an enemy attack?"[24]

For his part, Jinliang took pains, when he had the occasion, to extoll the energy and optimism of members of the Manchu community at Hangzhou, whose numbers grew from roughly two thousand in the aftermath of the Taiping War to about six thousand on the eve of the 1911/12 Revolution. He described them as enthusiastically supporting educational reforms, as very intensely loyal to the court, and as people who enjoyed the respect of their Han Chinese neighbors.[25] But it must have been true that by the time of his late adolescence Jinliang was aware that the economically deflated but egotistically inflated bannerman (*qiren*—no longer distinguished as Manchu, Mongol, Chinese-martial, active, cadet, reserve, or leftover) was a stock character of popular literature.[26] Wu Woyao (1866–1910) included a vivid recounting of some of these jokes in his contributions to the journal "New Fiction"(*Xin xiaoshuo*), then under the editorship of Liang Qichao; the episode was later included in Wu's collection, "Strange Things Seen in the Last Twenty Years" (*Ershi nian mudu guaixian zhuang*). In it the fictitious observer, Gao Sheng, notes a bannerman coming often to his favorite Peking tea house where, if one brought one's own leaves, the cost of a cup of tea was cut in half. The bannerman would regularly add only three or four leaves of common *xiangpian* tea to his cup and, when mocked by the other customers for it, would claim that it was a strong (and expensive) red tea from France; the onlookers only laughed at the spectacle of the man fussing over the colorless and tasteless liquid. Then the bannerman would buy the cheapest sesame bun in the house, munching upon it for hours, finishing by disguising his attempt to collect all the seeds fallen upon the table with a pretense of practicing calligraphy there with his finger. The story is capped by a scene observed one day when the bannerman's son comes into the teahouse, saying to his father, "Baba, go home right away. Mama wants to get up."

"So? Let her get up. What do I have to go home for?"

"You're wearing her pants. If you don't get home, she'll have nothing to wear."

The observers laugh in contempt, and the bannerman loudly upbraids the boy. "Cut the nonsense. Your mother's pants are in the leather bag, of course."

The boy fails to take the hint. "But Baba, I'm afraid you've forgotten that we sold that bag off. And the pants we pawned. For money to buy rice! And also, Mama wants me to tell you that we only have one handful of rice left, not even enough to feed the chickens. She wants you to buy a bag of rice for lunch."

"Now shut up!" The bannerman said furiously. "What's with you and your poor-talk (*qiunghua*)? Nobody here wants to borrow money from us. There's no cause for your carrying on."

When the boy had shaken his head, sighed in exasperation and left, the bannerman scurried over to the proprietor. "You have to forgive the child. There are so many people who wish to borrow from me, I have to keep up the poor-talk, as a decoy, you see? How could I be poor? We bannermen eat at the emperor's own table, you know. The children have got so used to hearing the poor act, they just blurt it out. You understand." Pressed to pay his bill of one penny (*yi wen qian*), the bannerman searches his belt pouch long and hard, finding nothing. He requests credit; instead, he is threatened by the proprietor if he does not make good. Finally a compromise is reached. The bannerman will leave his handkerchief behind as collateral, and pay his penny the next day. The proprietor holds the handkerchief up for the inspection of the crowd; it is revoltingly filthy. "Great," the proprietor sighs, "if you don't come back and pay, I'll use it as a dust rag."[27]

Satirizing Manchu commoners was not a form of *lèse-majesté*, but Jinliang later felt that Xiaoqin and her company were equally deserving of contempt, despite the protections of their exalted station. Eight years before, the officials of the court had threatened to throw Jinliang into jail. Now he took their dictation, waited in their background while they conferred, held their umbrellas as they shuffled from one drafty, unheated palace to another. It was not difficult for him to see in them the reflection of Lao She's hunchbacks and cripples, or Wu's shambling con man. A particularly hilarious joke, to him, was Xiaoqin's bold plan to modernize the Forbidden City and Summer Palace by installing electrical lighting. A generator was set up inside the Forbidden City, lamps strung through the imperial compound and out to the Qianmen marketplace. The glimpse of the modern marvel was truly a wonder to the residents of Peking since the lights shined so dimly that they could be considered as nothing other than an awe-inspiring, elaborate decoration. It seemed yet another wasteful bauble, dangled before the eyes of an anxious and deprived people. But the greatest clown of the Forbidden Palace, in Jinliang's view, was his old *bête noire*, the eunuch Li Lianying (d. 1911). Eunuchs as a class were an oddity of palace life for which his southern upbringing had not prepared Jinliang, and he found Li to be the single most repugnant person he had ever met. He detested the powdered arrogance of the man and the degree of influence accorded him by the Empress Dowager; at the same time, he agonized under the realization that expression of his disgust would be a grave error. Even the Guangxu emperor, who from youth had been a great hater of the eunuchs, had always been cowed by Li Lianying. Though the palace nobles professed horror at Li's cruel and tasteless pastimes—like tying firecrackers to the feet of crows and watching the birds blow themselves to bits high over the courtyards of the Forbidden City—they felt in no position to protest.[28] In later years Jinliang described his abhorrence of Li, with whom he often came into contact after being appointed to the censorial office: "I had no choice but to ask after his health, be accommodating toward him, sit by him at meetings. . . ." The ultimate outrage, for Jinliang, was the well-known photograph in which Xiaoqin and Li Lianying posed as the Buddhist goddess Guanyin and a hunchback attendant; their suggestive postures, Jinliang believed, were to close to the truths of court pastimes to which he was not privy.[29]

That the years following the profound humiliation of the country in the foreign occupation of Peking after the Boxer rioting should see the emergence of a radical rhetoric deriding the moral character of the Qing court and the Manchus could hardly have been a surprise to Jinliang, and he may even have considered more than a few of the charges to be justified. But it was also the case that he continued to be interested in reform. He had in fact already been lauded by Tang Shouqian for his youthful activism on behalf of the reformers' party in 1898, and like other educated, progressive, younger Manchus, he continued to seek a meaningful outlet for his political interests. Unfortunately, his was a constituency that was regarded with increasing wariness by reformers who found their more moderate avenues of dissent narrowing and disappearing altogether. The final break came with the suppression of the so-called Tang Caichang "rebellion" in 1900. Tang was an old associate of Tan Sitong, who had been executed in 1898 at the order of the Dowager Empress after the suppression of Zaitian's Hundred Days' Reforms. After the debacle Tang carried on the cause for constitutional monarchy. His "Assembly of China" (*Zhongguo yihui*) in Shanghai and the uprising of the "Independence Army" (*Zili jun*) in Hunan were the last manifestations of a movement openly centered upon the Guangxu emperor Zaitian. Though loyalist constitutionalists such as Kang Youwei and Liang Qichao remained active in the nationalistic movements that gained momentum after 1901, loyalism as a primary activist theme died when Tang was executed along with twenty comrades at the order of Zhang Zhidong, then the governor-general of the Huguang region. The drama of the Boxer Rebellion overshadowed the fact that 1900 was the year in which restorationist reforms lost their credibility permanently. In the years following, Xiaoqin and her counselors, primarily Zaifeng and Zaiyi, grasped the importance of convincing most sectors of the society, including the bannermen, of sincere intentions to institute widespread and deep reforms. During the first years of the twentieth century, conservatives, constitutionalists and radical nationalists entered a prolonged conflict that was at times rhetorically shrill and at others stunningly violent. Radical nationalism took on new energy with the appearance of a generation of students who were irreconcilably opposed to the Qing government, and determined to reject whatever form or reform it might try to assume. Zou Rong, author of "The Revolutionary Army" (*Geming jun*), died in prison in 1902; his comrade Chen Tianhua, equal in talent but somehow seeming to lack charisma, drowned himself in Japan in 1905, protesting the Japanese government's intention to curb the activities of the Chinese students who had flocked to Japan to drink in the secrets of their increasingly imperialistic neighbor while remaining safe from prosecution by the Qing government. Frustrations of this sort galvanized the movement, which reached a new plateau of organization with Sun Yatsen's creation of the Revolutionary Alliance (*Tongmeng hui*) in Tokyo on August 20 and the inauguration of the "People's Journal" (*Minbao*) in November.

The role of racism in the revolutionary movement has been debated often, and will be left for another part of this discussion. What is pertinent here is that the rhetoric emerging from these movements seems, on its surface, to be the sort of speech that should have disturbed Manchus profoundly. Lu Haodong (1866–1895), a revolutionary executed for subversive activity, left a testament that was published the year of his death in Hong Kong, in which he claimed that Sun Yatsen had named the Manchus as "the target of vengeance, from which they will be unable to escape." Lu's tract introduced what would become the stock phrases of the anti-Manchu writings of Zou Rong, Chen Tianhua and others: The Manchus, "the bandit spawn of Jianzhou," were the rapers of Yangzhou, a vile bestial race who exploited and continued to exploit Chinese civility for their own selfish ends. Lu asked "who lives on whose land, who eats whose fruits?" His excoriation of the Manchus was clearly not intended to take them as symbols of the Qing court or the troubles it had wreaked upon China, but directly condemned them as a race and demanded their elimination. Where Manchus existed, the Chinese would never be safe or prosperous: "It must be understood that today, without exterminating the [Manchu] Qing, the Chinese nation can under no circumstances be restored." The same year, Wang Xiuchou's "Memoir of Yangzhou," recounting in graphic detail the siege of Yangzhou in 1645, was reprinted by Feng Jingzhu in Yokohama together with a letter by the Ming statesman Shi Kefa.[30] Tan Sitong, executed in 1898, had described the Manchus: "Like thieves hating their masters they have always spun intrigues to close our eyes and ears, to fetter our hands and feet, to cut short the sources of our wellbeing, to desecrate our life, to cloud our mind." And Sun Yatsen, who later modified his racial rhetoric, still intoned, "Our ancestors refused to submit to the Manchus. Close your eyes and imagine the picture of the bitter battles, when rivers of blood flowed and the bodies of the fallen covered the fields, and you will realize that the conscience of our ancestors is clear."[31]

After the turn of the century, as the nationalists under Sun moved more toward issues of resistance to foreign imperialism, radicals writing under partial protection of the international settlement in Shanghai still continued to emphasize strong racist images. *Subao*, which would become a cause célèbre, particularly featured such writings: "Since all the Manchus are as stupid as deer and pigs, how could we refrain from making revolution?"[32] "Only when we have finished killing the Manchus will we stay our hands. Let us hasten to murder!" declared a famous essay of 1902, while another detailed the doctrine of "murderism" (*sharen zhuyi*)—a word that, translated as "terrorism," would lose its basic sense of satisfaction through the literal slaughter of one's oppressor: "There is an enemy with whom my 400 million brethren should not have shared the same sky during the last 260 years."[33] "Let us slay and exterminate more than five million of those beast-like Manchus," Zou Rong wrote in his "Revolutionary Army,"[34] and demanded, "Is there any disaster more heartrending and tearful than that of a reign of an emperor from among the Manchu thieves, despised race, wicked and wild-hearted sons of wolves, wandering herd of cattle raisers!"[35] Suggestions after 1901 that the Qing government might actually institute reforms were quickly denounced. "To this day the Manchus are as cruel and inhuman as in former times. Using the cover of false promises about introducing a constitution they seek to ward off the vengeance of the Han. In order to maintain their foul tribe of five million, 400 million Hans deny themselves bare necessitities, and exhaust all their spiritual and physical strength."[36]

It was Zhang Binglin, perhaps, who was most direct in a 1903 essay that led directly to his imprisonment: "Slay the Manchus! Slay the Manchus!" Zhang during these years was deep into the development of his polemics against the Manchus, or what he called "anti-Manchuism" (pai-man zhuyi). He had gone to Shanghai in 1900 to join Tang Caichang's "China Assembly" (Zhongguo yihui), had finally broken with the loyalist reformers and after Tang's death had gone into hiding again.[37] In truth, Zhang's sloganeering in Subao grossly simplified his views on the relationship of the Manchus to China, which were inseparable from his scholarly work generally and which could have been—there is reason to believe, they were in fact—appreciated in all their subtlety by Jinliang. Zhang was one of the leaders of a growing school of "national essence" (guocui) scholars, and it was from this realm of inquiry that he derived his political program of minzu zhuyi—nationalism, or an agenda for the creation of a state based firmly and exclusively upon the supposed racial solidarity of the Chinese. Rooted in scholarly techniques of etymology, paleography, and history, the scholars of this group (which at the turn of the century would have been hard to identify with precision) worked to discern essential and continuing features of Chinese civilization. On the basis of some very ancient Confucian traditions but also on the analyses that could be traced more directly to the early Qing dissident Wang Fuzhi (1619–1692), they had come to the conclusion that nature molds racial identity, racial identity informs culture, and culture defines moral character. The implications for the present situation were clear. It was no accident that the Qing dynasts were evil; the Manchu people from whom they sprang were evil, and to a man remained so. It was all very well for Jinliang to claim (as he often did to others and must have done to Zhang) that Manchus and Chinese were widely united by social customs in the nineteenth century.[38] Superficial similarities of mores were only that; moral identity was something much more profound, and something immutably determined by racial origin. Zhang had found the origins of the Manchus in the historical record; they were descended from the Jurchens, who were descended from the Wuji, who were descended from the Yilou, who were descended from the Yi of the classics, all peoples of barbarous character, which was what the Manchus continued to be. Zhang, indeed, went so far as to give philosophical justification to an equation commonly expressed among Chinese and Europeans (but not, it should be emphasized, among Manchus) long before his time. The Manchus must be resisted and ultimately expelled because of the "joint conspiracy between whites and Manchus" against the Chinese.[39] In a letter published August 8, 1900, in "China Periodical" (*Zhongguo xunbao*), he made his claims personal, with reference to the outstanding progressive Manchus of the time: "Among the Manchus, you may ask, are there not the surpassingly talented and wise, like Shoufu, Jinliang and others? But do you not know [the passage from the *Zuo zhuan*] 'He who is not of my people (*zu lei*), his heart must be alien'?"[40] Any claim of being integrated with the Chinese was a fraud—as would be any claim of intention to reform the government—perpetrated by the Manchus for the purpose of calming Chinese suspicions.

In 1901 Zhang returned from Japan to Shanghai and stopped to visit his old teacher Yu Yue, who was then in Suzhou. He may have been surprised at Yu's stern rebuke. The elderly scholar scolded Zhang for forsaking reformism and taking up the secretive life of a revolutionary, for seeking refuge in the lands controlled by China's enemies, for his racial invective: "Unfilial! Disloyal! Inhuman!"[41] But Zhang was undaunted, and continued his revolutionary propaganda; less than two years later he was in a Qing prison, refusing to flee arrest after the government had convinced the Shanghai mixed court to convict the staff and writers of the magazine *Subao* on charges of sedition. In ensuing years he became only more adamant in his insistence that in Republican China there would be no place for Mongols or Manchus.[42] They were unsuited to participating in the same polity with the Chinese because they were not Chinese and would never become Chinese.[43]

Jinliang saw Zhang Binglin in Shanghai between 1900 and 1902, and far from being repelled by his old idol's anti-Manchu passions, seemed moved by a spirit of amused indulgence of Zhang's political pretensions combined with a serious attention to his scholarly opinions. During his visits to Shanghai at this time, Jinliang was curious about the reform movements flourishing under the unfriendly but thus far impassive eye of the foreign authorities. Zhang Binglin, Jinliang claimed, introduced him to Tang Caichang, the last loyalist reformer whose movement had been suppressed by Zhang Zhidong so ruthlessly in 1900. Two years later Zhang Binglin introduced Jinliang to Chen Fan, the publisher of *Subao*, and Chen's daughter, a student at the Shanghai Patriotic Girls School (which was suspected of being a revolutionary front).[44] It is tempting to think that Jinliang's motives in socializing with this group were less than innocent, yet as a young reformer (this was three years before his assumption of official employment in Peking) there was much to provoke his honest interest in the publication. As late as June of 1903 *Subao* still published reformist articles and even essays explicitly condemning the anti-Manchu rhetoric affected by many revolutionary leaders.[45] There was also ongoing interest in protecting the Guangxu emperor from the evil intentions of Xiaoqin—who at the time of Jinliang's acquaintance with Chen Fan was still keeping the emperor with her in Xi'an and was believed to be considering his murder. Kang Youwei's "Protect the Emperor Association" (*baohuang hui*) was also active in the city. Jinliang, now a very young adult, a provincial degree holder and a man of somewhat precocious bearing, sometimes accompanied Zhang on his rounds and according to his own account helped the firebrand—who now wore his hair long, sporting a tattered monk's robe and rope sandals—evade the questions of suspicious policemen. It seems, too, that on occasion he felt the need to protect the revolutionaries from themselves, as on the evening he pacified a brawl between Zhang and Yamamoto Torajirō as they were in the process of smashing up the office of the "East Asian Gazette" (*Dongyin bao*) that they were publishing together.

If Jinliang regarded his acquaintance with Zhang in Shanghai as an extension, though a complex one, of their association in Hangzhou, it is clear that others regarded Jinliang's persisting interest in Zhang as peculiar and possibly dangerous to them both. In Shanghai he met one Song Yansheng, a friend of Zhang Binglin's who feared the worst from the friendship of Zhang and Jinliang and berated them for being seen together. Not long afterward Song maneuvered Jinliang into a tea house late at night and implored him to avoid Zhang, so anxious, apparently, that tears sprang from his eyes. Jinliang, mildly impressed by Song's solicitude but far less by his argument, "laughed a little and thanked him for his concern." Nothing seemed capable of puncturing Jinliang's blithe haze where Zhang was concerned. A few days after Jinliang's encounter with the tearful Song, "Zhang gave a speech advocating getting rid of the Manchus. My friend said that a certain Mr. Jin should be gotten rid of first. He wished, he said, that most of the Manchus were tyrants, as opposed to sages; so long as there were sages among the Manchus, revolution would be a very difficult thing. Ever after that, people jokingly called me 'the Manchu sage.' "[46]

There was more than a love of backward praise (though that in itself may have been no small factor) behind Jinliang's continued friendship with Zhang Binglin. Jinliang was not alone among the Manchus who, individually and as a group, would receive and ignore the bluntest possible expressions of Chinese hostility during the ensuing decade. Jinliang's smiling reception of Zhang Binglin's condemnation invites comparison to the attitude of Enming, the Anhui general-in-chief who was repeatedly warned by his colleagues that his aid, Xu Xilin, was a secret agent of the revolutionaries; Enming defended Xu and protected him from arrest, until the day in 1907 when Xu shot him eight times. The paternalism of Enming's treatment of Xu may have some reflection in Jinliang's fraternal vision of Zhang. Jinliang had been very young when he met Zhang as a student of Yu Yue's, and he clearly construed their friendship, in light of the relationship between Yu Yue and Fengrui—and common academic descent from Wang Yinzhi—as something close to familial. There is broad applicability of this model of the Manchu vision of Manchu-Chinese relationships. Not only had the emperors long styled themselves universal and impartial parents of the Qing household (*jia, boo*), but there were real and celebrated friendships, one of the more dramatic of which was that of the brilliant Manchu poet [Yehe Nara] Singde and Wu Zhaoqian. On a more general scale, it was certainly true that in the years of Wenxiang and Yixin, Manchu and Chinese cooperation had become standard practice, and since the disintegration of many garrison compounds Manchus lived intimately and on good terms with their Chinese and Muslim neighbors. Alterations in Manchu and Chinese relations after 1900 may have been subtle and slow; certainly they escaped the notice of Jinliang, and undoubtedly of a large number of other Manchus as well.

Jinliang's attitude toward Zhang Binglin had its corollary in the court's posture toward the small revolutionary outbreaks that occurred with increasing frequency after 1898. Though the government moved as swiftly and as ruthlessly as it could to punish the offenders (with a few exceptions, execution was the preferred expedient), there was sparse discussion of the content of revolutionary rhetoric. Little seemed new in the propaganda. Malcontents, in the view of the court, had been agitating against Qing rule ever since the conquest. On the surface this rhetoric bore great resemblance to the ancient slogans of the secret societies who swore to depose the Qing in order to restore the Ming; the similarity, in Jinliang's mind, was reinforced by Zhang Binglin, who on occasion cast himself as a Ming loyalist.[47] The new revolutionaries, like the Taiping rebels and the spectrum of Ming loyalists and scruffy bandits back to the time of Dorgon, harped constantly on the injuries inflicted on the Chinese in the conquest, and the ongoing crimes of the Manchus since. There was, perhaps, good reason for Manchus who managed to become aware of the specifics of subversive speech—and that was not always possible—to dismiss it as carrying the same message of categorical hatred for alien conquerors that had been supported for so long by the secret societies. Particularly in the immediate aftermath of the Boxer disturbances, there may have been little reason to fear that nationalists would attack Manchus instead of foreigners. Moreover, it may well have appeared that those who indulged in such rhetorical excesses as Lu Haodong's or Zou Rong's were systematically arrested, interrogated and executed; only in retrospect do we appreciate that for every Lu Haodong or Zou Rong there was a Sun Yatsen or Zhang Binglin who from the relative safety of a foreign enclave or colony could continue to proselytize.

But perhaps more important, the Manchus were not enraged by racism itself; on the contrary, the court had endorsed racial thinking in the eighteenth century, the importation of foreign thought in the late nineteenth century reinforced and refined it, and by the time the disintegration of the empire was imminent, racial identity appeared the only hope for a coherent future for Manchus as well as for Chinese. At heart, Jinliang considered that his and Zhang's views of the rules of the world and the meta-world were in harmony (if fine points, like the moral character of the Manchu race, could be debated). In fact Jinliang had picked up a new notion from Zhang, or from the intellectual and political trends that Zhang represented. He had arrived at the idea that the Manchus were a race. It was not necessary for him to look far for confirmation of this hypothesis. The means by which Zhang described the identity and delimitations of the Chinese, the clans, were in the forefront of every Manchu's view of his world.[48] In the same way that the Chinese clans and Chinese identity could never die, the Manchu clans, too, were eternal. Jinliang began to use a strange new word in referring to the Manchus. By analogy to Zhang Binglin's and other nationalists' imported term *minzu*, which meant both "race" and "nation," he began to call his own people *manzu*, the "Manchu race."[49] It was a new word for a new idea. Jinliang's acceptance of—or indifference to—Zhang's political ideas may have been connected with the fact that he knew that in addition to the attestable raciality of the Manchus, there were among the Manchus equally intense racial feelings. In the final years of the dynasty, his older brother Chunliang moved to the Northeast in anticipation of the fall of the imperial government; Jinliang's nephew Xiongwen, then a student at the Hangzhou prefectural school, gave a speech in the provincial assembly to which he had been elected as a delegate and insisted that, no matter what political reorganization might be coming, the Northeast, the "home of the Manchus," should never be a province, but an independent country.[50]

The rather logical extension of Chinese nationalist rhetoric in the early years of this century was in the end one of the sources of conflict between Zhang Binglin and the emerging revolutionary mainstream represented by Sun Yatsen and the Revolutionary Alliance (*Tongmeng hui*). If Manchus, Mongols, Uigurs, Tibetans and even Chinese Muslims were to be "races" with moral and cultural destinies distinct from that of the Chinese, it would be inevitable for them to seek (with, logically, Chinese encouragement) homelands equally distinct from China. In fact this was no matter of theory. Regionalist sentiments had smoldered long in Xin-jiang and Tibet, and with the moral and material nurturing of the Japa-nese it soon became clear, after 1905, that separatist movements in Mon-golia and the Northeast were inchoate. A comparatively small Chinese republic surrounded on three sides by independent and possibly hostile states ripe for cooptation by imperialist powers could hardly have been an attractive prospect for the revolutionary government. *Minzu zhuyi* was retained as one of Sun Yatsen's Three People's Principles (*san min zhuyi*), though its racial intentions were mitigated by a new language of nationalism as manifested by the Brotherhood of the Five Races of China. As Zhang intensified his racial polemic in the years leading to the revo-lution, he lost patience with the obfuscations of Sun's racial and cultural positions, which only recalled the forced integration under the Qing em-pire. Zhang was not, in any case, an enthusiast for Sun's idea of democ-racy; following the revolution he supported the forced presidency of Yuan Shikai until the latter's disgrace in 1916. After a brief rapprochement with Sun, Zhang left the political arena altogether and devoted himself to the private, and impecunious, pursuit of his iconoclastic scholarship; dire emergencies like the rumors in 1936 that the deposed Manchu em-peror was planning an invasion of Peking could, however, elicit bursts of admonitory epistles to military and political leaders, even literally from Zhang's deathbed.

It was soon after Zhang's retirement from public life in 1918 that Jin-liang, then living in the Northeast, received a letter from his old compan-ion of West Lake. While a police commissioner in Peking Jinliang had begun his writing career, in 1907 publishing his first volume of sketches on his life and observations on events in Peking. Now, years later, Zhang happened to see a copy of the work, and wrote to Jinliang that his atten-tion had been attracted by a passage "which mentioned somebody who was anti-Manchu and anti-Jinliang." In response, Zhang enclosed a short poem, which for Jinliang summarized much more than his relationship to Zhang Binglin:

> Heaven resolves the vengeance of drawn swords,
> Enemies and friends are even.

"Zhang understands," Jinliang concluded. "How could he not know that the two of us are above all things, and have travelled on a higher plane for a long time now? We are both pure and untarnished beings."[51] For all that, their youthful metaphysical argument was unfinished. Zhang Binglin was of the opinion that the Qing body had expired and it was time for the soul (the Manchu people) to hie back whence it came; Jin-liang was convinced that both were still united, and deathless.

FAVORABLE TREATMENT

To apply for a bureaucratic appointment in Qing China, which Jinliang did frequently between 1904 and 1911, one had to have a resumé. Specially formed little portfolios of fanfolded red paper with embossed black end pieces were purchased for the resumés, with custom red envelopes suitable for conveying the precious documents, together with whatever enclosures might be deemed advantageous. Like all good resumés, Jinliang's was a long one by the time he submitted it to Zhao Erxun, the governor-general of the Northeast, in 1911. Just thirty-four years old, Jinliang had taken every examination degree and served in a stunning variety of posts in the central bureaucracy. The object, however, was not to demonstrate the breadth of his experience. Jinliang had prefaced every single appointment in his record with the name of the individual who had appointed him, not altogether the usual way of presenting one's credentials; what he was offering was a encoded list of his sponsors in Peking.[52] The Qing government had withered away, and the men, with their august ancient titles, who had employed him in Peking were the very ones who would continue the north China power structure, whether revolutionaries or loyalists wielded the seals of legitimacy.

His appreciation of this fundamental truth had not made Jinliang indifferent to the fate of the empire. In the years since he had floated through Shanghai and seen for himself the radicalization of the reform movements, Jinliang had clearly come to identify himself ever more closely with the dynasty and with the political outlook of the men who controlled Peking and the Northeast. This was partly an accreditation process. He had taken the Zhejiang provincial degree (*juren*) in 1902, and only two years later attained the national degree (*jinshi*), the highest the empire had to offer and which he was the first of his lineage to achieve.[53] For almost one year he was able to bask in the glory of what for the better part of a millenium had been the nation's ultimate achievement, a prize that immortalized the recipient, elevated his ancestors and enriched his progeny. At the end of his year, a cascade of educational reforms swept away the entire traditional degree structure, and the meaning and advantages of the national degree along with it. For a man with as long and as intense a fascination with the symbols of elitism—both Chinese and Manchu—as Jinliang, the pain of having one's pretensions cancelled must have been acute. Later he was able to joke that his participation seemed to signal the end of every stage of the old examination process. His licentiate (*xiucai*) examination had been the last in which the "eight-legged" (*bagu*) style was required; his provincial (*juren*) examination had been the last in which strategic and statecraft issues figured in the questions; and his national examination (*jinshi*) had been the last ever administered.

"You could say I was an eight-legged *xiucai*, a strategic *juren*, and the ultimate *jinshi*."[54]

Jinliang had married a Manchu woman from the Hangzhou garrison at about the time he received the provincial degree, and in early 1905 he moved her, with his son Guandong and infant daughter, to Peking. He had been appointed an expectant secretary of the Imperial Household Department, which meant he received a small salary but as yet had no official duties, though a short time after his arrival at the capital he was assigned as a part-time clerk to the Outer City police department.[55] For additional income he also accepted students hoping to be tutored in philology, history and progressive politics.[56] He had time to explore Peking, as he had not during his rather hurried visit seven years before. The condition of the city may have impressed upon Jinliang how little of the old there was left to preserve. Whole neighborhoods were still in rubble from the Boxer fighting, and others had been demolished to make way for the railways connecting Peking with both Hankou in southern China and Tianjin on the coast. The Hanlin Academy, where the creme of the national degree holders had once managed the central communications process, had been destroyed and its grounds absorbed by the British legation; a new, smaller compound was being constructed for the Hanlin in the western quarter of the Inner City. The Tangzi, where the Qing emperors had performed their secret shamanist rites for two-and-a-half centuries, had been razed. The broad grounds of the Temple of Heaven were overgrown with weeds and the buildings themselves were darkened by smoke and soot. Here and there the city walls and gates had been pummelled away by bombs and cannon fire.

For Jinliang the destruction had a more personal side. He spent many months attempting unsuccessfully to trace relatives of Wang Yinzhi in Peking, but the great man's lineage had not thrived in the north. Still enchanted by his father's stories of the great Wenxiang, Jinliang sought out Wenxiang's mansion in the northeast quarter of the city; it was uninhabited, the courtyard overgrown with weeds, the wooden doors splintered on their hinges, the walls cracked and unrepaired. Several intersections away he found the mansion of the Suwan Gūwalgiya main lineage, as his father and grandfather had done. But the grounds had been sold to another family. The spirit pole of the Suwan Gūwalgiya clan stood forlornly in the courtyard, visible from the street; Jinliang and a cousin considered, then reconsidered, buying the pole and planting it elsewhere. Thinking daily of Fengrui lying terminally ill in Hangzhou, the sense of decay and morbidity for Jinliang was strong. It did not, however, overwhelm his youthful hopefulness or his confidence that the reign of stultification under Xiaoqin was drawing to a close and that new possibilities for reconstruction had only begun to be explored.

Jinliang, who had started writing in his spare time in hopes of documenting the transitional age and of augmenting his meager income, could not help noting the strangely conflicting trends around him. The Guangxu emperor was now kept virtually in perpetual confinement at a compound within the Yihe Summer Palace. Li Hongzhang and Ronglu were dead. Xiaoqin was decrepit, but very much alive, and Li Lianying, to Jinliang's dismay, showed no signs of expiring. But where, seven years before, Xiaoqin had been contemptuous of the reform programs promulgated by Zaitian, she had now decided to play the role of sponsor of a massive body of reforms, so untrammelled in scope as to be, in Jinliang's eyes and in the eyes of many others, meaningless. Since her return from Xi'an, Xiaoqin's appreciation of the seriousness of foreign and domestic demands for reform had deepened considerably, thanks to the efforts of a group of imperial princes who had assumed responsibility for the Peking government in her absence. Now generating a heightening mountain of reform plans, Xiaoqin seemed to consider no institution (including Jinliang's national degree) sacrosanct in her campaign to industrialize, modernize, rationalize and constitutionalize the Qing empire. For the princes Yikuang, Zaifeng, Zaiyi, Zaize and others, the future could be faced without trepidation. Yikuang in particular had been impressed with the manner in which the German imperial bureaucracy under Wilhelm II was dominated by members of the imperial family. He envisioned a similar plan for the new Qing order, with himself and other princes ensconced as the heads of the new departments and the majority of the cabinet. By the time Jinliang reached the Forbidden City, the race to produce reform plans, cabinet posts and new salaries for the Aisin Gioro clan was on.[57] The grasp of the conservative Manchu princes on the top government posts increased in direct proportion to the apparent restructuring of the government, and would become virtually complete with the announcement of the "princes' cabinet" of 1910. Intensification of conservative Manchu control over the shrinking central government did not mean continued protection of the traditional status of the Manchus as a group; on the contrary, the princes were more impressed with the bannermen as a drain on the state treasury and the imperial clan's public image.

The new enthusiasm for reformation of the state was due in part to foreign pressure, which the court found more credible after the occupation of Peking by foreign armies in 1900; in part to the Russian empire's dramatic defeat by Japan in the war of 1904–1905; and in part to a sense that dissident violence was exceeding the abilities of either the Qing domestic peace forces or the foreign police in the treaty ports to keep it in check. Xiaoqin's attention was finally drawn by Ma Fuyi, who aborted a plan to bomb a noble gathering on the occasion of her birthday in the autumn of 1904, was captured (apparently while planning another assassination), and was executed in April 1905. In protest, an uprising occurred in eastern Hunan that resulted in the execution of more dissidents. As the violence escalated, so did the government's efforts to publicize its almost feverish progressivism, to the point that the long-cried-for and long-promised constitution was pronounced forthcoming. In June of 1904 the Qing government, acting on the orders of Xiaoqin, announced that insofar as constitutionalism seemed to be the key to the power of Japan in defeating the Russian empire, the Chinese government would now study the phenomenon of constitutionalism by sending an embassy of investigators to Japan and various Western nations to observe that political system at work. The imperial prince Zaize was appointed to lead the group, which also included Shaoying, Dai Hongci (1853–1910), Xu Shichang (1858–1939) and Duanfang (1861–1911). Opponents of the government were immediately suspicious, seeing the dispatch of high ministers upon an extended tour abroad as a transparent scheme to defraud those agitating for constitutional reforms; action, it was assumed, would be indefinitely postponed, while the government would claim to be engaged in earnest reform. A young radical named Wu Yue, then residing in Peking, decided to kill the study group before they could leave the capital.

Wu Yue was almost exactly the same age as Jinliang. He was born in the prosperous Anhui city of Tongcheng, and in 1900, at the age of twenty-two, travelled through Shanghai on his way to Baoding, where several modern schools, including the officers' academy for the New Army, had been established. It was there that he became friends with Chen Tianhua (who would drown himself in Tokyo in 1905) and other young activists. By 1903 he was working as a teacher and was deeply involved with new nationalist organzations such as the "Military People's Education Society," based in Shanghai, and the editorial staff of the "Zhili Colloquial Gazette" in Peking.

On September 20, the official delegation gathered at the train station near the Chongwen Gate, prepared to board a coach of the Peking-Tianjin line for the coast, from which point they intended to continue by sea to Shanghai. Among their security guards was Sayintu, a graduate of the Peking garrison military college and colleague of Jinliang's at the Outer City police department. Wu Yue was also on hand, disguised as a waiter, with a bomb concealed in the front of his loose jacket. As the train pulled away from the long platform, Wu attempted to make his way to the spot where the delegation was seated; but he was prevented by the crowd from reaching them before a vibration in the train prematurely detonated the explosive inside his clothes. The blast disembowelled Wu instantly, and among the group of people injured in the explosion were Shaoying, Zaize and Sayintu, who received a shrapnel wound to the leg.

Sayintu's wound, from which he recovered two months later, was the subject of angry discussions in the constabulary. A plot was suspected and a large group of students—including a young Northeastern bannerman, Zhang Yong—were arrested and questioned; in the end they were all released, and responsibility was officially assigned to Wu alone. But a special public security bureau was formed within the police department, and another friend of Jinliang was appointed its first secretary. On the whole it did not appear to Jinliang that the ideology behind Wu's act was seriously examined. Wu's connection with revolutionary organizations and the New Army were not regarded as salient. What mattered was that for the first time since the Boxer fighting and in a perfectly peaceful situation a bomb had been exploded in the heart of the capital. The vectors of injury, the reverberation of the sound were what remained in Jinliang's memory, and he recalled it immediately when later in the year a moving picture projector that Duanfang had brought back from his constitutional study tour exploded: "The entire city was in panic. This was the residual echo of the Bombing."[58] To Jinliang, the Wu bombing, like the explosion of Duanfang's projector, framed the dangers of technology intruding into a fragile society. The Boxers had not been alone in their hatred of the extension of the railway system that was being developed in China on the basis of foreign loans and it was widely thought, purely to serve foreign interests. Hatred of the western contrivance was not lessened by the fact that railroads had been the chief means of conveyance for the Allied troops sent to Peking to quell the Boxers; the rebels had had strategic as well as nationalistic reasons for attempting to disrupt the Peking-Tianjin line, which despite their efforts was finally the means of bringing American marines from the coast to the capital. For Wu Yue, the symbolism of assassinating five ministers of state at the terminus of the despised Peking-Tianjin line must have been obvious.

The destabilizing powers of technology feared by the government authorities in Peking were in direct proportion attractive to the revolutionary underground. Wu's shockingly mutilated body was photographed by the authorities with shrewd attention to detail, and the photo was distributed in a modern mimesis of the traditional display of decapitated heads of the condemned; the price for attempting to bomb away ministers of state was graphically illustrated but the effect, apparently, was inadequate. Many who were later revered as early heroes of the revolution were incendiary terrorists who, with greater or lesser expertise, helped establish the gunpowder blast as a rhetorical device. Bombing was, in 1905, still a novel form of terrorism, imported with many other revolutionary techniques from Russia. The radical opponents of the Qing government adopted it despite the horrible risks that it posed for them personally. Huang Xing, Ma Fuyi, Wang Jingwei, Huang Fusheng and Lin Guanzi were later praised for their comparative specialization in the use of bombs. The dashing heroine of the Canton Uprising in March of 1911, Xu Zongshan—who helped Huang Xing escape to Hong Kong and later married him—was the leader of a legendary "bomb team" that helped soften up the Manchu elite in Canton just prior to the disastrous uprising. From 1907 on Manchu (or Chinese-martial seen as Manchu) leaders, particularly in the provinces, were slow-moving targets for proponents of "murderism."

The ideological and political developments behind the cresting violence continued to elude many observers, including Jinliang, who gives no hint that he was aware that in the very period in which he was beginning his friendship with Zhang Binglin, Hangzhou was becoming a center of radical anti-Qing activity.[59] Qiu Jin, the woman revolutionary who would be martyred for the cause in 1907, was born to a nearby Shaoxing family a year or two before Jinliang. At eighteen she married a minor bureaucrat and moved to Peking, where she, her husband and small children narrowly escaped the violence of the Boxer riots and their suppression. Later, with the aid of Jiang Kanghu (who still later would be an acquaintance of Jinliang), she arranged to travel to Japan, which was then a center of Chinese nationalist activity. In 1905 she returned to China, worked with underground revolutionary organizations, was active in the radical penetration of the New Army units in Hangzhou, and later began teaching at a girls' school in Shaoxing. On July 13 troops of the provincial governor Zhang Zengyang (1843–1921) discovered arms and ammunition cached on the school grounds; two days later Qiu Jin was beheaded at Zhang's order. Her remains were interred on the shore of West Lake, and though ordered removed by the provincial authorities shortly afterward would be returned there after the fall of the empire.[60] Qiu's cousin Xu Xilin shared in many of her revolutionary activities and in 1907 assassinated the Anhui governor Enming, for which Xu himself was speedily executed.[61] Cai Yuanpei and Chen Fuchen were among the intellectuals whose revolutionary thought pervaded the newly established Hangzhou academies of the turn of the century and contributed to the growth of interlocking journal editorial staffs, academic faculty and military organizers—most with links to the Chinese student community in Tokyo—who formed the infrastructure of the anti-Qing movement in Zhejiang.

Due primarily to his position in the constabulary Jinliang was as aware as anyone else in Peking of the unrest that was epidemic and accelerating in the country after the Sino-Japanese War of 1895, and certainly after the suppression of the Hundred Days' Reform. But after 1905 security measures at Peking were intense; primarily rumors and official reports conveyed to northerners the increasing chaos. "After the explosion [of the bomb thrown by Wu Yue at the ministers in 1905] the court strictly forbade talk in all the provinces of getting rid of Manchus. But at Liuyang in Hunan, at Pingxiang in Jiangxi, there were successive incidents by conspirators which were put down by the officials and soldiers of the area. This was the beginning of the revolution. . . ."[62] It was only with the benefit of a great deal of hindsight that Jinliang marked the beginning of the revolution to the Liuyang and Pingxiang uprisings of 1906. In fact, in this year of his father's death and his own appointment as an intendant of the Foreign Affairs Office (waiwu bu, established in the reforms in the stead of the old zongli yamen) and as a lecturer in the Imperial University (daxue tang), Jinliang saw the emergence of a new political structure at Peking. Xiaoqin was declining fast. The Guangxu emperor Zaitian, who in 1906 was only thirty-five years old, would soon be able to enjoy the restoration that had not been possible in 1898. Duanfang (1861–1911), a supporter of the constitution, of railway development and of Zhang Zhidong's military modernization, had just left his minister's post to become governor-general of Jiangxi and Jiangsu.[63] Xu Shichang (1858–1939) was about to become governor-general of the "Eastern Three Provinces" (dong san sheng) in a thoroughgoing reform of the administration of the Northeast. Both men had survived Wu's bomb attack and later continued their constitutional study tour abroad; they were progressive loyalists, in Jinliang's view, who could be counted on to support a constitutional monarchy under Zaitian.

Jinliang served under Xu in the new Ministry of the Interior (minzheng bu) created in 1907. After Xu's assumption of the governorship of the reorganized "Eastern Three Provinces" in 1907, Jinliang spent part of each year at Mukden serving in Xu's Bureau of Banner Affairs (qiwu si), which in 1909 was itself reorganized as the Department of Banner Affairs (qiwu chu). Natong was another traditionalist reformer in whom Jinliang had great hopes. In 1907 he had Jinliang assigned from Ministry of the Interior's foreign legation police force to act as deputy superintendent (zhishi) of the Inner City branch police force (neicheng xunjing fenting); the job soon evaporated along with the Inner City police force (which was absorbed by the constabulary), but the assignment formed the basis for Jinliang's first book of reminiscences, published the same year. By the beginning of 1911, Natong had new plans to send Jinliang to oversee agricultural education in Manchu and Mongolian for bannermen in the Northeast. Xiliang, the great Mongolian reformer who succeeded Xu Shichang as "Eastern Three Provinces" governor-general in February 1909, appointed Jinliang assistant secretary of the Banner Affairs Section of his administration and promoted him to superintendent of that office shortly afterward.[64] But perhaps Jinliang's most problematic attachment was to

Shanqi (1863–1921), Prince Su (*Su qinwang*).[65] It is probable that Jinliang had made Shanqi's acquaintance soon after arriving in Peking. In any event by 1908 the relationship was firm enough that Shanqi offered to write the introduction to a brief biography of Jinliang being published by Chen Xifu. In 1908 Shanqi joined an exclusive (and predominantly Aisin Gioro) group overseeing the Admiralty (*haijun yamen*), and later served overlapping terms at the Ministry of the Interior (where he appointed Jinliang to a series of Inner City police-force posts), and the Ministry of Dependencies (*lifan bu*).

Nearly all of Jinliang's appointments between 1906 and 1911 were in agencies, some more than a little ephemeral, that had sprung from the reform decrees of Xiaoqin (via Zaitian) in 1906 and 1907, particularly. In many of his capacities he was expected to take a first-hand look at the effects of the reforms on bannermen, both in Peking and in Mukden, where he began to spend more time in the successive administrations of Xu Shichang and Xiliang. The obvious problem with the Eight Banners was the amount of money spent on them; the princes had agreed, after all, to cut their own stipends in half (a first-degree annual stipend had fallen from 10,000 taels to 5,000, a second-degree from 5,000 to 2,500),[66] and with Xiaoqin gone there was no champion of continued banner support. In the overall context of Qing indebtedness at the beginning of the twentieth century, however, the banner stipend obligations could hardly have represented more than a fraction of the 46 million or more spent each year on servicing the outstanding foreign credit and indemnity payments alone.[67] The actual expense of the Eight Banner forces was no doubt magnified by new energies applied by the imperial clan, after 1907, to coopt the modernized provincial armies created by successive generations of governors.[68] The new reforms also paid little reverence to the ancient Qing concern with preservation of the Old Way (*fe doro*). Instead, the court for the first time was frank in viewing the bannermen as a social problem, and the princes were unsentimental in their determination to finally sever the ties of the bannermen to the state. Remaining legal distinctions between Manchus and Chinese were abrogated, all restrictions against marriage with Chinese were lifted. In 1902, bannermen were told to cease calling themselves slaves (*nucai*). The banners, the earliest institution in the formation of the people who would be the Manchus, were retained, and would in fact survive the fall of the empire. Schools were chartered (though it is difficult to see how many were actually funded and created) that would provide widespread instruction in Manchu as well as in a variety of practical trades. Workshops were instituted to allow bannermen to learn skills and at the same time earn money for the garrison administration.

The longstanding differences between China proper and the Northeast deepened even more in the early twentieth century. The Northeast, where many bannermen had retained their village economies and social structure, and where (thanks to large numbers of Chinese immigrants and distance from the Taiping War battlefields) agricultural development remained strong, began to industrialize in the very early twentieth century under the sponsorship of Russia, China and Japan, all of whom were competing for its control. Bannermen found employment in many of the new industries. Banner workshops were established in 1906 in Peking, Rihe, Mukden, Jinzhou, Jilin, Hunqun, and upper Heilongjiang, devoted to the apprenticing of bannermen in industries such as woodworking, lacquering, weaving, smelting, rugweaving, dying, tailoring, ceramics, soap-making, leatherworking, and glass manufacture. The shop at Mukden, which employed five hundred, may be a good example of the scale of enterprises. Like the old banner cadetships (which were disguised forms of subsidies to families with underage sons), these appointments were reserved for young men of thirteen or fourteen years of age. Bannermen were also given some preference in employment in Chinese-foreign jointly owned enterprises in the Northeast, particularly railroads and mines.[69]

The loss of an agricultural base and the distance of many garrisons from industrializing centers in China proper provided a less efficient environment for reforms there, although there were outstandingly successful reform generals-in-chief, like [Niohuru] Wenrui, who founded apprenticing workshops for bannermen seeking to escape opium addiction while he was general-in-chief at Suiyuan in Shanxi and at Xi'an in Shaanxi.[70] Efforts to educate banner women were primarily local initiatives, and partly for that reason were in some cases in advance of the government programs for men. At Hangzhou, a widow of a Gūwalgiya lineage, and possibly a distant relative of Jinliang, named Huixing rented a house in a tiny alley in the eastern part of the garrison and started a "practical literacy school for girls" in 1904. Her teaching was successful but within a year her funds had run out. She appealed to the general-in-chief Ruixing for aid. He refused, and in a protest suicide Huixing drank poison. Her note, "When the goose is gone the echo of its call remains, when the body is gone, the reputation remains. I take no pleasure in dying; but there is no choice!" evidently shamed Ruixing. Together with provincial governor Zhang Zengyang (who the next year would order the execution of Qiu Jin) he memorialized the court on Huixing's behalf, and she was posthumously titled "Pure heart, resolute effort (*zhen xin yi li*)." The people of the Hangzhou community themselves gathered the money necessary to continue the school; Jinliang, remembering his father's efforts to educate the women of his family, raised funds among his aquaintances in Peking and sent them to Hangzhou in Huixing's honor. In 1906 the Huixing School for Women (*Huixing nu xuetang*) was opened by the garrison community, two years before the state would mandate the opening at Hangzhou of the Eight Banners Elementary Preparatory School (*baqi chudeng xiaoxue tang*) and the Eight Banners Higher Preparatory School (*baqi goadeng xiaoxue tang*) for the garrison's young men.[71]

Xiaoqin died on November 15, 1908, but Jinliang's hopes for a Guangxu restoration were strangled when it was learned that Zaitian had mysteriously predeceased the empress at the Yihe Summer Palace. Xiaoqin had, during her lifetime, built for herself a mausoleum at the Eastern Tombs (Dongling) in Rihe, and her body was conveyed there on the first auspicious day. Zaitian thus far had no tomb. On January 5, 1909, a consortium of imperial princes, headed by Yikuang, was established to oversee a five-year construction project for Zaitian's mausoleum at the Western Tombs (Xiling). The imperial remains were conveyed to the subterranean chamber at the first opportunity, but construction of the outer complex was haphazard, and unfinished even at the time of the revolution. In the meantime, the business of choosing a successor was perfunctory; Xiaoqin had once again formed an alliance of interests before her death, and the princes fixed upon the three-year-old son of Zaifeng, little Puyi, as Zaitian's fictive heir. Jinliang was pleased to note that as the grandson of both Yihuan and Ronglu, Puyi united the Suwan Gūwalgiya and the Aisin Gioro clans in his person. Zaifeng was appointed his regent; the child's mother, Longyu, appointed as his tutors Lu Runxiang, Chen Baochen and Ikedan, a tenth-generation descendant of Fiongdon from the Xi'an garrison.

Though the flurry of business that accompanied the ongoing creation of reform programs in Peking may have obscured it, the fact was that from the deaths of Xiaoqin and Zaitian to the outbreak of the military violence that ended the empire was a relatively small step. The view from the provinces, Jinliang realized in retrospect, would have made this clearer. There, the New Army units with their Japanese-educated officers and conscripts from the secret societies made a potent combination of vision, confidence and passion. The Pingxiang uprising of 1906 could in fact have been an instructive paradigm for the coming struggle. Building on the base of traditional Gelao *hui* secret society cells with their ancient hatred of the Manchus, the Revolutionary Party (*Geming dang*) had supplied a second level of organization and ideology, publishing a manifesto detailing the crimes of the Manchus from Yangzhou to the present, calling for an end to the monarchy as an institution, and declaring "Not only will we drive out the Manchus, but we will never again permit minorities to usurp power."[72]

In the events that followed the October 10, 1911 Wuchang uprising that sparked the final chain of decisive confrontation between loyalist and revolutionary forces in the provinces, the promise to exterminate the Manchus directed much of the violence even though the quarries' relatively small numbers made them hard to find. In some regions Manchus were deliberately hunted and executed. At Wuhan, where the revolution began, the search for Manchus went on for days after the capture of the city; an eyewitness reported that he found "the streets deserted and the corpses of Manchus lying in all directions, fifty bodies being heaped together outside one gate alone. The rebel troops are still hunting for Manchus, of whom 800 are reported to have been killed. . . ." At Yichang, where the fighting had been relatively light, seventeen Manchu women and children were rounded up, and several days after the city had been secured they were executed, to, in the words of the Hunan Provisional Government established by the revolutionaries, "placate the troops."[73] In fact not all who were killed for being Manchu were in actuality Manchu. Chinese village girls with unbound feet, bearded men, people with fair complexions or "flat heads"—all traits of the mythical Manchu physiognomy—were snared in the revenge lust, just as three centuries before, Chinese settlers in the Northeast were sometimes submitted to the Ming government's collection of "Jurchen" heads. Three weeks after Yichang, the world was shocked by international press reports of the massacre at Xi'an of perhaps as many as 20,000 Manchus; after days of being surrounded in the garrison with all food supplies cut off, the community (led by the reformer Wenrui) was invaded by revolutionary forces, the Gelao *hui* in the forefront, who took another three days to pursue the last of the starving banner populace to the furthest corners of the garrison and slaughter them.[74] Jinliang was relieved to hear that Hangzhou, at least, had not suffered greatly in the revolution; the remnants of the garrison had been smashed but the last residents had fled with only a dozen recorded casualties.[75] Of his family, his nephew Xiongwen was wounded, in the neck.[76] The house in New Dragon Lane had been sacked by the revolutionary forces or the mobs following them. The belongings in the house, including books, engravings and paintings collected by Fengrui after his return from the war, were pilfered. But there was, perhaps, a hopeful omen: Thieves had attempted to drag the trunk containing Fengrui's jade collection down from the attic; they tripped, were badly bruised by the heavy trunk as it rolled over them to the ground floor and, realizing the uselessness of attempting to drag the thing away, fled the house before they could be apprehended by the servants. Jinliang made arrangements for the trunk to be transported north, to his home in Mukden.[77]

By January the court had realized the unstoppable momentum of the revolution. After brief negotiations, Puyi (aged six) abdicated his throne on February 12, 1912. He withdrew with his family to the Forbidden

City, where they were confined to the Kunning Palace and its adjacent compounds in the northern portion of the palace grounds. The Qing empire was no more. But the end of the empire did not mean the end of the dynasty, which at the time was an important distinction. Yikuang and the empress dowager Longyu bargained with Yuan Shikai and the revolutionary leaders. In exchange for a peaceful and orderly abdication, the Republic would guarantee two treaties. The first, the Manchu-Mongol-Uigur-Tibetan Articles of Favorable Treatment (*man meng hui cang youdai [daiyu] tiaojian*), protected the property and the political rights of these peoples. In seven articles, it promised equality between the Chinese (*han*) and the four peoples named (together these peoples constituted the "five races" of China); protections for their personal property; continued recognition for existing ranks and titles; means of livelihood for those in need; continuation of stipends for those who were receiving them (with the exception of the imperial household); lifting of all residence restrictions pertaining to the garrisons, and freedom to enter the civilian registers; absolute freedom of religion. "Favorable Treatment," in the case of the commoners of the four non-Han "races" in question, was actually a paper warrant against the unfavorable treatment that many had experienced in the revolution and still feared. Its one extraordinary provision was the inspiration of Yuan Shikai, who considered a portion of the bannermen to be superior soldiers and who wished to cement their loyalty to him. Unlike the imperial princes, Yuan was not confident of the loyalty of the bannermen without the enticements of stipends and recognition. First Yuan and then the Republican government felt that the cost of stipends was a reasonable expense in view of the probable avoidance of social disorder and possible real advantages of keeping a few militarily fit traditional soldiers on the rolls. Stipends were not universally abolished until 1924, the year the court was driven from Peking by Feng Yuxiang.

The second treaty, the Imperial Court Articles of Favorable Treatment (*huangshi youdai [daiyu] tiaojian*), was an elaborate agreement, amended the next year, that granted a remnant Imperial Household Department four million taels (to be changed in the early Republican period to "dollars"—*yuan*) per year, provided for the rent or purchase of imperial lands, guaranteed the private property of the imperial clan, sanctioned the maintenance in perpetuity of Puyi's personal bodyguard (though the individual guards would be enrolled formally in the Republican army) and permitted Puyi to reside in the Forbidden City for an indefinite period of time, after which he was to relocate to the Summer Palace at Haidian. In exchange, the court was to desist from naming years by the Xuantong reign period in all communications with the government or the public, to cease awarding new ranks and titles (existing titles would continue to be honored), to make honorary awards in commodities only (no cash), and to relocate to the Summer Palace as soon as possible.[78] This peculiar arrangement had two advantages to the new government. First, it circumscribed the uncertainties of loyalist resistance or the opportunistic pretension to loyalist resistance by the nobles and the northern warlords, and thus shortened the revolutionary struggle. Second, it prevented a concentration of loyalist energies in the Northeast. In the changing mosaic of factions and powers, Favorable Treatment may have seemed to have resolved at least one variable—armed, loyalist, Northeastern resistance—in the multiplex and self-perpetuating equation of political power in the early Republic.

The Articles of Favorable Treatment were taken, quite rightly, by the court and its supporters as acknowledgment by the Republicans of the continuing political capabilities of the restorationists. The revolution had been very much a phenomenon of south and central China. In the north the revolutionaries had made little progress in their attempts to enlist support among the men who had *de facto* control of the northern region. In fact the Northeast had begun a development away from the central government soon after the Boxer Rebellion, when Qing civil control over the region had disintegrated. Russia and Japan contended for strategic leverage there, and came to blows over the question in 1904. But local control rested with the bandits, or "redbeards" (*honghuzi*) who by force of arms managed the roadways and villages of the region. Many redbeards were former soldiers and bannermen who had broken away from the formal military and started operations on their own. Most attempted to play upon Russian and, later, Japanese interests in order to maintain or advance their own position. After 1905 the Japanese were laying railways and establishing factories at crucial points in Fengtian and Jilin provinces. Redbeards worked with Japanese liaisons to get themselves hired as spies, guards, drivers and—when Chinese property owners showed unreasonable resistance to encroachments by Japanese industrial or military agencies—goons. But they also needed to coordinate their operations with bigger redbeards and with the militarists who attempted to reestablish Qing control in the Northeast after 1906.

There was, perhaps, no better exemplar of redbeard ambition than Zhang Zuolin.[79] Zhang would later claim that he had been a Chinese-martial bannerman, and it was certainly possible that he or his proximate ancestors had been on the rolls. By 1903 Zhang had made himelf the head redbeard in the Xinmin, Fengtian region, and when Japanese troops seized control of the town Zhang was condemned to death. By some means he was able to convince the Japanese commanders that he could be useful to them, and thereafter he flourished under the unlegitimated but real Japanese control of the district. The local power balance had shifted, however, when Xu Shichang was commissioned by the Qing court to reestablish Chinese control over the Northeast and to create a consolidated governorship for the region. Zhang quickly bought his way into the graces of the Xu regime, which was absorbing the remaining Eight Banner and Green Standard forces of the Northeast into the reformed New Army. Zhang was given command of five battalions at Chengjiatun in Fengtian, and by parcelling out the troops to selected comrades was able to create a clique for himself that included his younger brother Zhang Zuoxiang.

When the decline and fall of the Qing was imminent in early 1911, several powerful militarists in the Northeast conceived of plans for establishing independent regional rule. That this plan happened to coincide with the long-term plans of some parties in the military and bureaucratic establishments in Japan (which had colonized Korea in 1910) was secondary; the collapse of the Qing had fueled simmering separatist movements in Mongolia, Xinjiang and Tibet, and the realities of local bases in the Northeast only made the proposition that much more reasonable there. The governor-general of the Eastern Three Provinces in 1911, Zhao Erxun of the Chinese-martial Plain Blue Banner, was however a staunch loyalist and an enemy of separatism in the Northeast. He suppressed efforts by several factions to incite separatist movements in the Provincial Assembly at Mukden, once even ordering the asssembly grounds to be surrounded by troops and guns to be drawn on the speakers. While "murderism" was the slogan of some constituencies of the republican revolution, "humanitarianism" (*rendao zhuyi*) was the motto of Zhao's modernized banner forces as they sought to quell fighting between contentious separatist factions and keep Zhao's command position intact. Zhao outlawed separatist leaders, and had himself elected head of the Peace Preservation Society (*bao'an hui*); local cells posted the aims of the society, which was protection of the lives and property of all local residents, "whether Manchus, Chinese, Muslims or Mongols."[80] The benevolence of the Peace Preservation Society's rhetoric was not seriously expected to disguise the ruthlessness with which Zhao intended to enforce what was now his personal regime in the Northeast. A young bannerman named Zhong Yong was murdered for challenging Zhao's rule, in an enigmatic case that dramatized the special tensions animating Northeastern politics as the empire evaporated.

The police had first taken note of Zhang Yong during the investigation of the Wu Yue bombing, and his radical contacts in the capital were well established. It was his opposition to Zhao and other loyalists in the Northeast that led at one time to Zhang's characterization as a revolutionary. While there were a small number of revolutionaries in the Northeast, they made few significant links with either the Japanese or the local miltarists, and were a relatively minor element in the political struggles of the time. A closer look revealed that Zhang was in all probability a separatist who on occasion clothed himself in revolutionary rhetoric, some of it extreme enough to disturb Zhao's henchmen. When Zhang Yong's speeches to the Provincial Assembly became too radical, Zhang Zuolin drew a pistol on him and forced him off the podium. Still, Zhang Yong continued through the late part of 1911 to contact and to cooperate with Zhao Erxun, hoping to convince the governor to make the Northeast independent from the moribund Qing regime. "There is no evidence," Gavan McCormack has noted, "that he conceived of the revolution as meaning anything more than that."[81] Materials published recently reveal the wisdom of this reassessment. Zhang was clearly playing a complex game of information and influence trading not only with Zhao Erxun and revolutionary activists, but also with Yuan Shikai, with unidentified Chinese conservative factions, and with the Japanese, a game that made him widely distrusted, even hated, by many of the parties involved.[82] Zhao Erxun may have feared that Zhang Yong would succeed in gaining significant power for himself, or he may have suspected that his interests were being betrayed to the Japanese. Whatever the reason, at Zhao's behest Zhang Zuolin's men murdered Zhang Yong as he left a dinner party with Yuan Jinkai (also a conspirator in the assassination) on January 23, 1912. In a hopeless appeal to the civil process, Zhang's older sister Zhang Wa attempted to press charges against Zhao and Zhang Zuolin for the killing. Her claims were investigated, and no grounds for charges were ever discovered.[83]

The murder of Zhang Yong was, as it happened, followed very shortly by the abdication of Puyi, which left Zhao Erxun as the unchallenged ruler of the Northeast. He remained an unwavering loyalist, dating his documents according to the Xuantong reign years, maintaining a reorganized Eight Banner force in his domain, and welcoming other loyalists from the Chinese provinces. Zhang Zuolin, in turn, was Zhao's second-in-command and enforcer. They were a strange pair in a strange scenario. Zhao was the epitome of a late Qing official, educated, urbane, experienced in a series of major governorships before being appointed to the Northeast in 1911. Zhang was uneducated, uncouth, and had few experiences beyond redbeard rivalries and the hostile cooperation with the Japanese that characterized life in the Northeast. Together, in the early years after the end of the empire, the two men controlled the new world that Jinliang, waving his list of degrees, offices and sponsors, attempted to enter.

For most Manchus, displaced and impoverished, flight to the Northeast—which they called "exiting the Pass" (*chuguan*) in ironic reference to "entering the Pass" (*ruguan*) in 1644—was impractical; the best hope for safety was to hide, keep a low profile, and wait for things to quiet down. Jinliang, however, lost no time in moving his household, including his mother Qian-shi, from Peking to his house in Mukden, and from there to the relative safety of Dalian on the Lushun peninsula, a region under firm Japanese control. Chunliang and Xiongwen, the latter once a separatist who was now modifying his rhetoric in view of the Northeastern regime's intolerance for such talk, lived at Mukden. Jinliang was still a young man, and had not lost hope for the dynasty. On the contrary he considered that the revolution provided the opportunity for a renewal, with the pernicious influence of the court denizens swept away. The child emperor Puyi was alive and well-cared-for in the imperial city. Powerful loyalists like Zhao and Zhang Zuolin only bided their time before effecting a restoration. In the meantime, Manchus like himself, his brother and his cousins could for the first time return to the Manchu homeland and enjoy its invigorating effects. He seems to have had no thought that the temporary eclipse of the Qing, whose creatures the Manchus were, boded the end of the Manchus as well. He had with him his son Guandong, and noted with pride Guandong's change of registration to the Northeast:

> Our Gūwalgiya clan is one of the ancient clans of the Changbai region. In the second year of the Shunzhi reign my ancestor Ubahai received assignment to the Hangzhou garrison, and in the seventh year of the Yongzheng reign my ancestor Jalangga was assigned to Zhapu. Then, in the third year of the Tongzhi reign my father was ordered to return to Hangzhou. In three hundred years we had three successive moves. Now after nine generations my youngest son Guandong is once again registered at Changbai, even though his ancestor's graves are still in Hangzhou and Zhapu.[84]

The home that Jinliang had established for himself and his family in Dalian was not retained for long; in late 1912 he moved back to Mukden and began work as curator of the former imperial archives there. This meant, in essence, that he had entered the personal governmental edifice maintained by Zhang Zuolin. Zhang was now the virtual ruler of Mukden, and over the coming fifteen years would eliminate other local rivals to dominate the Northeast, with only the Japanese to hinder him. Jinliang was affixed to Zhang's fortunes, whether he liked it or not. For the first few years he concentrated on enjoying the historical pleasures of the old imperial palace at Mukden, exploring and organizing the Manchu archives, travelling with his son to Nurgaci's old homestead at Xingjing (Hetu Ala). By 1917 he was also serving in civil posts, recommended by Zhang and ratified by the Republican government, as an official of the Mongol banners in the Northeast and as a judicial intendant at Xinmin prefecture, in the heart of Zhang Zuolin's realm. In addition, by this time he had begun tutoring Zhang's young son, Xueliang.

Jinliang was restless and unfocused during these years. He missed Peking and, during the winters particularly, thought of visiting Hangzhou. The ease with which he had moved between literati circles and Manchu enclaves during his youth was gone. His company was now divided between other former scholars and bureaucrats like himself who served their warlords in official or unofficial capacities, and the increasing number of soldiers, both local and Japanese, who formed Zhang Zuolin's inner circle. To his unending discomfort, Jinliang did not like Zhang Zuolin. The former redbeard was, to him, a diminutive, disreputable looking man, unhealthy, uncouth, and with little to recommend him beyond a certain vulpine intelligence.[85] Unfortunately Jinliang did not have the luxury of complaining to his family of his frustrations in dealing with the "old general." His mother, Qian-shi, considered Zhang a paragon and would not hear a word against him; when Jinliang resigned from Zhang's staff following a disagreement in 1917, Qian-shi browbeat him into going back. Jinliang fixed his hopes on the young Zhang Xueliang in hopes of forgetting his disappointment with the father. Chen Yuzhen, who had known Jinliang for twenty years, remarked the changes in his friend in a preface to a homily Jinliang was preparing in honor of the rather irascible Qian-shi. As a youth, Chen observed, Jinliang had been impetuous and prone to "comment on everything." As a mature man, Jinliang was gentle and sincere, but said little. Indeed, Chen was convinced that the older Jinliang grew, the more humane he became. Yet one could see that all was not right. "He is worried."[86]

Jinliang's mother may not have known that the loyalism for which Zhang had made himself known in the period immediately following the fall of the empire was waning in ensuing years as his personal ambitions waxed. In the Northeast, loyalism and restoration were serious topics, combining Japanese imperial designs, the ambitions of loyalists themselves and widespread sentiment in problematic mixtures. The demonstrated instability of the Peking regime and the sister republican government under Sun Yatsen in the south only fueled the intensity of restorationist expectations in the Northeast. In the early years the Nationalist Party was overburdened with the necessity of suppressing rebellions in the southern provinces, bargaining with provincial governors threatening to declare independence, and the attempts of Nationalist leaders to form a political coalition powerful enough to curb Yuan Shikai's increasing hold over all sectors of the new government. Nationalist attempts to dislodge Yuan had failed until his own monarchical coup brought him down. In the aftermath, the Peking order seemed even more volatile than before.

Restorationist sentiment had been galvanized in the Northeast in 1915, when Yuan was preening himself for the new emperorship. Japanese militarists were willing to back Qing restorationists who would oppose Yuan's seizure of power. In the spring of 1916 the Japanese cabinet had approved such activities, and through Kawashima Naniwa money and supplies were soon flowing to the Mongol prince Babojab, who vowed to mount a force to restore Puyi to the throne. Similar aid, also through Kawashima, was provided to Jinliang's old Peking sponsor Shanqi, who had been soliciting German and Japanese loans for years in order to create a private army for himself. Zhang Zuolin was not a friend to these movements. In response to Yuan's announcement of a new monarchy Zhang had begun to foment a "Fengtianese" independence movement, hoping to force Yuan to buy his neutrality or support by naming him to a variety of military and civil posts in the Three Eastern Provinces. The gambit worked, though as part of the price Zhang had to survive an attempted bomb assassination by a Japanese supporter of the restorationists in May of 1916. Babojab and Shanqi, on the other hand, were not successful. Soon after Yuan Shikai's death in June, Babojab led his three thousand Mongol horsemen and Shanqi his mixed squads of mercenaries in an uprising. The operation was confused, Japanese support that was expected did not arrive, and Babojab was killed in the fighting outside Zhangjiakou, south of the Great Wall; Shanqi fled to Japanese sanctuary in Lushun, where he died in 1921.[87]

In Peking, the poorly understood events of the Babojab and Shanqi uprisings did not create a backlash against the court or against the restorationists. The first ten years of the Chinese Republic were, inevitably, a chaotic period in which various warlords attempted to exploit the weakness and confusion of the unrealized parliamentary system to enhance their own personal power, while foreign states fished in the troubled waters for catch of their own liking. Loyalist elements were as sanguine and predatory as any other faction. Indeed, in the summer of 1917, shortly after the Babojab incident, Puyi was restored to the throne. Zhang Xun, a Zhili warlord who had kept his queue in reverence for the late empire, occupied Peking, dissolved the Parliament (which had only recently been reestablished after being dissolved by Yuan Shikai before his death) and declared the emperor restored. Zhang was received in the Forbidden City by Puyi, and it appears that Puyi's ministers may have hatched plans for creating a new regency headed by the "pigtailed general." For two weeks the restorationists held Peking, but were eventually driven out by bombs dropped from planes flown by the troops of Duan Qirui.[88] Coming in the wake of large-scale depredations by Yuan Shikai and increasing fears over the gigantic loans that Peking was obtaining from Japan and the Western powers to prosecute its territorial wars against the warlords of the west and south, Zhang Xun's restoration was regarded more as scandalous than dangerous, more interesting than terrifying. If Puyi's "memoirs" are to be credited, the occasion was one of merrymaking in Peking, as vendors rushed to sell souvenirs of the event and people dragged out their traditional garb to parade through the streets. Though the affair was of little immediate political significance, it sparked more than a few people's imaginations. The liberal reformer Hu Shih visited the palace more than once in the ensuing years, possibly to see if within the vessel of young Puyi there burned the soul of a responsible constitutional monarch. International celebrities like Rabindranath Tagore stopped by to chat with Puyi and to be photographed with him. People wrote letters to the paper speculating upon the possibilities of the monarchy as a unifying force. And, in Mukden, Jinliang began to feel that he was only biding his time until a return to the capital.

Zhang Zuolin visited Peking from time to time, and like many associated with the new civil government made "courtesy calls" upon the emperor. Jinliang accompanied Zhang on such a visit and made his first contact with the imperial adolescent, who was related to the Suwan Gūwalgiya through his mother. In 1923, when Puyi was eighteen, Jinliang moved back to Peking, probably for the purpose of cultivating the emperor and his circle. Certainly he spent his time with the loyalists who still lived in the vicinity of the Forbidden City; the same group now styled themselves *yilao*, "men living hidden lives," in solidarity with the intellectuals who before them had survived the collapse of the Song and Ming dynasties, in their hearts remaining true to their once-and-future rulers. His fellow Suwan Gūwalgiya clansman Ikedan was one of the first he approached; the greater part of Ikedan's lineage had perished in the catastrophe at Xi'an during the revolution, a tragedy Jinliang clearly saw as a parallel to that of the Zhapu lineage in the Taiping War. He revered Ikedan's wholehearted loyalty (as he perceived it) and would have collaborated with him on a Gūwalgiya genealogy had Ikedan not died in the summer of that year. Other loyalists and sympathizers were not in short supply, and Jinliang cultivated many of them; Wang Guowei (1877–1927) stayed in his house for a portion of 1923,[89] and Jinliang saw or corresponded with Zheng Xiaoxu, Shengyun, Zhang Zengyang (his former unwilling ally in supporting the Huixing school eighteen years before), among others. When, in 1924, Puyi at the age of nineteen began to assume personal control over the management of the court, he invited Jinliang to Peking to serve as one of four Grand Councillors (*dachen*) of the Imperial Household Department (*neiwufu*).[90] Jinliang could remember, as Puyi could not, a time when such an honor would have meant staggering wealth, political influence and eternal honor for the lineage. Certainly he was under no illusions that he would, at first, be doing anything more than participating in a small theater of actors with roles and costume, but no lines to speak. Still, with all hope and seriousness he moved his family to the imperial compound in February of 1924.

Puyi's invitation to Jinliang was motivated by the fact that he and his tutors, Reginald Johnston, Zheng Xiaoxu and Ikedan (before his death), were attempting to break the power of Puyi's father and regent, Zaifeng, over the Imperial Household Department, where all of the emperor's wealth was hoarded. Johnston and Zheng suspected that much of the wealth was already gone; priceless antiques and books from the imperial collections had been turning up in the city's emporia, evidently sold or pawned by corrupt officials of the household department, and Zaifeng had himself been spending freely of funds that in all likelihood were not his own. Puyi now appointed the outsiders Jinliang and Zheng Xiaoxu joint overseers of the Imperial Household Department. They were to be assisted by Luo Zhenyu, Wang Guowei, Shang Yanying and the Manchu [Gūwalgiya] Rongyuan, Puyi's father-in-law. Zheng Xiaoxu, Rongyuan and Jinliang were particularly fast allies. They apparently found themselves in agreement on basic ideas, which were laid out in Jinliang's second long memorial, of March 1924. It was a plan for a restoration, and the reflections of the youthful Jinliang's hopes for the Guangxu emperor in 1898 were apparent. They should work for Puyi's full assumption of responsibility within the imperial compound (that is, destruction of the regency of Zaifeng), reform of the Imperial Household Department and scrupulous management of its resources for the future, and the cultivation of a public image for Puyi that would arouse the affection of the population at large. Jinliang worked actively to build a political alliance outside the palace circles that could be used to aid in a restoration attempt, compiling long lists of politicians and intellectuals who might be sympathetic, and exchanging at least three letters with the socialist Jiang Kanghu in Shanghai.

The united and determined front presented by Puyi and his new ministers had provoked an equally determined reaction by Puyi's father Zaifeng, and Shaping, Qiling and others of the old guard of the Imperial Household Department.[91] The prince was particularly outraged at Jinliang's insistence that he should give up the regency and allow Puyi to manage the court.[92] Zheng Xiaoxu's difficulties derived in part from the political controversy growing around the court, which, the government noted, had now violated most of the requirements of the Articles of Favorable Treatment by continuing to number days according to the Xuantong reign, continuing to make rank awards to loyalists, refusing to acknowledge the new currency terms and failing to vacate the Forbidden City for the Yihe Summer Palace.[93] Pressure was gathering in the Yuan for repeal of the Articles of Favorable Treatment, and one of the accusations directed against Puyi was that, contrary to the rules of the department, he had appointed a Han Chinese, Zheng Xiaoxu, as director of the Imperial Household. Puyi accepted Zheng's resignation in hopes of quieting both the Imperial Household Department malcontents and anti-monarchists in the Yuan, and Jinliang was forced to resign shortly afterward.[94]

In the end the fate of the court was not decided by parliamentary politics. In September of 1924 war broke out a second time between Wu Peifu and Jinliang's former employer Zhang Zuolin. In late October the troops of Feng Yuxiang, allied with Zhang, made their way through the Shanhai Pass and moved toward Peking. During the first days of November they entered the palace compound, disarmed and dislodged the palace guard. On November 5 they finally presented to Puyi a government act, signed by acting premier Huang Fu, that abolished the imperial title. Though the imperial family was permitted to retain its property, Puyi and his entourage were ordered to vacate the Forbidden City. Through the good offices of Luo Zhenyu and Zheng Xiaoxu a residence was found for Puyi and most of the court at Tianjin. Appeals from the group to the Republican government for their reinstatement in Peking were firmly rejected, with extensive and heated discussion of particulars, by Sun Yatsen in the months before his death.

In 1925 "Documentary Evidence for the Secret Restorationist Plot by the Qing Court," (*Qingshi mimou fupi wenzheng*), a collection of letters and memorial concerning restoration recovered from the court archives after Feng's occupation of the palace, was published in Peking and aroused a public furor. The Republican government considered pressing charges of sedition against certain of the individuals involved, including Jinliang and Reginald Johnston. This plan was eventually abandoned, probably because most of the principals were living under Japanese protection in Tianjin.[95] It seemed the end, for the time being, of dreams of restoration. On Chinese New Year's Day, 1925, Puyi held a party for his former government in the hotel where he was staying. For Jinliang, the drama and disappointment were evidently too great. From the midst of those in attendance, a man in Qing dress suddenly emerged, the long sleeves of his robe covering his face. He pushed aside those in his path and fled out the door of the hotel lobby, issuing loud, long cries. Puyi was startled, and could not imagine the cause of such anguish. A bystander recognized the wraith as the former Imperial Household Councillor, Jinliang. Puyi's comment in his "memoirs" probably reflects more the later cynicism of himself or his editors than his real feelings at the time, though there must be at least a small element of truth in the suggestion of self-promotion: "The next day Jinliang had a poem published in the paper, and we all figured his antics were to call attention to his poem."[96]

Still, the resourceful Jinliang saw opportunities in the growing Japanese military presence in China and the Northeast; living under Japanese protection in Tianjin, the usefulness of the Japanese seemed only more apparent to him. For nearly twenty years they had been working to establish a military and commercial presence in the Northeast. Their colonization of Korea in 1910—the end of a long policy of military and commercial expansion there—together with the collapse of their great rival, the Romanov empire in Russia, intensified Japanese ambitions. Jinliang imagined that the Japanese might be able to effect a Qing restoration where the lesser powers of a Chinese warlord would certainly fail. Indeed he knew from his contacts with Japanese agents working for Zhang Zuolin in the Northeast that the Japanese favored separatist movements both in Manchuria and in Mongolia. They had great cultural and political sympathies, they claimed, with the peoples of these regions and could work very constructively with them for economic and industrial development. Jinliang reasoned that the future of the Xuantong emperor, Puyi, lay not in Peking but in the ancestral capital of Mukden. He himself prepared to return to Mukden—and his former employer Zhang Zuolin—in 1926. But before leaving he agreed to a request from Captain Doihara Kenichi, of the Kantōgun, that he arrange a meeting with the young former emperor.

The consequences of the meeting did not reveal themselves to Jinliang for some time. He returned to Mukden and assumed the post of curator of the imperial archives, entering into the great cooperative work that would become "Draft History of the Qing" (*Qingshi gao*). Zhang Xueliang, Zuolin's eldest son, was now grown, and in need of no tutor other than the Kantōgun agents who had annointed him heir apparent to his father as governor of the Northeast. Now fifty years old, Jinliang had become aware of but not resigned to the fact that what he had hoped would be a life of great deeds was quickly being reduced to a pile of rather mediocre writing. To supplement his income and assuage his loyalist yearnings, he joined the group hired by the aged Zhao Erxun (aged eighty-four), with the financial backing of a variety of lesser northern warlords, to write a draft history of the Qing dynasty. His impecuniousness evidently overcame his realization that by participating in the project he would, by all the symbolism that a literate man lived by, indicate his acknowledgment of the death of the dynasty. Jinliang's official position on the project as an assistant to the editor Yuan Jinkai, a Zhao Erxun crony and co-conspirator in the murder of Zhang Yong. Jinliang's was a lowly rank that was probably intended to allay the suspicions of the Republican government, to whom he was still an untried traitor. But Jinliang's ties to Zhang Zuolin gave him much more influence over the project than his official title would suggest. When the massive draft was finally completed in the spring of 1928 it was Jinliang who was entrusted with its final proofreading and delivery to the printers. He made, without the consent of his co-compilers, liberal emendations to the manuscript. Kang You-wei's biography, for instance, was revised in such a way as to emphasize his loyalty to the Guangxu emperor over his commitment to radical political change.[97] He also wrote and inserted a biography of Zhang Xun, the loyalist general who had occupied Peking for two weeks and effected the emperor's "first restoration" in 1917. In and of itself, this latter change meant the political doom of the publication.

Four hundred copies of Jinliang's version of "Draft History" had been distributed in the Northeast, Shanghai, Canton and Hong Kong before the other editors discovered what had happened. Distribution of any un-censored edition of "Draft History" had been prohibited by the Repub-lican government. As a consequence, the circulation of Jinliang's version was limited enough that the editors were able to round up a good number of the volumes, print the original text and submit it for government ap-proval. In late 1929 the work was finally permitted to circulate, after a preface of disavowal had been added by the censors and certain offensive passages annotated to point out the biases of the authors. Because Jin-liang's edition never had wide circulation outside the Northeast it is to-day known as the "Manchurian edition" (*guanwai ben*) while the original is called the "China Proper edition" (*guannei ben*). Throughout the 1930s a debate, often acrimonious, raged between Jinliang and his former col-laborators on "Draft History," particularly Peng Guodong. Peng claimed that Jinliang's influence over the standard work was slight, and that his major contribution had been corruption of the fruits of his colleagues' labors. In view of the inclusion in the China Proper edition of the biog-raphies of Guancheng, Fengrui, Xirui, Boliang and Hualiang, it could hardly have been the case that Jinliang had only slight influence over the content of the original "Draft History." But the suggestion of Jinliang that he was a major compiler, or even the real editor, of "Draft History," was certainly far from the truth, too.[98]

The year 1924 had been full of bad omens, as Jinliang had observed at the time. The last Qutughtu Khan installed by the Qing emperors in Mongolia was deposed. Puyi was expelled from the Forbidden City and his titles cancelled. The Leifeng Pagoda that had presided over the West Lake landscape for centuries fell down. But there had been cause for hope. The year that Jinliang sent "Draft History" to the printers, 1928, was different. Zhang Zuolin was murdered by the Japanese in June, his train bombed by Japanese agents while crossing a bridge just outside

Mukden. His son Zhang Xueliang, Jinliang's former pupil, was installed by the Japanese in his father's place, and the mourners for old Zhang, Jinliang among them, had bombs lobbed at them from Japanese planes while they attended Zhang's open coffin, set upon bare sawhorses in the middle of the floor. Shortly afterward came news even more shocking to Jinliang's sign-sensitivity. The Republicans under Chiang Kai-shek [Jiang Jieshi] had reached Peking with their "northern expedition," in an effective campaign to break the powers of the northern warlords. In the resulting warfare near Peking, a former bandit and now minor warlord named Sun Dianying descended with his troops upon the Eastern Tombs, the quiet valley where the Shunzhi, Kangxi, Qianlong and Xianfeng emperors as well as the dowager empresses Xiaozhen and Xiaoqin were buried. Cannons were used to destroy the huge sacred turtle guarding the spirit road into the tombs. Dynamite clusters were planted against the iron-bordered doors leading into the individual mausolea of Hongli and Xiaoqin, and pickaxes applied to pry them open. Inside, the wooden sarcophagi of Hongli and his two empresses, placed on their wide stone platform, were pounded open, their remains smashed and scattered as the vandals sought what valuables might have been buried on their persons; their grave goods were loaded into carts and baskets to be toted away as booty. Xiaoqin, who rested alone in her death palace, was dragged from her coffin in her gold-embroidered burial clothes and torn to bits in an orgy of ferreting for pearls, gold and jade. The doors of other tombs were assaulted with explosives and axes, pillars in sacrificial halls were hacked and gouged, ornamented ceilings were strafed by machine-gun fire, bronze and jade statuary were dragged away. Hearing of the sacrilege, Puyi was white with rage and mortification, a reaction that must have been shared by his entire entourage. His demands that the perpetrators be punished were humored but never satisfied by the Republican authorities.

Disconsolate, Jinliang assumed charge of a project to build a tomb for the unburied Zhang Zuolin. He also threw himself into a translation of a series of Manchu documents from the earliest imperial period; eventually the work became the *Manzhou bidang*, published in 1929, an important pioneering effort in the publication of Manchu materials. For two more years Jinliang clung to his hope that the Kantōgun would become the adopted warriors of the Qing emperor. But in September of 1931, when Japanese troops entered and occupied Mukden, he finally understood the true intentions of Japan in the Northeast. Unlike Zheng Xiaoxu, Shaoying, Luo Zhenyu and others who accompanied Puyi into the charade of the "Manchukuo" state, Jinliang, with his wife and three grandsons, fled the Northeast. They went first to Tianjin, and in 1934 to Peking, where

Jinliang, now fifty-six, would live a scholar's retirement for the next twenty-eight years.

Puyi was installed by the Kantōgun as President of the Republic of Manchukuo in 1932. Two years later he was made emperor of the Manchu Empire, and Zheng Xiaoxu, once Jinliang's ally in the teapot war against Zaifeng in the imperial enclave, became its prime minister. The League of Nations, after sending the Lytton Commission to investigate, denounced the embarrassing contraption that the Japanese army had created in "Manchukuo." Jinliang's oldest son Guandong stayed on in the new republic cum empire. For his part Jinliang grieved for the extinction of his hopes for a Qing restoration or at the very least a truly independent Manchu homeland in the Northeast. He could not return to the Northeast, and discovered that Hangzhou was no longer his home; the former banner quarter there, the *qixia*, had been razed and was now a marketplace, the old Manchu population having dispersed among the urban and suburban population of the region. He decided finally to settle with his wife and grandsons in Peking, where he had spent the better part of his adult life.

Jinliang had no money, and his political reputation was such that no government department, school or newspaper would dare to hire him. A good part of his income came from the demand in the bookmarkets of the city for his calligraphy, which featured large, simple characters. His style had a parallel in his writing, which was to a great extent unaffected by scholarly pretension. In collections such as "Strange Tales from the Melon Patch" (*Guapu shuyi*), which was the best and longest known of his writings, Jinliang drew upon the ghostly legends he had first heard from Fengrui and from other elders in the neighborhoods of the Hangzhou *qixia*. In his late years he was employed by historical commissions, notably that of the Yonghegong, or "Lamaist Temple," in northeast Peking, to work on histories of their institutions, and was paid a small monthly salary, though the works were never finished.[99] A small house in a poor neighborhood of the Dongcheng quarter of Peking was where he went to live for a time, later moving to Nanchang Street, not far from the present-day intersection with West Changan Street.

Jinliang did complete some important work as a historian, however. This was first of all based upon his knowledge of Manchu. In the 1930s in particular, ability in the Manchu language was uncommon and often denied by those who had it in any degree. Jinliang's unabashed advertisement of his knowledge led to grudging acceptance of his translations of the *Manzhou bidang*, which have since been surpassed by authoritative, team-researched editions done in Japan and in Taiwan. Jinliang could be a shrewd and careful handler of documents. It was he, for instance, who in the course of his work on "Draft History of the Qing" exposed as a forgery the famous "Jingshan diary," which supposedly elucidated the relationship between the Qing Court and the Boxers prior to the outbreak of the Boxer Rebellion in 1900. On the strength of Jinliang's revelations Ronglu has been exposed as not only a Boxer sympathizer but also the probable sponsor of the forged diary—which has since been attributed to Edmund Backhouse—for the purpose of diverting suspicion from himself in the aftermath of the foreign suppression of the movement.[100] In the middle 1930s Jinliang's vignettes, some of which contained very caustic commentary on his colleagues and acquaintances of the teens and twenties, became popular. Students of Qing history often visited Jinliang's home in the 1950s to interview him on the particulars of his experiences and his researches, but he was never officially restored to good political standing by either the Republican government or the People's Republic of China.

Although his supernatural and historical vignettes were popular, Jinliang seems to have exhausted his literary reserves in 1936, the last year he is known to have published any work. The man Chen Yuzhen observed in 1916 to be quieter and quieter, in 1936 became silent. In his late writings Jinliang often commented upon the antagonism he felt between himself and his society, and the ironic contrast to the circumstances into which he was born. Raised with a keen sense of the glory and immanence of his clan heritage, and having seen his father struggle with the memories of the Taiping War and the tasks of rebuilding his shattered community, Jinliang was educated for success in the traditional examination system that was abolished the year after he took his ultimate degree. He was appointed to a once-coveted position at a court controlled by vanity, corruption, and insularity at a time when to his young eyes opportunities for reform, revitalization and personal advancement lay everywhere. Cast into a world beyond the end of the world, where the emperor no longer reigned and those cultivated only to serve him catered instead to the whims of dirty, crude warlords whose "loyalty" was as inconstant as all else in the chaotic Republic, then reunited with the Qing sovereign, he engineered a realist's cooperation with the Japanese, only to be cheated by their ruthless imperialism in the sacred city of Mukden. Finally, he returned to Peking, broken, poor and without prospects, at fifty-eight a man too old to adapt to the world in which he had been imprisoned. The very constancy of his devotion to the ideal of progressive constitutional monarchy had transformed him from a public hero to a public embarrassment in the space of thirty years. He did not acknowledge the post-imperial world as being in any way legitimate or orderly. He was regarded, he knew, as a crank and an eccentric, but he was convinced that the oddity was all on the other side. "Nowadays," he wrote in 1936, "we take that which is not mad to be mad. I think people are strange, and they think I am strange. Strange here, strange there! It's hard to avoid nowadays, isn't it? . . . They all pretend there is nothing at all odd going on," he continued after a veiled reference to Japanese imperial expansion in the Northeast and to Communist growth in south China, "but the fact is that people are stranger than ever. And I—yes, I—am also stranger than ever. It's a wonder, isn't it?"

Jinliang died without publicity in 1962.

Conclusion

AN IRONIC OBSERVER of the Qing demise in 1911/1912 could hardly have refrained from noting that the dynasty had in the eighteenth century sanctioned the racial thinking that later contributed to the power of Chinese nationalist rhetoric; that its loyal servants Senggerinqin and Wenxiang had been fathers of the military reforms that had grown into the revolutionary armies; and that the court reactionaries of 1898 and 1900 had rooted out the last loyalist dissident movements in the land, leaving only radical opposition to grow. "Decline" seems almost too passive and mechanistic a term to describe the end of a political and social order that virtually spun itself apart. This book has stressed a Manchu search for self-identification amid the disintegration of the identity-giving structures of the Qing dynasty. The assumption, which might be challenged, is that all people crave a coherent sense of identity (that is, of fitting into the past and the present), which may be supplied in varying degrees by acts of external agencies (like states, societies and communities) or by personal acts of cognitive ordering of historical and cultural phenomena in such a way as to nourish an understanding of the general reasonableness of one's existence.

The "eccentricity" that Jinliang wryly attributed to himself was not entirely limited to his personal context. The period after the Republican revolution was indeed a strange and delicate one for Manchus. Most had lost stipendiary rights decades before (though they continued to be harangued for their parasitism), and found that the economic and political chaos of the early Republic only closed off further their abilities to provide for themselves; the communities formed in the later nineteenth century were subjected to even greater pressures, as the physical disruptions of the 1911/12 Revolution combined with the disappearance of court-sponsored education and reform programs to erode further the structures underlying Manchu cohesiveness that had evolved in the late nineteenth century. More important, the cessation of the empire and the suppression of many of its symbols undermined the historical foundations of Manchu identity and purpose.

Jinliang saw the effects of this directly. The last remnants of the Hangzhou garrison were destroyed in 1911 and the former inhabitants never returned. The garrison grounds became a marketplace in the 1920s, and after the communist revolution of 1949 were transformed into the public park, Hubin, that graces West Lake today; five or six hundred Manchus were reported living in Hangzhou before the Cultural Revolution of 1966–1976, and the latest census counted 1,220 Manchus for the entire province of Zhejiang. In Peking, Manchu settlement retained much the same patterns after 1912 as when the garrison was formally in existence; the quarters north and northeast of the imperial compound were densely Manchu and the relatively small Mongolian population resided there almost exclusively. The Manchu community unquestionably continued, but its poverty was striking and apparently irremediable; a 1919 study (which counted about 300,000 Manchus living in Peking) showed the Manchu family income at roughly half that of the Chinese, and those Manchus working for a living were concentrated in the lowliest and most poorly paid professions.[1] For the Peking population, there was little safety in numbers. As the Nationalist Republic experienced increasing frustration in its attempts to wrest control from the warlords and stabilize the nation's economic and political structures, intellectuals and journalists turned again and again to the Qing period as the source of China's troubles and to the Manchus as representative of the old evils. Manchus who could pass as Chinese did not advertise their Manchu ancestors, the small Manchu populations of areas outside of Peking and the Northeast did not attempt to reconstitute themselves for educational or welfare purposes. Most Manchus of the 1920s and 1930s developed a sharp dichotomy between their public and private identities. Many but not all could go about their business without encountering questions regarding their heritage. In their homes, however, the tendency was to keep the oral traditions of their ancestors alive. The result was a mysterious tension for their children and grandchildren, many of whom could have found themselves in awkward or damaging situations if their parents had decided, as Jinliang did, to emphasize their Manchu heritage.

We have some insight into this today because of the spoken and written testimony of young people who have decided to express a Manchu identity through instruments such as the Manchu Association (*manzu xiehui*), founded in Taipei in 1981.[2] Using the phrase *tongzu*, once a relatively technical term meaning "of the same *mukūn*," to indicate their fellow Manchus, the young people expressed relief at being able to openly proclaim their Manchu identity and compare notes on their home experiences. "I always felt that something was very strange about us," said a young man. "I thought maybe someone in our family was a criminal, or something very disgusting. But I never was able to ask my mother and father about it—I wouldn't have known what to ask. Suddenly, at a New Year's banquet, my grandfather was very drunk, and just before he passed out he shouted, 'We are Manchus, we are descended from the first Manchu through the Pass in the conquest.' I was really shocked. I didn't know what to do. But I was happy to know why my house had always been so strange." Another young man, who happened to be easily distinguishable from a Chinese in appearance and to come from a home in which the Manchu heritage was acknowledged, even emphasized, said, "I have never felt at home here in Taiwan. I've always found it easier to be friends with other minority peoples, like Mongols or Uigurs. One day a Uigur friend and I—both of us born here, raised here, speaking only Chinese, never even travelled abroad—went into a restaurant and sat down. The waiter brought us knives and forks. This had happened to both of us before. My friend called the waiter over and demanded to know why we had knives and forks. The waiter shrugged, 'I just thought you were foreigners.' My friend flew into a rage, we had to leave. I always thought if I went to Japan I would be less lonely. I thought that because of history and culture the Japanese would be more like us Manchus. So I went to Japan when I was twenty. But that was no solution. Next year I'm going to America."

Another young man, an accountant, was an amateur historian. "My father was extremely interested in history. I asked him many times why he was so fascinated with the Qing emperors until finally he said, 'Our family are mostly Manchus, with a few Mongols. I didn't want to tell you this when you were small.' He was very interested in the question of Yangzhou, always reading the history of the conquest there and saying, 'I wonder if it's really true. I wonder if it is.' Now, in college I made friends with another young Manchu, who told me angrily, 'The Yangzhou massacre never happened. It's a fable the Chinese have made up to justify their hatred of us.' He made me think. Now, I have spent many years researching this question of Yangzhou, and I'm telling you, *tongzu*, it happened. I'm happy, very happy, that finally we can be here together, and share our feelings, but we should never attempt to beautify history. You will hear people say that Yangzhou did not happen. But it did." There may be some profound delicacy regarding Chinese feelings in the psychology of Manchu ethnicity, or there may be considerable reverse-vanity; the sack of Yangzhou, of course, was primarily the work of the Chinese deserters who comprised the vaster part of the invading force.

Manchus from Taiwan and abroad—Australia, the U.S. and Europe—read of the formation of the association and wrote letters of greeting and support. Not surprisingly, many who retained pride in their heritage claimed noble descent, a reflection of the relative propensity of those with noble connections (however tenuous) to retain a consciousness of Manchu identity into the Republican period, and also a residual effect of the traditional Manchu emphasis upon class status. Some told of childhoods of alienation from their parents or their school friends, of surprising recitations from their grandparents detailing clan names, banner affiliations, garrisons, and the odds and ends of Manchu vocabulary. Outside of Chinese society, Manchu identity could take forms impossible within it. One European correspondent, for instance, who happened to be of the Gūwalgiya clan, signed his Chinese epistle with the surname Guan but included his European addresses which made clear that the surname he used was actually Guargias, and under his name had applied a chop imprint in Manchu. Many of the foreign writers specifically criticized the cultural attitudes of the Republic of China, comparing them unfavorably with the situation they perceived in the People's Republic. "Why can't we have a policy of 'nationalities unity' (*minzu tuanjie*), like they do on the mainland?" demanded a correspondent from Hawaii. "Last time I was in Taiwan, I watched a television series about the sack of Yangzhou. All of the Manchus were like animals. The Qing period is a common background for many of the historical series on television in Taiwan. Every one of them depicts the emperors and the Manchus as devils or beasts. We need a policy of 'nationalities unity' because it will make the students' study of history more objective. All of the textbooks need to be rewritten. Genghis Khan was not a monster, and the Kangxi and Qianlong emperors were great men. The Yuan period was a very constructive period in Chinese history, and so was much of the Qing period. The Manchus did not cause foreign imperialism to attack China in the nineteenth century! The Dowager Empress was not like all Manchus!" The People's Republic of China does indeed observe an official policy of "nationalities unity," but it does not necessarily make history more objective. A recent television serial produced in China on the life of Nurgaci depicts him not only as the conqueror of the Northeast but as its liberator from the clutches of corrupt Ming officials bent upon perpetuating the feudal order there. A Chinese educational official, when asked whether plans were in place for a further series on the conquest of China and, possibly, the sack of Yangzhou, declared it impossible because of "nationalities unity." In fact the treatment of Manchus in the People's Republic of China greatly simplifies and in some ways trivializes their story.

The experiences of the founders of the Manchu Association of Taipei were very closely parallelled by those of the founders of the Peking Manchu School (*manwen xuexiao*) in 1987. The government of the Peoples' Republic had originally commissioned the language school because of the critical need for readers of the two million deteriorating Manchu documents in the archives of the palace museums of Peking and Shenyang. Its faculty of eleven—ten Manchus and one Mongol—expected to have to recruit students for the school, but instead they ended up accepting 90 of 150 applicants. Of those accepted, more than half were formally registered as Manchus, but it is clear that only a small minority of the students saw themselves as without Manchu ancestral affiliation. A faculty member interpreted the school's mission in patent terms of ethnic identity. Referring to the seventeenth-century Jesuits who used Manchu to instruct the Kangxi emperor in mathematics and natural philosophy, he said, "If a foreigner could have a command of Manchu and teach our emperor, how can we of Manchu descent today remain unable to understand our ancestral language and leave numerous archives uninterpreted?" An elderly woman who was denied enrollment in the school continued to faithfully attend every class meeting and eventually was admitted to the final examinations. "I think I am obliged to recognize my ancestral language," said she. Like the founder of the Manchu Association, the head of the Manchu Language School was the recipient of letters from across the nation, from people "revealing" their Manchu identity for the first time. "The school helps to boost the sense of pride for an entire people," said the founder. "[Since the end of the Qing] many Manchus, though they had nothing to do with the toppled ruling class, have hidden their origin. Today we are excited that our Manchu culture is beginning to be well recognized and our Manchu descendants enjoy equal status in our motherland."[3]

Manchus are registered and counted as any other of China's "national minorities" (shaoshu minzu).[4] In the 1982 census their figures came out at roughly 4.3 million, of whom just under two million live in Liaoning province, just under a million in Heilongjiang, and 117,000 in Peking. This figure must be construed to include the descendants of the "New Manchu" peoples who were amalgamated with the bannermen and in many instances settled in China proper. The numbers for non-Manchu Northeasterners consequently remain very small. Sibos are counted at 84,000, Dagurs at 94,000, Evenks at 19,000, Orochons at 4,000 and Golds at 1,500. In total, the statistics present an intriguing contrast to the once-common assertion by Western scholars that the Manchus in China had disappeared—that is, they had become indistinguishable from the Chinese in dress, speech and manner, which raises the issue of what an *ethnos* is, and why. Ethnic categories in China are ratified by the state on the basis of anthropological and ethnographic consultation; new minorities may be authorized and old ones discontinued from time to time. In general the choice of registering as a Han Chinese or as an ethnic minority is left up to the individual, with certain fairly well-defined limits to the possible choices. Those who wish to register as a minority must demonstrate ancestry, and children of "mixed" marriages must choose the registry of one or the other of their parents; pertinent to the Manchus' instance, it is extremely irregular to attempt to claim the minority affiliation of a grandparent or great-grandparent.

The state position on the desirability of minority affiliation is decidedly ambiguous. On the one hand, a Leninist legacy has allowed the oppression of minorities to be seen as a historical phenomenon relevant to the dynamics of imperialism, and reporting oneself as a minority can be construed as a strike against the injustices of history. It would, moreover, be impossible for the state to demonstrate its good will toward minorities if there were none to be identified. At this time people registered as national minorities do receive some marginally preferential treatment, particularly in birth control policies and in certain areas of education and employment. On the other hand, there is an ancient prejudice in China against heterodox cultures, and a prejudice of more recent vintage against "ethnic sentiment" (*minzu ganqing*), which is always vulnerable to being ajudged bourgeois or worse. There appears, too, to be some impatience (among people registered as Han) with the present ethnic system, as it is felt that more people than ought to affect ethnic affiliations in order to draw attention to themselves or exploit the privileges available. In short, people choosing to register as national minorities (about 7 percent of the entire national population of the People's Republic) deal with a significant number of uncertainties, and are unlikely to make frivolous choices in a matter that will affect their children's fate as well as their own. This is particularly true for Manchus, who are a rather anomalous group among the "minorities." In general national minorities in China are administered under what is essentially a homelands policy, in which a critical mass continue to inhabit their traditional territories, some of which are autonomously governed, and retain to some extent their traditional economic and social lives while enjoying something of the educational and health benefits of the rest of the society. Urban Manchus, who do not inhabit a discrete homeland or attempt, as a group, to live in any "traditional" way, have been accepted as a minority without demonstrating a monolithic linguistic, cultural or religious difference from the Han Chinese.

The group gathered in Taipei in 1981 to discuss, for the first time, the particulars of their predicament were in agreement in their opinion that in many societies—they named the U.S. and Canada primarily, which few of them had ever visited—their problems would be nonexistent. They felt uncomfortable, alienated and constricted in Taiwan (without exception, their native country) because they were acutely aware that open expression of their family traditions would not be welcomed by the society at large. Stereotyping would be permissible, of course; in Taipei, for instance, those of Mongolian descent were allowed to dress in traditional garb and celebrate the birth of Genghis Khan once a year. But an attempt to be both "Chinese" in the sense of civic rights and political participation and "Manchu" in the sense of expressing the cultural sensibilities their parents and grandparents had repressed would be rejected, they feared. They did not wish, in other words, to wear sable robes, perform riding and shooting exhibitions and do Manchu shamanic dances once a year—these forms of identification had already been rejected by their eighteenth-century ancestors. They wished to announce themselves and their children as Manchus and also as complete citizens of China, without a fear that this would make their ancestors the whipping boys for all of China's lingering ills; they wished to go to restaurants without being handed knives and forks; they wished, not unreasonably, to feel that they were unconditionally accepted by the society they intended to inhabit, love and serve for the rest of their lives. But Taiwan, they suspected, was one of those places where total cultural capitulation was demanded, and even if offered might be ignored if the individual "looked" foreign.

The criteria by which Manchu identity has been detected in various contexts has been a subordinate theme of this study. Often authentic Manchu traditions are sought in those elements that are supposed to have typified Manchu life prior to the onset of Chinese influence. Horse riding and other aspects of military training, the speaking of the Manchu language, and retention of archaic social forms and sartorial practices are conventionally considered Manchu—as opposed to Chinese—traits. In the strictest terms, nothing before 1635 is actually "Manchu," since this rather opaque term was officially adopted by the court only in that year. It should not be forgotten that the identification policies of the seventeenth century were arbitrary; Jurchens of various cultural inclinations were incorporated into the Manchu banners along with many people of Chinese or Korean descent, for reasons ranging from acculturation to simple convenience, and many Jurchens went to the Chinese-martial or Mongolian banners. Manchu cultural antecedents, as they were construed in the eighteenth century, could be traced to the Jurchen peoples of the Northeast during the sixteenth century and earlier. Yet there is no period directly prior to the appearance of the Manchus in Northeast Asia when the region could be considered to be without influence from China. In historical context, Manchu life and culture were fundamentally shaped by two developments: first, the process of political integration and cultural identification that formed the Later Jin khanate (1616–1635) under Nurgaci and the Qing empire under Hung Taiji in the early seventeenth century; second, the long-term habitation of urban garrisons in the Chinese provinces by a major portion of the Manchu population after the conquest of China. Whether and to what degree archaic elements of Northeast Asian life retained functional or symbolic significance in Manchu society depended upon a great many factors, many of which have been discussed here. The primary consideration is that the culture of the Manchu bannermen was a subset of Qing urban culture, distinguished by a variety of enduring and self-conscious features. To seek Manchu ethnic standards in the Northeast, or in supposed primordial traits that could not possibly have survived the core Manchu experience in China would be to discuss Manchus in terms they themselves rejected in the eighteenth century. Ethnicity, sociologists would argue, is a matter of self-perception; it is a statement regarding the relationship of the individual to society and is made in a context—such as that of late nineteenth-century China—when the state no longer assigns racial or cultural identity by external mechanisms.

Beginning with Jinliang's father Fengrui, the Suwan Gūwalgiya lineage at Hangzhou—like the majority of Manchus of the time—experienced a progressive moulting of their traditional identity and status as Manchus. By 1864 they were no longer, in fact, the hereditary military slaves of the Qing emperors. Fengrui had taken the extraordinary step of becoming a volunteer cavalry expert in the irregular Chinese-led army fighting the Taipings. He made a conscious choice of refusing military and bureaucratic rewards from the state for his service, and built the most private of worlds for himself in the ruins of the Hangzhou garrison quarter. His voluntary service made him free, and there no question of turning back to his traditional status. Fengrui thereafter supported himself by private capitalistic enterprises: rent collecting and book printing. For his son Jinliang, traditional forms suggested by clan heritage and scholastic glory were modern appeals to status symbols from the past; on the sentimental level the intensity of their significance only increased after 1912 and the actual disappearance of the empire.

The shaping of a Manchu identity parallelled in its particulars the Chinese search for a vocabulary, a philosophy and a scholarship of an identity that would transcend the political structures that were in obvious danger of collapse. For the Chinese context of the late nineteenth and early twentieth century, one was nationalistic to the extent that one's sense of identity rested upon the criteria shared by others calling themselves "Chinese"—things like affirmation of the mythic value (or even the factuality) of descent from the Yellow Emperor, the moral value (if not the social acumen) of a rather truncated Confucianism, commitment to China's territorial reconstitution (along the lines of the high Qing imperium, paradoxically) and to political justice for the Chinese people in the international sphere. For at least a politically conscious, articulate group of Manchus, the fact was that Chinese nationalism had in the course of its formation galvanized an ethnic consciousness among the Manchus that had its roots in the Opium War and the Taiping Rebellion. The self-sufficiency that had grown up among the people as they were gradually abandoned by the court in the middle nineteenth century had produced not a general identification with the Chinese population, but its mirror-image: a sense of racial origin and destiny, with an ideology and a vocabulary borrowed from spokesmen for Chinese nationalism, like Zhang

Binglin. Thus, one was ethnic to the extent that one was distant from the values of Chinese nationalism but shared others with a constituent group.

But after the destruction of the empire in 1911/12, there came a period in which Manchu ethnicity, as we would now construe it, was incompatible with China's cultural agenda. Until the People's Republic again gave its sanction to the interpretation of individual historical condition through the phenomena of oppressed or dispossessed minorities, a self-identified Manchu in China was, at best, an eccentric. Manchus, Mongols, Muslims and other "minorities" were ethnicized in the process—they were pushed to the margins of a stage that was centrally occupied by Chinese nationalism, which would thereafter dictate the terms of political participation and social affiliation. The same processes driving Chinese nationalism—the refinement of international communications, the elaboration of foreign exploitative institutions in China itself, the inability of the dynastic form to accommodate the new demands of state management—produced ethnic identities, which superceded the cultural enclaves that had once been incorporated into the Qing imperial structure. Manchu communities, and not the Qing state, sustained and guided the emergence of the Manchu people in the late imperial era. Manchu ethnicity is as intimately associated with the modernization process in China as Chinese nationalism is accepted to be.

The world that the three generations of the Manchu Suwan Gūwalgiya clan discussed in this work inhabited can perhaps best be appreciated in light of the ongoing debate over Manchu "sinicization." The "sinicization" of the Manchus has been accepted as fact with too little sustained examination either of the "sinicization" concept itself or of the particulars of Manchu existence in the later Qing period. It appears that "sinicization" is used in preference to more definitive English terms such as "assimilation" or "acculturation" because it is intended to represent the Chinese phrase *hanhua*, "to become Han" or to become culturally indistinguishable from mainstream Chinese society. Qing official culture, of course, was not a duplication of the Ming, Song or any previous dynasty, whether "Han" or "non-Han"; as a group, it can hardly be argued that the Manchus of the Qing dynasty became duplications of the Chinese among whom they lived. While the Manchus created a culture very different from that of their ancestors in the Northeast, they were separated from the rest of China by barriers of masonry, law, social tension and self-identification. Quite apart from its failure to make much distinction between assimilation and acculturation, "sinicization" is silent on the self-identification that is so fundamental to a sense of ethnicity in China or anywhere else. The persisting use of the term has obscured many a discussion of the political and cultural development of the Qing dynasty and, more important, threatened to shackle Chinese identity to the rigid conceits of nationalist rhetoric of the early twentieth century.

That generalizations pertaining to the "sinicization" of the Manchus are common is due in large part to the discussion of Manchu assimilation in Mary Clabaugh Wright's classic work *The Last Stand of Chinese Conservatism*, first published in 1957. Wright was a revisionist, of a sort. Republican scholarship had fixed blame for China's nineteenth-century troubles upon the Manchus, implying that the interests of the Manchu court were dissimilar to those of the Chinese people as a whole, and that at crucial points the Manchus actually saw the goals of the foreign imperialists as roughly consonant with their own. The underlying assumptions regarding a fixed sense of Manchu distinctness were brittle, in Wright's view. In order to explain the workings of the Tongzhi "restoration," she had first to overcome the "symbiosis" theory of Karl Wittfogel, which itself had been a refutation of the biases handed down from early Republican Chinese scholarship. In 1949 Wittfogel and his collaborator Feng Chia-sheng had published *History of Chinese Society: Liao*, an annotated partial translation of the *Liao shi*, the history of the Liao dynasty (947–1123).[5] In a theoretical introduction, Wittfogel had argued against the conventional assumption that the "conquest dynasties," and particularly the Liao and Qing, had in fact been assimilated; it appeared that they had instead achieved a social and cultural symbiosis. In the case of the Qing, Wittfogel pointed out the legal and social restrictions upon Manchu contact with the Chinese, the apparent reluctance of the Qing court to adopt the Chinese tradition of primogeniture, and the persistence of the Eight Banners—the ultimate matrix of Manchu social and military organization—until the end of the dynastic period as factors preventing full sinicization of the Manchus.

Wright's counterargument was so incisive and so influential that it demands to be treated in some detail here.[6] She established that the Qing court had failed in its attempt to reserve a Manchu homeland in the Northeast; Manchus had instead melded into the general populace. In a discussion of the dismantling of the legal restraints against the intermingling of Manchus and Chinese she showed that the court had declined to pursue its earlier objective of legislating Manchu isolation after the middle of the nineteenth century. As for the apparent racial animosities that had pervaded bureaucratic life and spawned the growth of "Manchu" and "Han" factions, Wright saw these as virtually eroded away by the early nineteenth century. Indeed, she pointed to the Taiping War as exposing the basic agreement in cultural outlook and political interest between the Manchu and Chinese elites. Most important, Wright characterized the "Restoration" that followed the suppression of the rebellion as one in which Manchus and Chinese had become virtually indistinguishable, all united now in the effort to reestablish China's stability, sovereignty and prosperity. It was this "restoration" to which Wright intended to direct her thesis, and at the outset she wished to remove from the Manchus any special explanations based upon their supposed cultural or racial distinctness.

Many scholars who are doubtful of Wright's restoration thesis are still powerfully influenced by her premises on the Manchus. But there is surely no logical connection between Chinese immigration into the old Manchu homelands in the Northeast and the cultural life of millions of Manchus living for generations in closed communities within China proper. If conservation of the pristine traditions is in question, it may be answered that the most conservative Manchu community of the Qing period—and the one that is first to be investigated for its reflection of the old culture—was at Yili in Xinjiang province. More important, any argument that measures Manchu culture by the amount of military drilling taking place ignores the most basic reality of Manchu life in China: the enclosure of the population within the urban garrisons, and the likelihood that a family would inhabit a single garrison community generation after generation. Within the garrisons there emerged a culture that reflected the ancient traditions but more importantly was shaped by the exigencies and opportunities of forced urbanization. This distinctive garrison culture was the culture of the Manchus of China.

Insufficient interest in the life of the garrisons has led to another logical confusion, encouraged by Wright's usage but shared by many scholars today. Knowledge of life at the court sheds no light upon the life of the Manchu people in China. Wright's connection of the cultural condition of the Manchus with the political outlook of the court in the years during and after the Taiping War was specious and wholly unnecessary to her argument. Yet the idea that the emperor was the personal expression of Manchu culture is still very common. The behavior of the Qing emperors was not intended to serve as a model for the bannermen. The emperors were the dynastic rulers of the *Da Qing* empire and, to be sure, the descendants of the founder, Nurgaci; the bannermen were descendants of Nurgaci's followers, servants (they called themselves "slaves") of the Court, and were expected to preserve their Manchu heritage as part of their loyal service. The loss of the statutory identity of the Manchus after the Taiping War was real and, despite Wright's exposition upon it, is often ignored. Distortion of the status of the bannermen was a very late nineteenth-century development, whose influence has lingered in twentieth-century scholarship on the Manchus; Tan Sitong, Zou Rong, Wang Jingwei, Zhang Binglin and other spokesmen for anti-Manchu sentiment tended to characterize the Manchus of their time as enjoying all the ancient luxuries, despite the actual loss of much legal privilege and the materially destitute condition of the Manchus as a group. Qing intentions to disembarrass the government of the garrison populations after the Taiping War was in all probability spawned more by financial necessity than Wright's argument reveals. Most important, removal of statutory definition from the Manchus did not lead to their disappearance as an identifiable minority. Indeed the ability of the Manchu communities to continue on their internal strengths in the later nineteenth century contributed to the ease with which anti-Manchu activists of the early twentieth century targeted them for rhetorical and physical violence.

Whether or not the assumptions amalgamated under "sinicization" will continue as a single unit of discourse in modern Chinese history has significance for several interpretive problems. The perceptions of Manchu distinctness, both on their own part and on that of Chinese society, have not precluded the formation of a historical judgment regarding the degree of Manchu assimilation in the nineteenth century. It has been widely accepted that the loss of a martial tradition among the Manchus weakened the ability of the dynasty to respond to military challenges, both internal and external, in the late eighteenth and early nineteenth century. In addition, the assumption that Manchus were becoming less visible in the later Qing period has caused a correspondingly greater emphasis to be placed upon the ideological themes—as opposed to the "anti-Manchu" content—of various rebellions and the political movements of the nineteenth and early twentieth centuries. In particular, Chinese nationalism at the turn of the twentieth century is allotted greater weight than the "anti-Manchu" rhetoric with which it was often interwoven. Since 1949 Chinese scholarship has portrayed the events leading to the Revolution of 1911/12 as being characteristic of bourgeois nationalist revolutionary movements—"nationalist" because it emphasized the Chinese people as the basis of the polity and demanded a republican form to manifest the Chinese people's right to rule themselves, "bourgeois" because it limited its object to the creation of such a republic, without a thoroughgoing restructuring of the social economy. No historian has denied the "anti-Manchu" aspects of the rhetoric of the revolution. But some—perhaps the most prominent being Liu Danian—have characterized the anti-Manchuism of the revolution as a "veneer" over the true substance of the drive for a Chinese republic. Many Western scholars have, in the same vein, portrayed anti-Manchu sentiment as a minor propellant in the overall movement. This appreciation of the seriousness of ideas does much to clarify the intentions of the elite, although it will be remembered that Zou Rong, Zhang Binglin and others expressly rejected the notion that the Manchu people had been assimilated into Chinese society, and built their entire concept of modern Chinese identity upon the defining structures of both Chinese and Manchu racial history. How deeply such subtleties penetrated the thinking of the mass of supporters is still a question. The Taiping armies expressly targeted Manchu communities for extinction, and in cases such as the giant garrison at Nanjing were successful. In the course of the 1911/12 Revolution, Manchus of both sexes and all ages were slaughtered in their homes, hunted through the streets, and executed for spite after the fighting had subsided. Unresolved questions regarding the treatment of Manchus and other minorities in the Cultural Revolution linger—for instance, questions pertaining to the beating and drowning of Lao She in 1967. The motivations behind actions such as these are not explained by Christianity (even of the Taiping sort) or nationalism; something in the relationship between Manchus and Chinese society is still incompletely understood.

"Anti-Manchuism," most Western historians would be quick to point out, means two things here. On the one hand, it is opposition to the Manchu dynasty and the social and political order it by definition imposed upon China. On the other hand, it is hatred of Manchu people. But it is doubtful that this heuristic dichotomy has any real power to resolve basic questions about nationalist polemic at the turn of the century. In the thought of some revolutionaries, such as Zhang Binglin, the two meanings were inseparable. The Qing dynastic order was evil because it was the historical expression of the character of the Manchu people— immoral, rapacious, ungrateful to the Chinese who had taught them culture and righteousness. For others, one meaning could do without the other. The *Gelao hui*, for example, like other secret societies was fully capable of opposing the Manchus without reference to whether or not a republic would succeed them. For hundreds of years secret societies had sworn to drive out the alien overlords and restore the Ming dynasty to power. Sun Yatsen, though once eloquent on the subject of the evil nature of the Manchus, shifted his focus to opposition to the Qing dynasty in the late years of the nineteenth century because it gave the revolution the greatest possible base of appeal and it undercut separatist movements in China's border territories; in the end the revolutionary movement under Sun did indeed incorporate activists who agreed that the dynastic form was oppressive and outmoded. But Sun's ostensible ideal—how important it was to him personally can be debated—of a republic embracing all peoples indifferently was never realized. "Race" remained an issue throughout the 1920s and 1930s, and many would argue that it is an unresolved question in historical discourse even today.

A further difficulty with "sinicization" is the apparent fact that Manchu identity assumed a political charge in the early twentieth century. If we grant the existence of a reduced and rarefied Manchu community with its own sentimental attachments in the late Qing and early Republican years, it becomes possible to trace a politicization of a part of that community that rendered it susceptible to the overtures of the Japanese militarists who eventually established the Manchukuo state as part of their colonization of Northeast Asia. The crystallization of Manchu ethnic identity that began under the pressures of the Taiping War had, by the first decade of the twentieth century, gained expression in a new vocabulary of ethnicity—applied by Manchus to themselves as the Chinese applied similar terms to themselves—and in a demand that China's imminent political reorganization should make the Manchu homeland in the Northeast an autonomous territory, free of rule by the Chinese government.

The racial identity that most Manchus had become convinced of by the end of the dynastic period was, in the final analysis, a synthetic product of several forces in eighteenth- and nineteenth-century banner life. Most profound was the immuration process and the intensifying intermarriage between finite numbers of lineages within the garrisons; old differences among various federations, tribes and clans were worn away beneath the "Manchu," "Mongol" and "Chinese-martial" categories created by the court. Such labels, once based primarily upon cultural identity, were adjusted in the eighteenth century to accommodate the court's new emphasis upon genealogy and its formalization of Manchu culture. Those who could produce an account of their descent from a sixteenth- or seventeenth-century putative "Manchu" could enter the preferred Manchu banners, and many of the "Chinese-martial"—some of them descendants of the same Jurchens who later became "Manchu"—were dismissed from the rolls altogether on the mythicized assumption that they were really the same people as the conquered Chinese and therefore of less importance in maintaining the cultural vigor of the banners.[7] In the nineteenth century, the traditional racism of many of the Chinese secret societies beseiged the garrison communities for the first time, and though the Manchus reacted with fear and undoubtedly hatred of their own, the racism itself did not offend them, for both the realities and the court-sponsored ideals of Manchu identity had worked to make racial thinking not only acceptable, but required. As court sponsorship of Manchu livelihood and identity was withdrawn in the middle nineteenth century, the internal strengths of the cultures and communities of the garrison sustained the Manchus apart, and the repeated violence Manchus suffered in the social disorders of the nineteenth century and in the Republican Revolution undoubtedly worked to reinforce their separation. As the higher Qing political structures disintegrated, overt Manchu separatism and an ethnic discourse emerged. For a few, it was an overture to participation in the charade that was Manchukuo. For others, like Jinliang, it was the first step on the road to a perpetually incomplete existence in a society that had no ready mechanism for the acknowledgment and acceptance of an inner difference that has no outward sign.

Source Abbreviations

BMST	Ortai et al., *Baqi manzhou shizu tongpu*
BT	Ortai et al., *Baqi tongzhi* [*chuji*]
DMB	Goodrich and Fang, *Dictionary of Ming Biography*
ECCP	Hummel et al., *Eminent Chinese of the Ch'ing Period*
GCS	Jinliang, *Guapu congkan shulu*
GQL	Li Huan, *Guochao qixian leizheng*
GS	Jinliang, *Guapu shuyi*
GXQHL	Ding Bing, *Geng Xin qi Hang lu*
HBZY	Zhang Dachang, *Hangzhou baqi zhufang yingzhilue*
MJJD	Agui et al., [*Qinding*] *Manzhou jishen jitian dianli*
MMZ	Zhao Erxun et al., *Man mingchen zhuan*
MYK	Agui et al., *Manzhou yuanliu kao*
NZ	Wei Song et al., *Nanchuanxian zhi*
PZ	Peng Ranzhang et al., *Pinghuxian zhi*
QBT	Tieliang et al., [*Qinding*] *Baqi tongzhi*
QKZC	Zhang Zhongru et al., *Qingdai kaoshi zhidu ciliao*
QSG	Zhao Erxun et al., *Qingshi gao*
ZEDSS	*Zhao Erxun: Dongsan sheng*

Notes

Introduction

1. See, for instance, *QBT* 5:61b (Ming Rui and Meng Xi).

2. Yao Hui'an, *Xihu siyuan*, cites poems of Wu Yanzhen (128), Xu Hui (136), Fan Liang (195), Zheng Zai (194), Yan Kuisun (199), Deng Lin (207), Zhai Jing (221), Yao Yong (232) and Ye Xianggao (261), among others.

3. Wakeman, *The Great Enterprise*, 357.

4. I have argued elsewhere the fundamental artificiality of "race," together with the importance of race as an ideological construct, particularly during and after the Qianlong period. See "*Manzhou yuanliu kao*" and "The Qianlong Retrospect on the Chinese-martial (*hanjun*) Banners."

5. Nurgaci was inventor of the Aisin Gioro clan, first khan of the Later Jin and father of the first Qing emperor, Hung Taiji. See Yan Chongnian, *Nurhachi zhuan*; *ECCP*, 594–99.

6. Of Kharchin provenance, Sungyun had already distinguished himself for his work on regional history by the time of the writing of his work on Manchu folk culture. A very helpful review of Sungyun's work and some biographical background has recently been provided by Ji Dachun in "Lun Songyun." The date of Sungyun's original preface was 1789, and the work was reprinted later with two additional prefaces. There is more covert revelation of the conditions of garrison life in the admonitions of Sungyun's "old men" than there is overt exposure. The work has been well-known since its translation into Chinese by Sungyun's friend Fugiyūn in 1809, though there is much in its form that makes it problematical both as a text and as a historical source. Fragments of the text have been translated into Japanese by Ura Renichi and Itō Takao, and into Korean by Ch'oe Hakkŭn. A complete rendering into German by Giovanni Stary has been pointed out to me by Gertraude Roth Li. See also Kanda Nobuo, "*Remarks on Emu tanggū orin sakda-i gisun sarkiyan*," which is printed as the preface to a 1982 reprint of a complete Manchu copy of Sungyun's text.

7. See Tong Jingren, *Huhehaote Manzu jianshi*, and *Suiyuan cheng zhufang zhi*. I am indebted to Richard Bodman for directing my attention to these materials.

Chapter I
Peace and Crisis

1. Fang Chao-ying, in a classic essay, "A Technique for Estimating the Numerical Strength of the Early Manchu Military Forces," used the rule of 300 men per *niru* and 563 *niru* in the Eight Banners of 1644 to estimate a fighting force of slightly under 170,000. Wu Wei-ping and Gertraude Roth [Li] have both argued for lower enrollments per *niru*; see "The Development and Decline of the Eight

Banners," 100, and "The Manchu-Chinese Relationship," 35, n. 2 respectively. Zhou Yuanlian, in "Guanyu baqi zhidu de jige wenti," makes clear that even at the time of conquest the *niru* were still influenced by the population of the clans upon which they were in part based, and so varied radically in size. Li Xinda, in "Ru Guan qian de baqi bingshu wenti," 157–60, notes that for the period just prior to the conquest even the number of *niru* is in doubt, since the notation provided in the records is inadequate. A recent review by Guo Chengkang of the original materials collected in the *Mambun rōtō* and *shilu* has yielded the following estimates of the number of banner companies for the period just prior to the conquest of Peking: 250 Manchu companies, 100 (or very slightly more) Mongol companies, and 159 Chinese-martial companies, or a total of slightly more than 500 companies for all the Eight Banners, a figure significantly less than the earlier estimates of Li and Fang. See "Qingchu niulu de shumu." It is not likely that we will ever be precise in regard to the number of bannermen involved in the conquest of China.

2. The general history of the disposition of the garrison populations is given in *QSG* 95:3492–526, based on materials earlier collated for *Baqi tongzhi* [*chuji*] (1730) and [*Qinding*] *Baqi tongzhi* (1799).

3. The *hanjun*, despite their name, were quite different from the *hanjun* incorporated into the *minggan* organizations of the Jin Jurchens of the twelfth century; see Toghto et al., 44:1–4. On the *mouke-minggan*, see Tao, *The Jurchen*, 11–12. *Hanjun* was revived in the Qing reformation under Hung Taiji to indicate the incorporated "Chinese"—many of whom were of patently Jurchen descent but lived within the Chinese pale in Liaodong at the time of the Later Jin conquest of the area in the 1620s. The origins of the Chinese-martial Banners were in the *ujen cooha* units of Nurgaci's armies, artillery companies manned by deserters from the Ming army, or from the cities of Liaodong. Manchu *nikan*, depending upon context, translates either *han* (Chinese) or *hanjun* (Chinese-martial). See Liu Chia-chü, "The Creation of the Chinese Banners in the Early Ch'ing," 61–65; Gertraude Roth, "The Chinese-Manchu Relationship," 25; and Crossley, "The Qianlong Retrospect on the Chinese-martial (*hanjun*) Banners."

4. *BT* 1:2a. Nurgaci originally created four Banners in 1601, but in the Later Jin period the enlargement of the population led to the creation of four more units, so that the designations were Plain Yellow, Bordered Yellow, Plain White, Bordered White, Plain Red, Bordered Red, Plain Blue and Bordered Blue Banners. The Chinese-martial banners were created in 1642. Ultimately there were twenty-four regular Banners, eight for each of the three categories: Manchu, Mongol and Chinese-martial; additional companies were founded under the *butha* banners, under the jurisdiction of the Imperial Household Department (*neiwu fu*) and the Imperial Clan Department (*zongren fu*).

5. In using this term I follow Frederic Wakeman (*The Great Enterprise*, 44n), who explains his adaptation of this term from the work of Philip Curtin and Allan Isaacman. I have, however, limited it to immigrants to the Jurchen territories before the taking of Fushun in 1618, many of whom are noted in early records as *baisin*, or people lacking clan connections. See also Crossley, "The Qianlong Retrospect on the Chinese-martial (*hanjun*) Banners."

6. A final *juan* in *BMST* provides genealogies for this group. See also Widmer, *The Russian Ecclesiastical Mission*, 13–22; Mancall, *Russia and China*, 205–7; the biographies of Gantimur and Sabsu in *ECCP*, 269, 630 respectively.

7. An overview of Manchu-Mongol imperial clan marriages is provided by Hua Li, "Qingdai de Man Meng lianyin."

8. Hung Taiji (Qing Taizong) succeeded his father as second khan of the Later Jin in 1627 and later created himself emperor of the Qing dynasty. His biography in *ECCP*, 1–3 is under the doubtful name of "Abahai"; for comment see Gertraude Roth [Li] in Spence and Wills, *From Ming to Ch'ing*, 7. "Hung Taiji" is a romanization of the name as it occurs in the early Manchu records; see also Stary, "Abahai." For a recent biography, see Sun Wenliang and Li Zhiting, *Qing Taizong quanzhuan*.

9. On the categories of regular bannermen and banner households, see Fu Kedong, "Baqi huji zhidu chucao"; Hosoya Yoshio, "Shinchō chūki no hakki koseihō no henkaku."

10. The Three Superior Banners (*san shang qi*) were those controlled by the emperor personally after 1651. Nurgaci had originally been succeeded by three sons and a nephew, the "cardinal princes" (*hosoi beile*), each of whom controlled two banners. By a slow but steady process Hung Taiji eliminated his colleagues from actual power and established the emperorship in 1636. Thereafter the Bordered Yellow and Plain Yellow Banners that had belonged to Hung Taiji remained in the control of his son, the Shunzhi emperor (r. 1644–1661). Dorgon, Hung Taiji's half-brother and the Shunzhi regent, died in 1650; in 1651 he was posthumously denounced by the Shunzhi emperor and his Plain White Banner seized by the throne. Thereafter the Plain Yellow, Bordered Yellow and Plain White Banners, all controlled by the emperor, were known as the Three Superior Banners; the remainder were called the Five Inferior Banners (*wu xia qi*). The innovation was important, for it meant that future princes would have not whole banners parcelled out to them but companies of the Five Inferior Banners, which contributed to progressive fragmentation of princely power. See *ECCP*, 218; Kessler, *K'ang-hsi*; Huang, *Autocracy at Work*; and Spence, *Ts'ao Yin*, 9–11.

11. On servitude among the early Jurchens, see Wei Qingyuan et al. *Qingdai nupei zhidu*, 13–16, *MJ*, 14–31. For discussion of late Jurchen/early Manchu servitude, see Spence, *Ts'ao Yin*, 7–11, Chang Te-ch'ang, "The Economic Role of the Imperial Household (*Nei-wu-fu*) in the Ch'ing Dynasty"; Torbert, *The Ch'ing Imperial Household Department*, 53–59; the 1978 review of Torbert by Loh Wai-fong in *Harvard Journal of Asiatic Studies*; and Gertraude Roth [Li], "The Manchu-Chinese Relationship," 10–15. There has been debate over whether Jurchen population growth in the sixteenth century (that is, on the eve of Nurgaci's rise to power) was due to an increase in the number of agricultural slaves secured in raids against Koreans and southern Liaodong settlements. See Kawachi Yoshihiro, "Kenshū joshen shakai kōzō no ichi kosatsu," *Mingdai Mammōshi Kenkyū*; and Wada Sei, "Minhaji ni okeru joshen shakai no hensen," *Shigaku zasshi* 48 (1973): 9. A very useful technical discussion of Chinese terms related to Banner servitude and freedom is provided in Fu Kedong, "Baqi huji zhidu chucao."

12. The work of Guo Chengkang, "Qingchu niulu de shumu" indicates that

the number of Chinese-martial companies may have doubled sometime between 1640 and 1644, while an analysis by An Shuangcheng of the numbers enrolled in categories within the Chinese-martial banners suggests that the vast majority of additions to the Chinese-martial rolls may have been bondservants, who as late as 1720 represented half of all Chinese-martial bannermen. See An Shuangcheng, "Shun Kang Yong sanchao baqi ding'e qianxi."

13. Quoted in Denis Sinor, "The Inner Asian Warriors," 133.

14. See, for instance, Hongli's discussion of deserters in his *shengyu* reproduced in Meadows, *Translations from the Manchu* (Manchu text), 15: *ejen aha i sidede amba jurgan holbobuhabi* . . . , "Great loyalty has bound the master and slave together. . . ." Both "loyalty" and *zhong*, which is most often used to translate *jurgan*, omit or obscure the specifics of the master-slave relationship; *tondo*, "loyalty" (or perhaps more closely *comitatus*) is also rendered *zhong* in Chinese, but has its roots in the Northeastern hunting or warring collective, not in slavery.

15. The Jianzhou garrison, created in 1411, was part of the "garrison" (*weisuo*) system by which the Ming attempted to control the Northeast. In reality the garrisons were tribes or tribal confederations, and their commanders were tribal headmen. For background see Serruys, *Sino-Jürched Relations*; and Yang Yang et al., *Mingdai Nurhan dusi ji qi weisuo yanjiu*. It appears that even before the creation of the Jianzhou garrison the tribe upon which it was based was led by the father or grandfather of Möngke Temür, the first Jianzhou commander and later claimed as an ancestor by Nurgaci. See Chapter II of this work.

16. The name Jurchen (*ruzhi, ruzhen, nuzhi, nuzhen*) appears in Tang chronicles. Since Liao times (906–1125), Chinese records have distinguished between "tame," (or "cooked" or "familiar," *shou*) Jurchens and "wild" (or "raw" or "strange," *sheng*) Jurchens. As Chinese knowledge of and relations with various Jurchen groups became more elaborate in the fifteenth and sixteenth centuries, these terms lost some of their meaning and frequency; by the time of their sixteenth-century occurrence in *Liaodong zhi* 9.5a the vocabulary was disappearing. The constitution of the "tame" and "wild" classes changed over time, as new tribal peoples were discerned among the wild Jurchens (of whom the Chinese knew little) and previously wild peoples became "tame" by virtue of being economically integrated or politically familiar.

17. For a detailed discussion of the construction of identity as a by-product of the formation of the banners, see Crossley, "The Qianlong Retrospect on the Chinese-martial (*hanjun*) Banners."

18. Mo Dongyin, *Manzu shi luncong*, 128–39.

19. Levin, *Ethnic Origins*. See also Wu Yuanfeng and Zhao Zhiqiang, *Xibo zu jianshi*, written in Sibo by means of a modified Manchu script; Yang Yang et al., "Mingdai liuren zai dongbei"; Lü Guangtian, *Ewenke zu*, 3–6; Liu Zhongpo, *Hezhe ren*, 2–3; Feng Junshi, "oulunchun zu caiyuan"; Ling Chunsheng, *Songhuajiang*, 224–26; Shavkunov, *Gosudarstvo Bokhai*, 29–31.

20. Crossley, "An Introduction to the Qing Foundation Myth," 13–14.

21. Chai, *Qingdai Xinjiang*, 2–3; Shirokogoroff, *Social Organization of the Manchus*, 5; Kuang, *Xibo zu zi Fentian xi qian Xinjiang Yili zhi*, 3, 6–9.

22. Crossley, "The Sian Garrison," 29–34.

23. Lee, *The Manchurian Frontier*, 15–16; Lü Guangtian, "Qingdai buteha da xing Ewenke ren de Baqi jiegou."

24. Wu and Zhao, "Xibo zu you Kharqin Menggu qi bianru Manzhou baqi shimo."

25. For the most detailed history of the Green Standard Armies, see Luo Ergang, *Lüying bing zhi*.

26. The "Ode to Mukden" is remarkable as one of the last long works in Manchu and one of the first to have an impact upon Western readers. It was translated into French by Jean Joseph Marie Amyot in 1770, and later was retranslated and printed with the Manchu text in Klaproth, *Chrestomatie Mandchou*. Much of its language and possibly some of its form was adapted from the 1688 work of Umuna who had been dispatched to the Northeast by the Kangxi emperor, and may ultimately have derived from the work of the Chinese scholar Wu Zhaoqian during his exile in Ninguta. See also Etō, *Manshū bunka jō no ichi shinwa* and *Dattan*, 37–48; Stary, "L 'Ode di Mukden' "; Crossley, "An Introduction to the Qing Foundation Myth," 23–25, and "*Manzhou yuanliu kao*," 763, 774.

27. Yinzhen (1678–1735), fourth son of the Kangxi emperor, ruled 1723 to 1735 as the Yongzheng emperor. For biographical studies see *ECCP*, 915–19; Pei Huang, *Autocracy at Work*; Silas Wu, *Passage to Power*; Yang Qijiao, *Yongzheng di ji qi mizhe zhidu yanjiu*; and Feng Erkang, *Yongzheng zhuan*.

Xuanye (1654–1722), the third son of the Shunzhi emperor, ruled 1661–1722 as the Kangxi emperor. For biographical studies see *ECCP*, 327–31; Spence, *Ts'ao Yin* and *Emperor of China*; Kessler, *K'ang-hsi*; Meng Zhaoxin, *Kangxi dadi zhuan*.

28. See also Crossley, "*Manzhou yuanliu kao*," 779–81, and "The Qianlong Retrospect on the Chinese-martial (*hanjun*) Banners."

29. Chan, *Legitimation in Imperial China*; Rodgers, "The Late Chin Debates on Dynastic Legitimacy"; Bol, 1985 review of Hok-lam Chan in *Harvard Journal of Asiatic Studies*.

30. Crossley, "Tong in Two Worlds," "*Manzhou yuanliu kao*" and "Qianlong Retrospect on the Chinese-martial (*hanjun*) Banners."

31. The evolution of imperial ideology is complex and has not yet received comprehensive treatment. For a preliminary discussion, see Crossley, "*Manzhou yuanliu kao*," 779–81. On Yongzheng's argument see Feng Erkang, *Yongzheng zhuan*, 227–36 and Fisher, "Lü Liu-liang and the Tseng Ching Case." For more detailed discussion of the banners and Confucian ideology, see Crossley, "The Qianlong Retrospect on the Chinese-martial (*hanjun*) Banners."

32. For the portion of his military correspondence conducted in Chinese, Eldemboo was totally reliant upon a Chinese amanuensis, Hu Shixian. *QSG* 344:11153–54; see also *ECCP*, 222–24. On Hailancha, see *ECCP*, 273–74. On Fude, see *ECCP*, 262; *OSG* 314:10702.

33. Heshen, who inherited a very minor noble rank, managed to gain unprecedented personal power between 1775 and Hongli's death in 1799, following which he was forced to commit suicide by the Jiaqing emperor Yongyan. Heshen is blamed for isolating the elderly Hongli from the pressing problems of the day and creating a network of corruption that siphoned staggering amounts of money

and valuables from the imperial treasury and from the economy at large, to the point of protracting campaigns against internal rebellion to grotesque lengths in order to skim from the military appropriations. Fruitless bureaucratic attempts to prune Heshen's power only led to bloody factional strife that paralyzed the government in the later eighteenth century. More than any single individual apart from the Empress Dowager Xiaoqin [Cixi], Heshen is traditionally held responsible for the decline of the Qing dynasty. See also Kahn, *Monarchy*, 248–59. For biographical studies see *ECCP*, 288–90; Nivison, "Ho-shen and his Accusers"; Feng and Yang, "You guan Heshen chushen, qiji wenti de kaocha."

34. Precision is, again, impossible. In the early years of the dynasty only ablebodied males between the ages of fifteen and sixty were registered, and then, often only in their *niru* units. After the conquest a trienniel census was instituted, but its figures for garrison inhabitants are not reliable. Competition for stipends created pressures for over-registration of those eligible to receive them, while measures to account for non-combatants—who may well have represented up to 90 percent of many garrison populations—were never universally implemented. The problem is an important one and has been addressed often. Mo Dongyin's 1958 discussion in "Baqi zhidu," *Manzu shi luncong*, 130–35 has probably not been surpassed for information and common sense.

35. Liu Shizhe, "Manzu 'qishe' qianshu," 54 (from *MYK* 6:13b).

36. His successor Yongyan, the Jiaqing emperor (r. 1796–1820), exhorted the same community in 1807, "Manchu speech must be studied, and *qishe* must be strengthened." Hongli's son and successor, the Daoguang emperor Minning (r. 1821–1851), again chided the Canton bannermen in 1837: "Manchu speech and *qishe* are still the foundation of the Manchus, and every man must know it." Liu Shizhe, "Manzu 'qishe' qianshu," 53 (from *Zhu Yue Baqi zhi*).

37. Officers from the two garrison divisions at Mukden in 1691 were chosen ten candidates from each of the Eight Banners, of whom half would be instructed in Manchu and half in Chinese; but all would study equitation, infantry maneuvering and archery together. Liu Shizhe, "Manzu 'qishe' qianshu," 54. For more extensive background on the education of the bannermen, see Crossley, "Manchu education in the Middle Ch'ing Period."

38. Certainly this was the case with high-level Chinese-martial bureaucrats, who served disproportionately during the first twenty-five years after the conquest and whose percentages lowered gradually thereafter. See Kessler, "Ethnic Composition."

39. *QKZC* 4.78b–79a; 7.109a–b.

40. *QBT* 5:13a.

41. Hongli's language follows that of Yinjishan's earlier memorial: "The writings of the Manchus who study in order to pass the civil service examination have always been shallow and inferior. After they have passed the examinations and obtained their provincial (*juren*) or national (*jinshi*) degrees, they are at times asked questions about literature by Chinese scholars. They use being a Manchu as an excuse for their inability to answer the questions. When they are asked about the Manchu language and arts, or archery and equitation, they claim that, being scholars, they cannot possibly know things that are familiar only to soldiers.

They evade questions from both sides and always find themselves in a great dilemma. They have become useless people and incurred my great disgust." Chu and Saywell, *Career Patterns*, 52, quote from *Qingchao wenxian tongkao* (1935 Shangwu edition), 78:5582.

42. *QKZC* 1.40a–b.

43. *QKZC* 1.41a; 1.50b–51a.

44. Meadows, *Translations* (Manchu text), 5–6.

45. See Kahn, *Monarchy*, passim.

46. Chu and Saywell, *Career Patterns*, 52.

47. The extent of the remaining untranslated archival documentation in Manchu in China was first emphasized by Beatrice S. Bartlett. See "Learning from the Ch'ing Archives" and "Books of Revelations: The Importance of the Manchu Language Archival Record Books for Research on Ch'ing History." On particulars of the court's insistence that Manchu be used by the Grand Council, see also Ch'en Chieh-hsien, "Lun *Baqi tongzhi*," 5.

48. *QKZC* 1.60b–61a.

49. Jurchen and later Manchu are part of the Tungusic class of the hypothesized "Altaic" language group, unrelated to Chinese. As a Tungusic language Jurchen was related to Korean, Japanese (probably), and the languages of mainland Northeast Asia, particularly Sibo, Evenk and Gold. The Jurchens of the Jin period had used a "large character" script derived from the script of the Kitans, and a "small character" script introduced after 1145, both of which in turn derived from Chinese characters. The old writing system persisted into the fifteenth century and has been extensively studied. See Grube, *Die Sprache und Schriften der Jucen*, v; Kiyose, *A Study of the Jurchen Language and Script*, 21–22; Jin Guangping and Jin Qizong, *Nuzhen yuyan wenzi yanjiu*, 26–27. Apparently there also existed a cursive script, little studied as yet, of which surviving examples rested in the museum of the Leningrad Academy of Sciences; see Kiyose, 27.

50. The resulting phonetic script was not at first vocalized. After 1641 vowel marks were added. Today the original, unvocalized script is called Old Manchu in Chinese (*jiu manzhou*) and in Manchu "script without dots or circles" (*tongki fuka akū hergen*), in contrast to "dotted and circled script" (*tongki fuka i hergen*). It is quite possible that the inspiration for the vocalized script came from the Korean *han'gul* syllabary. See King, "The Korean Elements in the Manchu Script Reform of 1652."

51. The Mongolian bannerman Sungyun commented upon this fact in his 1789 work in Manchu, *Emū tanggō orin sakda-i gisun i bithe*, "Record of One Hundred and Twenty Stories from Old Men," 3.

52. There are many passing references to this practice, but see as an example *Qing Gaozong shilu* 1417.17a. This technique was also utilized by Chinese on the Manchu section of their *jinshi* examinations; examples may be found among the Manchu materials of the Han Yu-shan collection of the University Research Library at the University of California at Los Angeles. I am indebted to Professor Benjamin A. Elman and Mr. James Cheng for inviting me to examine these materials.

53. Wylie, *Ts'ing Wan K'e Meng*, iii, and Shirokogoroff, *Social Organization*

of the Manchus, 4. Since this is a syllabary, opinions may differ on how many discrete characters are actually present. I base the number of sixty-seven characters on the traditional chart presented in Chuang Chi-fa's introduction to *Lakcaha jecen*, iii.

54. See *MJJD*, "shangyu" .1a–b. Also Crossley, "*Manzhou yuanliu kao*," 779–80.

CHAPTER II
The Suwan Gūwalgiya

1. "Clan" is used throughout this work, it is hoped, with due respect for the occasional infelicities and ambiguities of the term. Those with specialized interests are also advised that this term's signification will waver, separately and with due notice, between Manchu *hala* and *mukūn* (and sometimes *aiman* or *tatan*), and between Chinese *bu* and *zu*. As will be discussed, the original meanings of *hala* and *mukūn* were distorted by the immuration process to the point that little precise correspondence between *hala* and *bu*, in the sense of "tribe," or *mukūn* and *zu*, in the sense of "clan," can be consistently found in Qing records apart from *BMST*, where the correspondence is often forced. Michael's retreat from characterization of seventeenth century Jurchen/Manchu society as a clan society (*Manchu Rule*, 80–91) was, in the opinion of this author, over-cautious and in all likelihood based upon an inadequate understanding of the work of both Shirokogoroff and what was then the forthcoming work of Wittfogel and Feng (*Chinese Society*, 1949). See also Crossley, " 'Historical and Magic Unity,' " 77–116; Shirokogoroff, *Social Organization*; and for a discussion of the heuristics of "clan" and "tribe," see Fried, *The Notion of Tribe*. Telford and Finegan, "Qing Archival Materials," provide a useful introduction to banner materials now available through the Genealogical Society of Utah; I am grateful to Mel Thatcher, Evelyn Rawski and Susan Naquin for having introduced me to these materials early in my research.

2. See, for instance, those preserved in *QBT* 5:3a (Niohuru) and 5:7a (Sumuru).

3. The three subjects were his grandfather Tašiha who died in the Xinjiang rebel suppression in 1830, his father Changshou and uncle Changrui, both of whom died fighting the Taipings in Guangxi in 1852. The compilation was not completed until 1890, and published later. *ECCP*, 405.

4. See Jinliang's introduction to his "Guarjia shi jiu zhong si jie san xiao tu bo" [Genealogical Chart of Nine Loyal Men, Four Chaste Women and Three Filial Figures of the Gūwalgiya Clan]," reprinted in *GCS* 45b–46a.

5. The portion of the Jianzhou federation that later came under Nurgaci's control had previously been governed by the "six princes" (*ningguta beile*), meaning Giocangga (Nurgaci's grandfather) and his five brothers. Nurgaci himself ruled as khan, but after the death of Cuyen seems to have intended power to pass to the "four cardinal princes" (*hosoi beile*), his sons Daišan, Manggūltai and Hung Taiji, and his nephew (Šurgaci's son) Amin. Hung Taiji soon emerged as khan, and in 1636 created himself emperor. Traditions of collegial rule may have continued to shape the workings of the emperorship and its attendant institutions through the

entire dynastic period. See also Kanda, "Shinshō no *beile* ni tsuite," and "Shinshō no gisei daijin ni tsuite"; Fu Tsung-mou, "Qingchu yizheng tizhi zhi yanjiu."

6. For his biography see *ECCP*, 78–80. Zhaolian identified the Eight Great Houses as follows: "Among the Manchu clans, the descendants of Fiongdon of the Gūwalgiya clan, Eidu of the Niohuru clan, Yangguri of the Sumuru clan, Gintaisi of the Nara clan, Hohori of the Donggo clan, Alantai of the Hoifa clan, Bujantai of the Ula clan, the various descendants of the Irgen Gioro, and of Tugai of the Magiya clan are considered to be the Eight Great Houses" (*Xiao ting za lu* 10:2a–b). Zhaolian's account of the *ba dajia* differs from that of Fang Chao-ying, who describes them (*ECCP*, 219) as "the Eight Great Families (*ba dajia*) or Princes of the Iron Helmet (*tiemao zi wang*), who enjoyed the right of perpetual inheritance. The founders of these families were, in order of their rank: Daisan (Prince Li), Dorgon (Prince Rui), Dodo (Prince Yu), Haoge (Prince Su), Jirgalang (Prince Zheng), Boggodo (Prince Zhuang), Lekedehun (Prince Shuncheng), and Yoto (Prince Keqin)" [romanization changed to conform to the present text]. This is almost a literal adoption of the passage from Brunnert and Hagelstrom, *Present Day Political Organization*, 9. Zhaolian's was the view of the imperial clan, and was also repeated by Yigeng (see Chapter IV).

7. The most thorough discussion of the difficulties of detailing the roots of the sixteenth-century Aisin Gioro remains Zhu Xizu, "Hou Jin guohan xingshi kao."

8. On Möngke Temür see *DMB*, 1065–67. Posthumously (by several centuries), Möngke Temür was recognized as the "First Ancestor and First Emperor" (*zhaozu yuan huangdi*) of the Qing dynasty. *ECCP*, 595. See also Rossabi, *The Jurchens in the Yüan and Ming Periods*, and Crossley, "The Tong in Two Worlds," 26–29. The evidence is circumstantial but consistent for identification of the Gioro with the earlier Jiagu. Various post-Jin variations of the Jiagu name, such as Juewen, a lineage name sometimes used by Möngke Temür, and Kalegu, glossed in the dynastic history of the Yuan dynasty (1280–1368) as Jiagu, are attested. Most important, however, are the cluster of citations affirming the use of the Tong lineage name by members of the pre-Aisin Gioro lineage consistently from Möngke Temür to Nurgaci. Tao Zongyi (*Zhuogeng lu* 1:"Shizu zhi") glossed Tong as the surname chosen by the Jiagu clan among the thirteenth-century Jurchens who had settled in China. For more discussion see Crossley, "Tong in Two Worlds," 46 and " 'Historical and Magic Unity,' " 123–28.

9. See Crossley, "An Introduction of the Qing Foundation Myth," 11–14 for a discussion of the Aisin Gioro clan history and myth, and more recently Jin Qizong, "Lun Fekulun." Important and relevant comparative reading on very early Northeastern myths is found in Pulleyblank, "The Chinese and their Neighbors in Prehistoric and Early Historic Times," 443–45.

10. According to legend the first shaman had indeed been a war leader, *cooha janggin*, who was captured by the Chinese and remained standing after being beheaded by them. See Nowak and Durrant, *The Tale of the Nišan Shamaness*, 97–98; Ch'en Chieh-hsien, *Manzhou congkao*, 19. See also Ling Chunsheng, *Songhuajiang*, 225, on the eligibility of "magic possessing" shamans for election as clan or tribe headmen.

11. The genealogies of *BMST*, which are not in all ways reliable, in the aggre-

gate give a convincing demonstration of this tradition very clearly and consistently, and it is suggested in the history of the Jurchen Jin dynasty (compiled in the thirteenth century) with reference to the origins of the Jin imperial clan in the late ninth century; see *Jin shi* 1:6–7. It was also observed by Shirokogoroff, *Social Organization*, 33. The sources on the splitting of the homesteads do not clearly state that the younger sons alone were expected to leave, although the implied birth orders in the genealogies suggest that this may well have been the case. Ultimogenitural rights were, according to Shirokogoroff, still recognized by the Manchu clans of the Aigun region in the early twentieth century. See Shirokogoroff, *Social Organization of the Manchus*, 140–41.

12. See Li Hsüeh-chih, *Cong jige manwen mingci*, 3; Crossley, " 'Historical and Magic Unity' " 84–86, based on Qianlong period glosses of "Jin guo jie" (*juan* 135) of the *Jin shi*. Li cites the Kangxi period *Qingwen jian*, where *mukūn* is glossed as *feniyen*, or a group of animals, people or inanimate objects (e.g. ships) that move together.

13. *ECCP*, 11.

14. *ECCP*, 897.

15. *BMST* "Fanlie". 1a–b.

16. Zhou, "Guanyu Baqi zhidu de jige wenti," 157–58.

17. Before the Second World War there may have been many spirit poles in Peking. Jinliang saw that of the Suwan Gūwalgiya inside the clan mansion compound, and an Aisin Gioro pole was still standing in the Forbidden City, outside the Kunning Palace in the palace grounds reserved for Puyi after 1912. Arlington and Lewisohn, *Old Peking*, 47–48 provide a description of the Kunning terrace and pole. The imperial clan remained practitioners of shamanism through the entire dynastic period; evidence for its practice among the garrison families is sparse.

18. Shirokogoroff, *Social Organization of the Manchus*, 16.

19. Shirokogoroff, *Social Organization of the Manchus*, 31. Emphasis follows original text. Shirokogoroff's emphasis here was partly pedantic, for he saw Manchu clans as classic representatives of the clan forms so important to ethnologists in his time; it happens, however, that his description of the Manchu clans was apt.

20. The best, recent, brief summary on Manchu clan names is Liu Qinghua, "Manzu xingshi shulue."

21. Crossley, "*Manzhou yuanliu kao*," 771–74.

22. The process is detailed in Pei Huang, *Autocracy at Work*, 168–84.

23. See also Crossley, "*Manzhou yuanliu kao*," 762–68.

24. For instance, the brothers Shi Tingzhu, Shi Guozhu and Shi Tianzhu all took the patronym Shi from their father Sigan of the Gūwalgiya clan, who immigrated to Guangning in Liaodong during the late Ming period. See Chen Wan, "Shi Tingzhu shiyi yu jiapu jikao"; Crossley, "The Qianlong Retrospect on the Chinese-martial (*hanjun*) Banners."

25. This is clearly shown in materials such as the necrologies published in honor of the garrisons communities that experience violence in the Republican Revolution of 1911–1912. See for instance Wu Qingdi, *Xinhai xunnan ji* (1916).

26. *BMST* 2.1a.

27. On Guiliang see *ECCP*, 428–30; on Yiliang, *ECCP*, 389–90. Their genealogy, *Zhenghongqi manzhou Hada Guarjia pu*, is the subject of Chen Jiahua's article, "Qingdai yibu guanliao shi zu de jiapu."

28. Written in *Jin shi* as Gulijia Shilun; see 111:1–7. The only other Gūwalgiya mentioned in the *Jin shi* is Puca, a *cishi* of Jiazhou (118:8).

29. The Aigun *mukūn* who called themselves the Sungyan Gūwalgiya were very likely Suwan. See Shirokogoroff, *Social Organization of the Manchus*, 44. A slightly different hypothesis regarding the early geography of the clan is forwarded in Mitamura Taisuke, "Manshū shizoku seiritsu no kenkyū," in *Shinchō zenshi no kenkyū*, 70.

30. *BMST* 1.1a. In the source, the list concludes with the words "and everywhere else." The Anjulaku Gūwalgiya, who were the clan of Loosa, may have been a branch of the Suwan Gūwalgiya. See *BMST* 1:8a: "Fiongdon Jargūci and the Songkoro Baturu, Loosa, of the Anjulaku Gūwalgiya, Bordered Red Banner, are of the same *mukūn* (*zu*)." Since Anjulaku was a part of the territory settled by the Warka tribe, it is not impossible that the branch were descendants of Juca who were not living together with the lineages descended from Solda (see below). See also *ECCP*, 541.

31. *BT* 54:1a–2b.

32. See Huang Weihan, *Heishui xianmin zhuan*, "Appendix," biography of Bayan Batu.

33. *Qing shilu* (*Taizu wu huangdi*) 1:8a. This is the first instance of the Gūwalgiya clan name in the Qing records, and it was written "Gergi." See also Liu Xiamin, "Qing kaiguo chu zhengfu zhubu jiangyu kao," 116, 118.

34. Liu Xiamin, in "Qing kaiguo chu zhengfu zhubu jiangyu kao," 129, notes the establishment of a Suwan garrison on the Suwayan River, 180 li (about 60 miles) from modern Jilin city. This river name, meaning "yellow," was apparently the origin for the name Suwan, now corrupted to Shuangyang, the "twin suns." Liu locates the Suwayan River on the upper Yitong, where there was also, in Qing times, a Suwayan Ridge and a Suwayan hamlet.

35. The Sibo, one of the Nine Tribes, were incorporated into Nurgaci's federation in the early 1600s, and are traditionally called "New Manchus" (an ambiguous term in many instances because of this). The great garrison established at Yili, in Xinjiang province, in the eighteenth century was predominantly Sibo, and remained a preserve of traditional Manchu culture well into the twentieth century. See Kuang Lu, *Xibo zu zi Fengtian qian Xinjiang Ili shi*, 1–3, and Chai Yüshu, *Qingdai Xinjiang*, 2. Shirokogoroff related a folk tradition, for which there is no historical evidence, claiming that the Sibo were remnants of the Jin Jurchens; see Shirokogoroff, *Social Organization*, 173–75. Their name is more frequently associated with that of the Xianbei (Hsien-pi, Hsien-pei) people of the Later Han and Six Dynasties period, and through them to the geographical term "Siberia." For a general history of the Sibo, see Wu Yuanfeng and Zhao Zhiqian, *Xibo zu jianshi*, 1984.

36. *BMST* 1:1a–3a. For what it may reflect of Jurchen taste in names, Nikan

and Solgo mean "Chinese" and "Korean" respectively. On *nikan* see also Crossley, "The Qianlong Retrospect on the Chinese-martial (hanjun) Banners."

37. Zhou Yuanlian, "Guanyu baqi zhidu de jige wenti," 145–46. The clan affiliations of Sando and Zhading, if they claimed any, are unknown.

38. *QBT* 11:3 and *BMST* 1:1a. See also Zhou, "Guanyu baqi zhidu," 145–46.

39. Solgo's were the type of *niru* classified by Ch'en Wen-shih as "A"—that is, "in the early years of the state, the various tribal chiefs led their relatives, clansmen and tribesmen in submission, or they were conquered but still remained a unit; after they had been organized into a *niru*, they themselves or their clansmen were given control. Originally they lived in the same place, had the same name and belonged to the same tribe." See Ch'en Wen-shih, "Creation of the Manchu *Niru*," 135.

40. For Fiongdon's biography see *MMZ* 1.1a–4a and *QSG* 225:9179–82; in English, *ECCP*, 247–48. Wakeman, *The Great Enterprise* includes several remarkable references to Fiongdon—the one on page 845 is correct.

41. On very early formation of the khanate, see two recent studies of chronology: Li Xinda, "Guanyu manzhou qizhi he hanjun qizhi de shijian shijian wenti" and Li Zhiting, "Ming Qing zhanzheng yu Qingchu lishi fazhan qushi."

42. *ECCP*, 21.

43. The special role of uncles (*ecke* and *nakču*) in Manchu life was detailed by Shirokogoroff (*avunkulat*), who considered it a remnant of matrilineal clan traditions, again in an interpretive twist that paid as much homage, perhaps, to early twentieth-century ethnological concepts as to his real subjects of study. For a recent retrospective on the problem of the avunculate see Guang Dong, "Jiufuquan de chansheng." See Shirokogoroff, *Social Organization of the Manchus* (82, 109, 142–46). Anecdotal evidence for the avuncular role among the Manchus in early Qing China can be found in cases other than Fiongdon's. For instance, Eidu's son Ebilun (d. 1674) was deprived of his post and ranks in 1637 for attempting to influence the trial of his niece for concealing a child's identity. *ECCP*, 219.

44. The structure of the state under Nurgaci and the earlier reign of Hung Taiji has been extensively treated in Roth [Li], "The Rise of the Manchu State." See also Wakeman, *The Great Enterprise*, 157–224.

45. *ECCP*, 694. Šurgaci had been individually entitled by the Ming government, and there is some contemporary evidence to suggest that he was highly regarded by the locals of southern Jilin, where the brothers began their conquests. Conflict between the brothers seems to have been open after 1607 and in 1611 Nurgaci had Šurgaci executed. See especially the 1597 report of Shin Ch'ungil, *Konju jichong dörök*, which has been summarized by Stary in "Die Struktur der Ersten Residenz des Mandshukhans Nurgaci"; and Ch'en Chieh-hsien, *Manzhou congkao*.

46. *ECCP*, 375–76. Hurgan's father Hulagu had joined Nurgaci the same year as Solgo, 1588.

47. Not all of the twelve sons of Solgo and ten sons of Fiongdon are accounted for in *BMST*. 1:2a–6b includes information on Solgo's sons Adu Bayan (eldest), Fiongdon (second), Indaguci (sixth), Urgan Mergen (seventh), Babun (eighth), Langge (ninth), Yarba (tenth), and Uici (eleventh); Šarguda and his son Bahai are

mentioned in *MMZ* 10.10b–12b. Of Fiongdon's sons, Nagai, Sugai, Tulai and To-hui are cited in *BMST*; Sunayan appears in *QBT* and *MMZ* 2.14b.

48. *QBT* 5:6a.

49. *QSG* 225:9182.

50. This and the slightly lesser rank *baitabule hafan* (Chinese *qiduyu*) were the normal perpetual hereditary ranks given to the early *nirui janggin*. Later these ranks became merely formal, and were awarded—often posthumously—for a fixed number of generations. See also Brunnert and Hagelstrom, *Present Day Political Organization of China*, 944.

On Nagai, see *BMST* 1:2b. After Nagai's death at Lushunkou in 1633, his company passed to his son Gurgan; after Gurgan's death, it passed to Nagai's younger son Gusu, who later was active in the Qing conquest of Fujian province, fought against Zheng Chenggong, and was eventually awarded the rank of third-class "baron" (*nan*); this rank later passed to Gusai's son Laxitai and grandson Yidonga.

On Sugai, see *BMST* 1:3b. Sugai's company was later inherited by his son Dupoluo, who served in the 1629 raid on Peking and was eventually raised to the military rank of *fudutong*; the company later passed to Duopoluo's son Duotair.

On Tulai, see *BMST* 1:2a–6b.

51. *QBT* 86.16b. This later passed to his son Wage, who served in the capture of Hangzhou, and to his grandson Furdan. Wage was also awarded the rank of first-class "viscount" (*zi*) and the third-class "duke" (*gong*), which later passed to Furdan (*BMST* 1:2b; see also *ECCP*, 264–65), to Furdan's son Zhaode and to Zhaode's son Hadaha.

52. *QBT* 86.22b. This passed to his son Mardu in 1659; to Mardu's son Made in 1704; and to Made's son Guanbao in 1728.

53. *BMST* 1.3b.

54. *BMST* 1.2b. Furdan was later the Qing commander in the disastrous defeat by the Oirat Mongols on July 23, 1731, and was deprived of most of his ranks and privileges; the major ranks of Fiongdon, in contrast to those of Oboi, were not cancelled but were transferred to another line of his descendants.

55. *BMST* 1.5b–6a and *ECCP*, 599–600. See also Oxnam, *Ruling from Horseback* and more recently Zhou Yuanlian and Zhao Shiyu, "Lun Aubai fuzheng."

56. *QBT* 5:25a.

57. *ECCP*, 219–21, 663. Khife's promotion to this triumvirate is at this moment a mystery to this writer.

58. Klaproth, *Chrestomathie Mandchou*, Manchu: 84, French: 261.

59. *GCS* 6b–7a.

60. No Gūwalgiya relative was too remote to merit citation, apparently; see for instance the separate resumés submitted to Zhao Erxun by the cousins Cun Xian and Cun Zhi, each of whom emphasize their Gūwalgiya step-great-grandmother. *ZEDSS* Box 517.

CHAPTER III
The Hangzhou Garrisons

1. Manchu edict of Yongzheng [Hūwaliyasun tob] 1:6:29. Meadows, *Translations*, Manchu text:1–2, English text:35–37.

2. A collection of fifty-seven documents related to Shunzhi period land enclo-

sures and the incorporation of the *daidi touchong* has been reprinted as "Shunzi nian jian de juandi he touchong": in *Qingdai dang'an shiliao congbian* 4:48–148.

3. See especially the carefully worded memorial, dated Shunzhi 11:1:24, to the *neiwu fu*, reprinted as document 43 (115–16) in "Shunzi nian jian de juandi he touchong."

4. See Guo Songyi, "Qingdai de renkou zengzhang he liuqian," 122–24. The opinion of the Kangxi emperor, as expressed during his revision of the land and head taxes in 1712–1713, was that at the time of the Qing conquest and the subsequent land seizures, arable land had been extremely cheap and plentiful; only in his own reign period, he claimed, had population growth caused land to become expensive, a situation aggravated by cash cropping (see, for instance, *Qing Shengzu shilu* 52 [1713]:10: *bingzi*).

5. It was not uncommon for total land grants to non-commissioned bannermen in a banner to equal that of a single officer from the same banner; population growth within the garrisons and alienation of the holdings could lower the average holding per non-commissioned bannerman to as little as a few square inches by the end of the seventeenth century. See for instance Crossley, "The Sian Garrison," 52; *BT* 57.2a–4a.

6. Chen Jiahua, "Baqi bingxiang shixi," 66, 69.

7. Im, *Rise and Decline*, 12–15.

8. Lee, *The Manchurian Frontier*, 36–39.

9. Details will be discussed below, but a good introduction to the policies and problems of garrison provisioning is provided in Li Qiao, "Baqi shengji wenti shulue."

10. Figures from Crossley, "The Sian Garrison," based on *Baqi tongzhi*. A *jalan* was a subdivision of a banner (*gūsa*). The Manchu and Chinese-martial Banners were each divided into five *jalan*, the Mongol Banners into fewer. The *jalan*, in turn, were divided into *niru*.

11. *QBT* 47:9a–b; 49:3b. English translations drawn from Brunnert and Hagelstrom, 719, 720, 722, 723, 726, 727, respectively.

12. Chen Jiahua, "Baqi bingxiang shixi," 63.

13. Im, *The Rise and Decline of the Eight Banner Garrisons*, 54–57.

14. Shen Qiyuan (1685–1763) on the condition of Peking Bannermen, in "Sishi wu ci," from *Huangchao jingshi wenpian* 35:10, quoted (but with an erroneous title for the source) in *Manzu jianshi*, 110.

15. A *sheng* being half a *dou*, and there being 10 *dou* in a picul. See Chuan and Kraus, *Mid-Ch'ing Rice Markets*, 79–98 on the complexities of the *shi* as a volume and as a weight (*dan*) measure for grain.

16. Im, *Rise and Decline*, 194. Chen Jiahua, "Baqi bingxiang shixi," 64–65. On political as well as economic motivations for this policy see Crossley, "The Qianlong Retrospect on the Chinese-martial (*hanjun*) Banners."

17. For a review of the literature concerning the effects upon China of the increase and subsequent diminution of silver flow in the seventeenth century, see Wakeman, "China and the Seventeenth-Century Crisis."

18. Chuan and Krause, *Mid-Ch'ing Rice Markets*, 92–98, 105ff.

19. It has been estimated that prices for most common items in the later Qing period increased 400 to 1,000 percent. Im, *Rise and Decline*, 144.

20. Im, *Rise and Decline*, 129–33.

21. *Manzu jianshi*, 110.

22. *BT* 67:23a, cited in *Manzu jianshi*, 110.

23. Im, *Rise and Decline*, 132.

24. Li Qiao, "Baqi shengji wenti shulue," 92.

25. Chen Jiahua, "Baqi bingxiang shixi," 66.

26. *QSG* 95:3497.

27. For instance, in the Canton garrison there were 400 *yangyu* in 1742, and 1,511 in 1884. See Im, *Rise and Decline*, 129. At roughly the same period, records indicate that of the 4,630 bannermen registered in the Manchu Plain Yellow Banner at Peking, 2,227—nearly half—were *yangyu*. See Li Qiao, "Baqi shengji wenti shulue," 98.

28. Chen Jiahua, "Baqi bingxiang shixi," 65.

29. Im, *Rise and Decline*, 133.

30. It would be easy to overstate the degree to which these large installations had preserved traditional society, and conditions there were certainly far from idyllic. A great deal of information on the plantations has been preserved in the *heturi dangse* (*heitu dang*), in Manchu, in the Liaoning provincial archives. A portion has been translated into Chinese and published (see for instance *Qingshi ziliao* 5:1–77) and more are in process.

31. *Manzu jianshi*, 111.

32. *Jilin tongzhi* 31:4, quoted in *Manzu jianshi*, 112.

33. *Qing renzong shilu* 324:8b–9a, quoted in *Manzu jianshi*, 113. The more alarming incident occurred when Eight Trigrams (*bagua*) rebels broke into the imperial compound in 1813. See also Naquin, *Millenarian Rebellion*, passim.

34. *Manzu jianshi*, 112. See also Lee, *The Manchurian Frontier*, 38–39. A small collection of documents dealing with the plans for the colonization of Shuangchengbao have been published as "Jiaqing ershi nian Lalin shi gen jihua ji zhangcheng shiliao" in *Lishi dang'an* 1987:3:47–50.

35. Yinsi (1681–1726), younger brother of the Yongzheng emperor, was executed at the emperor's order in 1726. *ECCP*, 926–27.

36. *Manzu jianshi*, 113.

37. A collection of 24 documents detailing such incidents has been published in *Qingdai dang'an congbian* 5:68–138.

38. The general problem of banner fugitives has been discussed in Li Qiao, "Baqi shengji wenti shulue," 97.

39. *Qing Gaozong shilu* 244:8a, quoted in *Manzu jianshi*, 114.

40. *Manzu Jianshi*, 113, 115.

41. See *ECCP*, 931–33. Yinghe himself would shortly see the effects of forced service; he was at work on the imperial mausolea in Rihe at the time of his writing, but in 1827 was banished to Heilongjiang for mismanagement of the construction.

42. *Qing xuanzong shilu* 81:29b–13a, quoted in *Manzu jianshi*, 115.

43. On Li's brief regime in Xi'an, see Wakeman, "The Shun Interregnum."

44. Zhu Youjian (1611–1644), the Ming Chongzhen (1628–1644) emperor, had committed suicide when Li's forces surrounded Peking in late April. His eldest son, Cilang (b. 1629), was executed by Dorgon in early 1645. *ECCP*, 1922.

45. See Struve, *The Southern Ming*; and Wakeman, *The Great Enterprise*.

46. Li escaped and was apparently killed later by villagers in Hubei. See *ECCP*, 491–93.

47. Dodo was the original lord of the Bordered White Banner. See *ECCP*, 215.

48. For Tulai's biography see *QSG* 235:9431–9435, *MMZ* 2.146–20a; and in English, *ECCP*, 247.

49. Wakeman, *The Great Enterprise*, 490n, 503, 509.

50. The original disagreement had by this time become overlaid with new grudges and rivalries. These have been treated in detail by Jerry Dennerline in his article "Hsü Tu and the Lesson of Nanking: Political Integration and the Local Defense in Chiang-nan, 1634–1645," in *From Ming to Ch'ing*, 92–132, and his book *The Chia-ting Massacre*. See also Struve, *The Southern Ming*, and Wakeman, *The Great Enterprise*, 321–31.

51. Bayintu was the son of Nurgaci's younger brother Bayara; see *QSG* 215:9863. For Ašan's biography see *GQL* 264:16a–b.

52. See Wakeman, *The Great Enterprise*, 306, 791.

53. Dennerline, *Chia-ting Loyalists*, 66.

54. The most famous account of the sack of Yangzhou is Wang Xiuchou, *Yangzhou shi riji*, which has been translated into English by Lucien Mao as "A Memoir of Ten Days' Massacre in Yangzhou," in *T'ien-hsia Monthly* 2:515–37. See also Zhang Defang, "Yangzhou shiriji bianwu," in *Zhonghua wenshi luncong* 5:365–76.

55. It was charged by Ming loyalists and later Chinese nationalists that many Yangzhou women were sent as concubines or female slaves to Manchu and Mongol princes after the pacification of the city. Wang Xiuchou, "A Memoire," 535.

56. *ECCP*, 652; Wakeman, *The Great Enterprise*, 588. In Qianlong times, the court would approve of a memorial temple to Shi (in 1768) and extoll him as the model of loyalty, which it was then attempting to promote as an absolute value. See also Crossley, "The Qianlong Retrospect on the Chinese-martial (*hanjun*) Banners," and Fisher, "Lü Liu-liang."

57. Tian later was appointed to first-class *amba janggin*, and in 1651 took part in the attack on the Zhoushan Islands. *HBZY* 4:3b;2:5a.

58. Wakeman, *The Great Enterprise*, 589, cites a noteworthy memoir by Dodo on the taking of Nanjing, making special mention of the dispatch of the *hung baturu* Nikan.

59. *QSG* 235:9434.

60. *ECCP*, 16–17; *HBZY* 1:1a–2b; 2:1a.

61. *ECCP*, 180–81.

62. *QSG* 226:9434.

63. Apparently Zhu was as interested in getting away from Fang Guo'an as he was in getting away from the Manchus. The general had already appropriated the

war budget for himself, and Zhu had very serious doubts about his loyalty. *ECCP*, 181. See also Wakeman, *The Great Enterprise*, 528.

64. Wakeman, *The Great Enterprise*, 771.

65. Ng, "Rape Laws in Qing China," 58.

66. See also Wakeman, "Localism and Loyalism during the Ch'ing Conquest of Kiangnan: The Tragedy of Chiang-yin," especially 43–45.

67. Quoted and translated in Li Chien-nung, *The Political History of China*, 207. Liang went on in the same quote to reject the proposition of racial war between Chinese and Manchus.

68. *HBZY* 18:1b.

69. *QSG* 235:9435.

70. Gusu was the son of Nagai and grandson of Fiongdon. *BMST* 1:2b.

71. *HBZY* 4:10b, 13b. See also *GQL* 270:23a.

72. *HBZY* 2:1a, 3b; 6:6a, 8b, 14a–b; 10:2b, 10b.

73. *HBZY* 16.6a.

74. *QSG* 95:3497.

75. Zhu Kezhen, *Wenji*, 31, 55.

76. Zhu Kezhen, *Wenji*, 18–20.

77. See *ECCP*, 399–402.

78. Sen-dou Chang, "The Morphology of Walled Cities," in G. W. Skinner, ed., *The City in Late Imperial China*, 90–91.

79. At the age of eighteen Singde had passed the first stage of the *jinshi* degree examinations of 1673, but was taken ill and had to complete the palace examination in 1676, when he was ranked seventh in the nation. His father Mingju (1635–1708) was one of the closest advisors to the young Kangxi emperor and may have devised the plan to strip Wu Sangui of his political powers over the southern provinces that precipitated the Rebellion of the Three Feudatories. As descendants of Gintaisi, Mingju and Singde enjoyed the political and social status of the "Eight Great Houses," but their fortune was considerably enhanced by the commercial acumen of Mingju and his bondservant An Qi. Like his father, Singde was a patron of Chinese writers in Peking, and used his inherited wealth to subsidize their efforts; his best known act of friendship, however, was his successful effort on behalf of his friend Gu Zhen'guan to have Wu Zhaoqian—a close friend of Gu's unknown to Singde—released from exile in the Northeast, and then engaging him as a tutor for Mingju's second son Kuixu (1674–1717), who like Singde was distinguished among the Manchu elite at Peking for both his enormous inherited wealth and his great talents in Chinese poetry. *ECCP*, 11–13, 430–431, 577, 662–63.

80. Xiaosheng was a great-granddaughter of [Niohuru] Eidu. *ECCP*, 369.

81. *HBZY* 16.10a. Specifically, governor-general Yang Tingzhang (1688–1772) requested that the previous order to expel the Chinese-martial be amended in such a way as to transfer a portion of them to the Green Standard Armies. In many garrisons Chinese-martial were offered a choice between becoming civilian or joining the Green Standard Armies, though it is unclear at this point whether this was a result of the initiatives of governors seeking to improve the numbers or the quality of the Green Standard recruits.

82. On the visits of the Kangxi emperor to Hangzhou during his "southern tours" see Spence, *Ts'ao Yin*, 129, 132, 147, and on the visits of the Qianlong emperor see Kahn, *Monarchy*, 92–94. The *Nanxun shengdian*, an illustrated record of the visit of 1765, provides some idea of the appearence of the Hangzhou environs at that time; two pages of it have been reproduced in Reischauer and Fairbank, *East Asia: The Great Tradition*, 384. The records of the imperial visits, including imperial commemorative poems, are reproduced in *HBZY* 7, and are the basis for this passage.

83. See document 50: (139–40), dated March 10, 1661. The plans for the boundaries had been drafted by the Board of Works (*gongbu*), and Kedo was instructed to follow them despite his protests. Details on the process of enclosure at Hangzhou are provided in *HBZY* 15.17b–24a.

84. The streets of Hangzhou no longer follow the irregular bends that characterized the city in traditional times. The garrison wall stretched from present Qingchun Road south to Kaiyuan Road, from Zhongshan Central Road westward to the edge of the lake. The present People's Conference Hall (on the corner of Kaiyuan Road and Yan'an Road) stands on the site of the former General-in-Chief's Residence. The original five gates were Hongzhen (in the northeast corner), Chengqian (in the northwest corner), Pinghai (in the eastern wall), Yangzhai (in the eastern wall) and Yanling (in the northern wall). Zheng Yunshan et al., *Hangzhou yu Xihu shihua*, 90. Wang and Zhao, *Hangzhou shihua*, 87.

85. *HBZY* 5:8a.

86. This is the estimate of Mo Dongyin, *Manzu shi luncong*, 20.

87. Records of the transfers, from the records of the Board of War (*bingbu*) and other previously collected in *Baqi tongzhi*, have been reprinted in *HBZY* 15.

88. Approximately the present site of Hubin Park and ferry launch. The district, with the blocks of modern shops around it, is still called *qixia*, "garrison ground," though no trace of the Qing edifices remains.

89. The approximate site of the *Liu gong yuan*, adjacent to Hubin Park.

90. The approximate intersection of Yuanchao Road and Xueshi Road today; like most of the canals of Hangzhou, all the canals of the old garrison quarter have been culverted.

91. That is, in the area roughly between Jiefang Road and Kaiyuan Road, west of Yan'an Road. Zheng Yuanshan et al., *Hangzhou yu Xihu shihua*, 92–93.

92. For an introduction to the state cult of Guan Di see Duara, "Superscribing Symbols." The Qing imbrications of Guan Di worship caused by court shamanism, folk shamanism, state sacrificial cults and Manchu oral traditions brought considerable complexity to an already tangled tradition. See also Jinliang, *Guan Xuan xiao ji*, 128.

93. Im, *Rise and Decline*, 16; the route of the emperor's tours is narrated and depicted in *Nanxun shengdian*, see n. 82 above.

94. *BT* 57:2a–b.

95. Brunnert and Hagelstrom, 570, comes closest to describing this office.

96. *QBT* 47:1–3.

97. The "supplementary salaries," as Ch'ü T'ung-tsu has called them (see *Local Government*, 22–24) were an innovation of the Yongzheng period and radically

increased government expenditure on provincial officials. Their purpose is conveyed by their name, but in the case of the garrison officers, at least, the same term had in earlier reigns indicated what for civil officials was a salary—as titular slaves, the bannermen were not in need of salaries, but were given "honesty-incentives" to defray their expenses. See also Zelin, *The Magistrate's Tael*; Xue Ruilu, "Qingdai yanglian yin zhidu jianlun."

98. *HBZY* 18:10a. For Nian's biography, see *ECCP*, 587–90.

99. A complete list and career sketch of the acting commanders and assistant commanders at Hangzhou is included in *HBYZ* 18. For comparisons, Zhang Bofeng, *Qingdai gedi jiangjun* has been consulted.

100. Li Shiyao (d. 1788) was a descendant of Li Yongfang (d. 1654), a Ming commander at Fushun who became one of the early Chinese-martial generals after his capture by the Later Jin forces. Li Shiyao was himself a garrison commander at Canton, and later served for a decade as governor-general of Guangdong and Guangxi, where he attempted to break up the early comprador system. In the late 1780s he became a victim of the political factionalism sparked by Heshen's rise to power. See *ECCP*, 480–82. Yuji was Li's younger son. After years of service as the *dutong* of Rihe (now part of Hebei province), he was appointed Hangzhou *jiangjun* in 1817, the year before his death. See also *GQL* 309:21a–b.

101. *HBZY* 1:1a.

102. Thomas Meadows provides a vivid description of nineteenth-century Zhejiang and Zhapu in *The Chinese*, 582–83.

103. Hall and Bernard, *The Nemesis in China*, 309.

104. Details on the process of the enclosure at Zhapu are provided in *HBZY* 15.24a–25b.

105. Hall, upon seeing the houses of the garrison at Zhapu, thought they were arranged like tents—he attributed this to the Manchus' "wandering pastoral habits." Hall and Bernard, *The Nemesis*, 316.

106. Quoted in Im, *The Rise and Decline*, 109.

107. *HBZY* 8.9a–b.

108. Chen Jiahua, "Baqi bingxiang shixi," 67.

109. *HBZY* 16.17b–19b.

110. *HBZY* 16.5a. Compare the more than one million taels reported spent on garrison provisions in 1785. *HBZY* 16.6a. Reports of garrison provisions, which were partially left to the discretion of the generals-in-chief, are full of overlapping, hidden and unreported expenditures, and so are very difficult to compare with much precision.

111. *HBZY* 16.21b–22a.

112. *HBZY* 15.17a. On Chengde see *HBZY* 18.14b.

113. *QBT* 5:30a–b.

114. *QBT* 5:19b.

115. *GCS* 48a–49b.

116. *HBZY* 25:32–37; *GCS* 6–7.

117. *GCS* 48a–b. Shutongga's tablet was in front of the Tufu monastery near the West Gate in Zhapu.

CHAPTER IV
Guancheng

1. Like Chinese women, Manchu women of the Qing period were known simply as Somebody-*shi*; married Manchu women were usually recorded as Maiden Name-Married Name-*shi*, although either single or married women might be known simply by the name of their original clan or family, as in the case of Wanggi-shi. Since in most banner and garrison records men are recorded only by their personal names, the names of their wives and daughters usually provide the only information on the clan and family affiliations of the men with whom they are associated.

2. *HBZY* 20.7a.

3. *HBZY* 25.34a.

4. *HBZY* 25.34b.

5. *HBZY* 20.10a–b.

6. *HBZY* 25.34b.

7. *HBZY* 25.35b.

8. Shao-shi appears on the widows and orphans awards chart of the Hangzhou garrisons as late as Jiaqing 21 (1816). Wanggi-shi appears on the charity chart twice, once referred to as Wang-shi in Jiaqing 18 (1813), and once for an unspecified Jiaqing year. *HBZY* 20.7a; 20.6b; 20.10a–b. Jinliang, who is not always precise about these things, stated that Shao lived to be over eighty, which would mean that she outlived Guancheng and died about 1854 or 1855.

9. Shirokogoroff, *Social Organization*, 103–6. Lao She noted (*Beneath the Red Banner*, 23) that "traditionally, Manchus respected the women on the paternal side of the family," which on its surface seems incongruent with Shirokogoroff's discussions of the esteem of the materline.

10. Quoted in Mann, "Widows," 45.

11. Mann, "Widows," 42.

12. Mann, "Widows," 38 reviews the opinions of Liu Jihua and Mark Elvin on the phenomenon and its possible meanings.

13. Specifically, it was requested that Wanggi-shi should be granted the fourth official rank (*pin*), a height to which the family could hardly have aspired in Wanggi's time. The court, at least partly in response to Fengrui's reputation, acceded to the request. *HBZY* 20.10b.

14. She is the subject of moralizing essays by Wang Yinzhi and others that Guancheng published in the 1830s; she is the only widow given extended biographical treatment in the charity charts of the Hangzhou garrison records; she was the subject of Zhang Yuesheng's "Wanggi jiexiao zhuan" (now found in *HBZY* 25.34a–36a); she was also the subject of Sheng Yuanyi's "Wanggi-shi jiexiao zhuan" (*HBZY* 25.33b–34a); she has an individual entry in the Pinghu county history; and she has an individual biography among the "virtuous women" of "Draft History of the Qing" (*QSG* 590:14077) thanks to Guancheng's grandson Jinliang.

15. Guan and Zhou, *Zidi shu* (frontispieces; 270–78; 771–814).

16. Lao She (Shu [Sumuru] Qingchun), a Manchu and twentieth-century writer who died in the Cultural Revolution, wrote of this in an unfinished novel,

Hongqi zhi xia, which has been translated into English as *The Plain Red Banner*. His narrative (see especially 192–93) makes clear that the speech of the banner communities in Peking was still marked by this admixture of Manchu vocabulary at the end of the dynasty.

17. Shirokogoroff, *Social Organization of the Manchus*, 149; Arlington and Lewisohn provide some details of court shamanic pageants on lunar new year's and imperial birthdays—see *Old Peking*, 48–49.

18. *ECCP*, 79. The *ECCP* biographer of Shu Wei (661) notes that Shu and his collaborator Bi Huazhen were "amply rewarded" for the works they produced for Zhaolian.

19. There are many vivid passages on Manchu love of the theater and street performing in Lao She's work. See particularly *Beneath the Red Banner*, 12, 18–19, 50. On Dejunru, see *ECCP*, 583. The street and teahouse entertainments are an underdeveloped field for research, particularly since some of these traditions are still alive and await greater probing by Western and Chinese scholars. See Guan and Zhou, *Zidi shu*, 1–18; Blader, "Yan Chasan Thrice Tested," and "*San-hsia wu-yi*." For redactions of tales see, among others, Blader, "*San-hsia wu-yi*" [Appendix A]; Nowak and Durrant, *The Tale of the Nisan Shamaness*; and Chuang Chi-fa, *Nisan šaman i bithe*.

China's best-known actor today, Ying Ruocheng, is a Manchu from a literary family. Ying's earlier career was perhaps most marked by his portrayal of the translator in the Chinese film *Jinian Bai Qiu'en* (In Memory of Norman Bethune, 1961). He oversaw much of the production of Cao Yu's play *Teahouse* in New York in 1981, played Genghis Khan in the internationally produced television mini-series "Marco Polo," and played the lead role in Arthur Miller's 1985 production of *Death of a Salesman* in Peking. Most recently he was seen, in some ironic casting, as the inquisitor of the former child emperor [Aisin Gioro] Puyi (John Lone) in Bernardo Bertolucci's *The Last Emperor* (1987). It is fair to say that his attempts to internationalize Chinese theater have made Ying Ruocheng one of the best known and most important actors in the world.

20. *HBZY* 22.1a–b.

21. *Huang huo* (from the cycle *Si shi tong tang*), 274. The passage goes on to discuss the influence of the pastimes of the Manchus on the twentieth-century popular culture of Peking. In another novel, *Plain Red Banner*, Lao She discusses frequently and at length the immersion of the Peking bannermen in the trivia of bird-raising, pastry cooking, cricket fighting and so on. Though he does not emphasize his Manchu viewpoint, Dun Lichen (*Annual Customs and Festivals in Peking*) incarnated the sensibility Lao She re-created in his fiction.

22. Im, *Rise and Decline*, 121.

23. Yang, "Ye lun Qingjun zai yapian zhanzheng," 92.

24. "Normal garrison ranks" means, here, the ranks universal throughout the garrison system by this time—*jiangjun, fudutong, chengshouyu, xieling, canling, zuoling, fangyu* and *xiaoqixiao*; there were a small number of ranks that were limited to the Northeast or to the Capital Garrisons. Information on the changes in quantities of appointments is summarized in Sudō Yoshiyuki, "Shinchō ni okeru Manshū no toku shusei ni kansuru ichi kōsatsu."

25. Lei Fangshen, "Jingzhou qixue de shimo."

26. *HBZY* 17.1b–2b.

27. For examples see Chapter II.

28. From Guandong's introduction to *GCS* 3a. Like most other Manchu clan names, Gūwalgiya had taken on many forms in Chinese transliteration, but had been standardized in the *BMST* as written with the "melon" initial character.

29. For Guancheng's collection at Hangzhou, see *HBZY* 21.7a.

30. Wang Yinzhi's essay survived and has been reprinted by Jinliang as "Jie-xiao zhuan shu," in *GCS* 5a–b.

31. The high period of woodblock printing had passed, and it seems clear that Guancheng's business centered upon the carving of standard characters and their fitting into set of page frames. Great examples of Ming and earlier printing blocks were preserved in the Wenlan Palace, however, and may have been consulted by Guancheng or his wood workers. For a catalog of surviving texts see Qu Wan-liang, *Ban ke zhi yi*. Some very fine examples of Chinese woodblocks are preserved in the Han Yushan Collection at the University of California at Los Angeles, and I am grateful to James Cheng for showing them to me. For remarks on xylography related to the case of Cao Yin, who was also a printer, see Spence, *Ts'ao Yin*, 157–65.

32. *HBZY* 22. Most of the titles of known works by Guancheng and his sons are missing.

33. On Tao Zhu, see *ECCP*, 710–711; on Dai Xi, see *ECCP*, 700–701; and *QSG* 399:11816–18; on Tang Yifen, see *QSG* 399:2818; and on Zheng Tingji, see *ECCP*, 400.

34. This is a simplication of a very complex policy development in the early and middle seventeenth century that repeatedly changed the sort of examinations the bannermen could take and the conditions under which they took them. *QKZC* 1.3a, 8b, 9a, 7a, 9a, 12b, 16b. See also *HBZY* 9.10–11, 101a; and Chang, *The Chinese Gentry*, 168.

35. See *ECCP*, 431–34; 944.

36. His fellow bannermen candidates ranked sixty-eighth and thirty-eighth. See *HBZY* 10.2b.

37. For his biography see *ECCP*, 841–42. On Wang Yinzhi's academic influence in the Yangtze delta region, see Elman, "Ch'ing Dynasty 'Schools' of Scholarship," 5–11.

38. *HBZY* 16.21a.

39. Wakeman, *The Great Enterprise*, 465–66.

40. *BT* 3.1–5.

41. A middle-nineteenth-century foreign estimate put the banner population of the Inner City at Peking at 150,000 and noted that although each of the ring garrisons of the Capital System was supposed to house 3,000 bannermen, in fact the populations were much larger, which means that at least 60,000 additional Manchus were living in the ring garrisons. Meadows, *The Chinese*, 31. Chinese records for the period are inadequate and, in any case, indicate only the number of "eating (*shi*) bannermen" present. In fact if the total number of Manchus of all ages and both sexes is to be estimated and the perennial problem of illegal mi-

gration to Peking considered, it would probably be wise to double the numbers, which means that as many as half a million Manchus may have lived in Peking in the middle nineteenth century.

42. Harrell, Naquin, and Ju, "Lineage Genealogy," 38.

43. Li Qiao, "Qingdai Beijing," 25.

44. Tun, *Annual Customs*, 12, 48, 68–69. Respectively the present sites: Dazhong si on West Beisanhuan Rd.; Diaoyu tai within Yuyuantan Park between Fucheng Rd. and Fuxing Rd.; and the approximate intersection of Shazikou Rd. and Outer Yongdingmen St.

45. Li Qiao, "Qingdai Beijing," 25–26.

46. Kovalesky, "Excerpts," 72.

47. The last of the original elephants died during the Daoguang period, and from then until 1874 there were no elephants in Peking. Twelve elephants arrived as tribute from Annam in the 1874–1875 period, but by 1887 they had all died of starvation, like the earlier inmates. See Tun, *Annual Customs*, 53–54. The general vicinity was heavily damaged in the Boxer Rebellion and the grounds were razed after the Republican Revolution to make way for the parliament buildings erected under Yuan Shikai. This is now the area bounded on the east by Inner Xuanwumen Street and on the south by West Xuanwumen Street.

48. Now a shopping district, showing something of its old dimensions, at the corner of East Sishitiao Road and Dongdan North Road.

49. On Yinlu, see *ECCP*, 925. Yigeng may be ranked with Han Xiaochuang as one of the most prolific *zidi shu* composers of his time; sixteen of his texts survive. See Guan and Zhou, *Zidi shu*, 234–52. In the 1920s Yigeng's papers, including his historical essays, came into the possession of Yanjing University in Peking, which published them in 1935 under the title *Jia meng xuan congshu*. See also *ECCP*, 926.

50. In translation it is difficult to get across the actual flavor of this question. Lore on the founding of the dynasty honored a group called "Notables Who Were Not Admitted to the Eight Places" (*bu ru ba fen gong*), who were rather better known than the group who evidently had been admitted (*ru ba fen gong*). Yigeng was being asked how this strange negative distinction came about. His reply touches on the question of collegial rule. See also Chapter II, nn. 5, 6 of this book.

51. That is, Möngke Temür (d. 1433, posthumously titled Zhaozu yuan huangdi); Cungsan (d. 1467, posthumously titled Xingzu gaohuangdi); Giocangga (d. 1582, posthumously titled Jingzu yi huangdi); and Taksi (d. 1582, posthumously titled Xianzu xuan huangdi).

52. From Guancheng's preface to the *Donghua lu zhuiyan*, published in 1838; reprinted in *GCS* 1a–b.

53. "Tong" referred to a Jurchen lineage of Liaodong, many of whom went over to the Later Jin soon after the founding of the dynasty in 1616. The Tong had become associated with the Aisin Gioro clan by marriage when the Shunzhi emperor accepted one of the daughters of Tong Tulai as a wife; the result of the union was the birth of Xuanye, who became the Kangxi emperor at the Shunzhi

emperor's death in 1661. See Hou Shouchang, "Kangxi muxi kao," 100–102 and Crossley, "The Tong in Two Worlds."

54. See Crossley, "The Qianlong Retrospect on the Chinese-martial (*hanjun*) Banners"; and Chen Wan, "Shi Tingzhu."

55. Fu Guijiu, "*Donghua lu* zuozhe xinzheng," 168.

56. This is the phrase of Ch'ü T'ung-tsu, *Local Government*, 213. In order to be eligible for the "great selection" (*datiao*), a man must have failed the preliminary *jinshi* examinations three times. Between 1819 and 1833 there were six administrations of the preliminary examinations, any three of which could have been failed by Guancheng.

57. Zelin, "The Rights of Tenants," 501.

58. *NZ* 3.3b–8a.

59. Bannermen represented about 5 percent of the magistrates of Nanchuan, compared to the 6.7 percent national average of bannermen among *xian* magistrates in 1750, and the 1850 average of 7.6 percent. See Ch'ü, *Local Government in China*, 22.

60. *NZ* 3.8a.

61. *NZ* 4.2b–4b; 5b–7a. See also Hsiao, *Rural China*, 91.

62. Ch'ü T'ung-tsu, *Local Government in China*, 22, gives a nationwide *xian* range of 400 to 2259 taels. Ch'ü, 22–26, discusses magistrates' salaries. See also Xue Ruilu, "Qingdai yanglian yi zhidu jianlun"; and *NZ* 4.1a–b.

63. *NZ* 4.1b, from an earlier edition of the *Chongqingfu zhi*. These are the figures given in the records, though their relative accuracy could be debated at length. For demographic discussion with special relevance to Sichuan (whose provincial archives have of late been opened to foreign scholars), see Skinner, "Sichuan's Population in the Nineteenth Century"; and Smith, "Commerce, Agriculture and Core Formation in the Upper Yangzi, 2 A.D. to 1948." Also of interest are Zelin, "The Rights of Tenants"; and Zhang Zhongren and Li Rongzhong, "Lishi de guizhen—Qingdai Sichuan Baxian dang'an."

64. According to the calculations of Paul Smith, cited in Zelin, "The Rights of Tenants," 501. See also Smith, "Commerce, Agriculture and Core Formation in the Upper Yangzi, 2 A.D. to 1948," 11, 14.

65. *NZ* 13.8b. Edmund Halley had noted the intervals of the great comet's sightings in the sixteenth and seventeenth centuries and, in 1707, predicted its return in 1758. The 1834 sighting recorded by Guancheng's staff was the next time "Halley's" comet returned.

66. *NZ*13.8b–9a. See also *ECCP*, 885.

67. *NZ* 13.9a.

68. *NZ* 3.5a; see also *QSG* 492:13614, from the biography of Xirui. The entry is anonymous, but was written by Guancheng's grandson Jinliang.

69. "Nanchuan gong," in *GS* 5a–6b.

70. A detailed history of opium use and the Qing government's attempts to stem it is provided in Spence, "Opium Smoking." On background to the Opium War, see also Yao Weiyuan's annotated edition of Wei Yuan's "Record of the Invasions by Foreign Ships during the Daoguang Years," '*Yapian zhanzheng*' *shishi kao*, 3–81; Chang Hsin-pao, *Commissioner Lin*, 1–119; Fairbank, *Trade and Di-*

plomacy, 3–73; Wakeman, "The Canton Trade," 163–85; Fay, *The Opium War*, 3–66; Inglis, *The Opium War*, 15–120; Beeching, *The Chinese Opium Wars*, 11–93; Hibbert, *The Dragon Wakes*, 1–102.

71. See Chang, *Commissioner Lin*, particularly his review of principal state proscriptions on opium import or use, 1729–1839, 219–21.

72. Quoted in Spence, "Opium Smoking," 150. Emphasis follows the Spence text.

73. The effect of the trade upon silver values is detailed by Chang, *Commissioner Lin*, 44–45. He notes among other problems that the once inflexible ratio of 1,000 taels of copper to one tael of silver was out of kilter, and by 1836 was already noted to have reached an actual rate of 1,650 to every tael of silver. The causes of the economic problems of the early nineteenth century were in fact complex, and even the most stridently anti-opium partisans recognized that such problems were related to general issues of foreign trade, internal markets, monetary policy and taxes. An in-depth reanalysis of the problems of factionalism and statecraft is in James Polachek, *The Inner Opium War* (Harvard University Press, forthcoming).

74. Wakeman, "The Canton Trade," 185.

75. *QSG* 372:11526–27. Guan was a Green Standard career man of humble origins who had risen high in the naval garrison ranks. He died attempting to defend the Qing battery at Humen (the Bogue) on January 7, 1841.

76. Graham, *The China Station*, 109.

77. Graham, *The China Station*, recounts the background to the British invasion at Zhapu in great detail. For the Chinese side, the most comprehensive account is still Arthur Waley, *The Opium War through Chinese Eyes*, especially chapter III.

78. Eden, the first Earl of Auckland, became governor-general of India in 1835, which gave him ultimate authority over military operations in China; he was later First Lord of the Admiralty. See also Fay, *The Opium War*, 81, 180–88. Lin Zixu suspected the British would attempt to move up the coast toward the Zhoushan Islands but apparently was unable to give the government any precise warning. See Waley, *The Opium War*, 108.

79. Graham, *The China Station*, 128, from Bremer-O'Ferrall, July 6, 1840. In regard to the occupation of Dinghai, Waley notes that the English accounts appear to carry the first recorded instance of the new slang word, "loot."

80. Graham, *The China Station*, 131–35, discusses Elliot's futile attempts to make direct contact with the Qing court.

81. This is Graham's word (*The China Station*, 150). There appears to be no exact knowledge of what sort of illness struck the English garrison.

82. Qimingbao of the Manchu Plain White Banner, a native of the Rihe garrison, served as *jiangjun* at Hangzhou from April of 1839 to March of 1842. Seventeen years before his assignment to Hangzhou he is recorded as serving as *fudutong* at Jingzhou, and just prior to assignment at Hangzhou had served as *jiangjun* in Heilongjiang. He died in 1842. *HBZY* 18.18b. Zhang Bofeng, *Qingdai gedi*, 242.

83. *HBZY* 11.1a. A suspicion that conquered Chinese would work to subvert

the Later Jin/Qing regime can be traced back to the earliest period of the state and became a subject of official discussion during virtually all military operations. An early discussion of the fear of traitors during the Opium War was provided by Fairbank in *Trade and Diplomacy*, 87. Wakeman, in *Strangers at the Gate*, 49–57, analyzes the fear of traitors at Canton, and in "Canton Trade," 206–7 presents an excellent discussion of the coastal concern with traitors during this phase of the war. This point has been explored more analytically by Zhang Yiwen in "Shilun Qingjun zai Yapian zhanzheng shibai di jiben yuanyin," 94/87. Further light on the particulars of the search for *hanjian* at Jinjiang is provided by Elliott, "Foe Within, Enemy Without."

84. *HBZY* 11.1a. Changxi had a *zi*, Yiting, and like Guancheng was registered in the Manchu Bordered Yellow Banner. In 1835 he had been *fudutong* at Jingzhou, and served as Zhapu *fudutong* from June of 1838 to his death. See *HBZY* 18.18b; Zhang Bofeng, *Qingdai gedi*, 243.

85. Qimingbao reported them to the Court as being Naigui of the Plain Red Banner, Hengquan of the Bordered Red Banner, Shiding and Quansheng of the Plain Yellow Banner (Guancheng's own banner at Zhapu) and two officers. *HBZY* 11.1b.

86. Hengxing had a *zi*, Shiguan, and was registered in the Manchu Bordered Yellow Banner. He served as Hangzhou *fudutong* from March 1837 to June 1843. *HBZY* 18.18b; Zhang Bofeng, *Qingdai gedi*, 247.

89. *HBZY* 11.1b–2a.

88. Yao Weiyuan, *Yapian zhanzheng*, 64. Yilibu was a descendant of Nurgaci's younger brother Bayara; the lineage was struck off the rolls in 1652 because of the affiliation of Bayara's son Gunggadai with the Dorgon faction, but restored in 1799, though permitted only to wear red belts, not yellow. Yilibu, a *jinshi* of 1801, had established his good name on military expeditions to the southwest in the early nineteenth century, and at the time of his appointment to Zhejiang was fresh from new rewards for his service in Yunnan. See *ECCP*, 387–89.

89. *HBZY* 11.2a.

90. Mujangga was registered in the Manchu Bordered Blue Banner and was the son of Guangtai, a middle-level military bureaucrat of the Jiaqing period. Mujangga was himself a *jinshi* of 1805, and had had a distinguished career in both the civil and military bureaucracies at Peking. See *QSG* 363:11415–17. On Qi Junzao, see *ECCP*, 125–26; and Polachek, *The Inner Opium War*.

91. *ECCP*, 513. In the most dramatic instance, the Kaifeng magistrate Wang Ding was supposed to have written a last testament for the emperor, proclaiming his suicide in 1842 to be in protest of Lin's dismissal, and that Mujangga had cowed Wang's son into concealing it.

92. Historical discussion of the "Chuenpi Convention" normally assumes that signatories from both sides endorsed the items in question, but circumstantial evidence recently reviewed by Zhuang Jianping suggests that Qishan may never have given written acquiescence to the provisions of the "convention." See "Qishan cong wei qianding 'Quanbi caoyue.' "

93. Yishan, registered in the Manchu Bordered Blue Banner, was a fifth-generation descendant of the Kangxi emperor; see *ECCP*, 391–93; *QSG* 373:11537–

40. Longwen, registered in the Manchu Plain Blue Banner, was a *jinshi* of 1808; see *ECCP*, 391; *QSG* 373:11540. On Yang Fang, see *ECCP*, 884–85.

94. Yuqian's original name was Yutai, and his original clan affiliation was Borjigit. He was registered in the Mongol Bordered Yellow Banner; was a great-grandson of Bandi, whose dukedom had been diverted to a collateral clan branch a generation before; a grandson of Balu, who had served as *jiangjun* at Suiyuan; and son of Qingxi, who had been the *fudutong* at Jingkou. *ECCP*, 939–40; *QSG* 372:11523.

95. Yilibu was formally ordered to resume his post as governor-general of Jiangsu and Jiangxi, but in March was ordered to the capital and sentenced to banishment; his governor-generalship as well as his intendancy went to Yuqian.

96. Yijing was a great-grandson of the Qianlong emperor, and was registered in the Manchu Bordered Red Banner. By adoption into an heirless uncle's family he stood second-in-line for a second-degree princedom (Xun junwang). Yijing's experience had been almost exclusively with the banner services and military bureaucracy until 1836, when he served as president of the Board of Appointments (*libu*) in addition to his post as commander of the Peking constabulary. After the Opium War he was imprisoned for a time, but eventually released and allowed to serve in several military and official posts before he died of malaria while fighting the Taipings. See Yao Weiyuan, *Yapian zhanzheng*, 129–32; *ECCP*, 377–78; *QSG* 373:11540–41; and Waley, *The Opium War*, 158–72.

Wenwei was registered in the Plain Blue Banner and had taken the *jinshi* in 1815. See *QSG* 373:11532.

Teyishun had a *zi*, Jiantang, and was registered in the Manchu Plain Blue Banner. He was a native of the Fuzhou garrison and spent the early part of his career in the southeastern coastal sector, including Taiwan. In 1838 he served as the *jiangjun* at Ningxia, and later, in 1846, would be appointed *jiangjun* at Urumqi. See *HBZY* 11.6a; 18.18b; Zhang Bofeng, *Qingdai gedi*, 250; *QSG* 373:11543–44.

97. *HBZY* 11.6b.

98. *HBZY* 11.7a.

99. A superb narration of Yijing's campaign is provided by Wakeman, "The Canton Trade," 204–6. Waley recounts the background in *The Opium War*, 158.

100. Those from Shaanxi and Gansu arrived most speedily, being entirely assembled in Zhejiang within ninety days. The Sichuan contingent was the slowest, their first representatives reaching the Zhejiang headquarters on the ninety-sixth day after departure and the slower units arriving on the 110th day. See Mao Haijian, "Yapian zhanzheng shiqi de Zhong Ying bingli," 35; and Yang Wei, "Yelun Qingjun zai Yapian zhanaheng zhong shibai de jiben yuanyin."

101. The contemporary records (selections collected in *HBZY*; *Daoguang yangsao zhengfu ji*) call these troops "people from Shaanxi and Gansu [provinces]," which indicates that they might originally have been Tibetan or Turkic speakers, or simply unfamiliar with the standard spoken language; the purported inability to understand Chinese also might have been merely one of the many excuses forwarded by the commanders to explain their repeated failures. The records are certainly vague on the identity of these auxiliaries in the battles in question. Wakeman, "The Canton Trade," describes the aborigines as being from

the Golden River in Sichuan, presumably on the basis of an equally contemporary description.

102. *HBZY* 11.8b; *MJ*, 120–21.

103. *HBZY* 11:9a.

104. *HBZY* 11:9b. This is a cliché, but would become an even more frequently repeated description of fighting Manchus in the later nineteenth and twentieth centuries.

105. Longfu, a *zuoling* of the Bordered Red Banner, has a biography and brief account of the battle at Tianzun Temple in *PZ* 35.23a.

106. *HBZY* 11.10b.

107. Hall and Bernard, *The Nemesis*, 312.

108. Hall and Bernard, *The Nemesis*, 314. *PZ* 3.23a–b includes biographical notices of several of the men who died at Tianzun Temple.

109. Soon after the distribution of guns to the bannermen it became the custom for each man to store his ration of gunpowder in small bamboo cases carried in a bag strapped to his torso, where it would be within easy reach for reloading. Despite the obvious danger of this practice and the frequent mishaps that it caused this remained the custom until nearly the end of the dynasty. It was precisely this kind of accident that killed Lao She's grandfather while he was fighting the Allied invasion during the Boxer Rebellion of 1900. See Hu Jieqing's introduction to the English translation of *Zheng hong qi xia* : "About *Beneath the Red Banner*," in *Chinese Literature* (February 1981): 3.

110. Holt, *The Opium Wars*, 144.

111. Hall and Bernard, *The Nemesis*, 316–17.

112. Graham, *The China Station*, 214, 233.

113. Yao Weiyuan quotes a passage from Zhu Xiangqing's *Maifu ji*, composed some years after the attack: "Among the pirates were two races, white and black, the blacks being obedient to the whites. . . . Of all the captured women and girls, the young and beautiful were supplied to the white devils, and the black devils consequently received the older and homelier. It then transpired that several persons would sequentially debauch one person to death." To my mind there is a strong stereotypical quality to this account, which is like many others of nineteenth-century encounters of the Chinese with foreign troops. This does not mean that in its essentials it is false, for such things undoubtedly happened many times, but whether the account describes accurate particulars of the taking of Zhapu may be open to certain questions. British sources are frank on the problem of looting by their forces, but naturally say little that would corroborate either the charges or the sociological observations of Zhu's narrative.

114. Hall and Bernard, *The Nemesis*, 314.

115. Holt, *The Opium Wars*, 142; see also Wakeman, "The Canton Trade," 208.

116. Hailing was enrolled in the Manchu Plain White Banner. For his biography see *QSG* 372:11531. Fairbank comments briefly on Hailing's conduct in his post (*Trade and Diplomacy*, 87) but Elliott, "Foe Within, Enemy Without," gives new and extended treatment to the problem and its impact upon local Chinese-Manchu relations. For more on Hailing's defense, see *MJ*, 121. The numbers

provided differ from, and I assume supersede, those reported in contemporary accounts, which claim two to three thousand soldiers in the Jinjiang garrison, of whom about five hundred were the famous Qingzhou transferees from Shandong. See also Luo Chenglie, "Ya pian zhanzheng zhong Jinjiang kang Ying de shiliao."

117. Gough comments that the aftermath of Jinjiang echoed those at Zhapu with reference to the abilities of the bannermen. See Elliott, "Enemy Within, For Without."

118. Yao Weiyuan, *Yapian zhanzheng*, 160.

119. *HBZY* 11.11a.

120. A later work by Shen Shipu, *Renyin Zhapu xunnanlu*, amplified the garrison's appeals. I have been unable to consult Shen's work, but it is extensively quoted in Yao Weiyuan, *Yapian zhanzheng*, see especially 147–49.

121. Similar frustrations were evidently felt at Jinjiang, where the local government financed a small memorial stele to the Qingzhou bannermen who fell in defense of the town, listing three hundred names. The Hangzhou memorial tablets have been lost but the Jinjiang memorial is preserved in the Yidu county museum. See Luo Chenglie, "Yapian zhanzheng zhong Jinjiang," 62.

122. "Daoguang gengzi renyin Zhapu manzhou zhufang xunnan lu." The text is reprinted in *GCS* 2a–3b.

123. Changxi has a biography in *PZ* 12:1161; see also *HBZY* 18.18a–b; Waley, *The Opium War*, 137.

124. "Zhapu manzhou zhufang xunnan lu," in *GCS* 3a–b.

125. Xirui, from the introduction to "Zhapu manzhou zhufang xunnan lu," reprinted in *GCS* 3a–b.

126. Of this range of weapons, it should be emphasized, firearms accounted for by far the smaller part during the Opium War. Zhang Yiwen has estimated that no more than fifty percent and perhaps as few as thirty percent of the regular armed forces were supplied with firearms. See "Shilun Qingjun zai yapian zhanzheng," 89.

127. The causes of the Qing defeat have been reviewed and analyzed anew by Zhang Yiwen ("Shilun Qingjun zai yapian zhanzheng") and Yang Wei ("Yelun Qingjun zai Yapian zhanzheng"). Zhang, while giving considerable weight to the technological disparities involved, nevertheless concludes that social and political factors were decisive. Specifically, he argues that the Qing provoked hostilities between themselves (via their representatives, the bannermen) and the Chinese people, particularly with the search for Chinese "traitors" (*hanjian*) at Guangzhou and elsewhere. In Zhang's view the Qing saw the Chinese as their enemy after the British invasion, and so sabotaged the unity in the face of enemy invasion that might have sustained a national struggle. He points to the fact that the Chinese had the advantage of fighting on their own soil and to possibilities such as Yijing's plans for a kind of guerilla warfare (*sangong*) in Zhejiang as hopes subverted by the state's alienation of popular feeling. Yang, on the other hand, rejects Zhang's social explanation and points to the insuperable structural obstacles to Qing success in this instance: a dramatically weakened financial apparatus, an inefficient and decentralized communications system, and total lack of technological preparedness. I must say that while tensions between Manchus and Chinese were re-

current in some localities through the Qing period and there is vivid anecdotal evidence for the obsession of some banner officials with the problem of real or hypothesized Chinese "treachery," there is equally suggestive anecdotal evidence for spontaneous cooperation between Chinese and bannermen, both at the official level and below, and for the overriding hatred of British and Indian invaders by Qing subjects of all statuses and backgrounds. The concrete factors cited by Yang are so self-evidently persuasive and the possibilities Zhang touches upon for Chinese success in this instance so unlikely that, awaiting further investigation into the social history of the Opium War in China, Zhang's work, it seems to me, must be viewed as an interesting summary (which in many particulars parallels some long-standing Western analyses) of unproved speculations.

CHAPTER V
Fengrui

1. On Ye Mingchen, see *ECCP*, 904–5.

2. Jingheng, a Manchu of the Plain Yellow Banner, had previously served as the *fudutong* at Chahar and at Mukden. In 1853 he was appointed *jiangjun* at Jilin. See Zhang Bofeng, *Qingdai gedi*, 255; *Manzu jianshi*, 129.

3. See the series of memorials reproduced in *Qingdai dang'an shiliao congbian*, 11:45–113. See especially documents 12, 13, 14, 19, 22.

4. *Manzu jianshi*, 158–59.

5. Yu Yue wrote of Fengrui dispensing his rent income to the poor (*GCS* 7b–81); Jinliang later mentioned his father having a rent income of two hundred *shi*, which I assume is an annual figure though Jinliang did not specify how frequently it was received (*GS* 5a).

6. All were direct descendants of Jigantai, the son of Ubahai who had founded the garrison lineage. Guanji and Jingcheng were the sons of Ubahai's son, the *dutong* Shutongga.

7. "Xian jiangjun," in *GS* 4b.

8. *GCS* 7b.

9. "Guihe tang san dai shicun," in *GCS* 8b.

10. Yu Yue—great-grandfather of the *Honglou meng* scholar Yu Pingbo—was three years older than Fengrui and would survive him by one year; the two were lifelong friends, and the *Hangzhou baqi zhufang yingzhi lue*, on which much of the present work is based, was probably published as a result of their joint financing. *ECCP*, 944–45; *QSG* 484:13298–99; and Jinliang's *Jinshi renwu zhi*, 138–39. See also Chapter V: The Enclave, and Chapter VI: Body and Soul.

11. Yu Yue, "Shudeji xu," now *GCS* 7b.

12. Yu Yue, "Shudeji xu," now *GCS* 7a–86; and "Xinyonggong fu," in *GS* 24b.

13. *GCS* 47b–48a. That is, each reign period to Guangxu (1875–1908); Fengrui died in 1906, two years before the beginning of the last reign, Xuantong (1908–1912).

14. Yu Yue's father was Yu Hongjian, Zhejiang *juren* of 1816. See Chapter IV: Sir Nanduan.

15. *GCS* 48b.

16. This is a simplified description of a complex and very important enterprise.

See, most recently, Guy, *The Emperor's Four Treasuries*. The northern repositories stood at Peking, Shenyang and the two imperial summer retreats at Yuanmingyuan and Rihe.

17. See Guy, *The Emperor's Four Treasuries*, 47.

18. "Hangzhou Wenlan ge," in *GS* 23a.

19. "Siku quanshu xuanxiu kao," in *GCS* 27a–28b.

20. Wang Shilun, *Hangzhou shihua*, 74.

21. *GS* 23a–b.

22. Kuhn, *Rebellion and Its Enemies*, passim.

23. Luo Ergang, *Xiangjun bing zhi*, 16.

24. *ECCP*, 700.

25. See Lin Fengxiang's remarks to his captor Senggerinqin, as quoted in Shu
Yi, "Taiping Tianguo beifajun ruogan shishi kaobian," 177. There has been considerable discussion among scholars over whether *yao* in the writings of the Taiping founder Hong Xiuquan refers specifically to Manchus or to evil spirits generally. Luo Ergang, in the introduction to his *Taiping tianguo shiwen xuan*
(1960), insisted that the term referred to the Manchus, but removed it one step
from being racist by characterizing the Manchus as a metaphor for "feudal society." Teng Ssu-yu, on the other hand, finds no racial animosity in the early writings of Hong Xiuquan; it is after 1851 that he detects the refinement of anti-
Manchu rhetoric, particularly with the appearance of *Bian yaoxue wen zuili lun*
in 1853. This reached its height after the rise of Hong Rengan in 1859. Hong's
short but intense *Chuyao jiwen* (1861) was explicit in its description of the Manchus' devil-nature and called for a renewed assault on the north after the death
of the Xianfeng emperor. See Teng, *Historiography*, 8–30. Luo Ergang's views
have recently been restated and amplified by V. P. Ilyushechkin ("Anti-Manzhou
Edge"), who nevertheless allows that the lack of a well-formed class consciousness may well have led many Taipings to express nothing much more than outright hatred of the Manchus in their writings and utterances. It is probable that
hatred for the Manchus, quite independent of opposition to the Qing regime,
was widespread in many parts of China in the nineteenth century and that the
Taipings may have woven this element of folk life into their theology by seeing
the Manchus as a manifestation of Satan, which is not to say that they did not at
times also consciously exploit these sentiments to intensify loyalty among their
own followers. Philip Kuhn's discussion of this problem in "The Taiping Rebellion," 276, is unusually and refreshingly direct in its assessment of the role of
racial animosity in Taiping rhetoric.

26. Ilyushechkin, "Anti-Manzhou Edge," 259–62.

27. Xianghou, a member of the imperial clan, had a *zi*, Kuanpu, and was registered in the Bordered Red Banner. Previously he had served as *fudutong* at
Shanhai Pass. See Zhang Bofeng, *Qingdai gedi*, 250.

28. Jen Yu-wen, *The Taiping Revolutionary Movement*, 118, gives details and
citations on the fall of the garrison at Nanking.

29. Ilyushechkin, "Anti-Manzhou Edge," 268.

30. *GXQHL* 7.2a–b.

31. In the winter of 1856, rebel foragers were driven from the city's perimeters

by banner patrolmen. In August of 1859 a rebel expedition headed for the city was suspended when its commander became ill. *HBZY* 13.1a.

32. Hake, *The Events of the Taeping Rebellion*, 151. See Jen, *The Taiping Revolutionary Movement*, 131–33, and Du Wenlan's "Jiang nan bei daying jishi benmo," 45–74. See also Curwen, *Taiping Rebel*.

33. *HBZY* 13.1b. Ruichang had a *zi*, Yunge, and was registered in the Manchu Bordered Yellow Banner. He had previously served as *fudutong* at Jinzhou and at Jilin, and had spent several years under Senggerinqin fighting the Taipings before being assigned as the Hangzhou *jiangjun* in 1856. *HBZY* 18.20a; Zhang Bofeng, *Qingdai gedi*, 257; *QSG* 398:11809–10; *Zhejiang Zhongyi lu* 2.1a–2a.

34. *HBZY* 13.2a. Of the Manchu Plain Yellow Banner. Laicun served as the *fudutong* at Zhapu from June 1856 to September 1859 before being transferred to Hangzhou; he was succeeded at Zhapu by Xilingga. *HBZY* 18.20a; Zhang Bofeng, *Qingdai gedi*, 242.

35. The Qing fear of internal spies was well justified in the case of Hangzhou; Li Xiucheng later claimed that he gained information on the conditions within the walls from spies (see Curwen, *Taiping Rebel*, 231), and the timing of the militiamen's revolt would be easier to understand if it was coordinated by Taiping agents from within Hangzhou.

36. *GXQHL* 7.6b.

37. Of the Mongol Plain White Banner. Xilingga had previously (1857) served as *fudutong* at Fuzhou.

38. *GXQHL* 7.7a.

39. Curwen, *Taiping Rebel*, 237, 243.

40. Jen, *The Taiping Revolutionary Movement*, 372–74; Hake, *Events of the Taeping Rebellion*, 176. Curwen, *Taiping Rebel*, passim.

41. *HBZY* 13.5b–6a; Curwen, *Taiping Rebel*, 237; *HBZY* 13.6a.

42. *GXQHL* 3.75a; 4.40a–41b; 6.1–2a; 7.7b. *GXQHL* 4.42a–b. Jen Yuwen's treatment of the "feigned attack" on Zhejiang, which he estimates took 60,000 lives in Hangzhou ("mostly by suicide") is not surprisingly different in many ways from that of *Geng Xin qi Hang lu*, which is based upon government dispatches and the private accounts of Hangzhou loyalists. It does not appear, for instance, to be the case that a small Taiping vanguard seized control of Hangzhou on March 19, or that the banner troops immediately retreated to the garrison to await the arrival of relief forces. But all accounts are in agreement regarding the fury of the townspeople at the mutiny of the militia troops (371–72).

43. *HBZY* 13.7a.

44. *HBZY* 13.6b.

45. *HBZY* 13.12a.

46. Boliang, later *dutong* at Hangzhou, has a biography in *QSG* 482:12592. The generational element in Boliang's name makes clear that he is of the generation after Fengrui, whose children would bear the marker in their names: Chunliang, Xingliang, Jinliang, Hualiang, Wenliang.

47. *HBZY* 13.12b.

48. *PZ* 12: 11811–12, and see biography of Huang Jinyou, 12:11812; also *QSG* 482:12590.

49. Accounts of his death conflict; one version states he was shot by a banner-man standing on the walls of Hangzhou, who mistakenly thought he was an invader. According to Curwen, Ruichang hoped that Zhang would stay at Hangzhou to defend against future attacks, and this may have been Zhang's intention at the time of his death. See Curwen, *Taiping Rebel*, 232.

50. After Zhang's death command passed to a series of incompetents. See Jen, *The Taiping Revolutionary Movement*, 440–41, and Du Wenlan, "Jiang nan bei daying jishi benmo," 52–53.

51. Curwen, *Taiping Rebel*, 259.

52. *GXQHL* 2.8a–9a.

53. Hake, *The Events of the Taeping Rebellion*, 176–77.

54. *QSG* 395:11784–85; *Zhejiang zhongyi lu* 2.6a–8a.

55. Curwen, *Taiping Rebel*, 127. Later, in his forced confession, Li explained what had been in his mind while trying to reason with Ruichang: "The people of Manchuria crossed into our great country and took the imperial throne; this was ordained by Heaven's will and was not achieved by them. Formerly Manchus treated the Han people well; but now we each serve a different Sovereign and there is nothing we can do about it. It was with this in mind that I did what I did." Curwen, *Taiping Rebel*, 128.

56. *GXQHL* 2.18b. The Taipings later claimed that surviving bannermen had begun to follow the rebel camp, and Li found several who took him up on his offer of travel money "home." Curwen, *Taiping Rebel*, 128.

57. His memorial to the throne, which later became his introduction to "Record of Martyrs from the Eight Banners of Zhejiang," is reprinted in *GCS* 3a–4b.

58. "Xianfeng gengshen xinchou Zhejiang Baqi xunnanlu" in *GCS* 3b–4a.

59. Luo, *Xiangjun bing zhi*, 43–44.

60. Tacibu was one of the Manchu Bordered Yellow Banners. His career was virtually created by Zeng Guofan, who recommended his appointment to brigade-general and then to general-in-chief of Hunan in the 1850s. Tacibu died of a heart attack during the attempt to recapture Jiujiang in 1855.

61. On Li Hezhang see *QSG* 433:12337–38; Spector, *Li Hung-chang and the Huai Army*, 100, 303; "San daren," in *GS* 8b–9a; Jinliang, *Jinshi renwu zhi*, 270–71.

62. "San daren." Fengrui and Number Three became good friends, and between the end of the war and Li Hezhang's death in 1880 they corresponded often. *GCS* 9a.

63. One of the war's many odd combinations: Cheng was a deserter from the Taipings and Guo was a traditionalist officer from Hunan. But they were united in their resistance to westernization of the Chinese military. See Spector, *Li Hung-chang and the Huai Army*, 20, 84. Smith, *Mercenaries and Mandarins*, 118–21, details the EVA difficulties under Holland.

64. Smith, *Mercenaries and Mandarins*, 119.

65. Jen, *The Taiping Revolutionary Movement*, 495–96.

66. Apparently the incident that led to He's outlawing was the unjust prosecution of his elder brother; it was this elder brother, and not Guoxian himself,

with whom Fengrui had been acquainted. *QSG* 499:13809 and *GS* 4b—note that these are essentially the same text, both written by Jinliang.

67. Afterward He Guoxian reentered official life, and served in the Huai army as a warrant officer. Fengrui earned enough merit to be appointed an honorary *fudutong*, and was awarded the peacock feather.

68. Jen, *The Taiping Revolutionary Movement*, 488.

69. *GXQHL* 7.27b–28b. Jen, *The Taiping Revolutionary Movement*, 489.

70. Hake, *The Events of the Taeping Rebellion*, 430.

71. Jen, *The Taiping Revolutionary Movement*, 489.

72. *QSG* 240. See also Spector, *Li Hung-chang and the Huai Army*, 100.

73. *GCS* 9a. Jinliang clearly echoed his father's sentiments ("the victory at Tai-cang was the work of Li Hezhang") in his later essay on Li Hezhang in *Jinshi renwu zhi*, 270. He went on to speak of his acquaintance with Number Three's son Jingxi, and his disappointment at never having met Jingxi's son, Guoying.

74. *GCS* 49a.

75. Wright, *The Last Stand*, 39.

76. *ECCP*, 853–55. See also Hong Liangpin et al., *Wen Wenzhong shi lue*.

77. For background on the *zongli yamen*, see Banno, *China and the West, 1858–1861*, passim. As for Peking Field Force, I follow the translation of Fang Chao-ying. *Shenji* literally means "spirit instrument," "supernatural device" or other occult connotations not generally associated with the western idea of "self-strengthening" in the 1870s. Its intention is to describe a military application with unprecedented speed, efficiency, intuition and so on, and unfortunately remains inaccessible to precise translation.

78. Wright, *Last Stand*, 71.

79. Kovalesky, "Excerpts," 75.

80. Meadows, *Translations*, viii.

81. Wright, *Last Stand* :181.

82. Banno excerpts unflattering portraits of Wenxiang from contemporary correspondence. See *China and the West*, 343.

83. Wright, *Last Stand*, 286–93.

84. Tan Yi, "Wan Qing Tongwen guan yu jindai xuexiao jiaoyu," 349–50.

85. Evans, "The Banner-School Background of the Canton T'ung-wen Kuan."

86. See for instance Lei Fangsheng, "Jingzhou qixue de shimo ji qi tedian," 57.

87. The Number One Historical Archives in Peking contains a collection of *Shenji ying* documents, including the complete roster of officers serving under [Murca] Tieliang (1863–1910), which places it well after Wenxiang's time; it is nevertheless the most complete document of its kind, and the present description of the recruitment is drawn from it.

88. His purpose for going to the Northeast is supposed to have been to escort his mother from Mukden to Peking, where she would live with him. The road was reported to be harried by bandits, and so Wenxiang brought his troops along, and in their midst he transported his mother safely to Peking. *ECCP*, 854.

89. Wright, *Last Stand*, 208.

90. Meadows, *Translations*, 19.

91. Kovalesky, "Excerpts," 84–85. The writer was bemused by his inability to solicit from his Chinese informant a conclusion that the "devil" in question was the Foreign Devil in Canton; it was rather *the* devil, the one who spoke to and through the Manchus.

92. *Manzu jianshi*, 150, 152.

93. Li Qiao, "Baqi shengji wenti shulue," 94.

94. *Manzu jianshi*, 153, offers a description of conditions at Qingzhou, from *Qing muzong shilu* 88:19b.

95. *Manzu jianshi*, 154.

96. This estimate comes from *Manzu jianshi*, 156.

97. See especially Wright, *Last Stand*, 51–67

98. *QSG* 240:13810.

99. *GCS* 49a.

100. *QSG* 499:13089.

101. Of the Manchu Plain White Banner, Liancheng served as Hangzhou *jiangjun* from 1865 to 1872. *HBZY* 18.20b.

102. *HBZY* 19:7b; 22:1a–b.

103. The most penetrating and vivid analysis of local Zhejiang conditions probably remains Ho Ping-ti's *Studies on the Population of China*, 153–58; 214–44. See also Rankin, *Elite Activism*, 55; 330 n. 35. On the apparently extreme degree of depopulation during the Taiping War, it is important to note the recent argument of G. William Skinner casting doubt upon the accuracy of the high population estimates of the pre-Taiping era; see "Sichuan's Population in the Nineteenth Century."

104. Efforts at civil reconstruction, which were sometimes integrated with garrison projects and more often presented a parallel to them, have been deeply investigated in Zhejiang. See Rankin, *Elite Activism*, esp. 92–135, and Schoppa, *Chinese Elites*, passim.

105. *ECCP*, 753.

106. On Ding's other contributions to local reconstruction, see Rankin, *Elite Activism*, 107–8.

107. Wang Shilun, *Hangzhou shihua*, 78, and *ECCP*, "Ting Ping," 726–27.

108. The Bao family of Tongxiang, who were also printers, had been among the leaders in the submission of review materials for the *Siku quanshu* project in the middle eighteenth century. They had been rewarded with a special edition of the Imperial Encyclopedia (*Gujin tushu jicheng*) and other valuable books. See also *ECCP*, "Pao T'ing–po," 612–13.

109. *GS* 35b.

110. *GCS* 49b.

111. Qian-shi was the subject of two pieces reprinted in *GCS* 10b–12b. Whether she was Chinese or Chinese-martial is unknown. Jinliang later claimed that his mother, grandmother and great-grandmother were all "Chinese" (*han*), clearly not distinguishing between Chinese and Chinese-martial.

112. *QSG* 499:13809–10; the text is by Jinliang. This Shi must have had the extraordinary experience of first helping Xilingga kill his women family members, then raising his son.

113. *ECCP*, 617–20; *QSG* 410:11995–12000.

114. "Peng Gangzhi," in *GS* 6b–7a.

115. *GCS* 5b. It is my belief that Dingchang was the last Suwan Gūwalgiya resident of the Fiongdon mansion in Chaoyang Gate Street.

116. "Ruru laoren meng Hua Guan shi xu," now *GCS* 9a–10b.

117. "Shudeji xu," now *GCS* 8a.

118. *GCS* 49a, 4b.

119. *HBZY* 25:32a–34a.

120. *GS* 5a.

121. Her collection *Chaofanshi huafan* survived to the end of the century; see *HBZY* 21:23a–b and *QSG* 508:14055.

122. *ECCP*, 755, 945.

123. After 1911 he went to live in the Northeast, and apparently died sometime around 1920. *GCS* 50b.

124. "Gaoyou Wang shi wudai hezhuan," now *GS* 26a–b. Besides intellectual kinship (also his bond to Yu Yue), Fengrui insisted that he had, as a very young man, corresponded with Yinzhi, his father's academic patron and business associate. The families ceased contact after Xirui's death in 1861. A summary of the textual analysis movement to the development of *hanxue*, its relationship to statecraft and an explication of techniques with special reference to Wang Yinzhi and Wang Niansun is provided in Huang Aiping, "Qian Jia xuezhe Wang Niansun," 267–304. See also Elman, *From Philosophy to Philology*, 112–29.

125. The *xiaoxue* traditions of Wang Niansun and Wang Yinzhi, with which the family rightly or wrongly identified themselves, have been summarized in Huang Aiping, "Qian Jia xuezhe Wang Niansun, Wang Yinzhi fu zi xueshu yanjiu," 280–98.

126. Many of these tales were the basis for Jinliang's supernatural vignettes, most of which were published in a volume called *Lingyin zhiyi* in the spring of 1936. This is now part of *Guapu shuyi* 44a–55b.

127. "Wen Wen Gong shilue bo," in *GCS* 14a–b.

128. As a grown man Jinliang did not lose his fascination with the Li-Xu story. After he began working in Peking and the Northeast and became acquainted with Luo Zhenyu, he asked the latter for more information on the two, and in 1923 published a set of essays on them, *Longchuo jian shang liang xiansheng yiji*; see *GCS* 25a–b.

129. *GS* 4a. Jin Nong, of Hangzhou (Renhe *xian*) was a poet who died in 1764. His best-known literary name was Dongxin, the name by which he was referred to in Jinliang's family.

130. "Zi shu," in *GS* 4a. I was told by someone in Peking who knew Jinliang when he was old that he "looked like a typical Manchu," from which I invite the reader to draw a conclusion. There were many stereotyped representations of Yue Fei in the Hangzhou environs (at one time during the nineteenth century at least five temples to him were in existence), and the massive image in the Yue Fei Temple just west of the Hangzhou Hotel is a modern echo of them.

131. *GS* 6b, 8b–9a.

132. *GS* 5b.

133. References to Jinliang as Jin Xihou are amply attested for the period after 1912. Wenliang's style name was Fuhou, and one may assume that if he had lived to adulthood he would have been known as Wen Fuhou by many people.

134. "Song Zhongcheng," in GS 7b–8a.

135. GCS 48b–49a. A supernatural sketch deals with Chunliang's arrangements for the burial of Wenliang. See GS 54a.

136. GCS 25b. The reference to Mt. Tai is a cliché—many readers will know it from Sima Qian's Bao *Ren An shu* and Mao Zedong's *Jinian Bai Qiuen*.

137. GS 26b. *linggan*, literally "a sensitivity between souls."

CHAPTER VI
Jinliang

1. From the introduction to *Linggan zhiyi*, now GS 44a.

2. Zhang's literary name was Taiyan. The political thought of Zhang Binglin has been the subject of a great deal of writing. For his memoirs see Tang Zhiyun, ed., *Zhang Taiyan nianpu changbian*; Rankin, *Early Chinese Revolutionaries*; Furth, "The Sage as Rebel: The Inner World of Chang Ping-lin"; and Luo Baoshan, "Guanyu Zhang Binglin zhengzhi lichang zhuanbian de jipian tiaowen"; the latter includes the text of two essays and a letter not included in Zhang's collected works. See also Onogawa Hidemi, *Shimmatsu seiji shisō kenkyū*, 398–482.

3. Furth, "The Sage as Rebel," 118.

4. GCS 50b. Jinliang's relationship with Zhang Binglin is not, so far as I know, independently corroborated in the extant papers of Zhang Binglin, though the fact that Zhang singled Jinliang out as a progressive Manchu in 1900—at which time Jinliang's only claim on the public attention was his arrest in 1898, which was noted and commented upon by Tang Shouqian—is suggestive. Zhang's writing, and even his correspondence, is almost exclusively devoted to discourse; his personal encounters and relationships figure only in relation to his discussion of political or scholarly matters. Jinliang's writing, however, is highly anecdotal and, apart from his small number of truly scholarly works, almost exclusively based on his personal relationships and experiences. Although in the Republican years Jinliang may have had good reason to play upon or, indeed, overplay his relationships with revolutionaries of the late Qing period, Zhang Binglin would not have been the most auspicious choice, and Jinliang made no pretense of having been acquainted with those who later became leaders in the revolutionary government. It should be noted that Jinliang's reminiscences of Zhang were written for publication, and were widely circulated while Zhang was still alive. To my knowledge no public refutation of Jinliang's claims in this regard was ever forthcoming from Zhang or his associates. This is a contrast to Jinliang's contentions regarding his participation in the *Qingshi gao*, which were refuted by Peng Guodong and others. In short, I credit Jinliang's account of his relationship with Zhang, though the reader is advised that there is no independent verification of it that I have been able to discover.

5. Liu and Smith, "The Military Challenge," 202–11; 243–50; 253–58; 266–73.

6. Shoufu was a tenth-generation descendant of Šurgaci. ECCP, 611–12. *Manzu jianshi*, 163–64.

7. See Kwong, *A Mosaic of the Hundred Days*, 243–45 for a discussion of the implications of the word "faction" as applied to the *qingliu* and others.

8. Borokh, "Anti-Manzhou Edge," 306.

9. We have begun to have a sense of Zaitian's individuality from two important recent works, Sun Xiao'en's *Guangxu pingzhuan* and Luke S. K. Kwong's *A Mosaic of the Hundred Days*. My characterization of the emperor follows these two works.

10. *ECCP*, 405–9.

11. Xiaoqin on this occasion received three "Women of the third class (*san pin fu*)": Miao Jiahui, the wife of Chen Rui (*zi* Suyun) from Kunming, for calligraphy and painting; Ma's wife Ruan, *zi* Binxiang, from Yichang, given the name Yufen; and Fuluojia's wife Wang Shao, *zi* Maoyun, and Manchu of the Hangzhou garrison, who had written *Dongqing guan shi*; Renxing's wife, of the Gūwalgiya clan, named Hualiang, also a Manchu of the Hangzhou garrison, whose writings include *Chaofan shi huafan*. *QSG* 295:14055. The text is by Jinliang.

12. On the background and aftermath of the Hundred Days, see Spence, *The Gate of Heavenly Peace*, 1–29. See also Lo Jung-pang, ed., *K'ang Yu-wei: A Biography and a Symposium*; and Kwong, *A Mosaic of the Hundred Days Reforms*.

13. For analysis of the regional impact see Rankin, *Elite Activism*, 193ff.

14. *Manzu jianshi*, 162, from Kang Youwei, *Gongju shangshu ji* 2b.

15. He claims he went there to present his own "ten-thousand word memorial" in protest against the government reaction to the "Hundred Days" reforms. It is not likely that he was in favor of any of the more radical suggestions made by the reformers. His objection, apparently, was to the conduct of the government by a small and corrupt group and their obstruction of the emperor's right to govern. The content of Jinliang's manifesto has never been reprinted, by himself or anyone else. His behavior, apparently, was what gained him attention, more than what was said. Jinliang was not the only person to publicly demand Li's execution. A man surnamed Shen was also arrested in Peking for making a demonstration similar to Jinliang's and according to Tang Shouqian, "People said, in reference to Jin and Shen, 'Our way does not advance alone.' " See Tang Shouqian's introduction to "Wuxu shangshu" in *GCS* 30b–31a.

16. Tang was another activist from Zhejiang in Peking for the occasion, and would later become part of the progressive Zhejiang elite. For background see Rankin, *Elite Activism*, passim.

17. Chunliang, according to Jinliang's later memoir on the events, went on to inform Ronglu that his younger brother was an extremely talented student and the son of an outstanding bannerman from the Hangzhou garrison, a decorated Taiping veteran (like Ronglu's own father) now living in retirement. "So," Ronglu sighed (in this account) on hearing of Jinliang's promise, "my clan has talent like this, and yet no use is being made of it. That is the fault of the officials." *GCS* 31a.

18. *GCS* 31a.

19. Jinliang states he arrived back in Hangzhou some time after Zhang Binglin. He knew that Zhang was staying not in his own home—where he was likely to be arrested—but at the Fenglin Temple south of West Lake. At one point, Jinliang

later claimed, Zhang's hiding place became known to a gang of youths from the garrison, who intended to go to the temple and beat Zhang up. "When I heard about it, I hurried over and tried to get the mob to disperse; fortunately, nothing happened. Zhang never knew anything about it." GS 10b.

20. See particularly Schrecker, "The Reform Movement of 1898 and the Meiji Restoration as Ch'ing-i Movements." See also Kwong, A Mosaic of the Hundred Days, 305.

21. See Kwong, A Mosaic of the Hundred Days, and Huang Chang-chien, "On the Hundred Days Reform." The contemporary debate shares some traits with the textual debates of traditional times; Huang's work—a repudiation, on the basis of internal evidence, of the applicability of certain of Kang and Liang's writings—has cast doubt upon their actual role before and during the reform period, and Kwong has consequently sought explanations for the origins and implementations of the reforms at the court level. There has been resistance to the revisions of both Schrecker (see above) and Kwong, the latter of whose work has recently been criticized as argumentative (see, for the latter, Tang and Elman, "The Hundred Days Revisited"). The materials and interpretations of the present work, however, suggest that both Schrecker and Kwong have opened up very useful avenues of analysis, even if in their criticisms of each other and in the evaluations they receive from others they are considered to have "oversimplified" their cases. Kwong's work in particular is a subtle, detailed, comprehensive reinterpretation of the complex forces at work in 1898.

22. Manzu jianshi, 143. Manchu attraction to the Boxer movement is the primary theme of Lao She's unfinished novel, Beneath the Red Banner.

23. See Esherick, The Origins of the Boxer Uprising, for a view of the social origins and political dynamics of the Boxer movement.

24. Manzu jianshi, 55.

25. From summary of a text, now lost, titled Hangzhou qiying jilue; the contents were characterized by Chunliang in his introduction to the work, now GCS 13a–b.

26. Scenes of bannermen being humiliated by their creditors had early attestations, from the other side, in Sungyun's Emu tanggū orin sakda-i gisun sarkiyan, translated into Chinese in 1809. This was a pervasive image in both Manchu and Chinese popular life for, perhaps, the whole of the Qing period and certainly from the middle eighteenth century on. The culture of indebtedness was old; the experience of casual degradation by the society at large was new.

27. Wu Woyao, Ershi nian mudu, 21–22. This translation is my own, but the passage is nearly as well known among Western scholars of late Qing fiction as it was among the fiction-reading Chinese of the time; the similarities to "Kong Yiji" can hardly be overlooked. It has been previously translated individually by Gloria Bien, see "A Bannerman at the Teahouse" and by Liu Shi Shun, see Vignettes from the Late Ch'ing.

28. Der Ling, Two Years in the Forbidden City, 117–18.

29. Guan Xuan xiao ji, 93.

30. Shi's descendant Shi Jianru was active in Canton and Macao in the 1890s, 1900s in the Xingzhong Hui. Wakeman, Great Enterprise, 549n.

31. Borokh, "Anti-Manzhou Edge," 298, 306, 309, 311.

32. Wang, "The *Su-pao* Case," 102–3.

33. Rankin, *Early Chinese Revolutionaries*, 40. Wang, "The *Su-pao* Case," 101.

34. "Five million" was the contemporary, conventional estimate of the number of Manchus around 1900. There are a number of problems with this convention. First of all, it surely indicates the number of bannermen, not the number of Manchus. The comparatively small number of Mongols involved in the banners from the beginning and the elimination of a large portion of the Chinese-martial bannermen in the eighteenth century worked to conflate, in current terminology, the identities "bannerman" and "Manchu"—all were now *qiren*, "bannermen"—and this confusion is evidently present in the "five million"; nevertheless the Chinese-martial, who represented 70 percent of banner enrollment in the late seventeenth century, must still have been numerous within the banners. At most 200,000 bannermen seem to have been enrolled around 1700, and though this number increased during the eighteenth century it was subsequently decreased, so that for the year 1840 one estimates 200,000 to 250,000 enrolled bannermen. There may have been a doubling of this figure (which would not have indicated a doubling of population) by 1864, due to the simultaneous rebellions and renewed threat from the West. Thereafter policy militated against a growth in enrollments—indeed, produced considerable pressure for derollment—and though at this time no precision is possible, the number of enrolled bannermen in 1900 probably fell within the range of 150,000 to 200,000. Population figures for the garrisons of China proper were never complete or accurate with regard to the number of banner dependents, but figuring an average of fifteen dependents per active bannerman, the number of bannermen and dependents could not have exceeded 2.5 million. On the other hand, an age had begun in which the "Manchu" identity was no longer limited to garrison residents and bannermen receiving stipends. Like the lineage of Jinliang, a population identified by others and now identifying itself as "Manchu" lived outside the legal institutions of banner status, but the proportions of this population are, with present knowledge, indeterminable, and in fact would have been indeterminable by the registration instruments of the time. The irony of the "five million" convention is that it must have encompassed the population of the Manchu homelands (where there were probably less than 1.5 bannermen in 1900), which the Qing had attempted unsuccessfully to insulate from Chinese settlement but where, by 1900, bannermen and native peoples may have represented less than one person out of five. See also Lee, *The Manchurian Frontier*, 78–79.

35. Wang, "The *Su-pao* Case," 93–94.

36. Belov, "The Xinhai Revolution," 332.

37. Luo Baoshan, "Guanyu Zhang Bingli zhengzhi lichang," 56.

38. *GS* 38a–40b.

39. Quoted in Wiens, "Anti-Manchu Thought During the Early Qing," 19, from *Zhu ke yu* (Dialogue between Host and Guest).

40. From "Qing yan ju man meng ren ru guohui zhuang," from *Zhongguo xunbao* 19, quoted in Luo Baoshan, "Guanyu Zhang Binglin zhengzhi lichang," 57.

41. Luo Baoshan, "Guanyu Zhan Binglin zhengzhi lichang," 61.

42. Zhang particularly pointed to the official distance kept by the Manchus and Mongols, maintaining that there would never be a significant number of Manchu and Mongol women married to Chinese, and therefore the aliens could never "become" Chinese. See Luo Baoshan, "Guanyu Zhang Binglin de zhengzhi lichang," 57; for the development of Zhang's thought, see Furth, "The Sage as Rebel."

43. Furth, "The Sage as Rebel," 134.

44. *GCS* 50b. See Spence, *Gate of Heavenly Peace*, 46–49.

45. Rankin, *Early Chinese Revolutionaries*, 70–71.

46. *GS* 10a–b.

47. Belov, "The Xinhai Revolution," 337.

48. Furth, "The Sage as Rebel," 131–33.

49. One of the earliest citations of the use of the word *minzu* is in fact from Zhang Binglin's work, the essay *Xuzhong xing shang*, composed not later than 1900, and reprinted in Tang Zhiyun, *Zhang Taiyan nianpu changbian* (Vol . II), 112–14. There is no question, however, that citations for earlier years can be found. Liang Qichao, for instance, employed the term in 1898 and it is possible that Kang Youwei used it as early as 1895. See Han Jiuchun and Li Yifu, "Hanwen 'minzu' yici de chuxian."

50. *GCS* 50a.

51. *GS* 10b.

52. Jinliang's resumé is to be found among those collected at the Number One Historical Archives in Peking (see ZEDSS 517), and reveals his unsuccessful attempt to join Zhao Erxun's government in 1911, before turning to Zhang Zuolin directly (a development to which Jinliang makes no reference in his own writings).

53. His original ambition was to sit for the national examinations during the 1900–1901 administration. The 1901 metropolitan examinations, which would normally have been held in Peking, were moved to Kaifeng because of damage to the examination halls in the capital. Jinliang, *Guan Xuan xiao ji*, 19.

54. Jinliang, *Guan Xuan xiao ji*, 20, 61–62.

55. Very large numbers of bannermen and former bannermen staffed the police departments (which had earlier been a true gendarmerie) at the capital in the late years of the empire and under the Republic. For the history of the Peking gendarmerie, see Dray-Novey, "Policing Imperial Peking." Former bannermen in Peking during the earlier twentieth century are among those whose lives have been brilliantly captured in Strand, *Rickshaw Beijing*; see particularly chapters 2 and 3.

56. One of his students, Chen Xifu, compiled Jinliang's chronology and published it with a preface by Shanqi in 1908. See *GCS* 28b–29a. On the basis of his Hundred Days' reputation, Jinliang was seen as a remnant of the Confucianist progressives, for a time.

57. Rhoads, "Manchu Ascendency in the Late Qing," has presented a penetrating analysis of the developments behind the appeerence of the "Manchu Cabal" in the very late dynastic period, and my discussion has been shaped by his work.

58. *Guan Xuan xiao ji*, 104.

59. Rankin has called Hangzhou "the first center of modern thought" as well. See *Early Chinese Revolutionaries*, 140.

60. *ECCP*, 169–71. See also Rankin, *Early Chinese Revolutionaries*, 38–47.

61. Rankin, *Early Chinese Revolutionaries*, 176–85.

62. Jinliang, *Guan Xuan xiao ji*, 104.

63. Duanfang was a Manchu of Chinese ancestry, his forebears being recorded as Ming immigrants to the Northeast who moved to the Manchu territories before the rise of Nurgaci. See also Crossley, "The Qianlong Retrospect on the Chinese-martial (*hanjun*) Banners."

64. For background on Xiliang, see Des Forges, *Hsi-liang and the Chinese Revolution*, passim.

65. The Princes Su were descendants of Haoge (1609–1648), first son of Hong Taiji. The mansion originally granted to the lineage in Peking, straddling the present Zhengyi Rd.—which at the time was the Jade Canal (*Yuhe*)—was sold in the nineteenth century to Britain and to Japan, who used the grounds for their embassies; the lineage estates in the Northeast were lost in the Russian and Japanese occupation of 1900–1901. There is strong evidence that the Japanese deceived Shanqi into believing that Japanese control of the Northeast would result in the restoration of his ancestral estates. Shanqi allowed his daughter Jin Bihui (Jin, "Gold," being the surname often assumed by members of the imperial clan after 1912) to be adopted by Kawashima Naniwa, and she was thereafter known as Kawashima Yoshiko. She later had a strange career as spy and cabaret entertainer; forthcoming work by Barbara Brooks will profile this extraordinary figure. See also Yang Xuechen and Zhou Yuanlian, *Qingdai baqi wanggong*, 412–20.

66. Yang Xuechen and Zhou Yuanlian, *Qingdai baqi wanggong*, 369.

67. If 300,000 "eating" bannermen remained on the rolls (the number may have been considerably less) and the stipends were paid regularly and in full (which they were not) at a hypothetical average of three taels per bannerman (which is rather above the average statutory amount for non-commissioned men at the end of the dynasty), the total annual obligation of the government in the 1905–1911 period would have been something on the order of 10.8 million taels. For debt and imdemnity service, see Feuerwerker, "Economic Trends," 67.

68. Ichiko Chūzō, "Political and Institutional Reform," 386.

69. *Manzu jianshi*, 153–54.

70. Wu Qingdi, *Xinhai xunnan ji*, 4a–5b.

71. The Huixing school was renamed the Huixing Girls High School (*Huixing nuzi ahongxue*) in 1949 and in 1956 was merged with another school to form the present Hangzhou Number Eleven Middle School. Zheng Yunshan et al., *Hangzhou yu Xihu shihua*, 94. On Huixing see *QSG* 296:[1977]14082. The text is written by Jinliang.

72. Kostyaeva, "The 'Down with the Qing' Slogan in the Pingxiang Uprising of 1906," 312–16.

73. *The London Times*, October 14, 1911:8.

74. *The London Times*, November 6, 1911:5.

75. Wu Qingdi, *Xinhai xunnanji* 33a–34b.

76. *GCS* 50b.

77. *GCS* 47b.

78. Yang Xuechen and Zhou Yuanlian, *Qingdai baqi wanggong*, 368–70; Zhang Shucai, "Sun Zhongshan xiansheng mishuchu," 6.

79. Zhang has a biography in *Biographical Dictionary of Republican China*, (115–19). See also McCormack, *Chang Tso-lin in Northeast China, 1911–1928*.

80. *Qingdai dang'an shiliao congbian* (Vol. 8):16.

81. McCormack, *Chang Tso-lin in Northeast China*, 26.

82. *Qingdai dang'an shiliao congbian* (Vol. 8):91, 93, 165–70.

83. *ZEDSS* 577.

84. *GCS* 49b.

85. "Zhang laojiang," in *GS* 17a–b; *GCS* 13b.

86. "Guarjia mu Qian taifuren shouyan le shu," written in 1916; now *GS* 106–12a.

87. These restoration uprisings were built upon a purported political organization called the "Party of the Aisin Gioro Cult," *Zongshe dang*. In ways reminiscent of the later attempts of Jinliang and his colleagues to make and exploit wide contacts, the party of Shanqi worked for some time to build up a base before taking up arms. A collection of recently published documents sheds some light. See *Qingdai dang'an shiliao congbian* (Vol. 8).

88. Jinliang later wrote of this as the "first restoration." *GS* 14a.

89. Wang had been born a year before and not far away from Jinliang, in Hangzhou. There were some (probably misleading) parallels in their lives; in any event it is hard to see the "peculiar and haunting poignancy" that Joey Bonner attributes to the story of Wang Guowei (*Wang Guowei*, xi) reflected in the story of Jinliang, who struggled energetically to preserve his status and the order that accorded it to him, losing hope only when realizing the power of the Chinese Republic—his acknowledged foe—was dwarfed by that of the Japanese imperialist machine that he himself had helped, in his small way, set in motion; thereafter Jinliang lived a bitter but stubborn life to its natural end. Wang drowned himself in 1927 in Peking, whether because of despair over his financial affairs, his personal relations or the general condition of the world is and will probably remain unclear.

90. Jinliang's plan is explained at some length in Puyi's "autobiography," *Wode qianbansheng* (155–56). The photo reprints of what are probably the original documents are the major portion of the collection *Jiazi Qingshi bimou fupi wenzheng*, published by the Peking Palace Museum in 1929. On Jiang, see *Biographical Dictionary* of the Republican Period, 339–44.

91. Puyi contrasted the complacency and pessimism of this faction to the com-

paratively enterprising group led by Jinliang and Zheng Xiaoxu. See *From Emperor to Citizen*, 157. Zheng Xiaoxu (1860–1938) later became a prime minister of Manchukuo. See *Biographical Dictionary* (271–75).

92. Jinliang's most insistent advice to Puyi was that he abolish his father's regency and take up rule himself. Puyi later claimed that Jinliang even tried to persuade him, at one point, to leave the palace and give up his title, using his wealth to found schools and charitable institutions, rather than let Zaifeng continue to manage the court finances. See *From Emperor to Citizen*, 178.

93. "Sun Zhongshan xiansheng mishuchu," 5–6.

94. Reginald Johnston, *Twilight in the Forbidden City*, 35–39; 42.

95. Johnston, *Twilight in the Forbidden City*, 43. Puyi, *From Emperor to Citizen*, 188–89.

96. Aisin Gioro Puyi, *From Emperor to Citizen*, 190.

97. The historians Wang Zongyan and Ho Lieh later studied these changes in great detail. See Wang Zongyan, *Du Qingshi gao zaji*, 33–45, and Ho Lieh (He Lie), *Liushi nian lai zhi Qingshi yu Qingshi gao*, respectively.

98. "The Draft History of the Qing" was the source for "The Qing History" (*Qing shi*) published by the National War College in Taiwan in 1961, and the original text was itself republished, with annotations and corrections, by Zhonghua Press in Peking in 1977. It is a master text for the study of Qing history, somewhere between an original and a secondary source, whose origins reveal a great deal about the world view that produced it.

99. The Yonghegong was the princely residence of the Yinzhen, later the Yongzheng emperor, and was the birthplace of Hongli, for which reason it was later made a temple. It is described in Arlington and Lewisohn, *In Search of Old Peking*, 190–96, and *Rixia zunwen lu*, 34 and may be visited today. The fragments of Jinliang's unfinished works are preserved in the library of the Yonghegong and in the library at Peking University (Beijing daxue).

100. See the comments of Trevor-Roper in *Hermit of Peking*, 48–51, 62–78, 85–86, 180–213.

Conclusion

1. Gamble and Burgess, *Peking*, 19, 51. See also Strand, *Rickshaw Beijing*, especially chapter 2.

2. I am grateful to Mr. Guang Shucheng [Khantinger Kunggur] for his kindness in inviting me to the opening sessions of the Manchu Association in 1981 as well as the subsequent meetings of the younger members, and for sharing with me the correspondence the group received. In 1987 Pan Zhe wrote of his accidental discovery of the existence of the Manchu Association in Taiwan, and recounted for his mainland audience the background of the association and its periodical publication, *Manzu wenhua*. See "Taiwan de Manzu xiehui he 'Manzu wenhua.'"

3. Zou, "Manchu Language Rescued," 6.

4. Slightly under 7 percent of the Chinese population is recognized as national minorities. See "Quanguo gesheng" and "Yijiubaer nian."

5. See Wittfogel, Karl A. and Feng Chia-sheng, *History of Chinese Society: Liao* (Philadelphia: American Philosophical Association, 1949).

6. See particularly "Manchu Interests and Chinese Interests," in Wright, *Last Stand of Chinese Conservatism,* 51–56.

7. On this process, see Crossley, "The Qianlong Retrospect on the Chinese-martial Banners."

Select Bibliography

PRIMARY AND CONTEMPORARY SOURCES

Agui et al. *Qinding manzhou yuanliu kao* [Researches on Manchu Origins]. 1783. Photo reprint of original. Taipei: Wenhai, 1966.

Aisin Gioro Puyi (Aixinjueluo Puyi). *Wode qian ban sheng* [My Earlier Life]. 1964. Reprint of Qunzhong edition. Peking: Zhonghua, 1977.

————. *From Emperor to Citizen: The Autobiography of Aisin-Gioro Pu Yi*, W.J.F. Jenner, trans. Oxford: Oxford University Press, 1987.

Bredon, Juliet. *Peking: A Historical and Intimate Description of Its Chief Places of Interest*. Shanghai: Kelly & Walsh, 1922.

Der Ling. *Two Years in the Forbidden City*. New York: Moffat, Yard and Company, 1912.

Ding Bing. *Geng Xin qi Hang lu* [Record of the Grievings for Hangzhou in 1860 and 1861]. 1896. Reprint. Taipei: Huawen, n.d.

"Dongsan sheng Xinhai geming shiliao [Collected Materials from the Archives of the Qing Period]." *Qingdai dang'an shiliao congbian* (Vol. 8). Peking: Zhonghua, 1982.

Hake, A. E. *The Events of the Taeping Rebellion*. London: W. H. Allen & Co., 1891.

Hall, W. H. and W. D. Bernard. *The Nemesis in China*. London: Henry Colburn, 1847.

Huang Weihan. *Heishui xianmin zhuan* [Biographies of Heilongjiang Ancestors]. Shenyang, 1924.

Jiang Liangqi. *Donghua lu* [East Gate Chronicles]. Reprint of Qianlong edition. Peking: Zhonghua, 1980.

Jinliang. *Dezong yishi* [Miscellanea on the Guangxu Emperor], n.p., n.d.

————. *Dong lu yin cao* [Jottings of the Hermit of Donglu], n.p., n.d.

————. *Dongsansheng zhi* [History of the Eastern Three Provinces], n.p., n.d.

————. *Fengtian gu ji kao* [Studies on the Ruins and Landmarks of Fengtian], n.p., n.d.

————. *Gengzi jingshi baoxu lu* [Record of the Violence at the Capital in 1860]. Taipei, 1968.

————. *Guang Xuan liezhuan* [Exemplary Lives of the Guangxu and Xuantong Eras]. Taipei, 1969 (reprint of 1934 edition).

————. *Guang Xuan xiao ji* [Notes on the Guangxu and Xuantong Eras]. Dalian, 1934.

————. *Guapu congkan shulu* [Prefaces and Narratives from the Melon Patch Collection], n.p. 1934.

————. *Guapu congkan shulu zhengxubian* [Continued Prefaces and Narratives from the Melon Patch Collection]. 1935.

Jinliang. *Guapu shuyi* [Strange Episodes from the Melon Patch]. Reprint of 1936 edition. Taipei, 1975.

————. *Heilongjiang tongzhi gangyao* [Digest of the Comprehensive History of Heilongjiang]. Reprint of 1925 edition. Taipei, 1969.

————. *Jinshi renwu zhi* [History of Important Persons of the Present Day], Reprint of 1933 edition. Taipei, 1955.

————. *Jin zhishi shou yu lu* [Jottings of Police Constable Jin]. Peking, 1907.

————. *Manzhou bidang xuanbian* [Selections from the Secret Archives in Manchu]. Taipei, 1968.

————. *Manzhou laodang bilu* [Secret Record of the Old Manchu Archives]. Reprint of Peiping 1929 edition. Taipei, 1967.

————. *Neifu yitong mitu* [Secret Illustrations of the Grounds of the Imperial Household], n.p., n.d.

————. *Qing di wai ji* [Unofficial History of the Qing Emperors]. Peking (Peiping), 1933.

————. "Qingshi gao huiyilu [Recollections of the 'Draft History of the Qing']," in *Yijing*[Traces], No. 10 (1936).

————. "Qingshi gao xiao ke ji [Memoirs of the Editing of the Draft History of the Qing]." In Zhao Erxun et al., *Qingshi gao* [Draft History of the Qing] (1928 guanwai edition).

————. *Qing hou wai zhuan* [Unofficial Biographies of the Qing Empresses]. Peking (Peiping), 1934.

————. *Renzi jiyoucao* [Haphazard Notes on the Events of 1912], n.p., n.d.

————. *Sanxitang fatie shiwen* [Translations from Regulations Hung in the Sanxi Pavilion], n.p., n.d.

————. *Shengjing gugong shuhualu* [Records of the Books and Paintings of the Palace at Mukden], 1924.

————. *Sichao yiwen* [Miscellaneous Essays on Four Eras]. Peking (Peiping), 1936.

————. *Xijiang jiaoshe zhiyao* [Digest of the History of Intercourse with the Western Regions], n.p., n.d.

————. *Yuanmingyuan Changchunyuan tu* [Sketches of the Yuanming yuan and the Changchun yuan], n.p., n.d.

————. *Yue mantang riji suoyin* [Index to the Yueman Pavlion Diary]. Hong Kong, 1977.

————. Untitled foreword to *Manzhou mingchen zhuan*, 1928 shanben edition only.

————. Untitled foreword to *Xinhai xunnan ji*, 1916.

————, ed. and trans., *Manzhou bidang* [Secret Archives in Manchu]. Taipei: Wenhai, 1966 (reprint of 1934 edition).

Johnston, Reginald. *Twilight in the Forbidden City*, 1934.

Klaproth, Jules. *Chrestomathie Mandchou, ou Recueil de Textes Mandchou*, Paris, 1828.

Kovalesky, Egor Petrovich. "Excerpts from E. P. Kovalesky's *Journey to China* [Puteshestvie v Kitai]," A. J. Dray, trans. *Papers on China* 22A (May 1969):53–88.

Ku-kung po-wu-yuan (Gugong bowuyuan). *Jiazi Qingshi bimou fupi wenzhong* [Materials on the Qing Entourage's Restorationist Plot of 1924], Peking (Peiping): Gugong, 1929.

Kuang Lu (Guang Lu). *Xibe zu yi bufen zi Fengtian xi qian Xinjiang Yili shi* [History of the Transfer of a Portion of the Xibo People from Fengtian to Yili, Xinjiang], Taipei, n.d.

Lao She. *Beneath the Red Banner*, D. J. Cohn, trans. Peking: Chinese Literature (Panda Books), 1982.

————. *Crescent Moon and Other Stories*. Peking: Chinese Literature (Panda Books), 1985.

————. *Huang huo* [Anxiety and Disaster]. Hong Kong: Weitong, 1972.

————. "The Plain Red Banner," *Chinese Literature*, February and March, 1981.

Meadows, Thomas T. *The Chinese and Their Rebellion*. Stanford: Academic Reprints, 1954.

————. *Translations from the Manchu with the Original Texts*. Canton: S. Wells Williams, 1849.

Ortai et al. *Baqi tongzhi* [chuji] [General History of the Eight Banners, Original Edition], n.p. 1739.

Peng Guodong. *Qing shi kaiguo qian ji* [A Preliminary Account of Early Qing History]. Taipei, 1969.

————. *Qingshi cuanxiu jishi* [A Memoir on the Collation and Revision of the History of the Qing]. Private printing, n.p., n.d.

Peng Ranzhang et al. *Pinghuxian zhi* [History of Pinghu County] (with Xunnan lu attached), 1886.

"Sun Zhongshan xiansheng mishu chu zhi Puyi 'neiwu fu' Shaoying deng ren huan" [A Letter from the Secretariat of Mr. Sun Zhongshan to Shaoying and Others of Puyi's 'Imperial Household Department']. *Lishi dang'an* [Historical Archives] 1981:3:5–6.

Sungyun. *Emu tanggū orin sakda-i gisun sarkiyan, Bai er lao ren yulu* [Record of One-Hundred and Twenty Stories from Old Men]. Reprint of 1791? original. Taipei: Chinese Materials Center, 1982.

Tieliang et al. *[Qinding] Baqi tongzhi* [Imperially Commissioned General History of the Eight Banners]. 1966. Taipei Reprint. 1977.

Toghto et al. *Jin shi* [History of Jurchen Jin dynasty]. 1261. Reprint. Peking: Zhonghua shuju, 1975.

Tun Li-ch'en [Dun Lichen]. *Annual Customs and Festivals in Peking as Recorded in the Yen-ching Sui-chih-chi by Tun Li-ch'en*, Derk Bodde, trans. Hong Kong: Hong Kong University Press, 1965.

Wei Song et al. *Nanchuanxian zhi* [History of Nanchuan Country]. 1851.

Wu Qingdi. *Xinhai xunnan ji* [Record of the Martyrs of 1911/12]. Reprinted 1924, 1935. Peking, 1916.

Wu ti Qingwen jian [Five-Part Lexicon of Qing Script]. Photo reprint of Qianlong period original. Peking: Minzu, 1957.

Wu Woyao. *Ershi nian mudu guaixian zhuang* [Weird Things Witnessed over Twenty Years] (2 vols.). Hong Kong: Kwong Chi, n.d.

Wylie, Alexander. *Translation of the Ts'ing Wan K'e Mung*. Shanghai: London Mission Press, 1855.

Zhang Dachang. *Hangzhou baqi zhufang yingzhilue* [A Selective History of the Management of the Eight Banners Garrison at Hangzhou]. Reprint of 1912 edition). Taipei: Wenhai, n.d.

Zhang Zhongru et al. *Qingdai kaoshi zhidu ciliao* [Materials on the Examination System during the Qing Dynasty], n.d. Photoreprint. Taipei: Wenhai, 1968.

Zhao Erxun et al. *Man mingchen zhuan* [Biographies of Famous Manchu Officials]. 1928. Taipei: Tailian Guofang reprint, n.d.

———. *Qing shi gao* [Draft History of the Qing]. Punctuated reprint of 1928 original. Peking: Zhonghua shuju, 1977

Zhao Erxun: Dongsan sheng [Zhao Erxun: The Three Eastern Provinces]. The Papers of Zhao Erxun in the Number One Historical Archives (diyi lishi dang'an). Peking (cited by box number).

SECONDARY AND COMPARATIVE SOURCES

Abe Takeo. *Shindai shi no kenkyū* [Researches on Qing History]. Tokyo: Sobunsha, 1971.

An Shuangcheng. "Shun Kang Yong sanchao baqi ding'e qianxi" [A Preliminary Analysis of the Eight Banners' Active Registration in the Shunzhi, Kangxi, Yungzhen Reigns]. In *Lishi Dang'an* [Historical Archives] 1983:2:100–103.

Banno, Masataka. *China and the West, 1858–1861: The Origins of the Tsungli Yamen*. Cambridge: Harvard University Press, 1964.

Bartlett, Beatrice S., "Books of Revelations: The Importance of the Manchu Language Archival Record Books for Research on Ch'ing History." *Late Imperial China* 6(2):25–33.

———. "Learning from the Ch'ing Archives." Paper presented at the New England Conference of the Association for Asian Studies, October 17, 1981.

Belov, Y.A. "The Xinhai Revolution and the Question of Struggle against the Manzhou." In *Manzhou Rule in China* [Manchzhurskoe bladichestbo v Kitae], S. L. Tikhvinsky, ed., 325–37. Moscow: Progress, 1983.

Bien, Gloria, trans. "A Bannerman at the Teahouse." *Renditions* 4 (Spring 1975).

Blader, Susan. *A Critical Study of San-hsia wu-yi and Relationships to the Lungt'u Kung-an Songbook*, doctoral dissertation, University of Pennsylvania, 1977.

Bol, Peter K. Review of Chan 1985 in *Harvard Journal of Asiatic Studies* 47(1):285–98.

Bonner, Joey. *Wang Kuo-wei: An Intellectual Biography*. Cambridge: Harvard East Asian Series, 1986.

Borokh, L. N. "Anti-Manzhou Ideas of the First Chinese Bourgeois Revolutionaries (Lu Huadong Confession)," D. Skvirsky, trans. In *Manzhou Rule in China* [Manchzhurskoe vladichestvo v Kitae], S. L. Tikhvinsky, ed. 297–311. Moscow: Progress, 1983.

Brunnert, H. S., and V. V. Hagelstrom. *Present Day Political Organization of China*, Beltchenko and Moran, trans. Shanghai, 1911.

Chai Yü-shu (Zhai Yushu). *Qingdai Xinjiang zhufang bingzhi de yanjiu* [Researches on the Military System and Garrisons of Xinjiang During the Qing Dynasty]. Taipei, 1969.

Chan Hok-lam. *Legitimation in Imperial China: Discussions under the Jurchen Chin Dynasty.* Seattle: University of Washington, 1985.

Chang Hsin-pao. *Commissioner Lin and the Opium War.* Cambridge: Harvard University Press, 1964.

Chang Te-ch'ang. "The Economic Role of the Imperial Household (Nei-wu-fu) in the Ch'ing Dynasty." *Journal of Asian Studies* 31:2 (February 1972):243–73.

Ch'en Chieh-hsien (Chen Jiexian). "Lun *Baqi tongzhi*" [On the General History of the Eight Banners]. Printed as front matter to [*Qinding*] *Baqi tongzhi.*

————. *Manzhou congkan* [Collected Works on the Manchus]. Taipei: Guoli Taiwan daxue, 1963.

Ch'en Ching-fang (Chen Jingfang). *Qingmo Man Han zhengzhi quanli xiaozhang zhi yanjiu* [Researches on the Growth and Attenuation of Political Power of the Manchus and the Han Chinese in the Late Han Period]. Taipei: Wenhua, 1961.

Chen Jiahua. "Baqi bingxiang shixi [An Analysis of the Military Supplies of the Eight Banners]." *Minzu yanjiu* [Nationality studies] 1985:5:63–71.

————. "Qingdai yibu guanliao shi zu de jiapu [Genealogy of a Family of Bureaucrats during the Qing Dynasty]." *Minzu yanjiu* [Nationality studies] 1983:5:39–45.

Chen Wan. "Shi Tingzhu shiyi yu jiapu jikao [A Study of the Descendants and Genealogy of Shi Tingzhu]." *Qingshi yanjiu tongxun* [Bulletin of Researches on Qing History] 1986:2:33–36.

Ch'en Wen-shih (Chen Wenshi), "The Creation of the Manchu Niru," P. K. Crossley, trans. In *Chinese Studies in History, XIV, No. 4,* P. Huang, ed. White Plains, 1981—originally published as "Manzhou baqi niulu de goucheng," in *Dalu zazhi* (1965) 31:9 and 31:10.

Chen Xulu et al. *Zhongguo jindai shi cidian* [Dictionary of Modern Chinese History]. Shanghai: Cishu, 1982.

Chu, Raymond W., and William G. Saywell. *Career Patterns in the Ch'ing Dynasty.* The University of Michigan: Center for Chinese Studies, 1984.

Ch'ü T'ung-tsu. *Local Government in China under the Ch'ing.* Cambridge: Harvard University Press, 1962.

Chuan Han-sheng, and Richard A. Kraus. *Mid-Ch'ing Rice Markets and Trade: An Essay in Price History.* Cambridge: Harvard University East Asian Research Center, 1975.

Crossley, Pamela Kyle. " 'Historical and Magic Unity': The Real and Ideal Clan in Manchu Identity," doctoral dissertation, Yale University, 1983.

————. "An Introduction to the Qing Foundation Myth." *Late Imperial China* 6:1[December 1985]:3–24.

————. "Manchu Education in the Middle Ch'ing Period." Unpublished paper, prepared for the conference "Education and Society in Late Imperial China," sponsored by the Joint Committee on Chinese Studies of the American Council of Learned Societies and the Social Science Research Council, with funds provided by the National Endowment for the Humanities and the Andrew W. Mellon Foundation.

———. "Manzhou yuanliu kao and Formalization of the Manchu Heritage." *Journal of Asian Studies* 46:4 (November 1987):761–790.

———. "The Qianlong Retrospect on the Chinese-martial (*hanjun*) Banners." *Late Imperial China* 10:1 (June 1989):63–107.

———. "The Sian Garrison," unpublished paper, 1979.

———. "The Tong in Two Worlds: Cultural Identity in Liaodong and Nurgan during the 13th–17th Centuries," in *Ch'ing-shih wen-t'i*, 4, No. 9 (June 1983):21–46.

Curwen, Charles A. *Taiping Rebel: The Deposition of Li Hsiu-ch'eng*. Cambridge: Cambridge University Press, 1977.

Dennerline, Jerry. *The Chia-ting Loyalists: Confucian Leadership and Change in Seventeenth-Century China*. New Haven: Yale University Press, 1981.

Des Forges, Roger V. *Hsi-liang and the Chinese National Revolution*. New Haven: Yale University Press, 1973.

Dray-Novey, Alison. "Policing Imperial Peking: The Ch'ing Gendarmerie, 1650–1850," doctoral dissertation, Harvard University, 1981.

Du Wenlan. "Jiang nan bei daying jishi benmo [Complete Chronicle of the Southern and Northern Grand Batallions]." *Taipingjun shiliao* [Historical Materials on the Taiping Army] 4:45–74.

Esherick, Joseph W. *The Origins of the Boxer Uprising*. Berkeley and Los Angeles: University of California Press, 1987.

Elman, Benjamin. *From Philosophy to Philology: The Evidential Scholarship Movement in Eighteenth-Century China*. Cambridge: Harvard University Press, 1984.

Elliott, Mark C. "Foe Within, Enemy Without." *Late Imperial China*, forthcoming.

Etō Toshio, *Dattan* [Tatars]. Tokyo, 1956.

———. *Manshū bunka shi jo no ichi shinwa*. Tokyo, 1934.

Evans, Nancy. "The Banner-School Background of the Canton T'ung-wen Kuan." *Papers on China* 22A (May 1969):89–103.

Fairbank, John K., ed. *The Cambridge History of China, Volume 11: Late Ch'ing, 1800–1911, Part I*. Cambridge: Cambridge University Press, 1978.

———, ed. *The Cambridge History of China, Volume 11: Late Ch'ing, 1800–1911, Part II*. Cambridge: Cambridge University Press, 1980.

Fang Chao-ying. "A Technique for Estimating the Numerical Strength of the Early Manchu Military Forces." *Harvard Journal of Asiatic Studies* 13:1 (June 1950).

Fay, Peter Ward. *The Opium War 1840–1842: Barbarians in the Celestial Empire in the Early Part of the Nineteenth Century and the War by which They Forced Her Gates Ajar*. Chapel Hill: University of North Carolina Press, 1975.

Feng Erkang. *Yongzheng zhuan* [Life of the Yongzheng Emperor]. Peking: Renmin, 1985.

Feng Guozhe, and Yang Naiji. "You guan Heshen chushen, qiji wenti de kaocha [An Inquiry into Some Questions Related to the Origins and the Banner Registration of Heshen]." *Qingshi luncong* [Reprinted Essays on Qing History] 4 (1982):141–51.

Feng Junshi. "Oulunchun zu caiyuan [Origins of the Oronchon]." *Jilin shifen daxue bao* [Jilin Normal University Journal] 1979:2:77–86.

Feuerwerker, Albert. "Economic Trends in the Late Ch'ing Empire, 1870–1911." In Fairbank and Twitchett, eds., *The Cambridge History of China: 11(2)*, 1–69.

Fisher, Thomas Stephen, "Lü Liu-liang (1629–1683) and the Tseng Ching Case (1728–1733)," doctoral dissertation, Princeton University, 1974.

Freedman, Maurice. *Chinese Lineage and Society: Fukien and Kwangtung*. London: University of London Press, 1966.

Fried, Morton. *The Notion of Tribe*. Menlo Park, Calif.: Cummings, 1975.

Fu Guijiu. "Donghua lu zuozhe xinzheng [New Evidence on the Author of the 'East Gate Chronicles']." *Lishi yanjiu* [Historical Studies] 1984:5:168–70.

Fu Kedong. "Baqi huji zhidu chucao [Preliminary Draft on the Eight Banners Household Registration System]." *Minzu yanjiu* [Nationality studies] 1983:6:34–43.

Fu Tsung-mou [Fu Zongmou]. "Qingchu yizheng tizhi zhi yanjiu [Studies on the Collegial Rule System of the Early Qing]." *Guoli Zhengzhi Daxue xuebao* [National Government University Bulletin] 11 (May 1965):245–95.

Furth, Charlotte. "Concepts of Pregnancy, Childbirth and Infancy in Ch'ing Dynasty China," in *Journal of Asian Studies* 46:1 (February 1987):7–35.

———. "The Sage as Rebel: The Inner World of Chang Ping-lin," in *The Limits of Change: Essays on Conservative Alternatives in Republican China*, 113–50.

———, ed. *The Limits of Change: Essays on Conservative Alternatives in Republican China*. Cambridge: Harvard University Press, 1976.

Gamble, Sidney D., and John Stewart Burgess. *Peking: A Social Survey*. New York: George H. Doran, 1921.

Gasster, Michael. *Chinese Intellectuals and the Revolution of 1911: The Birth of Chinese Radicalism*. Seattle: University of Washington Press, 1969.

Gernet, Jacques. *Daily in Life in China on the Eve of the Mongol Invasion, 1250–1276*, H. M. Wright, trans. Stanford: Stanford University Press, 1961.

Glazer, Nathan, and Daniel P. Moynihan. *Ethnicity: Theory and Experience*. Cambridge: Harvard University Press, 1975.

Goodrich, Luther C., and Chao-ying Fang. *Dictionary of Ming Biography* (2 vols). New York: Columbia University Press, 1976.

Graham, Gerald S. *The China Station: War and Diplomacy 1830–1860*. Oxford: Oxford University Press, 1978.

Grimes, Sara. *West Lake Reflections*. Peking: Foreign Languages Press, 1983.

Grube, Wilhelm. *Die Sprache und Schriften der Jucen* [The Language and Script of the Jurchens]. Leipzig: Harrassowitz, 1896.

Guan Dedong and Zhou Zhongming, eds. *Zidi shu congchao* [Collected Transcriptions of Zidi Tales] (2 vols.). Shanghai: Guji, 1984.

Guang Dong. "Jiufuquan de chansheng, fuzhan he xiaowang chu cao [Preliminary Draft on the Emergence, Development and Decline of the Avunculate]." *Minzu yanjiu* [Nationality studies] 1985:2:19–28.

Guo Chengkang. "Qingchu niulu de shumu" Numbers of Banner Companies in the Early Qing Period, *Qingshi yanjiu tongxun* [Bulletin of Research on Qing History], 1987:1:31–35.

Guo Songyi. "Qingdai de renkou zengzhang he renkou liuqian [Population Growth and Population Drift during the Qing Period]." *Qingshi luncong* [Reprinted Essays on Qing History] 5:103–39.

Guy, R. Kent. *The Emperor's Four Treasuries: Scholars and the State in the Late Ch'ien-lung Era.* Cambridge: Harvard University Council on East Asian Studies, 1987.

Hail, W. J. *Tseng Kuo-fan and the Taiping Rebellion.* New Haven: Yale University Press, 1927.

Han Jinchun, and Li Yifu. "Hanwen 'minzu' yici de chuxian chuqi shiyong qingkuang [The Circumstances of the First Attestations and Usages of the Chinese Word 'Minzu']." *Minzu yanjiu* [Nationality studies] 1984:2:36–43.

Hangzhou shi wenhua ju. *Hangzhou de chuanshuo* [Complete Narrative of Hangzhou]. Shanghai: Wenyi chubanshe, 1980.

Harrell, Stevan, Susan Naquin, and Ju Deyuan. "Lineage Genealogy: The Genealogical Records of the Qing Imperial Lineage." *Late Imperial China* 6:2 (December 1985):37–47.

Hibbert, Christopher. *The Dragon Wakes: China and the West, 1793–1911.* London: Penguin, 1984.

Ho Lieh (He Lie). *Liushi nian lai zhi Qingshi yu Qingshi gao* [Sixty Years of Qing History and Qing Draft History]. Taipei, 1968.

Holt, Edgar. *The Opium Wars in China.* London: Putnam, 1964.

Hong Liangpi et al. *Wen Wenzhong shi lue* [Chronology of Wenxiang]. 1882. Reprint. Taipei: Wenhai, 1966.

Hou Shouchang. "Kangxi muxi kao [On the Maternal Lineage of the Kangxi Emperor]." *Lishi dang'an* [Historical Archives] 1982:4:100–106.

Hsiao Kung-chuan. *Rural China: Imperial Control in the Nineteenth Century.* Seattle: University of Washington Press, 1960.

Hua Li. "Qingdai de Man Meng lianyin [Marital Connections between Manchus and Mongols in the Qing Period]." *Minzu yanjiu* [Nationality studies] 1983:2:45–54.

Huang, Pei. *Autocracy at Work: A Study of the Yung-cheng Period, 1723–1735.* Bloomington: Indiana University Press, 1974.

Huil, W. J. *Tseng Kuo-fan and the Taiping Rebellion.* New Haven: Yale University Press, 1927.

Hummel, Arthur W., et al. *Eminent Chinese of the Ch'ing Period.* Washington: United States Government Printing Office, 1943.

Ichiko Chūzō, "Political and Institutional Reform, 1901–1911" in *The Cambridge History of China* 11(2):375–415.

Ilyushechkin, V. P. "Anti-Manzhou Edge of the Taiping Peasant War." In *Manzhou Rule in China* [Manchzhurskoe vladichestvo v Kitae], S. L. Tikhvinsky, ed., and D. Skvirsky, trans., 257–73. Moscow: Progress, 1983.

Im, Kaye Soon. *The Rise and Decline of the Eight-Banner Garrisons in the*

Ch'ing Period (1644–1911): A Study of the Kuang-chou, Hang-chou, and Ching-chou Garrisons. University Microfilms, 1981.

Jen Yu-wen (Jian Youwen). *The Taiping Revolutionary Movement.* New Haven: Yale University Press, 1973.

Ji Dachun. "Lun Songyun [On Sungyun]." *Minzu yanjiu* [Nationality studies] 1988:3:71–79.

Jin Guangping and Jin Qizong. *Nuzhen yuyan wenzi yanjiu* [Studies on the Language and Script of the Jurchens]. Peking: Wenwu, 1980.

Kanda Nobuo. "Remarks on *Emu tanggū orin sakda-i gisun sarkiyan.*" Sungyun, *Emu tanggū orin sakda-i gisun sarkiyan,* iii–ix.

————. "Shinshō no beile ni tsuite [On the *beile* of the Qing Dynasty]." *Tōyō gakuhō* [East Asian Journal] 40:4 [March 1958]: 349–71.

————. "Shinshō no *yizheng daren* ni tsuite [On the Consultative Princes during the Qing Dynasty]," in *Wada Hakushi kenreki kinen tōyōshi ronsō* [Collected Essays on East Asian History in Honor of Professor Wada Sei], 171–89. Reprint. Tokyo: Dai Nihon Yūbenkai Kōdansha, n.p. 1951.

————, and Matsumura Jun. *Hakki tsushi retsuden sakuin* [Index to the Exemplary Lives in the General History of the Eight Banners], n.p. 1964.

Kessler, Lawrence. "Ethnic Composition of Provincial Leadership during the Ch'ing Dynasty." *Journal of Asian Studies* 28:3 (May 1969):489–511.

————. *K'ang-hsi and the Consolidation of Ch'ing Rule, 1661–1684.* Chicago: University of Chicago Press, 1976.

Kiyose, Gisaburo N. *A Study of the Jurchen Language and Script: Reconstruction and Decipherment.* Kyoto: Horitsubunka, 1977.

Kostyaeva, A. S. "The 'Down with the Qing' Slogan in the Pingxiang Uprising of 1906." In *Manzhou Rule in China* [Manchzhurskoe bladichestbo v Kitae], S. L. Tikhvinsky, ed., 312–24. Moscow: Progress, 1983.

Kuhn, Philip A. *Rebellion and Its Enemies in Late Imperial China: Militarization and Social Structure, 1796–1864.* Cambridge: Harvard University Press, 1980.

Kwong, Luke S. K. *A Mosaic of the Hundred Days: Personalities, Politics and Ideas of 1898.* Cambridge: Harvard University Council on East Asian Studies, 1984.

————. "On 'The 1898 Reforms Revisited': A Rejoinder." *Late Imperial China* 8:1 (June 1987): 214–19.

Lee, Robert H. G. *The Manchurian Frontier in Ch'ing History.* Cambridge: Harvard University Press, 1970.

Lei Fangsheng. "Jingzhou qixue de shimo ji qi tedian [History and Special Characteristics of the Banner School at Jingzhou]." *Minzu yanjiu* [Historical Studies] 1984:3:57–59.

Li Chien-nung. *The Political History of China, 1840–1923,* S. Y. Teng and J. Ingalls, trans. Stanford: Stanford University Press, 1956.

Li Hsüeh-chih [Li Xuezhi]. *Cong jige manwen mingci tantao manzhou (nuzhen) minzu de shehui zuzhi* [The Social Organization of the Manchu (Jurchen) Nationality as Extrapolated from Several Words in the Manchu Literary Language]. Taipei: Academia Sinica, 1981.

Li Huan. *Guochao qixian leizheng* [Categorical Biographies of Outstanding Men of Our Dynasty], 1890.

Li Qiao. "Baqi shengji wenti shulue [Narrative on the Livelihood Issue of the Eight Banners]." *Lishi dang'an* [Historical Archives] 1981:1:91–97.

Li Xinda. "Ru Guan qian de baqi bingshu wenti [Problems on the Numbers of Eight Banner Soldiers before the Conquest]." *Qingshi luncong* [Reprinted Essays on Qing History] #3 (1982):155–63.

Li Yaohua. "Guanyu 'minzu' yici de shiyong he yiming wenti [Problems on the Usage and Meaning of the Word *minzu*]." *Lishi yanjiu* 1963:2:175.

Li Zhiting. "Ming Qing zhanzheng yu Qingchu lishi fazhan shi [Historical Trends during the Ming-Qing Wars and the Early Qing Period]." *Qingshi yanjiu tongshun* [Bulletin of Researches on Qing History] 1988:1:7–12.

Ling Chunsheng. *Songhuajiang xiayou de hezhe zu* [The Golds of the Lower Songhuajiang] (2 vols.). Nanjing: Zhongyuanyan, 1934.

Liu Chia-chü (Liu Jiaju). "The Creation of the Chinese Banners in the Early Ch'ing," P. K. Crossley, trans. *Chinese Studies in History* XIV, No. 4, P. Huang, ed., White Plains 1981—originally published as "Qingchu hanjun baqi de zhaojian," in *Dalu zazhi* 1967, 34:11 and 34:12.

Liu Kwang-ching, and Richard J. Smith. "The Military Challenge: The Northwest and the Coast." *The Cambridge History of China: 11(2)*, 202–73.

Liu Qinghua. "Manzu xingshi shulue [An Account of Manchu Surnames and Lineages]" *Minzu yanjiu* [Nationality studies] 1983:1:64–71.

Liu Shih Shun (Liu Shishun), trans. *Vignettes from the Late Ch'ing: bizarre happenings eyewitnessed over two decades*. Jamaica, N.Y.: St. John's University Press, 1976.

Liu Shizhe. "Manzu 'qishe' qianshu [A Preliminary Account of qishe among the Manchus]." *Minzu yanjiu* 1982:5:48–57.

Liu Xiamin. "Qing kaiguo chu zhengfu zhu bu jiangyu kao [A Study of the Territories of Several Tribes at the Initiation of the Invasions by the New Qing State]." *Yanjing xuebao* [Yenching Journal] 23 (1936):6, reprinted in *Qingshi luncong* [Reprinted Essays on Qing History] 1 (1977):107–46.

Liu Zhongpo. *Hezhe ren* [The Hezhes]. Peking: Minzu, 1981.

Lo Jung-pang, ed. *K'ang Yu-wei: A Biography and a Symposium*. Tucson: Association for Asian Studies, 1967.

Loh Wai-fong. "Review of Torbert, The Ch'ing Imperial Household Department." *Harvard Journal of Asiatic Studies* 38 (1978):2:492–501.

Lowe, H. Y. *The Adventures of Wu: The Life Cycle of a Peking Man*, D. Bodde, trans. Princeton, N.J.: Princeton University Press, 1983.

Luo Baoshan. "Guanyu Zhang Binglin zhengzhi lichang zhuanbian de jipian tiaowen [Several Documents Relating to Changes in the Political Outlook of Zhang Binglin]." *Lishi yanjiu* [Historical Studies] 1982:5:56–62.

Luo Chenglie. "Yapian zhanzheng zhong Zhenjiang kang Ying de shiliao [Historical Materials on the Resistance to the British at Jinjiang during the Opium War]." *Lishi yanjiu* [Historical Studies] 1978:4:62.

Luo Ergang. *Lüying bing zhi* [Military History of the Green Standard Armies]. Peking: Zhonghua shuju, 1984.

————. *Xiangjun bing zhi* [Military History of the Xiang Army]. Peking: Zhonghua shuju, 1984.

Lü Guangtian. *Ewenke zu* [The Evenk Nationality]. Peking: Minzu, 1983.

————. "Qingdai buteha daxing Ewenke ren de Baqi jiegou [The Eight Banners Organization of butha Evenks during the Qing Period]." *Minzu yanjiu* [Nationality studies] 1983:3 23–31.

McCormack, Gavan. *Chang Tso-lin in Northeast China, 1911–1928: China, Japan and the Manchurian Idea.* Stanford: Stanford University Press, 1977.

Mancall, Mark. *Russia and China: Their Diplomatic Relations to 1728.* Cambridge: Harvard University Press, 1971.

Mann, Susan. "Widows in the Kinship, Class and Community Structures of Qing Dynasty China." *Journal of Asian Studies* 46:1 (February 1987):37–56.

Manzu jianshi [Short History of the Manchus]. Peking: Zhonghua, 1979.

Meng Sen. "Baqi zhidu kaoshi [A Study of the Eight Banner System]." *Lishi yanjiusuo jikan* [Proceedings of the Institute for Historical Research] VI (1936):3:343–412.

————. *Qingshi qianji* [Early Qing History]. Taipei: Tailian guofeng, n.d.

Mitamura Taisuke. *Shinchō zenshi no kenkyū* [Researches on Early Qing History]. Kyoto: Toyoshi kenkyūkai, 1965.

Mo Dongyin. *Manzu shi luncong* [Selected Essays on Manchu History]. Reprint of 1958 original. Peking: Sanlian, 1979.

Naquin, Susan. *Millenarian Rebellion in China: The Eight Trigrams Uprising of 1813.* New Haven: Yale University Press, 1976.

————, and Evelyn S. Rawski. *Chinese Society in the Eighteenth Century.* New Haven: Yale University Press, 1987.

Ng, Vivien W. "Ideology and Sexuality: Rape Laws in Qing China." *Journal of Asian Studies,* 46:1 [February 1987] 57–70.

Nivison, David. "Ho-shen and his Accusers: Ideology and Political Behavior in the Eighteenth Century." In *Confucianism in Action,* David S. Nivison and Arthur R. Wright, eds. Stanford: Stanford University Press, 1959.

Norman, Jerry. *A Concise Manchu-English Lexicon.* Seattle: University of Washington Press, 1978.

Nowak, Margaret, and Stephen Current. *The Tale of the Nišan Shamaness.* Seattle: University of Washington Press, 1977.

Onogawa Hidemi. *Shimmatsu seiji shisō kenkyū* [Studies on Late Qing Political Thought]. Kyoto: Toashi kenkyūkai, 1960.

Oxnam, Robert B. *Ruling from Horseback: Manchu Politics in the Oboi Regency, 1661–1669.* Chicago: University of Chicago Press, 1970.

Pan Zhe. "Taiwan de Manzu xiehui he 'Manzu wenhua' [The Manchu Association of Taiwan and Manchu Culture]." *Qingshi yanjiu tongxun* [Bulletin of Research on Qing History] 1987:4:53–55.

Pao Tso-p'eng (Bao Zuopeng) et al. *Zhongguo jindai shi luncong* [Reprinted Essays on Modern Chinese History], vol. 1. Taipei: Zhengzhong, 1966.

Peng Bo. *Manzu* [The Manchu Nationality]. Peking: Minzu, 1985.

Pulleyblank, E. G. "The Chinese and Their Neighbors in Prehistoric and Early

Historic Times." *The Origins of Chinese Civilization*, David N. Keightley, ed. Berkeley and Los Angeles: University of California Press, 1983.

Qian Shipu. *Qing ji xin she zhi guan nianbiao* [Chronological Chart of the Newly-Established Offices of the Qing Era]. Peking: Zhonghua, 1961.

———, ed. *Qing ji zhongyao zhi guan nianbiao* [Chronological Chart of Important Offices of the Qing Era]. Peking: Zhonghua, 1959.

Qingdai dangan shiliao congbian [Selected Historical Materials from the Qing Dynasty Archives] 11. Peking: Zhonghua, 1982.

Qu Wanliang. *Ban ke zhi yi* [Selections of Woodblock Texts]. Jinan: Jilu shushe, 1987.

"Quanguo ke sheng, shi, zizhiqu ge minzu renkou [The Population, by Nationality, of all Provinces, Municipalities and Autonomous Districts]." *Minzu yanjiu* [Nationality studies] 1984:6:70–77.

Rankin, Mary Backus. *Early Chinese Revolutionaries: Radical Intellectuals in Shanghai and Chekiang, 1902–1911*. Cambridge: Harvard University Press, 1971.

———. *Elite Activism and Political Transformation in China: Zhejiang Province, 1865–1911*. Stanford: Stanford University Press, 1986.

Reischauer, Edwin O., and John King Fairbank. *East Asia: The Great Tradition*. Boston: Houghton Mifflin, Co., 1960.

Rhoads, Edward J. M. "Manchu Ascendency in the Late Qing." AAS conference paper, 1984.

Rodgers, Michael. "The Late Chin Debates on Dynastic Legitimacy." *Sung Studies Newsletter* 13:57–66.

Rossabi, Morris. *The Jurchens in the Yüan and Ming Periods*. Ithaca: Cornell University China-Japan Program, 1982.

Roth [Li], Gertraude. "The Manchu-Chinese Relationship." In Spence and Wills, *From Ming to Ch'ing: Conquest, Region and Continuity in Seventeenth-Century China*. New Haven: Yale University Press, 1979.

———. "The Rise of the Early Manchu State: A Portrait Drawn from Manchu Sources to 1636," doctoral dissertation, Harvard University, 1975.

Schoppa, R. Keith. *Chinese Elites and Political Change: Zhejiang Province in the Early Twentieth Century*. Cambridge: Harvard University Press, 1982.

Serruys, Henry. *Sino-Jürched Relations in the Yung-lo Period (1403–1424)*. Wiesbaden, 1955.

Shavkunov, Ernst Vladimirovich. *Gosudarstvo Bokhai i pamyatniki ego kulturi v primor'e* [Monuments and Culture of the Bohai State found in the Maritime Province]. Moscow: Nauka, 1968.

Shin Ch'ungil (Shen Zhongyi). *Konju jichong dŏrŏk* [Illustrated Narrative of a Journey among the Jianzhou]. Taipei: Tailian guofeng, 1971 (photoreprint of 1597 original).

Shirokogoroff, Sergei Mikhailovitch. *Social Organization of the Manchus: A Study of the Manchu Clan Organization*. Shanghai: Royal Asiatic Society, North China Branch, 1924.

Shu Yi. "Taiping Tianguo beifajun ruogan shishi kaobian [A Substantiated Hypothesis on the Possibilities of a Northern Campaign by the Taipings]." *Lishi dang'an* [Historical Archives] 1982:4:117–22.

Sinor, Denis. "The Inner Asian Warriors." *Journal of the American Oriental Society* 101:2 (April–June 1981):133–44.

Skinner, G. William. "Sichuan's Population in the Nineteenth Century: Lessons from Disaggregated Data." *Late Imperial China* 8:1 (June 1987):1–79.

———, ed. *The City in Late Imperial China*. Stanford: Stanford University Press, 1977.

Smith, Paul. "Commerce, Agriculture and Core Formation in the Upper Yangzi, 2 A.D. to 1948." *Late Imperial China* 9:1 (June 1988):1–78.

Smith, Richard J. *Mercenaries and Mandarins*. New York: K.T.O. Press, 1978.

Sollors, Werner. *Beyond Ethnicity: Consent and Descent in American Culture*. Oxford University Press, 1986.

Spector, Stanley. *Li Hung-chang and the Huai Army*. Seattle: University of Washington Press, 1964.

Spence, Jonathan D. *The Gate of Heavenly Peace*, New York: Viking, 1981.

———. "Opium Smoking in Ch'ing China." In *Conflict and Control in Late Imperial China*, Wakeman, Frederic, Jr. and Carolyn Grant, eds. Berkeley and Los Angeles: University of California Press, 1975.

———. *Ts'ao Yin and the K'ang-hsi Emperor: Bondservant and Master*. New Haven: Yale University Press, 1966.

———, and J. Wills, eds., *From Ming to Ch'ing*, New Haven: Yale University Press, 1979.

Stary, Giovanni. "Die Struktur der Ersten Residenz des Mandschukans Nurgaci [The Structure of the First Residence of the Manchu Khan, Nurgaci]." in *Central Asiatic Journal* XXV (1985):103–9.

———. "L'Ode di Mukden' dell'imperator Ch'ien-lung: Nuovi spunti per un analisi della tecnica versificatoria mancese [The 'Ode to Mukden' of the Qianlong Emperor: New Beginnings for an Analysis of Manchu Versificatory Techniques]." *Cina* [China] 17:235–51.

Strand, David. *Rickshaw Beijing*. Berkeley and Los Angeles: University of California Press, 1989.

Struve, Lynn. *The Southern Ming, 1644–1662*. New Haven: Yale University Press, 1984.

Sudō Yoshiyuki. "Shinchō ni okeru Manshū chūbō no toku shusei ni kansuru ichi kōsatsu [An Investigation Relating to the Special Characteristics of the Manchu Garrisons during the Qing Dynasty]," in *Tōhoku gakuho* [North Asia Journal] 11:1:176–203.

Sun Wenliang. *Nurhachi pingzhuan* [A Critical Biography of Nurgaci]. Shenyang: Liaoning daxue, 1985.

———, and Li Zhiting, Qing Taizong quanzhuan Complete Life of Qing Taizong. Jilin: Jilin Renmin, 1983.

Sun Xiao'en. *Guangxu pingzhuan* [A Critical Life of the Guangxu Emperor]. Shenyang: Liaoning jiaoyu, 1985.

Tamura Jitsuzo et al. *Kotai Shimbun kan yakukai* [Interpretive Index to the Wuti Qingwen jian]. Kyoto: Kyoto University, 1966.

Tan Yi. "Wan Qing Tongwen guan yu jindai xuexiao jiaoyu [The Late Qing Foreign Language Colleges and Modern Schools and Education]." *Qingshi yanjiu* [Researches on Qing History] 5 (1986):344–61.

Tang Zhiyun, ed. *Zhang Taiyan nianpu changbian* [Chronology and Selected Writings of Zhang Taiyan] (2 vols.). Peking: Zhonghua, 1979.

——, and Benjamin Elman. "The 1898 Reforms Revisited." *Late Imperial China* 8:1 (June 1987):205–13.

Telford, Ted A., and Michael H. Finegan, "Qing Archival Materials from the Number One Historical Archives on Microfilm at the Genealogical Society of Utah." *Late Imperial China* 9:2(December, 1988):86–114.

Teng Ssu-yü. *Historiography of the Taiping Rebellion*. Cambridge: Harvard University East Asian Research Center, 1972.

Tong Jingren. Huhehaote manzu jianshi [Short History of the Manchus of Huhhot], n.p., n.d.

——. Suiyuan cheng zhufang zhi [History of the Garrison at Suiyuan]. Revision of 1958 original. Huhhot, 1984.

Torbert, Preston M. *The Ch'ing Imperial Household Department: A Study of its Organization and Principal Functions, 1662–1796*. Cambridge: Harvard University East Asian Monographs, 1977.

Wakeman, Frederic Jr. "The Canton Trade and the Opium War." *The Cambridge History of China* 11(1) :163–212.

——. *The Great Enterprise: The Manchu Reconstruction of Imperial Order in Seventeenth-Century China*. Berkeley and Los Angeles: University of California Press, 1985.

——. "Localism and Loyalism during the Ch'ing Conquest of Kiangnan: The Tragedy of Chiang-yin." In *Conflict and Control in Late Imperial China*, Wakeman, Frederic, Jr. and Carolyn Grant, eds. Berkeley and Los Angeles: University of California Press, 1975.

——. *Strangers at the Gate: Social Disorder in South China, 1839–1861*. Berkeley and Los Angeles: University of California Press, 1966.

Waley, Arthur. *The Opium War Through Chinese Eyes*. New York: The Macmillan Company, 1958.

Wang Shilun, and Zhao Zhenhan. *Hangzhou shihua* [A Colloquial History of Hangzhou]. Hangzhou: Zhejiang renmin, 1979.

Wang Xiuchou [Wang Hsin-ch'u]. "A Memoir of a Ten Days Massacre in Yangzhow," L. Mao, trans. *Tien-hsia Monthly* 4:5:515–37.

Wang, Y. C., "The Su-pao Case: A Study of Foreign Pressure, Intellectual Fermentation and Dynastic Decline." *Monumenta Serica* 24 (1965):84–129.

Wang Zongyan. *Du Qingshi gao za ji* [Miscellaneous Notes after Reading Qingshi gao]. Hong Kong: Zhonghua, 1977.

Wei Qingyuan et al. *Qingdai nupei zhidu* [The Slave System of the Qing Period]. Peking: Zhongguo Renmin Taxue, 1982.

Widmer, Eric. *The Russian Ecclesiastical Mission in Peking during the Eighteenth Century*. Cambridge: Harvard East Asian Research Center, 1976.

Wright, Mary Clabaugh. *The Last Stand of Chinese Conservatism*. Stanford: Stanford University Press, 1957.

————, ed. *China in Revolution: The First Phase, 1900–1913.* New Haven: Yale University Press, 1968.

Wu, Silas. *Passage to Power: Kang-hsi and His Heir Apparent, 1661–1722.* Cambridge: Harvard University East Asian Series, 1979.

Wu Yuanfeng, and Zhao Zhiqiang. "Xibo zu you Kharqin Menggu qi bianru Manzhou baqi shimo [A Narrative of the Transfer of the Sibo from the Kharchin Mongol Banners to the Manchu Eight Banners]." *Minzu yanjiu* [Nationality studies] 1984:5 (60–73).

Xue Ruilu. "Qingdai yanglian yin zhidu jianlun [A Brief Discussion of the Honesty Incentive Supplements of the Qing Period]." *Qingshi luncong* [Reprinted Essays on Qing History] 5[1984]:139–57.

Yan Chongnian. *Nurhachi zhuan* [Life of Nurgaci]. Peking: Beijing chubanshi, 1983.

Yang Li-ch'eng (Yang Licheng). *Siku mulue* [Catalogue of the Four Treasuries]. Taipei: Zhonghua shuju, 1969.

Yang Qijiao. *Yongzheng di ji qi mizhe zhidu yanjiu* [Studies on the Yongzheng Emperor and his Secret Memorial System]. Hong Kong: Sanlian, 1981.

Yang Wei. "Ye lun Qingjun zai yapian zhanzheng zhong shibai de jiben yuanyin [Reply on the Basic Causes of the Defeat of the Qing Forces in the Opium War]." *Lishi dang'an* [Historical Archives] 1985:4:(89–97).

Yang Xuechen, and Zhou Yuanlian. *Qingdai baqi wanggong guizu xinghuai shi* [History of the Rise and Decline of the Eight Banner Princes and Nobility of the Qing Period]. Shenyang: Liaoning renmin, 1986.

Yang Yang, Yuan Lukun, and Fu Langyun, *Mingdai Nurgan dusi ji qi weisuo yanjiu* [Researches on the Ming Period Nurgan Commandery and its Garrisons]. Zhumazhen (Henan): Zhongzhou shuhuashe, 1981.

————, Sun Yuchang, Zhang Ke, "Mingdai liuren zai dongbei." *Lishi yanjiu* [Historical Studies] 1985:4:54–88.

Yao Hui'an. *Xihu siyuan tiyin yange kao* [Selections from Literary Works Extolling the Xihu Environs]. Shanghai: Foxue shuju, 1934.

Yao Weiyuan. *Yapian zhanzheng shi shi kao* [An Investigation of the Facts of the Opium War]. Shanghai: Xin zhishi, 1965.

"Yijiubaer nian ge minzu renkou [The Population of the Nationalities in 1982]." *Minzu yanjiu* [Nationality studies] 1983:3:80–81.

Zelin, Madeleine. *The Magistrate's Tael: Rationalizing Fiscal Reform in Eighteenth-Century China.* Berkeley and Los Angeles: University of California Press, 1984.

————. "The Rights of Tenants in Mi-Qing Sichuan: A Study of Land-Related Lawsuits in the Baxian Archives." *Journal of Asian Studies* XLV:3 (499–526).

Zhang Bofen. *Qingdai gedi jiangjun dutong dachen deng nianbiao, 1796–1911* [Chronological Tables for the Generals-in-Chief, Banner Commanders, and Major Officials of the Qing Period, 1796–1911]. Peking: Zhonghua shuju, 1977.

Zhang Yiwen. "Shilun Qingjun zai yapian zhanzheng zhong shibai de jiben yuanyin [A Thesis on the Basic Causes of the Defeat of the Qing Forces in the Opium War]." *Lishi dang'an* [Historical Archives] 1983:1:87–94.

Zheng Yunshan, Xi Yanning, and Liu Zhengjiu. *Hangzhou yu Xihu shihua* [A History of Hangzhou and West Lake]. Shanghai, 1980.

Zhou Yuanlian, "Guanyu baqi zhidu de jige wenti [Several Problems on the Eight Banner System]." *Qingshi luncong* [Reprinted Essays on Qing History] 3 (1982):140–54.

———. *Qingchao kaiguo shi yanjiu* [Studies on the Foundation of the Qing Dynasty]. Shenyang: Liaoning renmin, 1981.

Zhu Xizu. *Hou Jin guohan xingshi kao* [Researches on the Lineage and Surname of the Later Jin Khan], n.p., 1932.

Zhuang Jianping. "Qishan cong wei qianding 'Quanbi caoyue' [Qishan Never Signed the 'Chuenpi Convention']." *Lishi dang'an* [Historical Archives] 1986:3:99–102.

Zou Jielan. "Manchu Language Rescued." *China Daily*, October 12, 1987:6.

Index